*Radical Change
through Communication
in Mao's China*

THE EAST-WEST CENTER, established in Hawaii by the United States Congress in 1960, is a national educational institution with multinational programs. Its purpose is to promote better relations and understanding among the nations and peoples of Asia, the Pacific area, and the United States through their cooperative participation in research, study, and training activities.

Fundamental to the achievement of the Center's purpose are the cooperative discovery and application of knowledge and the interchange of knowledge, information, ideas, and beliefs in an intercultural atmosphere of academic freedom. In Center programs, theory and practice are combined to help current and future leaders generate, test, and share knowledge about important world problems of mutual concern to people in both East and West.

Each year about 1,500 scholars, leaders, public officials, mid-level and upper-level managers, and graduate students come to the Center to work and study together in programs concerned with seeking alternative approaches and solutions to common problems. For each participant from the United States, two come from the Asian/Pacific area. An international, interdisciplinary professional staff provides the framework, content, and continuity for programs and for cooperative relationships with universities and other institutions in the Center's area of operations.

Center programs are conducted by the East-West Communication Institute, the East-West Culture Learning Institute, the East-West Food Institute, the East-West Population Institute, and the East-West Technology and Development Institute. Each year the Center also awards a limited number of "Open Grants" for graduate degree education and research by scholars and authorities in areas not encompassed by the problem-oriented institutes.

The East-West Center is governed by the autonomous board of a public, non-profit educational corporation—the Center for Cultural and Technical Interchange Between East and West, Inc.—established by special act of the Hawaii State Legislature. The Board of Governors is composed of distinguished individuals from the United States and countries of Asia and the Pacific area. The United States Congress provides basic funding for Center programs and for a variety of scholarships, fellowships, internships, and other awards. Because of the cooperative nature of Center programs, financial support and cost-sharing arrangements also are provided by Asian and Pacific governments, regional agencies, private enterprise, and foundations.

The Center is located in Honolulu, Hawaii, on twenty-one acres of land adjacent to the University of Hawaii's Manoa campus. Through cooperative arrangements with the University of Hawaii, the Center has access to University degree programs, libraries, computer center, and the like.

East-West Center Books are published by The University Press of Hawaii to further the Center's aims and programs.

Radical Change through Communication in Mao's China

GODWIN C. CHU

AN EAST-WEST CENTER BOOK 图
from the East-West Communication Institute

Published for the East-West Center by
THE UNIVERSITY PRESS OF HAWAII
HONOLULU

Library of Congress Cataloging in Publication Data

Chu, Godwin C   1927–
  Radical change through communication in Mao's China.

  "An East-West Center book."
  Bibliography: p.
  Includes index.
    1. China—Social conditions—1949–   2. Communication in politics—China. 3. Communication—Social aspects—China. 4. Social change. 5. Communism—China. I. Title.
HN677.C48   301.5'92'0951   77-3874
ISBN 0-8248-0515-1

Contents

Preface

A quarter century ago, the anthropologist Francis Hsu published his classic portrayal of Chinese life, *Under the Ancestors' Shadow*. Indeed, for centuries the Chinese dutifully followed the dictates of their ancestors. Today the ancestors themselves have faded into the shadows. The eight hundred million Chinese have worked and lived under the towering image of one man, Chairman Mao Tse-tung. In a process unparalleled in history, the ideals and aspirations of one man have jolted the Chinese away from their heritage of traditions and have pushed them toward a life of collective survival and development.

The ideas for this volume grew out of a curiosity that has lingered on for some two decades—a curiosity to understand some of the puzzling features in China's processes of social transformation. The China I knew prior to 1949 was a land of toiling peasants as well as of extravagant entrepreneurs, a land of homesick millions who yearned for a quiet family life after a generation of wars, a land of young men and women impatient with academic work in their universities and shouting angry slogans for peace and freedom. Except for the privileged few, it was also a land of poverty. How was this land transformed into the China of today?

The ultimate goals of Communism in China are stated to be both economic and ideological in nature: the equitable distribution of work and reward and the cultivation of new values and beliefs. The Party has been relying on social structural change as a major means of achieving these goals. This change is unique in a number of perspectives. It is penetrating in the sense that nearly every aspect of the traditional Chinese social structure has been affected. It is extensive, reaching every corner of China's vast area. It is swift and drastic, leaving the Chinese people with barely enough time to adjust. Above all, it is unique because the change has been brought about not by a revolution of technology, nor by the exclusive application of force, but rather, primarily by the skillful use of communication.

That a social structure can be altered through the means of communication is not surprising. A social structure is a structure of communication, and therefore it can be changed by communication. But it took the Chinese Communist revolution to demonstrate on a massive scale that communication (particularly when effectively employed in a group setting) can be a powerful mechanism to yank a traditional society out of its old routines and to put it on the road to development. Thus it is the purpose of this volume to demonstrate, even with the limited materials available, how communication has been used to bring about social structural change and development in China. It is not intended to examine the chronological events of China's development experience or to analyze the Party's economic policies.

Since this book discusses various aspects of social structural change and development, it is of necessity multidisciplinary, drawing on theoretical concepts and empirical findings from sociology, social psychology, cultural anthropology, economics, and political science. The main framework of analysis is that of communication.

The research perspective, however, differs from the general premises of communication research in a number of ways. The primary concern is to analyze the roles of communication in the processes of structural change, rather than to demonstrate discrete communication effects in terms of individual changes of attitudes and behavior. Thus, this research does not seek to establish relational propositions involving communication behavior and other individual traits, for instance, whether greater exposure to the official mass media is related to stronger ideological commitment. Rather, the primary interest is in the functional consequences of communication to individual members, their groups, and the social system in the processes of change. The enquiry does not start with the mass media and ask under what conditions mass communication is effective. Rather, it takes the various communication processes, through mass media as well as other channels, and analyzes how they are structured in the overall framework of societal change. Nor does the topical division follow the usual way of conceptualizing mass communication research, that is, newspapers, television, radio, traditional media, and interpersonal communication. Instead, the pertinent channels and patterns of communication are examined for their contributions to certain functional requisites of development.

In short, communication is not treated merely as a stimulus or as a change agent that brings about effects in terms of specific individual response. Rather, communication is conceptualized as the basic social process, encompassing an intricate entirety of verbal stimulus and response, the patterns of which change dynamically and concomitantly with changes in the social structure.

The author wishes to acknowledge a senior fellow grant from the East-West Center in 1973–1974, which enabled him to start on this project. The work was completed with the continued support of the Center. He feels particularly indebted to Wilbur Schramm, formerly director of the East-West Communication Institute and now distinguished researcher of the East-West Center, for his encouragement and extensive help throughout the preparation of this volume. Daniel Lerner of the Massachusetts Institute of Technology, while he was a consultant at the East-West Center from 1974 to 1976, gave invaluable advice and suggestions, which are reflected in many parts of this book.

A special note of thanks is also due John K. Fairbank of Harvard University, A. Doak Barnett of the Brookings Institution, Stephen Uhalley of the University of Hawaii, and Everett Rogers of Stanford University for their reviews and suggestions. Both William Rivers of Stanford and John Hulteng of the University of Oregon read the initial draft and made many helpful contributions. To all of them and to other colleagues who commented on various portions of this manuscript, the author is extremely grateful. However, he himself assumes sole responsiblity for any errors in facts and interpretations. This volume could not have been prepared without the encouragement and support of the author's wife, Julia, whose intuitive understanding of the Chinese culture has brought insight into the academic enigma that is China.

I
Introduction

July 10, 1921, was hardly noticeable as a day that would change the face of China. In an ornamented houseboat on South Lake, about an hour's train ride from Shanghai, eleven men—among them young Mao Tse-tung—had spent the day in heated discussions. By sunset they had reached a consensus. They agreed to form a Chinese Communist party.

Mao had come from Hunan to join delegates from five other regions for what was later to be known as the First National Congress of the Chinese Communist party.

There were twelve of them as they started their meeting on July 1, 1921, in a rented school building in Shanghai's French concession. After they narrowly escaped a police search on July 8, one delegate quit. The others decided to move the meeting to a sightseeing boat on South Lake, where their presence would not arouse suspicion. When the manifesto declaring the founding of the Party was adopted, only eleven delegates were present. At that time, the Chinese Communist party counted exactly fifty-nine members in the entire country.[1]

No one at the meeting could have foreseen the day when, some twenty-eight years later, Mao would make his one-sentence proc-

lamation at Peking's Tienanmen Square: "I declare the establishment of the People's Republic of China."

Historians will some day reveal the whole story of those twenty-
eight years: the founding and collapse of the Soviet Republic in
Kiangsi, the Long March to Yenan, the coup by young Marshal
Chang Hsueh-liang that kidnaped Generalissimo Chiang Kai-shek
and halted his military actions against the encircled Communists,
the devastating Japanese invasion, and the ensuing civil war that
ended with the Nationalist retreat to Taiwan. What perhaps has
most amazed the world outside is the almost magic transformation
of China from a war-torn country in 1949 to a world power today.
How did China develop herself from a "poor and blank" country
—in Mao's words—to her present status of near self-sufficiency?

This is a question of more than academic interest because many
emerging nations are looking for ways of improving their economic
productivity. It is no secret that some of their leaders are reluctant
to turn to the West for a model. Both their past experience with the
colonial powers and the seemingly impracticable pattern of Western economic development may have discouraged these new nations from taking the Western model seriously. They cannot afford
to wait for a hundred years. What they want is a speedy transformation from poverty to self-sufficiency. In this context, the experience
of China seems to offer promise.

In a strict sense, no country's experience can be a model for any
other country because of differences in cultural and social structural
backgrounds as well as leadership style. The Chinese experience has
its own peculiar characteristics and, without Mao, the Chinese
Communist Party could not have expanded from fifty-nine members to its present power. However, it is possible to examine some
of the broad steps taken by the Party leadership in the past quarter
century in order to understand China's processes of socialist transformation and development.

In an oversimplified sense, the Chinese model of development
has drawn its strength from the participation of the people, rather
than from the use of materials and capital. According to Mao,
development must start with the people, "the people, and the people alone, are the motivating force in the making of world
history."[2] In order to initiate participation, two conditions must be
achieved. First, there must be a change in the major social institutions to remove the old barriers that stand in the way of mass

mobilization. This would require a social structural change. Second, there must be a transformation of the traditional values and beliefs that hold the Chinese back from fully utilizing and organizing their own resources. This would require a change of cultural ethos, of personality; in short, the creation of the New Chinese Man.

These would be immense tasks for any societies, and particularly so for China upon the Communist takeover in 1949. The Chinese social structure at that time still retained many of its rigid, traditional features that had persisted for centuries. In the rural countryside the kinship system and the land-owning gentry dominated the villagers' social-economic life. The gentry class owned most of the arable land and maintained influential connections in the officialdom.[3] The tenants often had to pay as much as 50 percent of the crop as rent for cultivating the land. Even tenantry of this nature was not readily granted. According to a survey made in 1934–1935, only seven out of a hundred farm laborers could expect to rise to tenant status after working from boyhood to the age of 31.[4] Agricultural productivity was generally low. However, the close kinship relations, under which elders and authority figures like landlords were respected, gave the social system a relatively high stability. To the average person, life had very few choices. One must obey and follow the footsteps of his father, and submit to other persons of authority. Ready acceptance of one's status quo and a reluctance to depart from the kinship network contributed to a low mobility, both socially and physically.

In towns and cities, the small businessmen and proprietors were held to a low status in comparison with that of the gentry. They had to struggle to maintain their inherited trades under the constant demands for taxes and levies from the bureaucrats. These problems were further aggravated in big urban centers like Shanghai, where the foreign imperialists and their affiliated commercial firms had a dominating influence on both the local government and commerce. The idea of development, of improving the livelihood of the common people beyond what little they already had, appeared to be alien to the majority of the ruling class.

For many years, however, the Chinese had not only survived under that system, but had also learned to live with both the limited material subsistence and tolerable inequities it entailed. Compatible with the rigid social structure was a stable personality that enabled the Chinese to gain a sense of security from authoritarian submission, but made them feel alienated by innovation.[5] Conformity to customs and traditions was so overwhelming that a mere suggestion of departure would be psychologically disquieting. Any change in the old, accepted way of life was to be strongly resisted. To those intellectuals who took a special pride in the Chinese cultural heritage, the idea of replacing the old with something new borrowed from the alien West was particularly humiliating.

Furthermore, the nearly half century of wars had had the effect of impairing some of the major functional capabilities of the Chinese social system without reducing much of its rigidity. Because of the extensive war destruction and the depletion of economic resources resulting from excessive taxation in some regions, the Chinese social-economic structure in the late 1940s no longer provided the same degree of security and stability as before.

It is in this perspective—a traditional social structure in a stage of disturbance and unsettlement—that one has to view the task of structural change and development that the Chinese Communist party took upon itself. This was a task others had attempted before, but failed. There was a need for change, but the Chinese people, bound by their traditions, were unable to initiate actions and unwilling to depart from their old way of life. The unique instrument the Party has skillfully employed to bring about change and development, one that was missing in previous efforts made by others, is communication—the sharing of messages, sentiments, and intent among the people so that they could be aroused to act like one man, in a way desired by the Party authorities.

The Chinese Communist way of communication, as we shall illustrate later, is not just a few leaders talking to the populace through the mass media about what they should do. Rather, it is a case of almost everyone talking to everyone else, horizontally as well as vertically, upward as well as downward, regarding the ends and means of mobilization and development. It involves a high intensity of interpersonal communication at the grassroots level as well as mass media communication at the national level. It represents an integrated use of the media, the schools, the cadres, and above all, the local small groups. Participation in this gigantic communication network is both a right and an obligation. There is definitely control, but the control works primarily through communication among the people.

Communication of such intensity has been a novelty to the

Chinese, whose world prior to 1949 was rather severely confined, both geographically and psychologically. Facilities for mass communication had been few and underdeveloped. Most of the larger cities had been served by newspapers and radio broadcasts for a number of years, particularly since the war with Japan. But in the vast rural regions, communication, largely by word-of-mouth, was both slow and limited. The peasants were neither informed nor allowed to participate in the discussion of affairs that would affect them. For all practical purposes, the majority of Chinese at that time were kept outside the networks of public communication. To initiate the kind of communication that the Chinese engage in today, the Party had no hesitation to use coercion as a means of removing some of the barriers in the traditional social structure and getting the peasants and workers involved in the process of change. Once a new structural framework has been established, it provides the channels to keep the dynamic communication process moving. Partly persuasive and partly coercive, communication of this nature has sought to mobilize the energy and enthusiasm of the Chinese masses for changing the structural and ideological basis of China in order to maintain the pace of socialist transformation and development.

The primary purpose of this book is thus not to present a chronological account of China's development experience, nor to evaluate some of the economic policies the Party has pursued for development. Rather, our purpose is to analyze the unusual ways in which communication has been used in China (1) *to bring about the major social structural changes necessary for development, (2) to integrate and maintain the new social structure after it has been instituted, and ultimately, (3) to bring into being the New Chinese Man as the foundation of the New Chinese Socialist State.* The planners in a developing nation can consider whether any of the measures of change employed by China might be feasible within their own cultural and social structural context and compatible with their modes of leadership.

Development and Alternatives

A brief review of the concept of development and of two major alternative models will help answer the *why* of Chinese Communist approach before we discuss the *how*.

Development can be viewed both as an economic end product and as social processes of change.[6] As an end product, development represents a higher level of productivity achieved through a new combination of production factors—labor, materials, and equipment. Capital is essential as a medium for securing these production factors.

Underdevelopment, both from a historical and an analytical perspective, can be seen as a result of underutilization of production factors due to inadequate use of manpower, inefficient division of labor, and poor technology. This situation is often aggravated because of exploitation of labor, either by colonial powers or by native capitalists. Imperial China in the last decades of the Manchu dynasty was a classic example. Part of the huge pool of manpower lay idle. The crude division of labor then in effect, handed down through the ages, proved to be inadequate for large-scale productive activities. The level of technology was so low that Manchu China had to hire foreigners to run her newly acquired machines. The foreign settlements in Shanghai and other major cities attested to the exploitation by colonial powers, primarily the British and the French from Europe and the Japanese from East Asia. The indigenous capitalists showed not much more concern for the welfare of the Chinese people in general than did the compradores.

The case of imperial China illustrates that among the problems of development are (1) *how to correct underutilization of production factors and,* (2) *how to minimize exploitation.* When development is viewed in these perspectives, it becomes a matter of social processes for change rather than an end product. In order to create employment opportunities, there must be reallocation of material resources. There must be savings for investment. These and the minimization of exploitation—essential for rewarding productive activities—often require a change in the basic social structure. Efficient division of labor needs the support of a new, task-oriented social organization as well as managerial skills. To motivate the full use of manpower, some of the old cultural values and beliefs, for example, fatalism, may have to be changed. Use of machines requires technological training, which also may necessitate a set of new values and beliefs. Without these social structural and cultural changes, abundant resources may lie unused. The task of development, in that sense, is how to bring about these changes so that production factors can be fully utilized and exploitation minimized.

Chinese leaders who were anxious to rebuild China out of the tattered Manchu regime faced two available alternative models for development. One was the capitalist, free enterprise model of the West, largely founded on profit-oriented investment. According to Schumpeter, the economic development of Western countries gained its impetus from profit-seeking. Keynes sees Western economic development as a result of investment, the pooling of resources for productive activities.[7] Capital as a medium holds a key in this model, because with enough money the necessary equipment and materials can be procured and labor can be motivated, trained, and organized. The profit motive is assumed to be strong enough to induce an accumulation of capital. The same profit motive, operating through interest rates, provides a source of savings. The level of investment, according to Keynes, thus depends on the interest and the profit rates. Because this model is based on profit, the social system must provide a structural basis for protecting investment and profit.[8] The profit motive also needs a basis in cultural values—for instance, the Protestant ethic.[9] As Schumpeter has pointed out, the foundation of this model is entrepreneurship, which must have its basis in social structure and cultural values.

A major problem of this model, when applied to countries like China in early stages of development, is capital formation. The low income level, the low rate of accumulation of savings, and the low level of productivity form a vicious circle.[10] When people have barely enough to eat, even a strong profit motive will not be sufficient to induce savings. Another drawback of this model is its inattention to problems of exploitation, as reflected in an inequitable distribution of the fruits of labor imposed by the investors. Once savings are accumulated, they must be used to bring up underutilization of production factors and to achieve high productivity. However, unless exploitation is minimized—for instance, by a progressive income tax—the inequitable distribution of reward will persist. If the initial fruits of investment are not shared on a broad basis, there will not be a general rise of demand level to stimulate sustained development and there will not be a sufficient motivational basis to turn high aspirations among the people into productive labor.

In short, the free enterprise model is a better guide for maintaining an already highly developed economy than for transforming a social system from underdevelopment to development. An attempt at promoting development by strictly following this model is likely to run into difficulties, because the social structural and cultural conditions that characterized Western countries more than a century ago are generally not present in most of the developing countries today.[11]

The other major alternative approach to development is represented by the economic theory of Karl Marx. The Marxist theory purports to explain the origin as well as the operation of capitalism. It analyzes a highly developed economy, and seeks to eliminate exploitation by the capitalists through class struggle. The key concept of Marx is surplus value, defined as the difference between the "use value" of labor, that is the value-creating capacity of labor, and the "exchange value" of labor, that is, the market price of labor expressed in wages. Labor is held to be the most crucial element in production.[12]

Because of overconsumption of surplus value by the ownership class, Marx contends, the labor force, which makes up the bulk of society, would be unable to accumulate savings. The investment process would be slowed down, and the level of productivity would be curtailed. These observations, however, have not held true in all capitalist countries. Marx suggests that once surplus value and exploitation are eliminated, full use of manpower can be developed, presumably because an equitable distribution of the fruits of labor will follow, and that, in turn, will provide enough motivational support. However, the experiences in countries that profess Marxism do not seem to bear out these predictions.

Marxism recognizes the impetus for development originating from the elimination of exploitation, but provides few practical suggestions as to how an underdeveloped country can move ahead in its economic growth once exploitation is removed. The vital aspects of organization and technological know-how seem to be taken for granted. Inasmuch as the free-enterprise model is built upon the profit motive, by denying the pursuit of profit Marx seems to have cast out one propellant to development without offering a functional substitute.

The Chinese Approach

Dr. Sun Yat-sen, founder of the Republic of China, sought to develop China's economy not by following either the capitalist free-enterprise model or the Marxist model, but by adapting some features of both to China's own situation.[13] The basic problems he faced were the same that confront many national leaders today: how to accumulate enough capital for the procurement of essential equipment and materials, and how to effectively organize the people of the country for the best use of their resources.

Recognizing that any effective development program for China must benefit her teeming rural population, he proposed a "land-to-the tiller" reform which would redistribute agricultural land to the peasants, with compensation for landlords. To prevent accumulation of undue profits by urban land owners in the process of urbanization and industrialization, he proposed a heavy progressive tax system. He sought to maintain a balance of the public and private sectors of the economy by allowing private capitalism in industry and business and by placing major utilities and public services under state management. His objectives were to correct underutilization of production factors and to minimize exploitation, in this order. His ideal was to provide room for anyone capable of making a contribution to China's development without seeking excessive profit. Dr. Sun Yat-sen died before he had a chance to test his ideas.

When the Chinese Communists came into power in 1949, they rejected the free-enterprise model and turned to the Marxist model. In a sense, the Communist leaders shared Dr. Sun Yat-sen's objectives. However, they followed a different set of priorities in dealing with China's material and human resources, and employed different means of achieving their objectives. Elimination of exploitation was to take top priority, according to the Marxist theory, as a means of releasing human energy for development. This the Chinese Communist party promptly undertook by expropriating the rural landlords and urban businessmen. What was uniquely Chinese, reflecting the thinking of Mao rather than of Marx and Lenin, was the manner in which the landlords and businessmen were removed from their positions of wealth and influence. It was not so much the use of force, which was present, but rather the mobilization of social pressure from the mass of people—the peasants and workers—through a combination of group communication and coercion, that toppled the landlords and businessmen and eventually led to a fundamental change in the social structure.

These steps were only the beginning of China's process of social change and development. With the major sources of exploitation eliminated, the Party then turned to the difficult task of accumulating savings for capital investment from a population exhausted after years of war. How could the vicious circle of low income, low savings, and low productivity be broken? What could be done to increase productivity and curtail consumption so that the surplus could be channeled into investment? The solutions of these problems would be essential to the full use of material resources.

There were manpower problems too, having to do with organizational features as well as with the intrinsic qualities of productive labor. In terms of organization, the productive activites among a huge population must be coordinated and supervised. This requires an effective national communication network for transmitting the directives to the people, eliciting their support, and relaying their feedback to the policy-making body. The immense geographical size of China and the lack of transportation facilities made communication difficult. But the major obstacle seemed to be the old Chinese bureaucracy, which maintained no effective communication with the people. What were the Chinese Communist leaders going to do in order to transform the old, inept bureaucracy into an effective network of communication?

Furthermore, an efficient division of labor in the performance of tasks requires a system of cooperation and competition that is conducive to productivity. Bound by strong kinship ties, the Chinese in the past found it difficult to engage in cooperative efforts that required the pooling of manpower and resources outside the kinship network. Within the kinship structure, the predominant atmosphere was one of coexistence and seasonal mutual help rather than intensive competition, lest the internal harmony be disrupted. Large-scale competition outside the kinship realm was rare, too, because the overall Chinese social structure provided little reward for such behavior. Since business success and entrepreneurship were not highly regarded, there was little to compete for other than the glory of the ancestors, which was usually achieved through literary accomplishments leading to a position in officialdom. Given such a cultural background, how would the Communist leaders proceed to institutionalize a socialist system of cooperation and competition? How would the Party organize the traditionally passive Chinese people into functioning groups capable of pooling their resources and managing their local affairs in a manner that would improve productivity?

Regarding the intrinsic qualities of productive labor, the prob-

lem is essentially one of manpower training in terms of technological competence as well as supportive ideology and value orientations. China's old educational system had not been able to fulfill
the function of training adequate manpower for the tasks of development because of the traditional concept that "scholarly achievements lead to official positions." How could the system be overhauled in such a manner as to promote the learning of practical
skills and technology, and also to inculcate new goals, new values,
and new ways of thinking—in short, to create the New Chinese
Man? How could these objectives be achieved?

There are two other problems crucial to the developmental process although they do not directly promote the accumulation of
capital or the utilization of manpower. One concerns the process of
decision-making regarding the allocation of manpower and resources. Major decisions in Chinese history had typically been made
without seeking input and understanding from ordinary people.
The social and economic reforms proposed by Wang An-shih (A. D.
1021–1086) contained many promising features. They failed partly
because no attempts were made to obtain the understanding and
support of the people whom the reforms were intended to benefit.
What kind of decision-making process which at least takes into account the needs of the populace and gives them some sense of participation in the direction of development has been followed by the
Communist party leadership? Once a decision is made, how is it explained to the people in order to enlist their support?

The other problem concerns conflict resolution. Development efforts tend to aggravate conflicts because they disrupt the existing
social equilibrium and leave varying impacts on different segments
of the population. The situation of conflict in China during the last
quarter century seems to have been particularly pronounced because conflict has been more than a by-product of development; it
has been actively employed as a major instrument of change. By
conflict, we are referring not to the internal power struggle within
the Party, but to the contention among people over the limited resources and status. The old mechanisms for conflict resolution built
into the kinship structure were no longer functioning after the removal of landlords and other influentials. Thus, there became necessary new social mechanisms that would enable the Party to
manage social conflict, giving it timely attention and resolving it
somewhat to the satisfaction of the parties concerned. Conflict reso-

lution of this kind is considered by the Party to be important to prevent an accumulation of tension and friction and to maintain social integration in the course of change and development. How is it done?

These six problems are considered to have cross-cultural generality in the sense that a developing country must solve them in one way or another. Many other problems of an economic nature—such as control of inflation, priority of resource allocation for industry versus agriculture, establishment of financial institutions, regulation of foreign trade—are of vital importance and must be given full attention by each developing country. Health and population programs are crucial too. We have, however, chosen to limit our investigation to those six because they are related to the fundamental social structural fabric for economic development.

Of the six problems, four bear directly on the development process involving the use of material and human resources. They are: capital formation, communication networks, cooperation and competition, and manpower training (see figure 1). Of the remaining two, decision-making has to precede each development effort while conflict resolution is essential in order to keep up the momentum of development. (These major concepts are defined in later chapters.) No clear and ready solutions can be found in either Marx or Lenin to these problems. The Chinese Communists have had to find their own way. Before considering in the following chapters how the Chinese have been organized to solve these structural problems of development, we shall discuss briefly the meaning of communication, a key concept in our thesis, in the perspectives of social system and social change.[14] We shall then examine the Chinese communication system—its mass media and interpersonal networks—in the light of its roles in China's structural change and development processes.

Communication and Social Change

By *communication* we mean the symbolic behavior of man. It has long been recognized that human society functions through and by communication. The British sociologist Herbert Spencer, writing a century ago, spoke of the means of communication as a major coordinating and controlling apparatus of society. Charles Cooley was among the first American scholars to emphasize communication as the very mechanism through which human relations

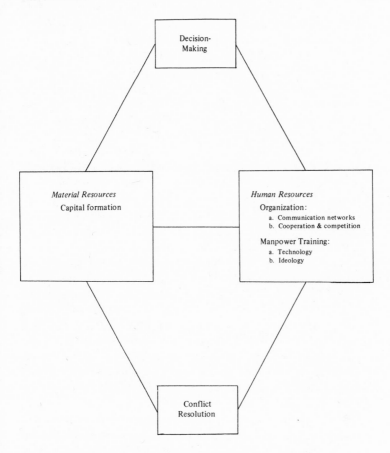

Figure 1. Social Structural Fabric for Development

exist and develop. The anthropologist Edward Sapir conceived of society as a network of relations maintained chiefly by communication. "Every cultural pattern and every single act of social behavior," Sapir observed, "involve communication in either an explicit or implicit sense." Dewey and Park, among others, held similar views.[15]

The thinking of those early theorists has had considerable influence on empirical research in communication, which has emerged as a discipline in the last quarter century. To both Daniel Lerner and Wilbur Schramm, the study of communication is inseparable from the study of people. Lerner regards communication as the means of exchange and the measure of value in social life.[16] According to Schramm, "When we study communication, we study people—relating to each other and to their groups, organizations, and societies, influencing each other, being influenced, informing and being informed, teaching and being taught, entertaining and being entertained."[17]

The societal functions of communication implicit in the early theorists have been more specifically enunciated by Harold Lasswell, a political scientist and a pioneer in communication research. In his essay that has since become a classic, Lasswell proposes three functions of communication: (1) surveillance of the environment, (2) correlation of the different parts of society in responding to environment, and (3) transmission of social heritage.[18] Schramm has discussed these functions in terms of their relevance to the political system, the economic system, and the social system in general.[19]

Structure and Content of Communication

Because communication is pervasive, the concept is also somewhat elusive. The classic paradigm, originally proposed by Lasswell and expanded by Lerner, conceptualizes communication in terms of six variables: who (the source) says, what (the content), to whom (the audience), why (for what purpose), how (through what media), and with what effect?[20] Following the distinction between the patterns and content of culture in anthropology, we can categorize the six variables into (1) the patterns of communication, as they exist in the network of channels, and (2) the content of communication. Having observed the channels and the content, we can then make inferences regarding the purposes and effects of communication.

By communication network, we are referring to the regulated paths along which messages flow in a society between the source and the audience, in oral or written form, through interpersonal contact or the mass media. That the communication network is an integral part, although not the whole, of social structure is suggested by the French anthropologist Claude Levi-Strauss, who conceptualizes a social structure in terms of what he calls the communication of goods and services, the communication of women, and the communication of messages. These may be approximately identified as the economic system, the kinship system, and the commu-

nication system. Lucian Pye, a political scientist, considers the
"structure of a communication system with its more or less well-
defined channels" to be "the skeleton of the social body which
envelops it." Understanding the patterns of communication will
take us a long way toward understanding a social system.[21]

The content of communication is the very substance of human
intercourse. Given the extreme variety of messages in human interactions, however, a clear, unambiguous classification of communication content that lends itself to fruitful analysis would seem
to pose considerable difficulty. From the work on human communication in psychology, sociology, and communication research,
it seems that at least four categories can be distinguished.[22]
Although a communication act most likely involves more than one
category so that the four are not completely independent of one
another, it is possible to identify the predominant category by its
relative weight.

Four Categories of Communication

When people get together, they often transmit factual information, or what purports to be factual information, about their physical and social environment. This may be called *informational communication*. Communication of this kind assumes a prominent role
in the surveillance function, and is essential for the survival of individuals as well as groups.

Factual information is presumably either true or false, and its
validity should have a basis in physical reality. However, two obstacles usually exist in a social group to make the test of validity by an
individual difficult. First, not all individuals can have full access to
all the relevant information that is essential for their functioning in
the group. Secondly, among those who have full access, not all are
intellectually equipped to effectively assess all the information.
Because of these inherent limitations, informational communication is usually differentially distributed in a group, giving certain
individuals an advantage over others because of their greater access
to information. The validity of factual information to the other individuals and their subsequent behavior often rests on the judgment of those who are more centrally located in the information
network. Gaining control of informational communication thus
becomes instrumental to gaining control of the group.

At other times, the act of communication involves not so much the transmission of information as the application of social pressure. This is primarily an act of beseeching, requesting, demanding, or even threatening. Apart from selective dissemination of information, it is largely through communication of this kind that a group maintains control over its members and directs them toward specified tasks. The pressure may be exerted directly and backed up by group actions against the deviants, or it may be applied indirectly by creating in each member an awareness of the expectations of others in the group. While all communication takes place in a social context, the existing social relations among the group members become particularly critical to the effectiveness of this kind of communication. The application of social pressure is effective only if the person to whom the pressure is directed wants to maintain social relations with the others and does not intend to leave the group. This type of communication either seeks to sustain existing group relations by bringing the deviants back into the mainstream, or represents an attempt by the deviants to create new normative relations in place of the old. In either case, it seeks the acceptance of certain behavioral norms and standards by some members of the group. We shall call it *normative communication*, which serves primarily the function of correlating the different parts of society in responding to environment.

Every society, indeed every group, has a set of values, which spells out what is good, right, and desirable. According to the American anthropologist Clyde Kluckhohn, values are important because they influence the selection from available modes, means, and ends of action by groups and individuals.[23] The Communist ideology is a set of values that defines certain indisputable ends as well as preferred means of achieving these ends. Even though values cannot be totally divorced from reality, their validity is supposed to be accepted without questioning. It is not to be tested on an objective, utilitarian basis. The code of seppuku (hara-kiri) among Japanese samurai is an example. It was accepted as the ultimately desirable, and indeed the only feasible way of maintaining the honor of a samurai under certain circumstances. Whether there might be less painful ways of resolving a problem was beside the point.[24]

In any society or group, its members engage in a variety of communication acts that are intended to imbue the new recruits with the distinctive values they must accept. The transmission of cultural heritage from one generation to the next is accomplished primarily through this kind of communication. The socialization of new members in a group follows the same route. We shall call it *value-oriented communication*. While social pressure functions as an external behavioral restraint, effective only when the individual has to rely on his group for acceptance and survival, values are an internal behavioral regulator. An individual is guided by his values because he has voluntarily accepted them. When a person is under social pressure, he *has* to do what he is expected to do. When a person is guided by values, he *wants* to do what he is expected to do.

However, social pressure and values do not function in complete independence of each other. Normative communication, which applies social pressure, is a process which relies for its effectiveness on the manipulation of reward and punishment. Sometimes, the reward or punishment is presented in terms of material incentives or affiliative relations. If one resists the social pressure, one may stand to lose either useful goods and services, or the goodwill of friends and associates, or both. At other times, the pressure is exerted in a value-oriented framework. A person can be told by others in his group that it is morally or ideologically wrong to do this and not to do that. In other words, *values can give concrete content to social pressure, while social pressure can operate as an enforcer of values.* Thus, normative communication and value-oriented communication can, and often do, function in a complementary manner even though they are conceptually distinctive from each other.

There is a fourth category of communication that involves not so much the transmission of factual information, exertion of pressure, or inculcation of values, as the expression or arousal of emotion. The expression of love, hatred, joy, and anger are examples. While the other kinds of communication deal largely with cognitions, whether informational, normative, or evaluative, a communication act in this category involves primarily affection. We shall call it *affective communication*.

Both informational and normative communications are generally considered instrumental in nature, in the sense that they are used as a means for achieving an end. Value-oriented communication may be considered either a means or an end, depending on the situational context in which it takes place. The teaching of moral principles to children, for instance, could be primarily an end, while political indoctrination is generally employed as a means. Affective communication is often considered to be an end in itself. Love, for instance, is supposed to be selfless. Thus, affective communication is said to be expressive and consummatory rather than instrumental.[25] This basic nature of affective communication, however, need not imply that emotional expression and arousal cannot be used as a means for achieving an end. In fact, emotional arousal has been an indispensable component of almost all mass movements, whether religious, social, or political.

Purposive Use of Communication for Change

These four types of communication are part of the fundamental social processes that maintain the functioning of groups. As vital to society as air and water are to the life of organisms, these communication processes may be considered "natural," being part of the existing cultural dynamics of a social system. In this sense, we can analyze a social system in terms of the structure, content, and flow of communication.[26] A conceptual scheme in this perspective requires an analysis of the *networks* of communication that constitute the basis of role relations, as well as an examination of the *patterns* in which the different *contents* of informational, normative, value-oriented, and affective communication flow through the networks. The implications of the structure and flow of communications to the functioning of the social system can then be observed. This perspective follows broadly the structural-functional approach in anthropology and sociology, but makes communication the focus of analysis.[27]

The same communication processes, however, need not be viewed only as social mechanisms for maintaining the status quo. They can become effective instruments for the specific purpose of inducing change in the social system. First, because the communication structure is an intrinsic part of social structure, it would be reasonable to assume that change of a social system will not likely occur without concomitant change in the patterns of communication. In other words, systemic social change will generally involve communication change. This point has been well illustrated by Lerner, among others. If this assumption is valid, then one can hope to change a social system by first changing the patterns of communication. That is, the means and channels of communication can be effectively utilized as instruments to induce planned social change. Among scholars interested in social and economic development,

Schramm has argued vigorously for this proposition.[28] Finally, once a social system has been initially changed, it may become necessary to control the patterns of communication in order to prevent the reversion of the new social system to its old form. It is these *purposive uses* of communication, rather than the existing communication processes in a society, that will be the focus of our analysis with respect to China's experience in social change and development.

Communication and Change Processes

In general, we assume that a social system consisting of inter-related institutions will remain viable as long as sufficient people participate in the institutions and derive satisfaction from them. Tha lack of a basis of economic efficiency and social justice need pose no immediate threat to the system as long as the participants do not subjectively feel deprived. The situation in the traditional Chinese villages provides an illustration. The tenants labored hard and tried to eke out a living on what little was left after the landlords had collected the rental. These conditions of inequity were endured without challenge for centuries. It was not until strong dissatisfaction had been activated among the tenants and the prospect of change held out to them, that change became possible. In this sense, dissatisfaction, reflected in both rising expectations and rising frustrations, would be a necessary condition before a major institutional change could occur.

When this stage is reached, then an acceptable alternative institution must be made available to fulfill the expectations of the dissatisfied majority role participants. For instance, a land reform could change the landlord-tenant relationships to provide more benefits for the tenants. Such new institutions, being a network of new role relations, cannot be established by administrative orders or political means alone. They will become established only through sustained behavioral participation as well as firm value-attachment by the participants involved. Well-intended programs of national development have sometimes failed despite strong political backing, partly because of insufficient support of resources and services, but more importantly, also because of the planners' inattention to the need to generate popular participation and induce value change.

If we assume that political and economic supports are available —a precondition that is often unfulfilled—we can then analyze the roles of communication in facilitating the processes of social structural and value changes.

First of all, informational communication can be used to change the perception of the old institutions among the disadvantaged participants. By presenting information that alters the basis of a relative sense of deprivation, what was previously perceived as satisfactory, or at least tolerable, will now be seen as unsatisfactory and intolerable. The peasants can be reminded, for instance, that the landlords in their own village live a comfortable life without doing much work while the peasants themselves toil in poverty. They can also be reminded that peasants like themselves have in some instances taken actions that resulted in an improvement of their livelihood.

However, because a social institution is supported by value-attachment—for instance, acceptance of misery as fate, submission to existing authorities—factual information alone may not be sufficient to change individual perception. Emotional arousal is often necessary in order to commit individuals to some irreversible overt action as a prelude to perceptual change. This can be seen by the fact that a revolution involving the masses inevitably has an emotional foundation, whether it be nationalism or intergroup antagonism based on class enmity or ethnic division. Once the individuals have taken the first step of behavioral commitment, further involvement and eventual perceptual change will become easier. In time, the old institution, previously accepted as given, will be considered potentially changeable.

At this point, adequate informational communication will be necessary to present an alternative institution that has a high degree of technical feasibility and greater reward. For instance, the peasants may be asked to pool their resources and form a cooperative. However, because an existing institution generally has a basis of social reality, in the sense that people other than oneself are also seen to be engaged in it, an individual alone will hesitiate to deviate from the old institutional patterns even if he wants to. The use of informational communication to assure him of the technical feasibility and increased benefits may not be enough to change his behavior. Normative communication in the group then becomes essential, both to create social pressure and to generate a basis of social support in order to steer the individuals away from the old institution and, subsequently, to elicit their active participation in the new institution.

Once individuals begin to participate, their conforming behavior needs to be rewarded and their deviant behavior punished. Partly, this is a surveillance problem—just knowing who is conforming with the new behavioral patterns and who is not. An adequate network of informational communication is required for monitoring. As a follow-up of surveillance, normative communication can be used to convey social approval and disapproval. Also, control of informational communication may become necessary in order to prevent the perception of other, alternative institutions.

To build a firm basis of the new institution in place of the old, however, requires more than overt conformity. There must be a change in the foundation of value-attachment, through genuine acceptance of the new values and new ideology. Only then will the new behavioral patterns become internalized. Value-oriented communication is required to achieve this end. Like a religious conversion, this process can be aided by affective communication to arouse emotional commitment, and by normative communication to create a new basis of social reality.

In short, all four types of communication can play essential roles in the processes of planned social change, although how they are used and organized would vary from one social system to another.

Value-Oriented Communication in China

The concept of using communication for social change is almost as old as Chinese civilization. Confucius (551–479 B.C.) was in effect advocating the use of value-oriented communication, through moral teachings, rituals, folk music, and ancestor worship, to change what he considered to be an unhealthy contemporary society back to its old form in the early Chou Dynasty.[29] While many philosophers in Chinese history shared the concern of Confucius about bringing back the old, thus blocking the road to reform and progress, there have been a few notable exceptions. The most radical was Mo Tzu (468–403 B.C.), a scholar with a working-class background who gained a national reputation shortly after Confucius' time.[30] Completely rejecting Confucius' ideal of restoring the old through rituals and music, Mo Tzu wanted to revolutionize Chinese society and remove social inequities through preaching of

disciplined life and universal love. However, the influence of Confucius was so overwhelming throughout the centuries that the voice
of Mo Tzu was largely drowned out. It was the invasion of Western
imperialism toward the end of the nineteenth century that finally
awakened the Chinese intellectuals to the need for social reform.

Dr. Sun Yat-sen was among the first to make a bold attempt to
change the Chinese social system, again through the use of value-
oriented communication embedded in the teaching of his Three
Principles of the People. The New Life movement by the government of the Republic of China before the Sino-Japanese War had a
similar though more limited objective, and followed a similar approach. These attempts were not highly successful because they
employed communication in a segmental, but not comprehensive
manner. They preached value-orientations and relied on the emotional appeal of nationalism, but generally made little effective use
of informational and normative communications that are vital to
mobilizing mass participation. It remained for Mao Tse-tung to
take hold of the age-old Chinese tool of value-oriented communication and the newly awakened nationalism, and to blend them
with the Leninist version of agitation and propaganda.[31] The result
has been a powerful instrument of persuasion and organization that
reflects both the traditional Chinese emphasis on value-oriented
communication and the coercive pressure of Leninist tactics.

The Communist ideology as espoused by Mao contains notable
parallelisms to several schools of Chinese philosophy, although its
overall emphasis is different from any of them.[32] Ideological conversion is highly important to Mao, as it was also to Confucius. Law
and punishment, according to Confucius, are not adequate for
achieving a perfect social order. At best they can convince the people that they dare not violate the law. A perfect society can be built
only upon the foundation of perfect men. For this objective to be
realized, the people must be taught the doctrine of *jen* ("love,
humanity") so that harmonious human relations can be cultivated.
At the same time, they must be taught to "feel shame" *(chih)* so
that they will refrain from undesirable behavior. The Confucian
motto "Do not do unto others what you do not want others to do
unto you " embraces both the positive reward of jen and the
negative restraint of chih. Confucius emphasized *li* ("rules of pro-
priety") and advocated the practice of rituals and music as the

means of achieving his perfect society. Like Confucius, Mao wants to build the New Chinese Socialist State on the foundation of the New Chinese Man. However, Mao has relied on self-criticism and mutual criticism in a group setting to bring about his version of ideological reform.

The Maoist ideology stresses the importance of the people, as well as two-way communication between the people and the government. These same concepts were emphasized by Mencius (390–305 B.C.), a later disciple of Confucius.[33] The people are the most important element in a state, wrote Mencius, whereas the government is the next important, and the emperor the least important. The concept of two-way communication was prominent in the teaching of Mencius, who considered it necessary for the ruler and the subjects to share each other's happiness and worries. Mencius used the term *people* to include everyone. According to Maoist ideology, only the proletariat are considered qualified to be the "people."

Although both Confucius and Mencius have been severely criticized, Hsun Tzu (340–245 B.C.), another Confucian philosopher, has won praise from the Chinese Communists.[34] A near contemporary of Mencius, Hsun Tzu believed that human nature is evil, and therefore must be restrained and reformed by external forces.[35] This is clearly what the Party has been trying to do with the Chinese people over the last quarter century. The Party's ultimate objectives, however, are quite different from those of Hsun Tzu. Hsun Tzu advocated the use of ritualistic indoctrination in the Confucian tradition to achieve a perfect social order, in which everyone knows his rights and obligations and observes them rigidly. The Chinese Communist party wants to reform the people in order to establish a proletarian dictatorship.

Some of the radical revolutionary ideas and practices followed by Mao can be found in the writings of Mo Tzu mentioned earlier. Mo Tzu wanted to remove exploitation and to correct unjust distribution of wealth. He established himself as The Master *(Chu Tzu),* and imposed rigid discipline over all his followers, who were expected to forego freedom of thought and movement and live a spare life of material scarcity. His disciplinary requirements were so demanding that the disciples had to be prepared, upon an order of The Master, to "jump into boiling water and walk into burning

fire, and meet death without a hesitating step." Mo Tzu considered selfishness to be the origin of all human conflicts, a view the Maoist ideology seems to share. The similarity, however, ends there. Mo Tzu sought to negate selfishness by preaching "universal love," believing that only mutual love would bring about mutual benefit. He was against all conflicts, particularly war. On the other hand, the Chinese Communists have relied on conflict and class struggle, rather than love, as a means of establishing a collective, selfless social order.

Even some of the practical implementations of development and the exercise of political authority by Mao can be identified in the writings of early Chinese philosophers. For instance, Han Fei Tzu (280–233 B.C.), a disciple of Hsun Tzu and a founder of the legalist school, regarded the army and the peasants to be the cornerstones of national development.[36] Mao has followed the same approach. According to Han Fei Tzu, there can be no binding love and deep trust between the ruler and his followers. A stable political structure can be maintained only through mutual surveillance and a delicate balance of control and delegation of power. Events in China during the last quarter century seem to reinforce his view.

It is difficult to say whether and to what extent Mao and other Party leaders have been influenced by ancient Chinese philosophers of different schools. Whatever influence, if any, seems to have been selective.[37] But the possibility remains that because these ideas and views have been part of the Chinese culture, not alien, their infusion into the Chinese Communist ideology may have made it less difficult for the Chinese people to accept the indoctrination and pressure tactics employed by the Party.

The Communication System in China

Back in the Yenan days, Mao once made the following remarks on mobilizing the masses of China:

> We should go to the masses and learn from them, synthesize their experience into better, articulated principles and methods, then do propaganda among the masses, and call upon them to put these principles and methods into practice so as to solve their problems and help them achieve liberation and happiness.[38]

This, in essence, has been Mao's way of bringing about structural and ideological transformation in China. Communication is at the

very center of the whole approach. Over the years, Mao and his Party have relied on a highly efficient, well-controlled communication system to achieve their objectives of development.

The Chinese communication system consists of two major components: the extensive and ever-present mass media, and a tightly organized network of interpersonal channels built around small groups. Both are closely supervised by the Party. China's mass-media system has been analyzed in detail by a number of scholars, notably Frederick Yu.[39] Before we present the highlights of that system, as it has been developed since the early days of the People's Republic, we shall briefly note the difference between the Western concepts of communication and the Chinese approach, particularly its reliance on small groups.

In Communist ideology, communication media are an important means of class struggle because they can be used to support the change of the material base of the social structure and cultivate a favorable ideological consciousness as well. The Chinese Communist philosophy for the purposive use of communication differs rather pointedly from the Western philosophy.

Communication, as employed in Western countries for purpose of persuasion, involves primarily dissemination of information. Whether in a political campaign, commerical adverstising, or international propaganda, Western communicators assume that if the right kind of information is disseminated to the right audience, taking into account its existing predispositions and group affiliations, it will change the audience's perception of the environment, and consequently also its motivation and behavior. The task of the communicator is to maintain a high degree of source credibility, select the most attractive appeals, choose the right channels, and organize the message in a style that would achieve the maximum effects.[40] Care is taken not to challenge the basic values and group affiliations of the audience. The final choice is presumably left to the person who is the target of the message, with the expectation that he will change his perception, motivation, and behavior in the direction suggested by the communicator.

Because of the large size of the audience that can be reached, the mass media are usually chosen as the primary channels. Interpersonal communication is not overlooked, but is treated as a side benefit if it can be brought around to aide the mass media, either as an aid for transmitting information or, sometimes, as a means of normative communication for generating social support. The fact that it is considered the second step of the "two-step flow" hypothesis reflects the Western evaluation of the role of interpersonal communication, which is usually not tightly organized.[41] The media channels are open to anyone who has the financial resources to buy time or space. Divergent views as well as different commodities are allowed to compete within the limits of their financial capabilities. Western communicators, whether politicians, advertisers, or evangelists, generally work on the basis of existing values, rather than seeking to change them. Intensive emotional arousal on a massive scale is employed more by evangelists, less by politicians, and much less by advertisers.

Group Communication

To the Chinese Communists, purposive communication goes far beyond dissemination of information. Although communication research as it is conducted in the West does not seem to exist in China, the Party leaders have apparently accumulated considerable practical experience in the art of mass persuasion.[42] They are certainly aware of the importance of information to one's perception of environment. Because of this awareness, they have been highly selective in the dissemination of information, so that the people will not be confronted with divergent views, but will perceive their environment only in the manner encouraged by the Party. This end is facilitated by screening information input from without and discouraging the expression of major dissent from within. The masses speak with "one man's voice," as it were, creating a sense of unanimity and popular support.

However, the Chinese Communist leaders apparently do not regard perception of environment alone as capable of regulating or changing the behavior of the audience. For behavioral change and regulation, the Party relies heavily on normative communication within the group setting. What Mao means by going to the masses is simply to generate and mobilize social pressure, through normative communication within the group, in order to elicit and regulate the correct behavioral patterns. In the Party's view, the most important part of communication is what goes on within the group under the supervision of Party cadres. The mass media, by comparison, play a secondary support role. To use an analogy suggested by Wilbur Schramm, interpersonal communication is the infantry, while the mass media are the artillery.[43]

The relationship between mass media and interpersonal communication was clearly spelled out by Mao in his talk to the editorial staff of the *Shansi Suiyuan Daily* in 1948:

> The role and power of the newspapers consist in their ability to bring the Party program, the Party line, and the Party's general and specific policies, its tasks and methods of work before the masses in the quickest and most extensive way.[44]

How the masses are going to carry out the Party programs and policies is left to the groups to work out, as long as they stay within the Party's guidelines. The major mechanism for fulfiling this function of implementation is the small study groups, which have been instituted all over the country, in rural production teams, in factory and mining work shifts, in government offices, military units, schools, and in urban neighborhood resident groups.[45] Everyone, young or old, man or woman, belongs more or less permanently to some group upon which he depends heavily. Numbering anywhere between ten and thirty in membership, the study groups meet regularly, usually two or three times a week or whenever there is a need to get together. Information on Party policies and programs reaches the group through the mass media and is quickly transmitted to all members. Under the guidance of local cadres as group leaders, the members discuss and digest information in the light of the task that confronts them, whether it be a production campaign, family planning, or a movement to criticize Lin Piao and Confucius. In discussion, the information emanating from the mass media takes on local relevance and directs the group toward performance of its task.

The groups provide an effective setting for normative communication. By participating in the group discussion and by voicing his individual support, each group member contributes to a perception of consensus regarding the means and ends available to the group. In essence, the group members generate social pressure to bear upon themselves. In the case of production, group objectives are set and accepted. In the case of behavioral modification, right is differentiated from wrong, for all members to observe.

In contrast to the Western practice, the Chinese Communist

party chose to challenge directly the old values. Because of its ability to generate a perception of unanimity, the small study group has been employed as a mechanism of value-oriented communication for the purpose of providing ideological support for behavioral conformity. By requiring the Chinese to study a uniform text of Chairman Mao's thoughts, and by relying on the strength of assertions repeated again and again in a group setting, where deviance is readily exposed and punished, and conformity publicly approved, the Party expects communication of this nature to be effective some day in changing the deeply rooted traditional values and beliefs of the Chinese.

The emphasis on value-oriented communication appears to be a major difference between the Chinese approach and the Russian model. Both the Chinese and the Russian Communists apply social pressure through normative communication. In the Russian case, the social pressure is backed up largely by the threat of force without an excessive concern with ideological conviction. In the Chinese case, the threat of force is ever present too, and has been invoked, as in the antirightist campaign following the Hundred Flower movement, and in the Cultural Revolution. However, the Chinese Communists seem to emphasize ideological conviction more than the Russians do, perhaps because of China's traditional reliance on value-oriented communication.

As part of China's communication system, the small groups provide a setting for emotional arousal that seeks to facilitate the pace of ideological conversion. That an intimate, small group possesses an enormous power of emotional arousal can be illustrated by the behavior of the Holy Rollers, a movement that became popular in the United States during the Great Depression.[46] Confronted by an outpouring of emotional confessions by his peers in the movement, a person would gradually work up his own feeling of guilt and inadequacy until he too made a full admission of sins in a cathartic outburst. A similar pattern has been followed by the Chinese in self-criticism sessions, in which the sense of guilt arising from self-abasement is mingled and reinforced by a strong feeling of shame (chih) activated by public mutual criticism.

In short, through a minimum amount of coercion and skillful use of communication—informational, normative, value-oriented, and affective—the Party has been able to organize the vast Chinese population into its respective groups. The groups are kept alive and busy with a constant flow of tasks and campaigns. Propelled by fuels largely generated through communication within the groups, they are running like local engines, carrying on the development programs along the tracks laid down by the Party.

Mass Media

While interpersonal communication in the group is supervised by local cadres, mass media communication is controlled by the Party hierarchy. China's communication media are tightly organized into three layers, the national, provincial, and local, for the purpose of guiding the perception and behavior of her eight hundred million people. The Party's Central Committee, through the Department of Propaganda, controls all the national media, including the *People's Daily,* the monthly magazine *Red Flag,* and Radio Peking. The Party's provincial committees perform the same function for the provincial newspapers and provincial radio stations. Except for local news which varies from province to province, the same kind of information and views are disseminated by the New China News Agency (Hsinhua) to the entire population.

Hsinhua is a national news agency operated by the Party to serve all the mass media in the country as well as Party-affiliated newspapers overseas. It has correspondents all over the country, down to the commune level, and in some of the capital cities abroad. Its selection and presentation of news are closely supervised by the Party.[47] It monitors and coordinates the contents of all media, whether national, provincial, or local. The flow of information through Hsinhua is both downward and upward. News and features originating from Hsinhua's local correspondents are often given prominent display in the *People's Daily* if the contents are considered worthy of nationwide attention.

The process of news management at the provincial level seems to be somewhat less rigid, as told by Huang Ling-ling, a former reporter of the *Canton Evening News:*

In reporting local news, the emphasis must be placed on "good" news. Bad news is toned down or not carried at all. The reporter has to tell the editor how and where he got the story. If the editor thinks the material worthwhile, he will instruct the reporter in detail how to write the story. The reporter writes it accordingly and the story is usually

published with little editing. However, if the intended story touches on
politics or policy matters, then the editor has to obtain approval from
the secretariat of the local Communist Party Committee before
publishing it.[48]

Editors are Party members of sufficient standing to publish
routine items without seeking approval. They are held responsible
for the editorial content of the newspaper entrusted to them. Two
channels keep them informed of the Party's policies and background events. One is the weekly study sessions during which the
Party's latest instructions are discussed. All editorial staff members
must attend. The other channel is a tabloid of four to eight pages
published six days a week by Hsinhua for internal distribution
among Party cadres. Known as *Chan Kao Hsiao Hsi* (Reference
News), it primarily contains news about world events, both favorable and unfavorable to the Communist cause, as well as foreign
press comments on China. It occasionally carries a foreign wire service report on some domestic event. It was from one of these information sheets that former reporter Huang learned about the defec-
tion of Chinese Communist jet pilot, Lt. Liu Cheng-szu, in a
MIG-15 in March 1962.[49] The current circulation of *Chan Kao
Hsiao Hsi* is estimated at six million copies.[50]

The Chinese Communist Party has put together a gigantic mass-
media system at relatively low cost. Television, a medium that requires a huge initial capital outlay, began in 1958, but is apparently not given top priority.[51] According to American editors who
visited China in 1972, the country had about one hundred thousand black-and-white television sets, mostly in big cities. The press,
on the contrary, is highly developed. The *People's Daily* itself has a
circulation of three million copies.[52] The total number of readers
reached by the official newspaper is much greater than its circulation figure would indicate (by Western standards) because of
several factors. One is the large number of bulletin boards where
the official paper is posted for the reading public in cities and
towns.[53] Second, the Party has initiated a practice of allowing people to "rent" a copy for a maximum of two hours at half the street
sale price. The post office handles this service, which is apparently
used by many. Third, all over the country there are newspaper reading groups, in which a student or someone else reads the stories
from the *People's Daily* to his illiterate neighbors. Although the

circulation figures for the provincial newspapers are unknown, they are most probably not small.[54]

Several recent developments may be noted about the mass media of the People's Republic. In content, there has been a much stronger emphasis on value-oriented communication. According to a special article published in the *People's Daily* during the Cultural Revolution, the mass media "must carry the voice of Chairman Mao to all corners of the land."[55] Since then an unmistakable change has been noted in the official newspaper, emphasizing the role of the mass media as carriers of ideological admonitions rather than as sources of news and information. Most news items now generally concern visits to China by foreign dignitaries, itineraries of Chinese missions visiting other countries, and world events that are favorable to the Communist cause. Ideological discussions and reports on production models dominate the rest of the official paper. There is little else about what is happening in the country.[56]

Radio broadcasting facilities have increased rapidly to give the Party a powerful tool of informing the people, organizing mass actions, and teaching ideology down to the village level. In 1956 China had only 1.5 million receiving sets for a population of six hundred million.[57] Although latest statistics are not available, visitors to mainland China have generally come back with the impression that most urban families have radio sets.[58] Perhaps more significant is the expansion of broadcasting services in rural villages. The government began developing radio facilities for rural areas in 1955, using primarily radio-relay stations and wired louspeakers. A plan drawn up in 1955 projected nine hundred line-broadcasting stations, with a total of four hundred fifty to five hundred thousand wired loudspeakers within one year.[59] We have no data on the progress of expansion in the ensuing years. According to an official announcement on September 21, 1974, all counties and cities now have broadcasting stations. Line-broadcasting facilities have been installed in more than 90 percent of the production brigades and production teams, and 63 percent of the present homes now have their own wired loudspeakers.[60]

The expanded wired broadcasting facilities have enabled many counties and cities to organize broadcast meetings, for instance, to criticize Lin Piao and Confucius. Radio has been extensively used for broadcasting lectures on the writings of Marx, Lenin, and Mao

Tse-tung. In Hsiangtan, Hunan, more than twenty-three hundred poor and lower-middle peasant cadres were trained by radio lectures during a 1974 campaign. Party secretaries at various levels often used wired broadcasting to explain the Party's policies, organize production campaigns, exchange experiences, and publicize model cases.[61]

Since the Cultural Revolution, the Party has taken steps to develop a local print medium at the production brigade level to serve as a vital linkage between the national media and the small groups. Sometimes called the *war bulletin (Chan Pao)*, this is a mimeographed information sheet edited and put out by peasant correspondents in the brigade. With "mud on their feet and callouses on their hands," they are said to be comparable to the barefoot doctors.[62] At Huang Lou Commune near Shanghai, for instance, there were some 150 peasant correspondents in 1968. Because they work on farms, they understand the problems of peasants in a way the urban reporters cannot. Most of them are sons and daughters of poor and lower-middle-class peasants, who have no training other than in elementary or junior high school. A peasant correspondent must, first of all, be completely loyal to Chairman Mao. He or she must be a capable and diligent worker, and must have close relations with the mass of people in the commune. Whether one can write well is of secondary consideration.

At Huang Lou Commune, the peasant correspondents also wrote articles for the commune's line-broadcasting station and submitted local features about the commune to newspapers and radio stations in Shanghai. According to incomplete statistics reported by *Wen-hui Pao* of Shanghai, more than twenty of their articles were published in Shanghai newspapers in 1968. Out of some four hundred articles submitted to the county radio station that year, more than one hundred eighty were used. In general, the peasant correspondents act as opinion leaders in the village, disseminating information from the national mass media, eliciting local support for Party programs, and organizing normative communication through interpersonal channels in the village to sanction undesirable behavior.[63]

To sum up, the Party has developed a highly efficient communication system. The mass media use a variety of means including the press, radio, line-broadcasting and wired loudspeakers, bulletin boards, and a small television network, supplemented by news bulletins in the communes. These media are supported by a network of interpersonal communication at the grassroots level. The entire communication system is closely supervised and monitored: the media by the Party committees, and the interpersonal communication by local cadres in the small groups.

Hypotheses

Unlike most other developing countries, China has placed communication at the very center of her development processes. Out of these processes, we have chosen six research problems that seem to have broad cross-cultural generality: capital formation, establishment of communication networks, cooperation and competition, ideology and manpower training, decision-making processes, and conflict resolution. These problems are reflected in the following hypotheses:

1. Development in China started with a radical social structural change that removed the old institutional barriers and helped mobilize the energy and resources of the masses for productive efforts.

2. Communications—informational, normative, and affective—functioned as catalytic factors in bringing about the initial social structural change that was essential for China's development.

3. Once instituted, the new social structure has made it possible to generate those processes of communication that are instrumental in keeping up the pace of productivity, coordinating the development programs, and maintaining the integration of the system.

4. Value-oriented communication, though extensively employed for the long range goal of changing the traditional Chinese values and beliefs and creating the New Chinese Man, has thus far been less vital than normative communication to the integration and functioning of the Chinese social system.

More specifically, we hypothesize that it was primarily through the skillful use of communication that the Party was able to hasten the downfall of the rural landlords and urban business owners, paving the way toward instituting a new basis of social relations as well as capital formation. In a similar manner, an efficient and extensive network of local communicators was established all over the country, particularly in the vast and previously neglected rural sector, to support and coordinate the tasks of development and socialist transformation. In the absence of strong material incentives, it is largely the use of communication in the group setting that generates enough social pressure for maintaining a level of competition and cooperation sufficient for development. Communication has also been used adroitly, with varying degrees of effect, for ideological indoctrination, for changing the institution of manpower training, for speedy dissemination of major policy decisions, and for resolving conflicts that are inherent in the process of turbulent change, in a manner that contributes to the viability of the social system as a whole.

How communication acts of various kinds—informational, normative, value-oriented, and affective—have been structured and used in China for these purposes will be illustrated in the following chapters.

II
Communication, Social Structural Change, and Capital Formation

In general, economic development requires efficient utilization and organization of manpower and resources. Manpower is essential not only in the form of an abundant supply of labor but also in the quality of technical know-how available to a country. Major resources include land, raw materials, and production equipment. An underdeveloped country is usually deficient in most of these aspects: insufficient supply of labor because of the poor health of many people, low quality of technical know-how because of illiteracy and lack of training, and shortage of raw materials and production equipment because of inadequate savings and investment. In some cases, land is available, but not fully cultivated.

The conditions of China on the eve of the Communist takeover had a number of characteristics perhaps not uncommon in other underdeveloped countries. There was no serious shortage of labor, although the general level of technical know-how was not high. Unlike some countries in Africa and elsewhere in Asia, China did have a sizable, though probably inadequate, group of engineers and managerial personnel. There was no grave shortage of land. The most serious deficiency for China was in the supply of raw materials and production equipment. An effective strategy would therefore be to try to make the most efficient use of what China did have, that is, labor, land, and limited technical know-how, in order to accumulate enough capital to buy raw materials and production equipment.[1]

Capital formation thus held a key to economic development in China. Two necessary conditions can be identified for capital formation: the level of consumption must be less than the level of production, and the surplus must be channeled into investment. Both conditions are related to cultural values as well as social structure. The relation between cultural values and productivity is well illustrated by Weber's discussion of the Protestant ethic.[2] Cultural values are related to consumption. Assuming that the level of productivity in a country is not so low as to provide the barest minimum consumption, then the size of the surplus depends on the readiness of the people to defer gratification.[3] In some cultures, however, predominant values may not favor deferred gratification. Extensive feasts and celebrations tend to minimize or even eliminate any sizable surplus. Even when a surplus is made available, it may not be channeled into investment, but kept immobile in the form of gold, jewelry, or unproductive land holdings because of cultural beliefs and values.[4]

The relation between social structure and capital formation is perhaps even more pronounced. It has been suggested that one major factor for the different rates of economic development of China and Japan during the past could be their social structures, the patterns of interactions involving the rights and obligations of the role participants.[5] The Japanese social structure, characterized by primogeniture, did not permit the division of land among all sons, but allowed only the eldest son to inherit the land. The other sons had to find work elsewhere. Even when they had accumulated some wealth, there were restrictions on purchasing land. Accumulated wealth, not being convertible into land, often became capital for investment in business. In the old Chinese social structure, however, all sons were entitled to a parcel of the father's land, so that there was less structural pressure to engage in other forms of productivity. On the other hand, there was no structural restriction on the purchase of land, which was valued as a status symbol. Thus, much of the wealth generated outside the rural economy was not channeled into investment, but tied up in the purchase of largely unproductive real estate. Capital formation greatly suffered.

Another structural barrier to capital formation, according to

Marxism, is inherent in both the feudal and the capitalist systems.[6] As Marx has theorized, those who engage in productive labor generally do not own the major equipment of production. They work for wages and receive only a minor share of the fruits of their labor. The major share, including the surplus value, is divided among the owners of the production materials. Because a disproportionate share of the surplus value is consumed by the owners, the Marxists contend, the majority of the labor force is unable to accumulate savings.

Due to its rather complex cultural and social structural basis, capital formation could conceivably be approached in a number of ways in a country that wants to develop its economy. In mainland China, as we shall demonstrate, capital formation was achieved by first changing the economically relevant social structure so that the surplus value was no longer held by the ownership class but channeled by the state into investment. Once the state gained control of the surplus value, it then proceeded to further augment the amount for capital investment by increasing production and curtailing consumption. We shall outline the main programs that the Chinese Communist authorities have undertaken toward achieving these objectives. We shall discuss the patterns in which various kinds of communication were utilized, through both the mass media and interpersonal channels, to remove the influentials from the old social structure, to stimulate productive activities, and to induce curtailed consumption. It is our purpose to illustrate how communication following these patterns played an essential part in the processes of structural change and capital formation for economic development in China.

Social Structural Change
Land Reform

The Chinese Communist leaders considered a change of social relations for production to be a prerequisite to increasing productivity. In the predominant rural regions of China, this was achieved by the agricultural land reform program started in June 1950. The objective of land reform was to end the dominance of the landlord class over the major resource of China's economy, that is, agricultural production. By 1952, when land reform was pronounced as successfully concluded, approximately 737,300,000 *mu* (about 123 million acres) of farm land previously owned by landlords had been confiscated and redistributed to a peasant population estimated at approximately three hundred million, or about 90 percent of the entire agricultural population at that time. Some of the peasants also acquired cattle, farm tools, and houses that formerly belonged to the landlords.[7]

The Land Reform movement was officially declared to be a "fierce class struggle," carried out through the combination of Party direction and mass participation by the peasants.[8] Communication both through the mass media and at the interpersonal level played essential roles in the entire movement. The directives of the Party were published in the newspapers and broadcast over the radio. Acting according to the directives, land reform work teams were sent to the villages to organize the peasants. In the outskirts of Peking, for instance, 469 cadres were assigned to the work teams, including 135 who had had land reform experience in old liberated territories occupied by the Chinese Communists before the war.[9] They were organized into teams ranging from five to nine members. In the whole country, more than three hundred thousand cadres took part in the work teams during the entire period of the movement.[10] In general, when a team had arrived in a village, the cadres first made a public announcement of the objectives of land reform, with a warning to the landlords that they must cooperate fully. The cadres then went to visit the poor peasants and tenants to make their acquaintance and to learn about their sufferings. Then the peasants were called together to share with each other their past experiences. In this way a core group of supporters having a common orientation was formed. The core group of poor peasants and tenants was then expanded to absorb the middle peasants, and together they were organized into a peasant association. A number of meetings were then held, at which the peasants were asked to "spit bitter water," that is, to tell their own stories in order to convince each other why the old system must be changed. This step, intended to cultivate class consciousness among the peasants, was considered highly important. Only after the achievement of this stage were the peasants thought to be ready to take action against the landlords.

The first confrontation between the peasants and the landlords was considered crucial. Its specific course usually depended on what appeared to be a pressing local need of the peasants and thus most likely to get them actively involved. Often it took the form of a mass trial of those individuals who had exploited the peasants. They were referred to as *eh pa,* that is, villains. In the 264 villages outside Peking, 66 villages started the land reform with mass trials of villains.[11] Other villages began by bringing the landlords to a mass rally and making them promise to repay the tenants for the excessive rental they had charged over the years. In a few cases, the peasants were mobilized into action through first participating in the village's production relief work. According to an official report, when the first action fulfilled a popular need in a village, the peasants tended to participate in the movement more actively and the land reform work was more successful.[12]

The mass trial of a villain usually began with public accusations by peasants and concluded with a conviction by the people's court right then and there. Speedy action was deemed necessary in order to maintain the spirit and participation of the peasants. At first the peasants were not sure what to say at a mass rally, and did not show the enthusiastic response the Party expected. They began to participate more actively when it was suggested that silence could be interpreted to mean siding with the landlords.[13] Acting upon the cues given by Party cadres, a number of peasants would speak up at the rally to expose the wrongdoings of the landlords, and other peasants would voice their approval. An intense atmosphere of mass involvement was gradually built up to create a sense of urgency and legitimacy for whatever actions were taken against the landlords. In most cases, the landlords surrendered their land and properties. According to Liao Lu-yen, the highest ranking official in charge of agriculture, those landlords "who had committed serious crimes, with stains of blood debt, against whom the people are furious, and those who attempted to resist or destroy the land reform," were sentenced to death and executed.[14] Outside Peking, for instance, of the 130 villains brought to mass trials, seven were given the death penalty, one was sentenced to life imprisonment, and twenty-six were given prison terms of varying severity. Other cases were judged to be mild and let go for the moment.[15] Although no national statistics were released, Liao noted that the execution of those landlords divided the landlord class and effectively reduced resistance to the movement.[16]

Meanwhile, public meetings continued among the peasants to determine their class identification and to dispose of the properties seized from the landlords. The class identification was a step of lasting importance. While landlords and tenants were relatively easy to identify, the categories of rich peasants and middle peasants were more ambiguous. In theory, a land-owning farmer who rented to others more than 25 percent of his land was considered a rich peasant. If the land rented out did not exceed 25 percent, he would be classified as a middle peasant.[17] The actual application of this criterion, however, presented many technical problems because of the varying fertility of the land and because of side incomes.

The Party found a solution in a method of public communication known as "democratic evaluation."[18] The peasants were called together, and each in turn declared his own class identification, which was then evaluated by the others. During the course of public evaluation, a number of concrete cases were established as bases for comparison. A person could dispute the result of the evaluation if he was not convinced, and the discussion would go on till the dispute was resolved. This method of public evaluation, however, was not fail safe. In the Peking area, for instance, there were cases in which middle peasants were forced to admit that they were either landlords or rich peasants.[19]

Following identification of classes, the peasants proceeded to dispose of the seized land, cattle, and other properties. Outside Peking, the peasants association first ordered the landlords to make an inventory of everything that was to be confiscated, and to assume responsibility for its safekeeping. The peasants association then organized three teams, one to check the inventory, one to take care of transportation, and one to handle storage. These steps made it unlikely that the confiscated properties would be destroyed by the landlords or stolen by others during the process.

Redistribution of the land and properties was the last step. Those peasants who had no land were given top priority. The actual redistribution was worked out also through "democratic evaluation." Each eligible peasant declared what he considered to be his fair share. Usually, there was not enough to go around. A method of paired comparison was devised. Using the lowest claim as the basis, the peasants and cadres compared each pair of claims and made adjustments accordingly till most people were satisfied. The results of redistribution were posted in public. The final act of the land reform was the issuance of the "certificate title of land usage" to the peasants.

The importance of communication and organization to the Land

Reform movement was fully recognized by the Party. Liao Lu-yen, who was in charge of agriculture, pointed out:

> Our experience in the last three years proves that without organizing and releasing the vast rural masses, the land reform could not have been brought to a true fruition. If we had not organized the masses, and only depended on administrative orders to bring about the so-called "peaceful land reform," or "bureaucratic land reform," we could not have truly destroyed the landlord class, or truly carried out the land reform, let alone setting the land reform upon a solid foundation.[20]

Although the Land Reform Law provided that landlords could retain some land for their own use, the movement in effect eliminated them as an influential social class and completely altered the social structure in rural China. Before the land reform, the agricultural population in China was estimated to consist of less than 10 percent landlords and rich peasants who owned about 70 to 80 percent of the arable land. The remaining 90 percent included some 70 percent tenants and poor peasants, and about 20 percent middle peasants. After the land reform, the composition was estimated at about 80 percent middle peasant and 20 poor peasants.[21]

Wu Fan Movement

A similar change of production relations took place in the cities shortly after the rural Land Reform program. Officially known as the *Wu Fan* (Five Anti) movement, it started as a mass campaign to stamp out such practices as bribery, tax evasion, pilfering of public property, profiteering, and stealing of economic information.[22] It ended as a purge of industrialists and businessmen, and paved the way for the eventual nationalization of all industries and business in 1956. Because the use of communication in Wu Fan was highly indicative of the patterns of many other mass campaigns, here is a brief account of what happened in Shanghai, the focus of that movement.[23] By January 1952, two years after the establishment of the People's Republic, the nation had just witnessed a mass campaign directed against widespread practices of corruption and extortion among Party cadres of different levels.[24] On January 13, 1952, the *People's Daily* published a short editorial entitled "Resolutely Suppress the Attack from the Capitalist Class," which criticized several businessmen who had involved Party members by offering them bribes in return for illegal profit. Following this official lead, the media in big cities quickly joined the movement by exposing and denouncing the illegitimate practices of bribery and profiteering in business circles.

The Party used the media to set the framework of the Wu Fan movement by casting industrialists and businessmen in the role of public enemies. This can be illustrated by the case of Wang Kangnien, owner of a large pharmaceutical company who was accused of making huge profits by selling fake medicine to the People's Liberation Army. Once Wang's case was chosen as a prototype, the newspapers in Shanghai were saturated for weeks with stories exposing his crimes. Radio stations broadcast plays in which Wang's case was dramatized. Stage shows and musicals were presented by the East China Experimental Operatic Troupe. Even the comedians joined in by telling jokes about Wang Kang-nien. Thus every conceivable channel was utilized to publicize his case.[25]

At the same time, face-to-face communication was organized on a massive scale to apply pressure to industrialists and businessmen. On January 15, 1952, more than sixteen hundred attended a meeting of representatives of industry and business in Shanghai. Several prominent industrial leaders were asked to make confessions. The meeting lasted three days and established the ground rules for fighting corruption, deception, profiteering, and tax evasion. On January 18, similar meetings were held for different trades, and committees were formed to carry out the campaign of confession. Audit teams, known as Tiger Beaters, were organized among Party members, professors, and college students to examine the books of factories and stores. Many "broadcast stations," each equipped with a microphone and loudspeaker, were set up on street corners. Day and night, the loudspeakers broadcast demands for confession: "Owner so and so, we have all the evidence of your wrongdoings. You had better confess." After the name of a particular store owner was broadcast, a small team would go to that store and demand an immediate confession. Depending on what the owner might say or do, the broadcast would sound again: "Owner so and so, you have not been frank enough. Confess more." This would continue until the team was satisfied with a complete account of misdeeds. In addition to face-to-face confrontation and street corner broadcasts, *tatzepao* (big character posters) were used extensively. Walls and windows were covered with posters of all kinds: For instance, "Store owner, have you confessed everything?" or, "All Shanghai workers unite and direct your fire at your boss!'' or, ''We have covered the entire heaven and earth with a net; you have no escape.''

Unlike the Land Reform program, the Wu Fan movement was not proclaimed by law. In fact, the government ostensibly took no initiative. However, enormous pressure was applied through a coordinated use of mass media and face-to-face communication. In a way, the individuals singled out were not unlike the naïve subject in Asch's well-known psychological experiment on line judgment.[26] When placed in a situation in which everyone else said a short line was long, some of the naïve subjects agreed with the majority judgment. In the Wu Fan movement, each of the Chinese industrialists and businessmen faced the crowd all by himself. From all the channels of communication he heard only one version. The media, the street-corner broadcasts, and the tatzepao, his colleagues, and workers in his factory all said he was guilty. Whether any of the business owners actually came to believe their guilt could not be ascertained. At least overtly, they all admitted their guilt, which provided a basis of legitimacy for later action. Everything confessed was placed on record. If the owner of a factory admitted that he had stolen public funds in a contract with the government or evaded taxes, he was required to repay the state. In the end, many industrialists and businessmen surrendered virtually all the mobile assets they had: cash, foreign currency, gold, and jewelry. The total value of private properties and other assets diverted to the government during the Five Anti movement was estimated at 850 million to two billion U. S. dollars.[27] Industrialists and businessmen were still allowed to retain the ownership of their businesses, but the movement had stripped them of any prestige and credibility in the eyes of their former subordinates. In effect, the Wu Fan campaign removed these individuals from the management of their own businesses.

Socialist Transformation

The Wu Fan movement in 1952 paved the way for the socialist transformation of all private enterprise during the Public–Private Joint Management program carried out from late 1955 to early 1956. More than seventy thousand private factories and some two million stores were converted into joint enterprises.[28]

The socialist transformation of private businesses into joint enterprises represented a novel use of communication. A participant-observer account by Robert Loh, a representative of private business who took an active part in carrying out the transformation in Shanghai, described what happened.[29]

Shortly after the Chinese Communists came into power, it was made known that all private industries and businesses would be nationalized gradually over the next twenty-five years. The Five Anti campaign, however, had made most businessmen in Shanghai uncertain about their future. One day in December 1955, about eighty of Shanghai's top businessmen and industrialists were called to a meeting with Chairman Mao Tse-tung. Mao began by praising them for their contributions, and then said that many businessmen had been asking that socialist transformation of private business be hastened. Mao himself expressed reluctance, but since he was not well informed on the subject, he had come from Peking to seek their advice.

The industrialists and businessmen protested that the progress of socialist transformation thus far had indeed been too slow. All who spoke expressed a desire for nationalizing private business with the least possible delay. Some suggested that the transformation could be made in as little as five years. After listening attentively for two hours, Mao thanked them and said he would give serious thought to their opinions. The consensus among the businessmen after the meeting was that socialist transformation would take place within six years. A couple of weeks later came the official announcement. Joint state-private management was to be effected in six days.

Shock-attack teams were quickly organized in Shanghai and throughout the nation. In Shanghai, the teams were composed of members of the Working Committee of Young Businessmen, which was affiliated with a Communist-front organization, the Democratic Youth Association of Shanghai. Working with the state-controlled Federation of Industry and Commerce, the shock-attack teams called businessmen to special meetings and explained the purposes of the campaign. The teams helped businessmen fill out applications for joint state-private management and put pressure on the few who were reluctant to join.

Meanwhile, speeches by prominent business leaders supporting the campaign were publicized in the newspapers and over the radio. Slogans were posted and placards printed for distribution. A competition was started for the different trade groups to challenge each other, to see which would be the first to achieve 100 percent application. As soon as one particular trade or guild had turned in applications for all its members, a big parade was staged, with banners, bands, drums, gongs, firecrackers, and slogan-shouters. Students and members of women's organizations lined the parade route to cheer the procession, which was led by businessmen carrying stacks of red envelopes containing the formal applications. The parade first went to the Federation of Industry and Commerce, where the envelopes were ceremoniously delivered, then to the respective government and Party headquarters to report the good news.

Instead of encountering resistance, the Party had turned the massive takeover of private business into a celebration. The experience of the Wu Fan movement had probably convinced most businessmen that resistance would be futile. Yet had it not been for the fanfare and the holiday mood of popular involvement and celebration created by the Party, it would probably not have been possible to achieve the formal transformation within a week. The businessmen and industrialists were swept off by a gigantic tide, as it were, which they themselves had helped generate. After all, one could hardly complain about something that he himself was celebrating.

It should be pointed out that no direct force was applied if a business owner should refuse to join. According to Loh, of some 165,000 firms in Shanghai, he knew of only one whose owner refused to apply. This was an elderly man who operated a medium-size papermill. After the campaign he could not get raw materials and lost all orders. No banks would extend him loans. He was bankrupt within two months. He was sued by the labor union and the tax bureau, arrested, and sentenced to labor reform.[30]

After the celebration, the business owners were required to evaluate their assets, generally at about one fifth of the market value, and then turn the assessments over to the state as their shares in the joint enterprises. The state awarded them an annual interest of 5 percent, to be paid for seven years. The owners were given the same salaries they had been receiving before. Otherwise, they were separated from the business they had previously owned. Some industrialists were given management jobs elsewhere. Owners of small businesses were sometimes permitted to work in their former stores. Through the Wu Fan movement and the Joint Management program, the government gained control of every industry and business in the country. More significantly, these programs eliminated the urban social class that had held the major share of what Marxists call the surplus value of labor.

Surplus Value and Investment

Elimination of landlords and urban business owners did not mean, however, that the surplus value was to be distributed among peasants and workers.[31] Rather, the state took over the surplus value and channeled much of it into capital for investment. For the Chinese Communist party, the question then was how to generate the maximum possible amount of capital, given the available resources and manpower. Once a state has gained control of the surplus value, it can generate more capital by either increasing production, or limiting consumption, or both. The Chinese Communist leaders chose both. This is apparent in a statement by Sung Shao-wu, a high level official in charge of economic planning, "The main sources of capital funds are the steady increase of production and the practice of economy, thereby creating new wealth for the nation."[32]

One effective way of increasing production is through industrialization, which has been the long-range objective of China. However, industrialization requires a massive amount of initial capital investment, which China did not have, and a high level of technical know-how, which China had yet to develop. The technological and economic aid from Soviet Russia undoubtedly helped.[33] Yet much of the burden of capital investment had to be borne by China herself. When Party leaders looked around in the early 1950s for ways of generating surplus value for capital investment, it is not surprising that their eyes fell on China's main resources, peasant labor and land.

Production Organizations and Campaigns

In a major policy speech on New Democracy delivered in Yenan in 1940, Mao had envisioned Dr. Sun Yat-sen's "land to the tiller" program to be the goal of rural reform for China.[34] The land reform essentially achieved this objective. The program had been successful in restoring agricultural production to the prewar level. It had lifted up the spirits of the peasants who now tilled their own land. But production was considered not high enough, partly because of a shortage of cattle and farm tools in the aftermath of war destruction. According to a report by Minister of Agriculture Li

Shu-cheng on agricultural production from 1950 to 1952, the total number of farm cattle was 16 percent below the prewar level, and major farm tools were 30 percent short.[35] Another factor considered to be holding down the level of production was the relatively little division of labor inherent in the small-farm, private-ownership system. A peasant working in his small paddy field has to do practically everything by himself.

Furthermore, after the removal of the landlords, some of their former functions, particularly in providing rural credit, marketing, and coordinated use of farm tools, were also left unfulfilled. In the confusion after the land reform, some of the Party's rural cadres took advantage of the situation to buy up land and issue high- interest loans. Thus, the result was not the establishment of egalitarian independent farming that Dr. Sun Yat-sen had envisioned, but rather the emergence of agricultural petty capitalism controlled by rural cadres.[36]

In a sense, this development was not surprising. The land reform eliminated the landlords as an influential and stabilizing element in the villages, but did little to change the behavioral patterns of the peasants. For ages they had been accustomed to relying on their superiors when they needed help. They never learned how to organize themselves for group action other than in the kinship framework. Now that their kinship superiors were gone, they had to turn to somebody having authority. The Party's rural cadres simply filled that vacuum.

Perhaps these situations as well as its long range ideological commitment to Communism led the Party to depart from Mao's earlier pledge and to experiment with a series of measures that progressively changed the institution of agricultural production till it culminated in the communes of 1958. These measures were intended to make the maximum collective use of land and rural manpower and to achieve the highest possible level of agricultural production. Judging from the bumper crops between 1953 and 1957, the results were largely positive. It was only when the Party tried to push agricultural production beyond the limits of human endurance—in the Commune movement—that adverse effects began to set in.

It is important to note that the Party did not attempt to build its new rural institution from scratch. To ease the process of transition, it took as a basis an old institution which had existed in rural China for centuries: that of informal mutual help among peasants.

Chinese peasants have always extended help to each other in the form of labor, cattle, tools, and occasionally credit. This is known as *hu tung yu wu,* that is, exchange between the haves and the have nots. In the past, such exchanges were made generally between persons within the kinship network when the need arose. The exchange was informal and regulated by reciprocity rather than by contractual stipulations. The recipient of help knew when and how much to repay according to age-old norms in the villages.

The Communist party expanded this old institution by organizing the peasants into mutual aid teams. In most areas, beginning in the spring of 1953, the peasants were first organized into temporary mutual aid teams for a seasonal, simple exchange of labor, following the patterns of earlier experiments tried by the Communists in North China back in 1943.[37] The purposes were to share the use of draft animals and farm tools and to pool labor resources, generally among friends and neighbors, during the busy sowing time, summer cultivation, and autumn harvesting. During the slack season, when there were only odd jobs to be done, the peasants would do them separately and individually. Seasonal mutual aid did not change the basic characteristics of individual farming. But it helped relieve shortages of cattle and labor, and more importantly, prepared the peasants for the eventual collective farming.

When the peasants had become more or less accustomed to this new form of labor relations, the mutual aid teams were converted from a seasonal to a regular, year-round basis. Membership in a regular mutual aid team was meant to be permanent. Peasants in the same team helped one another at all times. They worked according to simple production plans and began learning to manage their local affairs. As a result of the division of labor, production efficiency was described as greatly increased. In eight experimental counties in North China, the yield per unit of land of the mutual aid teams was reported to be 50 percent higher than that of individual peasant households.[38] Some teams used their increased income to buy farm implements and draft animals as common property.

In December 1953, the Peking government announced its Agricultural Cooperative movement, which converted the mutual aid teams into larger units known as Agricultural Producers' Cooperatives, with an average size of about 160 families. Altogether, more than 740,000 cooperatives were eventually organized.[39] While the Mutual Aid program was built upon the traditional Chinese norm of reciprocity among peasants, the Agricultural Cooperatives called for collective planning of production and collective use of cattle, farm tools, land and manpower. The cooperatives were characterized by the peasants' contribution of land as shares and centralized management by the cadres. In the elementary cooperatives, which initially replaced the mutual aid teams, the titles to land usage, cattle, and farm implements remained with the peasant members. The distribution of crop income among the members was based partly on the number of shares each member had acquired by transferring his land to the cooperative, and partly on the amount of labor he and his family had performed. In the advanced cooperatives, which replaced the elementary cooperatives in late 1956, the number of shares no longer made any difference. The distribution of crop income was based solely on labor. Except for private plots around the houses and small numbers of livestock, all land, cattle, and major implements were collectively owned. Based on initially released results from eight experimental counties in North China, the cooperatives were said to have a unit productivity twice as high as that of individual peasant households.[40]

In the whole process, the mass media, particularly the newspapers, largely played the roles of announcing the general directives, providing specific instructions, and serving as a mechanism of feedback from the grassroots level. Throughout these movements, the problems and difficulties of transition experienced by peasants in various localities were rather openly reported and discussed in news and feature stories. Among the major obstacles were the conflict between collective labor and self-interest among the peasants, and the tendency of some cadres to rely on coercion in organizing mutual aid teams and cooperatives.[41] These issues will be further discussed in subsequent chapters.

The economic significance of these organizational changes lies in the fact that they provided the group setting that made production campaigns possible. Once the peasants were organized into production units, not operating as small, independent farmers, they could be mobilized to join group production competitions. The main task of motivating and organizing the peasants was carried out through face-to-face communication. After a village had been assigned a production quota, the peasants were called together by the local cadres to discuss the ways and means by which the quota could be achieved. Everyone was urged to express his views, to criticize others, and to engage in debates. This was known as *ta ming* (big blooming), *ta fang* (big airing), and *tapienlun* (big debate). In this way all conceivable difficulties were discussed and solutions considered. The face-to-face communication was supported by tatzepao, the big character posters which were the only print medium available at the village level that could be exclusively employed to publicize events and programs in the village. Through the discussion and debates, the production quota assigned by the hierarchy became accepted as a group goal, and group norms and standards emerged to govern the behavior of individual peasants for fulfilling the group goal. The process was not unlike what has been observed in group dynamics in the tradition of Kurt Lewin.[42] Meetings and discussions of this kind were held not only at the village level, but at levels all the way from the rural district up to the province, where problems of different scope were discussed.

To stimulate rural production, the Party employed a method of group competition known as "grasping the advanced and bringing up the followers," and "grasping the followers and pushing the advanced."[43] The idea was to select a village that had achieved success in some aspect of production or innovation. A meeting was then called in that village, and attended by representatives of other villages. The experience of the model village was thoroughly reviewed and possible difficulties of application to other villages discussed. The representatives would return to their own villages to try the program out. In this way, those villages that were behind could "grasp" the village that was more advanced in order to bring themselves up. But once the experience was shared with other villages, the advanced village would soon lose its leading position. Therefore, the more advanced village was constantly under pressure to work even harder in order to stay ahead. It was "pushed" by the followers.

Essentially the same methods were used to organize and stimulate industrial production. In a continuing program of "labor contests" started in 1950, a number of production units with outstanding records were designated as pioneering models for each manufacturing industry, and their production achievements widely publicized, either locally in tatzepao or nationally through feature stories in the newspapers. On-the-spot demonstrations were organized and attended by workers from other units. In this way, these other units could "compare with the pioneers, learn from the pioneers, and catch up with the pioneers."[44]

Whenever a production mission was assigned, the first move was to call a mass meeting of workers to explain the task. Then the leaders organized the same kind of discussion practiced in the villages—ta ming, ta fang, and tapienlun—during which the workers raised questions, proposed plans of production, and suggested ways of improving techniques and saving raw materials. All workers were required to participate in prolonged discussions. New ideas arising in the discussions were written up and posted in tatzepao. Millions upon millions of tatzepao were said to have been posted to disseminate such technological innovations.[45] In the ten years of labor contest movements form 1950 to 1959, more than thirty-one million feasible suggestions and new ideas were said to have been proposed in this manner, and some 5,690,000 workers were voted labor pioneers by their colleagues.[46]

Restricted Consumption

In order to generate huge savings, the government also took steps to hold consumption to the lowest possible level. Food, the major item of consumption, was thus strictly rationed. A food rationing system would function effectively only if the government could gain complete control of all foodstuffs at the source, that is, in the vast peasant population. To achieve this, several programs were carried out, largely through the use of persuasive communication.

The overall objective of these programs was to enable the government to collect nearly all the foodstuffs produced, leaving the peasants barely enough for their own consumption. A major portion of foodstuff collection came from the levies that the peasants were required to pay in kind in lieu of cash taxes. During the initial period before food rationing was strictly enforced in November 1953, the peasants were allowed to do whatever they pleased with the rest of the crop after the levies had been paid each year. For instance, they could sell it to private stores. They were not obliged to sell any surplus food to the government. However, the government ended up being the main buyer through the use of personal persuasion on a massive scale.[47] First, Party cadres went to the villages to find out how much food had been produced that year and how much was available for sale. This was called "feeling the bottom."

Then, using all available channels of interpersonal communication, that is, friends, relatives, or local cadres who had the confidence of the peasants, a persuasive campaign was launched to pressure the peasants to sell their surplus foodstuffs to the government. In effect, the peasants were obliged to persuade one another. Competition was encouraged by publicizing a few model peasants in each village and by urging the others to emulate them.

After full-scale rationing was proclaimed in November 1953, the peasants were no longer allowed to sell their foodstuffs to private stores, but were required to sell to the government only. The problem then became how to work out an effective yet flexible criterion which, depending on varying sizes of crops in different locations, would leave the peasants with just enough for their own use. Again, communication was extensively employed. Instead of using a formula, the government allowed each village to work out its own criteria within a general quota. The method was "democratic evaluation." All families in the agricultural cooperative were informed of the quota assigned to their village and asked to declare how much food each would volunteer to sell. A series of meetings was then called to discuss each case until a final agreement was reached on the quantity of sale by each family.

In areas where food was not produced in sufficient quantities and where the peasants had to buy food from the government, the same method of democratic evaluation was employed to determine how much they could buy. Through group discussions, the peasants would agree on the minimum each family would require. The total was then presented to the local government for approval.

The peasants were not encouraged to spend the money they received from their grain sales. If they had obtained production loans from the village credit union, the amounts were automatically deducted from the cash payment. The prompt collection of loan repayments was emphasized by the central government.[48] Of the remaining amount, the peasants were urged to deposit a portion in the People's Bank as savings. They were asked to pledge their deposits during the same group discussions in which they volunteered the amounts of grain sales.[49] Through the same process of democratic evaluation, each peasant was asked to pledge an amount that was judged by the group to be adequate and equitable.

Instead of waiting for the peasants to come and make the deposit, the People's Bank and the credit unions jointly sent work

communication to give the peasants this clear message: the perennial situation that had existed in their villages was about to change. At this point, the peasants in each village were still an aggregate of unorganized individuals having a commonality in poverty that had just been brought to the focus of their attention. They were not yet an interacting group capable of taking collective action to change their situation. But a significant point is that they were beginning to see their situation as potentially changeable.

To create an active group out of an aggregate of passive peasants, the Party cadres moved to bring them together, initially not to ask for any action but merely to strengthen their bond by sharing their sufferings with one another in "spit bitter water" sessions. Two factors that had important implications to the subsequent turn of events may be noted about these sessions. First, the affective communication in these sessions provided a basis of collective identity for the peasants by accenting their common misery. This identity is essential for group formation. Second, the emotional arousal through the same process of affective communication laid for the emerging group a sufficient motivational basis for future actions.

Now the nature and source of the peasants' grievances had been identified for them—in the exploitations by the landlords. Having acquired a common identity and a basis of motivation, the new group was ready for action. The critical task was the class struggle against the landlords as the first major behavioral commitment by the peasants in the change processes. The important factors at this stage were the acceptance of the task by the peasant group and the adoption of group norms regarding ways of implementing the task. Prior to the mass rally at which a landlord was to be tried, the cadres applied pressure on the peasants to secure their participation. Coercion was implied, if not always used. The peasants complied by attending. At the rally, the emotion-laden accusations and demands for action against the landlords were presented by a select few in an atmosphere of unanimous group approval, signifying to the peasants the new behavioral patterns expected of them.

The adoption of new norms was not achieved without difficulty. During the initial stage of the land reform, there were indications that the peasants did not quite know what they were supposed to do or how far they should go in pressing the landlords. Evidently there was nothing in their previous experience that would suggest the appropriate patterns of behavior. In the setting of face-to-face communication during the struggle, the peasants learned to speak out against former superiors and to voice their approval when actions were proposed. The new norms gradually emerged and became adopted. It was a classic case of role playing guided by strict norms that developed through a skillful combination of affective communication and normative communication. The accusations were intended to keep the peasants in a state of hatred and excitement, while the vocal support by those who spoke at the rally contributed to a perception of legitimacy among the villagers for the purge of the landlords. These affective and normative processes, aided by the appeals of equity and justice and buttressed by the force of implicit coercion, worked effectively to overcome the traditional passivity of the peasants and to elicit their behavioral commitment.

In retrospect, perhaps no other tasks ever assigned to communication could match in difficulty and in scope the ones that the Chinese Communist authorities intended to achieve in their land reform. Here was a vast social class of individuals, most of whom were illiterate, and who had been for generations subservient to those who wielded enormous influence in their villages and controlled their economic life. Now these individuals were asked to stand up and strike down this powerful group of landlords. If the peasants had not been emotionally and motivationally roused during the mass rallies and the prerally group sessions, if they had not been placed under considerable pressure by the cadres, it is doubtful that the material rewards alone could have induced them to act.

After the expropriation of the landlords' properties, the disposition of the same was achieved by the use of both informational communication and normative communication. The peasants were fully informed of the nature of the task. Through public discussions in the groups, they were directed to work out their own standards and procedures for redistribution.

Broadly speaking, the same processes we have observed in the land reform can be identified in the confrontation between the workers and the industrial owners during the Wu Fan movement. Informational communication from the mass media and group meetings provided a new definition of the situation for both the workers and the owners. Thus a rigid social context was created, in which pressure generated through normative communication among the workers was applied to the owners to induce their behavioral compliance, that is, admission of guilt and submission of assets. Affective communication played the role of keeping the workers in a state of animosity and agitation, for instance, by calling the industrial owners public enemies, by identifying the workers themselves as "tiger beaters," and by using abrasive language in street corner broadcasts. It seems as if the workers had to indulge in an intense emotional arousal in order to be sufficiently motivated to confront their erstwhile superiors, whom they had always before obeyed.

It may be noted that the Party relied on emotional arousal more heavily in the inital rounds of class struggle than in the subsequent stages of structural transformation. In the villages, once the landlords had been removed from their positions of influence and wealth, the task remaining was to reorganize the peasants into networks of new role relations, changing progressively from small independent farmers through mutual aid teams and cooperatives to communes. These changes were achieved largely through the use of informational communication and normative communication. Generally, informational communication transmitted through the mass media and the local cadres defined the task for the peasants, whether it was to organize a mutual aid team or to start a cooperative. Then, through normative communication within the groups, the new role relations were discussed and accepted, and ways of implementation were proposed and adopted. Group pressure was continuously applied to prevent dissent and deviance. In the cities, the Public–Private Joint Management program that nationalized all industries and businesses was carried out in a similar manner.

Informational and normative communications were extensively used to organize and coordinate the productive activities both in agriculture and industry. Whatever the task might be, the workers and peasants were thoroughly briefed and urged to express their views and raise questions. Through the process of face-to-face communication, the group generally seemed to accept the task as a collective objective and worked out its own ways and standards for achieving it.

The Party uses normative communication to pressure the peasants and workers to compete against each other in a group context for higher productivity. Equally important, and perhaps more intriguing, is the way it uses normative communication to achieve involuntary deferred gratification through curtailed consumption. As understood outside the Communist world, deferred gratification refers to the voluntary postponement of immediate reward in return for a possibly greater reward in future. The postponement springs from an individual motivational basis, whether the beneficiary is the person himself or someone dear to him, such as wife or child. Since there is no outside restraint on immediate gratification, other than one's own motiviation, those who lack a sufficient motivational basis tend to squander their extra income and thus slow down the overall process of saving. The Chinese Communist leaders solved this problem not by cultivating individually-oriented motivation, but by allowing the barest minimum level of consumption, and thus achieved involuntary but effective deferred gratification on a mass basis. Again normative communication played a major role in bringing it about through the process of group discussion known as the democratic evaluation.

A general pattern can be seen from the processes of communication as employed by the Chinese Communist authorities. The initial impetus usually comes from a high-level policy decision of the Party. The mass media—newspapers, radio stations, and sometimes magazines—take over from there to disseminate information and interpret Party policy, to provide feedback from the grassroots on the problems and difficulties encountered, and to supply reinforcement by publicizing cases of success. Implementation of the policy, however, is achieved through normative face-to-face communication in closely supervised group networks. Within each network, the peasants and workers are called upon to play their designated roles, whether purging landlords, denouncing business owners, or contributing their labor. Although different situations call for different role performances, the networks appear to be sufficiently well organized to accommodate all of them.

III
Communication and Political Socialization of Cadres

Economic development, in a practical sense, requires new programs that will increase a nation's total productivity. Sound planning is important. So is technological training of manpower. Equally important, however, is a national communication network that will (1) solicit initial input from the people regarding development needs, (2) transmit policy decisions and other relevant information to the people, and (3) initiate among the people, in their respective groups, favorable social processes for implementing the new programs. When the people carry out the action programs, the network must relay feedback about problems to the different levels of government for revision and adjustment whenever necessary. Without such a communication network for transmission of information and organization of action, the most careful planning for development would be unproductive.[1] As Schramm and Lerner have pointed out, effective communication in this sense would be a functional requisite for national development.[2]

There is little doubt that a communication network approximating these capabilities has developed in China. Television news programs showing thousands of Chinese quietly sweeping new snow early in the morning during Richard Nixon's visit to Peking illustrate the efficiency of China's communication network. In the current planned-birth movement, the same network assigns a birth quota to each neighborhood and makes sure that it is followed.[3] Recalling the old Chinese bureaucratic structure, in which anything except routine administrative orders hardly ever traveled far beyond the city gates, causes us to wonder how this new national communication network developed. How is it possible for someone in Peking to push a button, as it were, and set the whole country to work on any project that the Party has chosen?

We have at least the beginning of an answer because we know that an effective communication network geared to promote change must have a chain of communicators who can pass the directives from top to bottom. They must understand and support the directives to relay them accurately from one link to another in the entire social system. The most important link in this chain of communicators is the lowest level. There the communicators must face the people whose behavioral support is crucial. They must know how to explain the programs convincingly, how to solicit and obtain cooperation, and how to organize for action. These grassroots communicators must also originate information to start the flow of feedback. While communicators at the grassroots level play important roles in any national networks, they are particularly vital to the Chinese Communist system because of its reliance on social pressure and emphasis on ideological indoctrination. Functioning as local leaders, they hold the key to the small-group communication processes that are essential to China's patterns of development. It is through them that the Party has been able to reach the masses down at the village level and mobilize them for collective actions. It is through them that the Party has been making an effort to seek ideological conversion of the Chinese people and to understand their moods and needs in the rapid processes of change. Indeed, the success or failure of China's development has depended in a large measure on the organizational ability and ideological conviction of the grassroots communicators.

We shall analyze in this chapter how Chinese Communist authorities developed their communication networks. We shall examine how the communicators were trained at the different levels, particularly in the villages, and how their work was organized and supervised. We shall see how the peasants, who constituted the majority of China's population, were initiated into the vast communication networks to facilitate program input as well as to effect implementation of development projects. This analysis should help us understand why the group communication network in China works so effectively as an instrument of social change and development.

Our focus is on the birth of the network within the Chinese Communist party during the formative years after the establishment of the People's Republic. It was during that period that the foundation for an effective communication apparatus was laid on a national scale. Subsequent attempts to improve the network have essentially followed much the same tactics developed in the initial phase. They will be briefly discussed.

Party Apparatus after 1949

The Chinese Community party today operates through a vast network of well-organized individuals known as *kanpu,* or cadres.[4] They are administrators at various levels who are at the same time communicators, organizers, and supervisors. During the early years of the revolution, before the Communist party came into power in 1949, most of the cadres were intellectuals with a high degree of enthusiasm for the revolution. In the late 1920s, when the Chinese Communists were fighting in the mountainous regions of Kiangsi, Hunan, and Fukien, and later, after the Long March, when they had retreated from Kiangsi to Yenan, the Chinese Communists were more concerned with survival and military strategy than with administrative affairs and social reform. During those years reform programs such as land redistribution were tried, but such early experiments cannot be compared in scope and complexity with those that began in 1949. Thus the problems of administrative manpower and organization did not become a serious Party concern until after the People's Republic had been established.

In 1949, there were approximately 720,000 administrative cadres, excluding those in the military.[5] The increasing demand during the first three years brought the total number of cadres up to 2,750,000 by late 1952. The new cadres were recruited from the following sources: (1) peasants and workers who distinguished themselves in various mass campaigns and purges, (2) college and high school students who had been assigned to various organizations after short courses of indoctrination and training, (3) intellectuals who had held administrative positions in the old society. The Party's personnel policy during the early years of transition seemed to be one of adjustment and accommodation. So as to restore order to a war-torn country, the Party used any available administrators who would cooperate with the new regime. Most of the previous government employees were temporarily retained because their services were needed.

Propaganda Network

The Communist leadership had recognized the importance of communication as early as the 1930s. After conducting a survey at Changkang Village in Kiangsi Province in 1933, Mao Tse-tung was impressed with the success of the village's propaganda team in publicizing the expansion of the Red Army and local economic development.[6] When the Party took power, the leaders foresaw the obstacles, particularly the widespread bureaucratic practices, to carrying out its programs of socialist transformation. Apparently persuaded by the Kiangsi experience that adequate dissemination of information and correct interpretation along the Party line would help enlist the support of the people, the Party leaders established a nationwide "progaganda network."[7]

The function of this network was to carry out constant "agitation," following the instruction of Stalin, except that the Chinese Communist party considered the term "propaganda" *(hsuan chuan)* to be more appropriate than "agitation" *(ku tung)*, when rendered into Chinese.[8] The propagandists were recruited from among Party members, members of the Communist Youth Corps, school teachers, model workers, women's representatives, and neighborhood section leaders. They were stationed in each of the Party's branch headquarters below the level of the city and county.[9] According to the Party directives,[10] a propagandist was supposed to:

1. constantly explain to the people in his area, in simple and popular forms, the current events at home and abroad, the policies of the Party and government, the people's tasks (particularly the immediate local tasks at that time), and model experiences of the masses of people in production and other work;

2. refute reactionary rumors and erroneous ideologies current among the people;

3. encourage the masses of people to learn from model experiences in order to accomplish their tasks; and

4. report regularly the conditions among the people to higher Party officials, so that the officials could decide on adequate propaganda content and methods from time to time.

Even though the propagandists took part in such mass movements as land reform, the new marriage law, and summer grain collection, their primary task during the initial period appeared to be promoting anti-American feelings.[11] Since the end of the Korean War, not much has been heard about the propaganda networks. From all indications, the original concept of depending on a special group of propagandists to achieve communication objectives proved to be impracticable without the organizational support of other cadres. What the cadres in general communicated by their deeds apparently carried far more weight with the people than what the propagandists communicated by their words.

Bureaucratic Practices

The behavior among the rank and file of the Party cadres pointed to many problems of communication breakdown. Some of the problems could be traced to arrogance or indiscretion of the cadres, as later investigations revealed. According to an offical report by An Tze-wen, then minister of personnel, some of the cadres "beat up people, arrested or detained people at will, interfered with the freedom of marriage, persecuted those who criticized them, framed good people, or even protected counterrevolutionary elements, raped women, caused people to commit suicide, or killed people."[12] Serious cases of extorting money and accepting bribes were also discovered. During the *San Fan* (Three Anti) movement in early 1952, more than 105,000 Party cadres were found to have accepted bribes in excess of ten million yuan. These cadres represented 2.7 percent of approximately 3,836,000 Party members investigated during the movement.[13]

Other problems were more general and seemed to reflect the nature of the old Chinese bureaucracy the Communists had inherited. One was nepotism. Some cadres in high positions preferred to employ their own relatives, friends, and individuals from their home towns. The labor minister of Manchuria employed forty-two such individuals in his organization. "As a result," according to An Tze-wen, "many Party organizations and government offices had a great atmosphere of harmony, but lacked political awareness. Their organizations were unsound. They could not push forward with criticism and self-criticism, but rather protected each other."[14]

Another common ill was known as "commandism"—relying on mass obedience of administrative orders for carrying out new programs. Compliance was expected even though many of the orders were unrealistic and could not be carried out on schedule. This led to the practice—from the highest-level cadres to the lowest unit—of filing false reports and faking statistics.[15] Some cadres followed orders to extremes. For example, during the movement for the improvement of cotton seeds, the peasants of Szushui had already sown their cotton before they received the new seeds. The local cadres ordered them to dig up the cotton plants. Those who refused were bound and beaten by the village chief cadre. In a Well Drilling movement in Shangtung Province, cadres in several counties simply drew a number of circles on the ground according to the quotas assigned and ordered the peasants to dig wells. Most of these wells were unusable.[16] During the Mutual-Aid Team movement, the Party secretary of Pai Yao Village, Yang Wei-hai, called the peasants together and said: "Now I order you to join the mutual-aid teams. Whoever does not join does not love our country." In Shansi Province, where Pai Yao Village was situated, commandism was said to be practiced by about 21 percent of rural cadres.[17]

Rich-Peasant Thinking

Some problems appeared to be a result of waning revolutionary fervor. After land reform, many of the Party cadres in the rural areas considered the revolution to be over. Now that the exploiter class of landlords had been purged and arable land distributed to farmers, these cadres began to turn their attention to cultivating their own plots and regarded political work as an unproductive and undesirable burden. Family prosperity became more important than revolution. This tendency, decried by the Party leadership as "rich-peasant thinking," was typified by the much publicized case of Li Ssu-hsi, a rural cadre in Hunan. Li was quoted as saying, ". . . all my life I have suffered hardship. Now that I have been given land, I am completely satisfied, so why continue to make re-volution.''[18]

As the Party publicly acknowledged, many rural cadres took ad-vantage of the confusion following land reform to buy land from other peasants. Some even employed hired hands to work in their land, thus establishing themselves as new landlords.[19] In Hopeh Province, for instance, 31 rural cadres became landlords, another 36 invested their newly acquired capital in private business, and 1,003 were making profits from the age-old practice of lending money to peasants at prohibitively high interest rates.[20] Such practices were apparently so widespread that the Party had to draw special regula-tions to deal with them.[21]

There was evidence that many rural cadres, both the new recruits and those of long standing, were ignorant of the Party ideology other than the ultimate goal of "Communism." For instance, a survey conducted in 1951 of 109 Party members in four Shansi vil-lages showed that none had any idea how the goal of Communism was to be reached. Some expressed satisfaction with the way things were in their villages and saw no need for change. Their ignorance was attributed to a lack of systematic study of Marxism-Leninism and the thought of Mao Tse-tung.[22]

Inadequate Communication

The lack of revolutionary fervor and ideological understanding was paralleled by an inadequate communication system within the Party. Both supervision from above and feedback reports from be-low appeared to be lacking. High-level cadres made little effort to understand and supervise the work of their subordinates. Many at high levels only periodically checked the file cards and work reports and made no field visits. Lower-level cadres who prepared false favorable reports were commended, and those who actually worked hard and reported realities were blamed. As a result, the lower-level reports soon included only good news.[23]

Some cadres in responsible positions not only failed to seek fac-tual reports, but suppressed complaints and suggestions from the mass of people. The Party had encouraged the people to write let-ters, but many letters were relegated to the "complaint letter boxes" and remained unopened for years. Some were hardly legi-ble because of rain stains and other damage. In 1953, for instance, the Shangtung Province People's Government was found to have put aside more than seventy thousand such letters from the people. An incomplete tally made in thirty-one organizations in Shanghai found more than twenty-two thousand letters ignored.[24]

Some cadres who criticized their superiors soon became victims of covert retaliation. A high-level Party cadre could easily find seemingly justifiable excuses to remove those who criticized him. The victim knew that the boss was out to get him, but could do nothing.[25]

In general, the administrative structure of mainland China in the early 1950s appeared somewhat similar to that of some developing countries: a structure of bureaucrats characterized by widespread corruption, heavy reliance on administrative orders, and blatant insensitivity to the needs of the people. Directives and messages from the top Party hierarchy proceeded, often without needed explanation and interpretation, through a chain of cadres till they reached the lowest level. At this critical point, the communication stopped. The people received orders but often did not understand why they should do what they were told to do. There was virtually no feedback from the masses.

San Fan Movement

The Party's first action against corruption and bureaucratism among its members was taken by Premier Chou En-lai at a cabinet meeting on December 7, 1951. A special committee was organized under the central government with the specific duties of practicing economy, increasing production, and fighting corruption, waste, and bureaucratism. Po I-po, a ranking official, was appointed committee chairman. Almost from beginning the Party turned its attention away from economy and production and focused on its campaign against the three evils: corruption, waste, and bureaucratism. Thus the campaign was known as *San Fan,* or Three Anti movement.

Widespread Corruption

In his report delivered at the first San Fan rally for northern China six days after the cabinet meeting, Po acknowledged widespread practices of corruption in the Party, the People's Government and the People's Liberation Army.[26] Some cadres, according to Po, had become thieves who specialized in stealing public properties. Many who knew how to pad their expenses and fake accounts had money to squander, and were regarded by their colleagues as clever and generous. Those who followed the regulations strictly were called stingy. Organized graft was widespread.

An editorial in the *People's Daily* reported that in the month of November 1951 alone the People's Court in Peking tried 231 cases of corruption involving more than 100 organizations in Peking. Even the judicial branch was not immune. For instance, Ku Shang-yu, an official of the People's Supreme Court took bribes totalling 59,600,000 yuan. Yang Chan-ao, of the Central Security Bureau, stole 23,000,000 yuan of public funds and spent them on sightseeing and prostitutes in Shanghai.[27] The most serious cases that were nationally publicized concerned two high-level Party cadres in Tientsin City: Liu Chin-shan and Chang Tze-shan, who were Party secretaries of the Tientsin Municipality. Both had been with the revolution since the early days. Between them, they had stolen 17,162,720,000 yuan from public funds earmarked for such projects as airport construction, river dike repair, disaster relief, and subsidies for Party members' families. The attitudes of many cadres at the time seemed to by typified by Liu's remarks: "We won the revolution. We get to enjoy it."[28] Both Liu and Chang were convicted and sentenced to death.

Criticism Tactics

While the newspapers and radio were publicizing cases like those of Liu and Chang, the people were urged to write letters of complaint about such dishonesty to newspaper editors. During the height of the San Fan movement in early 1952, the newspapers were full of such letters. Most dealt with extortion and the acceptance of bribes by Party cadres at the middle and lower levels. Meanwhile, in public offices from the central government down to the county level, in schools, state enterprises, and civic organizations, meetings were called to investigate employees. Some were public rallies, but most were closed meetings.[29]

A standard procedure was followed. First, the Party's work team in charge of the movement in a particular organization would explain the objectives. The employees of that organization were urged to put aside all hesitations and engage in unreserved criticism of themselves and others. At each meeting, a few cadres would be designated as the "heavy points"—the focus of severe criticism and abuse. Harsh language and physical punishment were common.

For instance, Chang Nai-chi, vice chairman of the Democratic National Reconstruction Association, went through such an ordeal for eight days and nights. Lin Chung-yi, general manager of Peking's *Kuang Ming Daily News,* was forced to kneel at a public rally. Those who were not the heavy points would criticize them as severely as they could, even though they were all colleagues in the same organization. This was considered necessary in order to demonstrate their own innocence, loyalty to Party doctrine, and progressiveness. Mild cases were allowed to "pass" after thorough self-criticism and confession. More serious cases required immediate arrest. Suicides among cadres were reported to be common.

After each meeting those who had criticized others were required to stay and examine themselves, to see if any of them might be susceptible to the same charges. Generally, members of the work team, the tiger beaters, would lead the after-session examination by declaring that they themselves would need to be alert against similar errors of thought and conduct. This would be followed by similar statements from other cadres. They dwelled on their own minor errors and emphasized their eagerness for continuous improvement.

The severity of the punishment for a culprit was generally determined before the session by the work team, although the penalty had the appearance of spontaneity. According to an expatriate who presided over many such meetings, he would lead off by declaring the official charges against the victim. The others would then begin their criticism and finally demand punishment. Sometimes, they misread the cues and asked for a penalty more severe than the one officially intended.[30]

The San Fan movement seemed to put a stop to widespread corruption among middle-level cadres. It relieved the attitudes, then current in the Party's rank and file, that the revolution was over and that it was time to harvest a little reward. The movement also eliminated many of the administrative personnel left from the previous regime whose loyalty was questionable and whose service was no longer essential. The purges clearly persuaded the remaining cadres to abandon some of the old practices of bureaucratism and carry out the Party directives more seriously. In general, the San Fan movement strengthened the Party's control over its administrative organization by reducing corruption and minimizing waste and bureaucratism in public offices from the county up to higher administrative organizations. It was the first step toward establishing an effective national communication network.

Rural Rectification Campaign

The Party then turned its attention to the rural districts and villages, vital contact points in the communication network. In early 1952, while the San Fan movement was still being carried out at the county level, some rural districts started applying the same tactics to their cadres. Considerable distrubances in the villages interfered with farm production.[31]

The Village Situation

No official explanations were given as to why the pressure and purge tactics that succeeded at the county and higher levels were ineffective at the rural district and village levels. At the central and provincial government levels, public condemnation of corrupt officials was largely carried out in the press and by radio. Such publicity set the stage for the mass movement of criticism and self-criticism among Party cadres in those offices. Later, the same patterns were applied to cities and counties. The movement inevitably slowed down, and in some cases halted, the operation of the various offices. But since these offices were in charge of administrative affairs, not production, the effects were not serious.

The situation in the rural districts and villages was quite different. Due to the enormous number of units involved, the mass media could not effectively provide a basis of localized support. Furthermore, in a rural district or village there were relatively few cadres and they were often scattered over a large area. The Party could not single out a few scapegoats in each district or village, as it did in the larger administrative units, because an unduly large proportion of its rural cadres would be purged. Using the severe purgative tactics of San Fan at the rural district and village levels would have paralyzed local leadership. Production stopped in the few villages where the San Fan tactics were tried.

Moreover, the problems in the rural districts and the villages were different. Corruption and bribery were not serious, since the rural cadres had little access to public funds. The problems among the rural cadres were reflected in the practice of commandism, bureaucratism, and violation of law. The rural cadres did not always understand the Party's agricultural policy, and showed a lack of motivation to carry out collective farm programs, and a lack of ability to communicate reciprocally with the county level above and the peasant level below. At the rural district and village levels the Party had to achieve the political socialization of its cadres and eliminate undesirable individuals.

Campaign Objectives

The San Fan struggle tactics were therefore discarded for the rural areas as too severe and not suited for Party objectives. Instead, when San Fan was terminated, a new movement of rural rectification was started in the winter of 1952 and concluded before the spring planting of 1953. The primary objective was educational as well as purgative. Although most rural cadres had had some experience in mass rallies during the rural land reform and the subsequent movement for suppressing counterrevolutionaries, this was the first time the Party had attempted a nationwide program to teach its base level cadres how to play their roles as communicators and organizers.[32]

Another objective was to tighten up the organizations in rural districts and villages. At the time the campaign was started, many rural districts were said to be drifting without any leadership. In some places, the Party members in the district or village had not held a meeting for many months. Many members did not pay their Party dues and for all practical purposes were not related to the Party. In some cases, the Party secretary in the county did not know how many Party members he had in the villages. Sometimes an official who was not a Party member had gone to a village and dismissed the village Party secretary for poor performance. The situation was described as being intolerable to the Party hierarchy.[33] It seems that the most important link in the communication network, the link involving cadres in the rural districts and villages, also happened to be the weakest. The Rural Rectification campaign was planned to strengthen that link.

That campaign was also intended to correct the traditional peasant ideology and clear the way for agricultural collectivization. Having acquired their own land through the land reform, the peasants were beginning to work as independent farmers. Rich-peasant thinking soon prevailed among the peasants as well as the rural cadres and left them with little enthusiasm for changing their status quo. After all, peasants, whether Chinese or otherwise, generally have a strong love for the land they work on. When the Party started the Mutual-Aid Team movement as the first step toward agricultural collectivization, it was given a cool reception by many rural cadres. A survey conducted in the spring of 1953 in 3,847 villages in Shantung Province showed that only 30 percent of the rural Party members had joined the mutual-aid teams despite repeated calls by the Party.[34] The Party realized that unless rich-peasant thinking was eliminated from among its rural cadres, the agricultural collectivization programs would fail.

Political Socialization and Growth of Communication Systems

According to criteria published in 1952, a Party member should dedicate his life to establishing Communism in China. No matter how difficult the obstacles, he should not retreat or surrender to the class enemy. He should obey the Party's leadership absolutely, renounce all individual incentives, and wholeheartedly serve the interests of the people. To cultivate and achieve these ideals, Party members must constantly study the thought of Marx, Lenin, and Mao Tse-tung. To control deviation, they must continuously engage in self-criticism and criticism of others.[35]

The Rural Rectification campaign was planned according to these ideals and strategies. The Party recognized that the family and social backgrounds of many of its members made them susceptible to the influence of the old society. The task was to transform the mass of rural cadres, who reflected at least some of the characteristics of the traditional Chinese bureaucracy, into a solid corps of dedicated and faithful Party members.

Communication Tactics

It is indicative of the Chinese Communist philosophy and operations that the Party did not rely primarily on the informational and persuasive effects of the mass media. Nor did it depend on formal schooling. Instead, the Party put heavy emphasis on interpersonal channels of normative and value-oriented communications, involving both the cadres and the mass of people, as a major instrument of policial socialization. By requiring its rural cadres to communicate continuously both with the county cadres above and the peasants below, the Party created a structure in which the rural cadres could learn to perform their roles through actual experience. Constant supervision from above and criticism from below would make sure that errors in ideology and conduct would be spotted and corrected. Through this process, the Party apparently hoped, the desirable behavioral patterns and values for an ideal Party member could be created. Meanwhile, an effective communication network would be established.

The first step was to recruit and train an initial core of trusted communicators who could be sent out to the villages to conduct the massive campaign of political socialization. Toward the end of 1952, more than one hundred thousand such cadre members were selected from the rank and file by provincial and county Party secretaries all over the nation and organized into work teams.[36] The objectives of the campaign were explained to them. To give them actual experience, the provincial and county secretaries led their work teams to a number of selected areas to experiment with rural rectification. Problems encountered during the experimental stage were discussed, then the procedures were revised and tried again until they were judged to be appropriate and effective for the local situation.

Local Party authorities were given considerable flexibility within the overall policy and objectives. It is symptomatic of the loose control of the Party's central hierarchy at the time that the official guidelines were not strictly followed. In many areas the cadres who were supposed to educate others were themselves ignorant of the roles required of them. They attended training meetings for a few days and then started on their jobs. In other cases the experimental stage was omitted because of insufficient time. Some of the cadres recruited to train others were not even Party members. In Shangtu County, for instance, of the 286 cadres assigned to rural rectification, 109 were later discovered not to be members of the Communist party.[37] These problems, however, did not slow down the movement; the Party's strategy was to move ahead and do whatever it could under the circumstances.

The general tactics of rural rectification were as follows:[38] After a work team had arrived in a village, it would call a meeting of the village cadres. The objectives were explained and the procedures for implementing them discussed. Then the village cadres, not the outside work team, would call a meeting of all the Party members in the village. The work team would begin the meeting by criticizing themselves. The team members would admit that many problems in the villages were the result of their own lack of responsibility and supervision. This step was considered important in order to minimize resentment of local Party members and set the tone of normative communication within the group. The work team then emphasized that the only way to develop a healthy, efficient Party organization was for each member to engage in voluntary self-criticism, and mutual criticism.

Then came a series of criticisms. In an atmosphere of group pressure, the political consciousness and job performance of each Party member were thoroughly examined for error, first by himself and then by others. A number of criteria were employed: whether the deficiency was in political soundness or in administrative efficiency; whether the mistake was committed in the past or persisted; whether it was a first offense or a case or incorrigibility; whether the individual made a voluntary confession or refused investigation; whether the individual initiated the corruption or acted as an accomplice. Applying these criteria was largely left to the village cadres themselves, who were supervised throughout by the work team. Depending on the seriousness of the case, the Party member involved was either given a chance to reform himself, asked to withdraw from the Party, or dismissed.

No overall statistics were announced, but a few are available. For example, of the 60,360 rural Party members who took part in the initial phase of rural rectification in Shantung Province, 2,363 were found to be counterrevolutionaries (meaning that they were in some way related to the former regime), or landlords, or rich peasants, or undefined "rotten elements." These were expelled. Another 5,892 were asked to resign from the Party, and 1,856 were given educational reform. The number of disciplinary cases totaled approximately 15 per cent.[39] Thus did the Party purge itself of the undesirable members in its rural organizations.

Political Socialization

The primary objective, however, was political socialization, particularly with reference to rich-peasant thinking. By publicly exposing to the rural Party members cases and individuals that were considered undesirable and intolerable, the campaign in effect set certain behavioral boundaries that the rural cadres must not trespass. It is important to note that these boundaries were not set by laws or regulations that might not be clear or locally relevant. Rather, they were defined by actual cases from the cadres' own villages, which everybody could see and understand. Furthermore, since all Party members in the village participated in the self-criticism and mutual criticism, these boundaries had the appearance of being worked out by themselves, and thus were more likely to be followed.

The nature of the political socialization was both positive and negative, that is, it spelled out the do's as well as the don'ts. The characteristics of an ideal Party member were explained in three units, covering the ultimate objectives of Communism, the selfless dedication of a Party member to serve the people, and subordination of individual interest to collective interest. Again, these characteristics were presented, not in abstract terms, but through living examples with whom the rural Party members could identify.

The prototype examples were selected according to the following criteria: The case chosen should not only clarify the characteristics of an ideal Party member but should also help solve a realistic ideological problem. The case must not be too long and involved lest the educational effects be lost in a complicated story. The case should be one familiar to the local cadres.

An example illustrates how these criteria were applied. The collective farm movement had been an unresolved problem with both practical and ideological implications. Many peasants were hesitant to support it. So at a rural rectification training session, a model peasant, Ho Feng-shan, who had recently visited Soviet Russia, was invited to tell his experience. While he was visiting a Soviet collective farm, said Ho, he asked the chairman of the farm: "Do you have rich-peasant thinking here?" A member of the collective farm said: "Let me ask you a question. Do rich peasants in China have tractors, electricity, running water, automobiles, two-storied houses, radio sets, couches, and carpets?" Ho said: "None of these." "Well," said the Russian, "we have all of these things, and your rich peasants have none. Why should we follow the rich peasant road?" That convinced Ho to support the collective farm movement. This story was told numerous times, and was said to have had great effect.[40]

The Communication Network

Besides ideological rectification, the campaign sought to tighten up communication between the village and the county. By sending the county cadres to the villages instead of allowing them to remain in their offices, the Party established a channel of interpersonal communication between these two levels. Once established, the channel had to be constantly used. The county cadres could no longer be just paper pushers. Nor could they excuse themselves for not knowing what went on in the villages.

For the first time, the campaign also established the norm whereby peasants who were Party members in the village could criticize the mistakes of their superior cadres. This changed the previous pattern of relations in which the village cadres could claim a position of superiority and issue orders to both peasants and other Party members in the village without giving an explanation. The structural basis of commandism was weakened, if not totally removed. The village cadres were made clearly aware of the fact that now they were not only closely supervised by the county cadres, but were also constantly watched by the mass of people. False reports became rather difficult to maintain. That the provincial cadres could reach over the county and communicate directly with village cadres had the same restraining effects on the county cadres. At each level, supervision from above and criticism from below held the cadres within an overall network of surveillant communication.

Part of the socialization functions of rural rectification were instructional. Before this campaign, the rural cadres had attended mass rallies where landlords and rich peasants were opposed in struggle meetings. But relatively few cadres had conducted meetings in which practical problems were reviewed and solutions proposed. Rural rectification provided the rural Party members with an opportunity to learn how to conduct a meeting, how to lead a group discussion, and above all, how to criticize themselves and others.[41] Self-criticism and mutual criticism were particularly difficult because at first few people knew what to say. One participant said he was so nervous at his first self-criticism meeting that he coughed and kept going to the toilet while waiting for his turn.[42] While self-criticism would be ego threatening, criticism of others could damage personal relations. The general rule appeared to be: stick to the issues and avoid personal shortcomings not related to ideology or the task involved.

Follow-up Campaigns

Some cadres evidently learned role playing too well. As told by An Tze-wen, then minister of personnel of the central government:

> When a campaign comes, there are people who would prepare themselves in every conceivable way. They pretend to be progressive and sincere, as if they were really engaged in a relentless struggle against all

wrongdoings. At a mass meeting for self-criticism, they would cry, moan, and confess all their mistakes. After the campaign is over, when the "storm has calmed down" they go back to their old selves. Their self-criticisms are tossed aside, and they do whatever they want to do.[43]

This makes it apparent that the Chinese Communist party did not consider the San Fan movement and the Rural Rectification campaign to be a complete success in the political socialization of its cadres. These campaigns were just the beginning of a long process, even though they had the effect of pushing through three major agricultural collectivization programs within the short span of four years: the Mutual-Aid Team movement in 1953, the Elementary Agricultural Cooperative movement in 1954 and 1955, and the Advanced Agricultural Cooperative movement in 1956. However, while the earlier practices of corruption and violation of law had abated considerably by 1957, commandism was still strong, as the nationwide Anti-Rightist campaign of 1957–1958 demonstrated.[44]

The Commune movement and the Great Leap Forward of 1958 brought the nation's production system almost to the verge of chaos. By mid-1959, the Party retreated from the Commune movement as it was originally conceived, although without public announcement.[45] A period of consolidation appeared to have prevailed from 1960 to 1965. The central government under Liu Shao-chi seemed to be somewhat less actively concerned with mass movements than with the routine tasks of production and management. In an atmosphere of relaxed control, many of the bureaucratic practices had apparently crept back. According to secret military papers captured by Khamba guerrillas in Tibet in 1961, many cadres were charged with extreme forms of misdeeds and cruelty. A large number of cadres misused their authority.[46] The Party leadership responded by launching in the spring of 1963 the Socialist Education movement, a campaign which aimed at rectifying the excessive behavior of the cadres and keeping open the lines of communication from the central administration down to the local units. By late 1964, the movement had gained full momentum in the vast rural regions, having taken on the name of *Ssu Ching* (Four Clean-ups).[47]

Following essentially the same tactics employed in the Rural Rectification campaign of 1953, Party work teams were sent from counties to villages. The work team cadres lived with the peasants. They had door-to-door talks with the poor and lower-middle peasants and asked them to pour out their woes. In this way they learned the peasants' problems. Then in closed meetings, the work team members confronted the village cadres with the peasants' complaints and required them to "clean up" themselves in four aspects of their work: political, financial, ideological, and organizational. The Party's main concern appeared to be the financial aspect, involving misuse of public funds and accumulation of private wealth. The village cadres had to show how they had handled the accounts, the warehouse management, and the work-point system in their respective production brigades and teams. They must explain how they acquired their private properties. The number of village level cadres dismissed during the campaign was not disclosed, although the Party's goal was 5 percent of cadres and 5 percent of the middle-class peasants. Some of the poor and lower-middle-class peasants were promoted to cadre positions in their villages. Toward the end of 1965, the Ssu Ching campaign was applied to county level cadres, many of whom were singled out for criticism by their subordinates for their errors of commandism, bureaucratism, and revisionism.

Both at the village and county levels, the cadres were required to go through the same self-criticism and mutual criticism procedures. After a cadre had satisfactorily gone through the clean-ups, he became eligible for "three renewals," that is, renewal of study, renewal of ideological reform, and renewal of Party membership. Although by 1965 Liu Shao-chi was apparently taking advantage of the clean-up campaign to consolidate his power base at the grass-roots level, the movement did have the effect of curtailing the corruption that had again become current among many cadres.

The Ssu Ching movement was cut short in the summer of 1966 by the Cultural Revolution. Many senior cadres were accused of being "capitalist roaders" following the line of revisionism, and were removed. By early 1969, when the severe disturbances of the Cultural Revolution had subsided, the Party began to restore most of the cadres at the provincial and county level who had been demoted during the previous couple of years. Before their reinstatement, these Party cadres were required to go through a stage of reform education by going to the mass of people to admit their errors and to learn from the experience of the peasants.[48]

May 7 Cadre Schools

The typical process of this reform education was described by the *People's Daily* in an article on the first May 7 Cadre School.[49]

Started by the revolutionary committee of Heilungchiang Province on May 7, 1968, in response to Chairman Mao's instructions issued on May 7, 1966, the school consisted of 504 provincial-level senior cadres who were sent to Liuho Village, Chin An County, to start a farm according to the instructions of Chairman Mao. While they labored on the barren land, these high-level cadres engaged in a series of self-criticism and mutual criticism meetings to prevent the reemergence of revisionist thinking. Their actions were published in newspapers and by radio, and similar May 7 cadre schools were started all over the country. In neighboring Kirin Province, more than forty May 7 schools were established before November 1968, enrolling some ten thousand provincial-level cadres.[50] In Kwangtung Province in South China, more than one hundred thousand cadres above the county level were undergoing labor reform in some three hundred such schools in early 1969.[51] The Party was apparently depending on the same tactics employed in rural rectification as well as on manual labor to invigorate the cadres.

The loss of revolutionary zeal due to long years of administrative work was indicated by the inital complaints and lukewarm reactions among the rank and file. Some cadres were described as initially "unhappy" but later developed a "warm enthusiasm."[52] Others complained because they considered the labor reform in May 7 Schools to be a form of punishment.[53] Still others took an attitude known as "Let's just hang around for one year." This attitude was severely criticized.[54] Some cadres had become tired of heavy administrative work and took the May 7 Schools as a welcome relief. The Party reminded them that doing labor at the school did not exempt them from their responsibilities to the Party.[55] The greatest evil the Party wanted to eradicate through labor at the May 7 Schools was an attitude that "joining the Party is a sure way of acquiring high official status."[56]

In a special article published on May 6, 1974, the *People's Daily* noted the success of the May 7 schools in reforming the cadres.

> Among the cadres who have attended the May 7 schools, those of the older generation have regained revolutionary youthfulness, those of the younger generation have become more vigorous and enthusiastic in their work, those of worker and peasant origins have preserved their true color of the proletariat, and those of intellectual stature have integrated more closely with workers and peasants.[57]

However, the *People's Daily* noted the pernicious influence of the revisionist line that had not been fully wiped out. Some cadres wanted to move the May 7 Schools from the countryside to the city, while others in responsible positions attempted to direct the schools away from ideological struggles. "Only in struggle," said the *People's Daily,* "is there progress. Without struggle, there will be retrogression, bankruptcy, and revisionism."[58] To operate the May 7 Cadre Schools properly, the Party must carry out a persistent struggle against all the erroneous tendencies, as represented by Liu Shao-chi, Lin Piao, and Confucius. The campaign against Lin Piao and Confucius, in that sense, can be seen as a continuation of the ideological reform that began with the Cultural Revolution.

Communication and Institution Building
Removing the Old

The first step the Communist authorities took in establishing an effective communication network for the nation was to eliminate the influentials in the old social structure. Through rural land reform the Party removed from positions of relative wealth and authority the landlords, rich peasants, and those who had worked closely for the previous regime. In their place were installed Party members who had either fought in the revolution or distinguished themselves in the early mass campaigns after 1949.

The Party's elimination of undesirable elements during the first couple of years was not complete. Many administrators from the previous regime were allowed to remain. Among the long-time Communist members were those who began to turn their attention to accumulating individual wealth. Symptoms of the old bureaucracy soon began to surface. The communication networks which the Party was attempting to establish were obstructed. For a while the Party had apparently considered the ills of bureaucratism to be the result of inadequate information. It therefore initially counted on a national propaganda network to get the right kinds of information promptly to the people. It did not take the Party leadership long to realize that beneath the corruption and bureaucraticism of the cadres was a lack of ideological understanding and organizational ability.

Thus the Party found it necessary to conduct a nationwide rectification campaign soon after it came into power. At the higher level, this campaign took the form of a severe and extensive purge in the San Fan movement. Shortly afterwards, the Party began its rural rectification in order to expel from among its village cadres the former landlords, rich peasants, and those once connected with the previous regime. In essence, anyone who had some vestiges of influence or power derived from the past was effectively isolated from the village social structure. This action laid the foundation for the establishment of a Party-controlled, national communication network.

Establishing the New

While the Rural Rectification campaign sought to eliminate the last remnants of the old influentials, its primary objective was one of political socialization. The Party realized that its rural cadres must be educated in Communist ideology before they could play their roles as effective communicators and organizers. The tactics of self-criticism and mutual criticism are essentially a combination of normative and value-oriented communications for achieving this objective. Actual cases from the peasant population were used as concrete examples of the new values and the new ideology, to show the rural cadres what Communism meant and what they were supposed to do and not to do. These cases provided an ideological framework for the normative processes of self-criticism and mutual criticism that followed. Through self-criticism, each cadre then searched in himself for those asepcts of thinking and behavior that were judged to be undesirable by the standards of the new ideology. These were brought to the open in order to be examined by his peers in the group. Engaging in self-criticism also amounted to a public commitment to the new values. The subsequent mutual criticism among the cadres brought additional pressure to bear on one another, creating through the process of normative communication a basis of social reality for the new values and beliefs. This is a clear example of how social pressure generated by normative communication within the group functions to guide the learning of new value-orientations, which in turn provide an ideological basis for subsequent normative communication to apply further pressure (see figure 3).

The criticism sessions also provided practical training for the rural cadres in chairing meetings and conducting discussions. The cadres began to learn how to exercise their leadership and organize the peasants for action programs. As a result of the campaign, a communication network was established linking the county cadres, the village cadres, and the peasants into a vast net of surveillance by

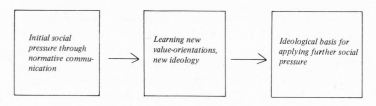

Figure 3. Interaction betweeen Normative and
Ideological Communications

which the performance and thought of each cadre could be constantly watched from both above and below. For the first time,
upward-directed criticism came to be accepted as a normative
means of communication.

A latent function of the Rural Rectification campaign appeared
to be the political socialization of the peasants in general. The
Chinese peasants had been aroused to take part in the rural land
reform that led to the downfall of the landlords. Much of their participation in that movement, however, appeared to be directed by
the Party's land reform work teams. Once the Land Reform movement was over, most peasants seemed to have lost interest in further
involvement. Their lack of concern could be explained by two factors. With the redistribution of land, a traditional source of social
grievance had been eliminated. Furthermore, while in the mass
rallies for land reform the peasants had been required to act as ac-
cusers and revengers, the roles they were supposed to play after the
landlords had been removed were ambiguous.

The Rural Rectification campaign defined for the peasants their
roles in the overall network of small group communication and provided some incentive for continued participation. They would be
allowed, and indeed required, to keep a watchful eye on the work
of the cadres in their villages. The disciplinary actions taken by the
Party during rural rectification indicated to the peasants that their
role performance would not be futile. Within the ideological
framework and the general constraints of the Party's production
goals, the peasants were permitted to voice their opinions regarding
the practical aspects of implementing these goals. Through guided,
actual experience with the campaign, they were given opportunities
to learn how to play their new roles.

We have outlined the processes by which the Communist party
purged its ranks of serious cases of corruption, eliminated the rem-

nants of undesirable elements at the grassroots level, and tightened up the channels of communication from the central government down to the Villages. The Party also institutionalized the practice whereby cadres and Party members were required to engage in continuous self-criticism and mutual criticism so that they could maintain a firm ideological commitment to the cause of Communism. It is this ideological commitment—a set of internalized values—combined with close surveillance from above and below that keeps the gigantic networks of communication operating as they do today. The institution of criticism in the group setting is essential to the functioning of the entire communication system. It shapes and reinforces the cognitive foundation of the system by inculcating the Party cadres in the correct beliefs and values. At the same time, it provides the social mechanism for the group members to apply pressure and exercise constant surveillance over deviant behavior and erroneous thought.

The Communist Chinese case is an unusual system of communication in which a directive from the top hierarchy, whether it is for the eradication of rodents or reduction of the birth rate, can rapidly reach the lowest level of administration. The directive does not end up on the bulletin board. The local cadres take up the directive and, through interpersonal communication with the peasants in the village, plan a way to carry it out locally. Feedback regarding practical difficulties flows through the same channels to higher administrative levels. The San Fan movement and the Rural Rectification campaign marked the beginning of a long process whereby this communication system was developed into a fairly effective, operational network. The subsequent purges, the Cultural Revolution, and the campaign against Lin Piao and Confucius can be seen as continuous attempts to discover and cleanse the system of its unhealthy elements, some of which seem to persist. The nature of the problem was rather candidly described by Chairman Mao in an internal Party document made public in 1967.[59] (See Appendix A.)

Comparisons

A number of characteristics of this system can be noted in comparison with the adminstrative structure that existed in old China and the Western version of bureaucracy.

The administrative structure of old China bore some similarities, but many differences, when compared with the Chinese Communist system today. The old Chinese bureaucracy consisted of a hierarchy of office holders, from the cabinet ministers to the governors, regional administrators, and magistrates. In the rural districts *(Hsiang)* and villages, a system of mutual surveillance and self-governance known as *Pao-Chia* existed.[60] A cluster of families, generally several dozens, were organized into a Chia, and several Chia were designated as a Pao. Both Pao and Chia had their administrators, usually influential local residents who carried out their duties part time. The major duties of the entire bureaucratic system were collecting taxes and levies and maintaining law and order. The old Chinese system was distinguished by relatively little program-oriented communication, if any, and hardly ever in an upward direction. The stable Chinese social structure founded on a kinship basis and the general lack of external disruption enabled the old Chinese bureaucracy to carry on its minimal functions of administration.

Officials in the old Chinese system were not initially recruited on the basis of their administrative competence. Rather, most were chosen through highly competitive statewide examinations on their knowledge of Confucian classics and literary works. Thus, many Chinese bureaucrats were talented, but did not necessarily have the special qualifications for the jobs they were assigned. They learned on the job, so to speak, and their responsibilities were largely diffuse, rather than specific. Promotion seemed to be based on personal relations, seniority, and subsequent demonstration of administrative competence.

Whereas the old Chinese bureaucracy was loose, the new administrative structure today is characterized by a tight network of communication that flows both horizontally and vertically, downward and upward. The old Chinese bureaucrats were only minimally supervised from above; the cadres today are constantly watched from both above and below. In addition to the general duties of collecting taxes and maintaining law and order, the cadres are now responsible for carrying out new programs of all kinds. Whereas the old political system generally left the people alone as long as they paid taxes and caused no trouble, the new system continuously organizes the masses for ideological indoctrination as well as action programs.

The similarities are remarkable. Like the bureaucrats of the past, the cadres today are not recruited on the basis of specific qualifications. The major criterion of selection in the current system is ideological and class purity, which, like knowledge of Chinese classics and literary works, is largely unrelated to job requirements. As in olden days, the cadres today have to learn on the job. They are generalists and perform diffuse rather than specific duties. While absolute submission to the emperor was required of bureaucrats in the past, the cadres today must continuously demonstrate their unquestioning loyalty to the Communist ideology, the Party, and Chairman Mao Tse-tung. Both in the past and in the present, some version of ideological commitment seems to weigh more heavily than administrative competence.

The current Chinese system is quite different from the Western version of bureaucracy.[61] The Western bureaucracy operates along rigid procedures; the Chinese system relies on mass movements. The Western system functions on the basis of role specialization in a hierarchy of office holders; the Chinese system draws its strength from the pooled contributions of individuals having diffuse roles. In the Western system, communication extends to the lowest level of bureaucrats; from there on the system depends primarily on compliance with the laws and regulations on the part of the citizens. In the Chinese system, communication goes all the way to the mass of people. Implementation of new programs and regulations is achieved though the mobilized zeal and participation by the subordinates as well as by the people at the grassroots level.[62] Western bureaucrats are supervised from above; Chinese cadres are placed under surveillance from above and below. The Western bureaucrats are protected by tenure and promoted largely on the basis of seniority. The Chinese cadres have no tenure and live under constant threat of criticism by their colleagues. They can be demoted or dismissed for no fault of their own. Seniority is no guarantee of promotion and hardly counts positively in a rectification campaign. Most Western bureaucrats are recruited on the basis of specific qualifications and job competence. The Chinese cadres are chosen by virtue of their ideological commitment. The Western bureaucrats are free to change jobs; the Chinese cadres are bound to the system unless dismissed. The Western bureaucrats are generally not inclined to accept innovation in government. The Chinese cadres are prepared to adapt to a constant demand for change.

All this suggests that an administrative structure that grows out

of Chinese roots and bears little resemblance to Western bureaucracy plays an important role in the course of China's development.
The point is that both the Chinese cadre structure and the Western
bureaucratic organization are communication networks that perform certain essential and similar functions despite their structural
differences.

IV
Competition and Cooperation:
Processes of Task-Oriented Communication

Competition and cooperation are perhaps the most fundamental processes upon which society is founded. Man has always had to compete for a limited supply of desirable goods and services. Yet the objectives that man competes for often cannot be achieved by solo efforts, but require cooperation. The very fact that human beings survive in groups would suggest that cooperation is essential not merely as an instrument of competition, but equally importantly, as a prerequisite for group existence. An examination of competition and cooperation processes would be fascinating in any society, but particularly so in present-day China because such an examination can shed light on the impact of systematically applied social change on one of the world's oldest civilizations.

The old Chinese social system could be characterized as more cooperative than competitive. Even though institutionalized channels did exist in China, by which children of certain classes—primarily the landed gentry—could achieve prominence through competitive examinations, the general social structure that was built around the extended family seemed to foster cooperation within the group far more than competition.[1] In a sense, the hierarchical kinship relations were so rigid that one's position within the extended family was fixed at birth, even though wealth and influence could sometimes be advanced by one's own efforts. Even the social recognition and material reward to be gained were regarded more as reflections on the honor of the extended family than as personal achievements. The general nature of the social structure was such as to discourage competition on an individual basis and to encourage cooperation within the context of kinship relations. Interactions between groups, whether cooperative or competitive, were infrequent and limited because of the lack of communication channels. Thus the China of old was compared to "a sheet of loose sand."[2]

The conditions today are quite different. For a quarter of a century, the Communist authorities have been trying to replace the old kinship-based system with a new social order founded on Communist ideology. A number of questions can be asked:

What are the normative patterns of cooperation and competition in China today? By *cooperation* we are referring to patterned role interactions in which two or more individuals work together to achieve a common end. By *competition* we are referring to patterned role interactions in which two or more individuals strive to achieve the same end, each to the exclusion of the others.[3]

What are the objectives of cooperation and competition? Are they individual achievement, glory for the extended family, the collective good of the country, or a mixture of some sort?

How are the behavioral patterns of cooperation and competition reinforced? What are the incentives for conformity, the sanctions for nonconformity? Are the incentives and sanctions material in nature, in terms of provision or denial of goods and services, or are they symbolic, in terms of social recognition and rejection?

What are the relations among role performers (defined as individuals who occupy certain positions in the social system with their rights and obligations)? These relations arise out of role interactions and at the same time govern role interactions. Are these relations specific and clearly spelled out, or diffuse and ambivalent?[4]

How are role performers recruited? Perhaps no recruitment process is ever completely open, since social structural restrictions of one kind or another tend to favor certain individuals. What structural restrictions, if any, exist in China today? Are the criteria for recruitment largely oriented toward achievement or ascriptive backgrounds?[5]

In what group contexts do cooperation and competition take

place? What are the implications of the group contexts to the normative patterns of cooperation and competition that prevail?

Finally, what are the communication patterns that arise out of and give support to the processes of cooperation and competition? In the Chinese case, these task-oriented processes include the following: perceiving and defining the task, searching and finding ways of implementation, setting the desired level of performance for individuals as well as for groups, evaluating the role performers, providing social recognition and applying sanctions, maintaining cohesive relations within the group, and above all, laying an ideological basis so that cooperation and competition will not become matters of expediency but will be accepted as a moral duty.

Informational communication will be essential regarding both task definition and implementation. The performers need to know what is to be done, and find out ways of doing it. Equally important for cooperation within a group is normative communication. The performers need to reach a group consensus on the desired level of performance, and work out acceptable criteria for evaluation and distribution of reward and punishment. Lest severe internal competition impair group unity, the members need to agree on normative standards of conduct and performance in order to maintain congenial relations. Also, both informational and normative communications are required for intergroup competition—knowing how one's own group is doing in relation to the performance of other groups and what general norms to observe.

Nearly all task-oriented efforts require a supportive basis in values and beliefs, whether the Confucian ethic or Communist ideology. When the general patterns of cooperation and competition in a society are changed, as they have been in China, there must be congruent changes in relevant values and beliefs. Fatalism and traditionalism, for instance, are not compatible with a system of cooperation and competition that calls for self-reliance and innovation. Thus, value-oriented communication has become necessary in order to lay a new ideological foundation for the patterns of task performance desired by the Party leadership.

How are the various processes of communication—informational, normative, and value-oriented—organized in China? We shall examine whatever materials are available regarding these and other aspects of cooperation and competition in the Chinese system. The picture we put together should be seen not as something definitive, but hopefully as the beginning of a broad outline in which many gaps still need to be filled.

Normative Patterns
Cooperation

Cooperation in China during the past, particularly in the rural segment, was largely based on reciprocity within a context of close kinship relations. In a Western capitalist society, cooperation generally takes place on the basis of mutuality of profit, and personal relations are of lesser importance.[6] The radical change of social structure in China, as discussed in chapter 2, has seriously weakened the kinship foundation and eliminated nearly all avenues of individual profit. The control of material resources and employment by the state has resulted in new patterns of cooperation that are different from those of old China as well as those of the West.

The norms of cooperation advocated by the Communist party leadership can be summarized as: (1) others first and self last, and (2) subjugation of individual interest for the sake of collective benefit.[7] This is seen from a discussion of cooperation by a high official in transportation:

Cooperation in a capitalist enterprise is entirely different from cooperation in a socialist enterprise. In the former, cooperation within and between units is built on profit-motivated contractual relations. The foundation of a socialist economy, however, ensures uniform benefit for individual, production units and collectives in the interest of building socialism. Cooperation is selfless and voluntary. This demonstrates the superiority of the socialist system.[8]

This norm of selfless cooperation is most likely an ideal rather than a reality. As the Chinese Communist authorities have openly admitted, one of the problems that have kept plaguing the Party is the rather widespread phenomenon known as the *Peng Wei* principle. *Peng Wei,* meaning "own unit," may be roughly translated as "groupism." This is manifest in a tendency not so much to look after one's individual interest, which is not permissible in China, but to look after the interest of one's group, thereby indirectly advancing one's own interest within a group context. In the transportation industry, for instance, some organizations were so bent on achieving outstanding records for their own units that they fought each other and stood in each other's way. If a freight train from one bureau passed through the territory of a different bureau, the local workers simply refused to make the connection. Problems like this were publicly deplored:

In our midst there are those who do not understand the nature of socialist cooperation. They see only a limited group interest but ignore the interest of the entire collectivity. They only know how to follow the regulations and impose fines, but do not practice political leadership and ideological unity. What they are doing benefits neither themselves nor others.[9]

Although adequate data are not available, groupism most probably exists at different levels, in which each unit tries to improve its own welfare within a larger organization, often at the expense of other units. In the aftermath of the Cultural Revolution, when control by the central government slackened, many state enterprises pushed hard to promote their own interests and ignored the overall planning by the central government.[10] The same phenomenon was reported at the small-group level, as seen in an official account of a nationwide production campaign started by the steelworkers of Peking in 1969. The report said the workers had to fight "self-interest in themselves and struggled to replace it with wholehearted service to the people."[11] Up until that campaign, the different shifts were uncooperative with each other. For instance:

Revolutionary mass criticism transformed C shift's thinking. Uncooperative with other shifts in the past, now they saw that good emulation meant good unity and cooperation. They made a resolution: "Leave things easy for the next shift and take the hard things from the last shift." They actively looked for ways to cooperate.[12]

Competition

The phenomenon of the Peng Wei principle was noted at about the same time as the promotion of the Great Leap Forward, when intense intergroup competition was demanded by the Party. The objective of the competition, which later came to be known as the general line for socialist construction, was "Go all out, aim high and achieve more, faster, better and more economical results in building socialism."[13]

Ever since the Great Leap Forward movement, the Chinese have been challenged to better each other's task performance, as in the steelworkers' competition campaign. They are "dared to think, dared to speak up, and dared to act." While the Chinese in the past were to some extent dominated by fatalism and were hesitant to try anything new, the spirit encouraged by the Party is one of self-reliance and defiance of obstacles. It is exemplified by Chairman Mao's much quoted parable of Yu Kung (the Foolish Old Man) who, with the help of others, removed a mountain by sheer determination. That is, nothing is impossible. Old regulations and traditional ways of doing things are to be swept away, so that new norms may be established. Disorder during the transition is regarded as a normal phenomenon, not something to be afraid of. Chairman Mao was quoted as saying:

[The Great Leap Forward] is not like inviting someone to dinner, or writing a polished article, or painting a fine picture, or embroidering flowers. You cannot do it in a slow, leisurely, and cultivated manner.[14]

According to the same source, Mao's way was to make "a hell of a mess," in which the workers were required to "learn from the pioneers, compare with the pioneers, and finally surpass the pioneers." In other words, compete as hard as possible and break the records whenever and wherever you can.

The same patterns of intense competition were urged upon the peasants as well as the workers. As a high official in charge of agriculture noted, the Chinese peasants were traditionally conservative, unwilling to part with the past, and contented with what little they had. They dared not speak their minds. The Communist party wanted to change all this and involved the peasants in massive campaigns of production competition.[15] The Agricultural Producers' Cooperatives and the Commune movement were examples.

Resentment

Though vigorously encouraged by the Party, this kind of pushiness in competition not only seems incompatible with the principle of cooperation but was apparently resented by some workers and peasants. Take the case of Su Kuang-ming as an example. Su, 61, was a model worker who had risen to be an engineer at the Harbin Rolling Stock Plant in Manchuria. He began at the plant as an illiterate worker many years ago and became a milling-machine operator. After the Communists had taken over the plant in 1945, the cadres invited him into the manager's office to discuss with him the production plan of his unit. "Speak out whatever's on your mind, Old Su," the new leaders urged him. Su cast a glance about the room and said with deep feeling, "Before, I wouldn't have even dared look at the door of this office, to say nothing of sitting in it discussing production plans!''[16]

From then on, Su Kuang-ming devoted all his time to the plant and developed a number of new methods of production. Several times he was chosen a national model worker, and in 1960 was promoted to the position of engineer at his plant. His eager and outstanding performance, however, aroused resentment among his fellow workers. One day he received an anonymous letter, obviously written by a bad egg, saying that if he made any more technical innovations, he'd better watch out.[17]

At that time, Su was organizing a survey group to visit other plants and to learn about their improvement of cutting tools. A rumor soon started circulating in the plants that the members of the survey group were ''trying to do something big to show off.'' Su, however, refused to give up and the survey was eventually carried through.

Another example of resentment of the competitive spirit was furnished by the experience of Lu Yu-lan, a female Party cadre. Born of a peasant family in East Liushanku Village, Linhsi County, Lu was elected head of an agricultural producers' cooperative at the age of fifteen, and became party secretary of a commune production brigade at nineteen. Now thirty-two, she is the party secretary of Linhsi County and concurrently a deputy party secretary of Hopei Province. When she returned to her village from schooling at fifteen, Lu tried hard to organize other young women in order to turn a sandy wasteland into green fields. She had some initial success. This aroused so much jealousy and resentment from among one segment of the villagers that, while Lu was away from the village at a meeting, they cut down trees that had grown to timber size and dug up the saplings that Lu and other women had planted.[18] However, Lu, according to the report, won out at the end.

A report in the *People's Daily* in 1968 would suggest that such resentment is probably not atypical. Deploring what it termed a tendency of anarchism among the peasants, the report said:

Some peasants spend their time playing cards, or visiting relatives and friends; some refuse to obey the correct leadership of the cadres. They argue over work points and complain about wages. They pick the light work and avoid the heavy work. They even find excuses for such erroneous behavior by saying they are merely ''breaking the old bondage'' and ''fighting against slavism.''[19]

Objectives and Incentives

The objectives of competition and cooperation in China today are clearly meant to be collective. Everything is done in the name of socialism. The peasants, for instance, are told that they work not primarily to feed their families, but for the sake of the socialist revolution.[20] However, the possibility that full acceptance of this objective is still a hope rather than a reality is suggested by the unabated official criticism of self-centered individualism that has persisted through all these years. In an editorial published in 1958 in the *People's Daily,* entitled "Mess Up Capitalist Individualism Till It Stinks," the Party left no doubt that individualism is the worst enemy of collective Communism.[21] During the Cultural Revolution, capitalist individualism was labeled a "big poisonous weed" that must be uprooted. This theme has been renewed in the current campaign against Lin Piao and Confucius. A report in the *People's Daily* in July 1975 deplored the behavior of some commune members "who hoist the flag of collectivism but mess around with capitalistic individual activities to fatten themselves."[22]

Material Incentive

The primary characteristics of capitalist individualism are said to be striving for money, position, and social recognition, which the Chinese Communists have strongly condemned. Despite their public condemnation, however, the Chinese Communists have not found it possible to do away entirely with monetary gain as an incentive. For instance, when the Weihsin (Sputnik) Commune of Honan Province was established in 1958, it employed eight different grades of wages, distributed as shown in the accompanying list.[23]

Grade	Work Points per Day	Percent of Work Force
Grade 1	4	8.0
Grade 2	5	14.7
Grade 3	6.5	23.0
Grade 4	7.5	23.0
Grade 5	9	18.2
Grade 6	10	11.8
Grade 7	12	1.1
Grade 8	15	0.2

The monthly wages were calculated on the basis of work points, ranging from slightly over 2 JMP for grade one, to 7.6 JMP for grade eight. The differentials were based on the following criteria, in descending order of importance: (1) ideological consciousness, (2) work attitudes, (3) productivity and technical proficiency, (4) physical strength. Further eligible for bonus distribution would be those who would: (1) obey leadership and follow orders, (2) vigorously compete in production and surpass production quotas, (3) protect public property and expose bad behavior, (4) make progress in ideological study and production techniques, and (5) work at least twenty-eight days a month.

The actual income distribution among peasants is most likely much less varied than implied by the eight grades because wages earned through work points usually constitute only a portion of the family income. At the beginning of the Commune movement, the Sputnik Commune and many others offered peasants free supplies of food and miscellaneous services in addition to work points. This practice was soon dropped as being impracticable. Although the communes now have considerable flexibility with regard to the distribution of their income, a general system has emerged through trial and error. The case of Pung Tao Commune, Nan An County, Fukien, provides an example.[24] According to a former member of the commune, its total crop output for the second season of 1964 was divided into the categories shown in the accompanying list.

Total crops of second season, 1964			14,900 catties
Less:	Levies in kind (remainder of 1964 quota of 10,000 catties)	2,000	
	Sales of surplus grain to state (exempt because of poor crop)	—	
	Seeds	1,800	
	Reserve	500	
	Bonus	500	
Leaving for general distribution to members			10,100 catties

Out of the 10,100 catties for general distribution, 10 percent was given as compensation to those commune members who had contributed manure as fertilizer. The bulk of the total crop—70 percent—was distributed free among all members according to their family sizes. Each adult in the commune received 54 catties of grain for that seven-month season, about 8 catties a month. The remaining 20 percent was distributed as wages according to work points earned. Income differences among peasants would thus be rather minimal. At the Red Star Commune near Peking, for instance, the highest household income in 1971 was only 80 percent more than the lowest.[25] No national statistics are available on the cash value of peasants' income. If we take the peasants in the outskirts of Peking as an example, the average income of an agricultural laborer in 1957 was about 110 JMP a year.[26] The corresponding figure could be lower in outlying areas.

Current data on factory wages are not available. One article in the *People's Daily* suggests that uniform wage scales applied to workers in the whole country, since even though one particular factory was making a huge profit, it could not raise its own pay scale because of national regulations.[27] According to statistics in 1957, workers were paid in eight grades of monthly wages: 35 JMP (grade 1), 41 JMP (grade 2), 48 JMP (grade 3), 56 JMP (grade 4), 65.5 JMP (grade 5), 76.7 JMP (grade 6), 89.6 JMP (grade 7), and 105 JMP (grade 8).[28] Over the years wages for workers have increased moderately. One article revealed that the average wage for workers in a motor repair factory went up from 57.94 JMP in 1950 to 71.30 JMP in 1957, an increase of approximately 3 percent a year.[29]

Although we have no up-to-date data, it seems that the wage level for workers has not changed greatly since 1957. If we take Peking's First Textile Factory as an indication, in 1965 worker Chang Yung-hua and his wife Cheng Chih-li together made 180.50 JMP a month, out of which approximately 115 JMP went for food for their family of six. Family income at this level was said to be common among urban dwellers in China.[30]

Symbolic Incentives

Material incentives, however, are used reluctantly—as a necessary evil. Over the years, the Party has been alternating between denunciation of and reliance on material incentives. From 1950 up to the establishment of the communes in 1958, the Party, in an attempt to adhere to its ideology, had been gradually limiting the material rewards for peasants and workers. The unfavorable popular reactions to this austerity policy were suggested by a campaign around 1959 in which the Party took pains to denounce a tendency known as *"Jen Ming Pi* in command," meaning "doing everything for money."[31] In the aftermath of the commune failure, when the country began to recover from the calamities of 1961 and 1962, the Party under Liu Shao-chi decided to make some concessions by restoring material rewards. The peasants were allowed to retain their small private plots, and a bonus system for meritorious performance became more widespread for both the peasants and workers. The bonus system came under severe attack during the Cultural Revolution. Though greatly curtailed as a result of the Cultural Revolution, material incentives have apparently come back in recent years. A provincial radio broadcast from Kansu in July 1974, for instance, acknowledged that the practices of "putting work points in command" have appeared again.[32] The problem, as seen by the Party authorities, is how to draw a clear line between "proper compensation for labor" and undesirable material incentives. The solution offered is to emphasize political consciousness and ideology.

With the general deemphasis of material incentives, the Party has had to rely on symbolic incentives by extending social recognition, and with it, eventually, access to membership in the various Party apparatuses. For instance, at Tung Ching Commune, Kuei County, Kwangsi Province, out of sixty-nine urban students sent to the commune for permanent settlement since 1970, by August 1974, three had acquired Party membership and another thirty had been admitted into the Communist Youth Corps.[33] Workers and peasants who achieved excellent performance were elected to be Labor Pioneers or Model Peasants. Some of them are periodically chosen for publicity in the mass media. A recent example is Yu Fang, a nineteen-year-old girl who was elected a Model Communist Youth Corps member in the spring of 1973, and awarded the title of Model Worker that fall. This girl grew up during the Cultural Revolution and became the captain of the women's brigade in her commune at the age of seventeen. She was described as being totally obedient to the Party and working for the collective interests only.[34]

The Party authorities apparently saw a subtle contradiction between their condemnation of capitalist individualism (because it is based on a quest for money, prestige, and position), and their own use of social recognition and Party membership as symbolic incentives. At a forum on the Red and Expert controversy (see below) sponsored by Peking University, a senior Party official offered this explanation in a concluding speech:

> The recognition and position we are talking about are different from the recognition and position in the old society. Anyone engaging in any labor can have recognition and position. We are not using recognition and position as objectives of our labor. Rather, they can be the consequences of our labor. We are definitely not seeking recognition and position by choosing to do this and refusing to do that. Rather, when the Party assigns us to do something, we'll do it; if we have done it well, the Party and the people will give us recognition and position, but not as reward for any particular individuals. This is entirely different from setting up recognition and position as the goals of our struggle.[35]

The moral seems to be clear. Strive for the collective interest; social recognition, position, and even some material reward will come as a result. But one must not labor for the sake of these rewards. However, the collective objectives do not seem to be widely shared by the people, who have yet to give up their concern with individual welfare.

Role Relations in Cooperation and Competition

The role relations in cooperation and competition, which reflect the task-related social organization of a country, pose another perennial problem for the Party. The overall objectives of mainland China are industrial development and large-scale collective farming. Both would call for a relatively high degree of division of labor and specific role relations. An unrestrained movement in this direction, however, would place the technicians and managerial personnel in a position of prominence, and minimize the importance of ideology. Nevertheless, the Party leadership must have recognized that ideology without technical know-how cannot achieve the objectives of economic development. Both are obviously necessary. This question of relative priority has become known as the battle between "the Red and the Expert."

Ideology and Technology

The Party makes no secret of the fact that it does not trust the technicians and specialists, most of whom come with a class background contaminated by bourgeois thinking. Meanwhile, before a new generation of uncontaminated specialists can take over, the Party still needs the present group of technicians for performing certain necessary tasks. The ideal solution of the problem would be to reform these technicians so that they will be "saturated with Redness" while developing a high degree of specialty.

One way to combine redness with specialty is through the eradication of self-centered individualism, which is considered the source of many bourgeois evils. Before this reform can be achieved, the Party must use the talents of the technicians without giving them the importance that would generally come with their role performance. The problem facing the Party leadership is represented in a choice between specific relations and diffuse relations of cooperation, particularly with regard to decision-making. In an organization characterized by a high degree of division of labor, it seems that the best efficiency can be achieved by specific role assignments and role relations, where each role performer has his rights and obligations clearly spelled out. As long as he stays within the boundaries of his rights and obligations, he can make decisions without referring them to other role performers in the same system. Only when the rights and obligations of others are involved will he find it necessary to consult them. It follows that if the task involved calls for a high level of technology, then those role performers who possess that technology will generally assume considerable importance because of their necessary participation in most matters of decision-making.

An organization characterized by diffuse role assignments and relations is structured in a different manner. Few role performers are given specific rights and obligations. When a decision needs to be made, generally no one is in a position to make it all by himself, because it is not clear whether he would be acting within his rights and obligations. Nor is it clear what specific others need to be consulted in this decision-making process. As a result, practically all role performers in the system need to be brought into the process through which a collective decision can be reached. Few individuals will rise to prominence within the group by virtue of their exclusive access to decision-making. On the other hand, efficiency will most likely suffer because of the need to involve many individuals in reaching a decision which would otherwise be made by a few individuals.

Diffuse Relations

When confronted with a choice between the two, the group leadership under Mao apparently preferred the diffuse rather than the specific patterns of role relations. This was evident in the attempt of the Great Leap Forward and the general line of socialist construction. It was the Reds, the mass, rather than the specialists and technicians that the Party would depend on. When Liu Shao-chi took over the leadership in the aftermath of the failure of the Great Leap Forward and the Commune movement, he showed a tendency to rely on the "specialty" rather than on the Red. This tendency of preferring specific rather than diffuse relations constituted one of the major grounds of criticism against Liu Shao-chi during the Cultural Revolution.

Since then the emphasis has been reversed again. Operating under the diffuse pattern, the specialists and technicians are brought to contribute their technical know-how in overall cooperative efforts, but are not given any specific authority. All important decisions are reached through a process of participation involving many individuals, including the Party cadres who are ideologically dependable but not necessarily technologically qualified. When there is a conflict between ideology and technology, specialty can give way to redness.

Under this system, there is a lack of clearly defined role responsibilities for individuals occupying different status positions. Neither the managerial cadres, nor the technicians, nor the workers have any specific roles that are exclusively their own. Rather, according to the principle of the "three-in-one" union—meaning a union of cadres, workers, and technicians—the cadres and technicians are required to perform manual labor, and receive recognition for doing so. For instance, the deputy party secretary of Hsiang Huan County, Li Hsin-cheng, was praised for personally delivering human waste to peasants for use as fertilizer.[36] A female model worker, Ho Chien-hsiu, who rose from illiterate farm girl to the position of engineer because of her invention of a cotton spinning device, was given publicity when she chose to join her former fellow workers at the factory where she had started out as a laborer.[37]

Workers, on the other hand, are allowed to participate in the decision-making process and contribute innovative ideas of management and technology. For instance, when the Ma-anshan Iron and Steel Company formed a technical innovation group, it was composed of workers and Party cadres as well as technicians in a three-in-one union. At the Shenyang No. 3 Machine Tool Plant, workers, technicians, and administrative cadres worked together on a new design.[38] Workers, as well as cadres and soldiers from the

People's Liberation Army, served on revolutionary committees such as the one at the Tientsin Textile Factory No. 2.[39]

Dependence on technology is strongly denounced in agriculture as well as in industry. Leadership in agricultural production, according to the Communist policy, must be assumed by ideology, not technology.[40] Due to the relatively low level of technology required in agriculture, the role relations of cooperation in the villages are not the same as in the factories. Modern industrial production demands a level of technical specialty that the ideologically conscious Party cadres may not have the ability to master. Thus, the technicians are allowed a place in the cooperative efforts of industrial production, although they are given no access to important decision-making. For agricultural production, the technology required is much less complex, so the tendency is for the cadres themselves to learn the new techniques first and then teach it to the peasants. For instance, when an experimental farm is started, it is the cadres who are directed to work on it first. If the experiment is successful, the technique is then disseminated to the peasants through on-the-spot demonstrations.[41]

The role relations in the villages are largely diffuse because of the Party's policy to merge the management role and the technician role into one for the cadres, who are also required to perform manual labor just like other peasants. However, unlike the industrial cadres whose authority is to some extent shared with the technicians and workers, the rural cadres appear to have a greater concentration of power by virtue of their administrative postition and control of technical know-how. In a sense, they may be the true "Red experts."

Recruitment of Role Performers
Recruitment and Mobility

Recruitment of role performers appears to follow a number of well-structured channels. The state through its various organizations decides the training and assignment of jobs for all individuals. Each year, the factories, communes, and various other organizations submit their needs of manpower to the state. Depending on the levels of technology required, either the central government or the provincial government works out plans of manpower training to meet the requirements.[42] Nearly all manufacturing, mining, and transportation industries operate their own training schools for skilled and semiskilled workers. This system of factory-school "hook-up" was introduced in the 1950s, and has been more widely practiced since the Cultural Revolution.[43] Many communes have short-term training courses of their own. Sometimes the factories and communes can approach the colleges or vocational schools directly to arrange training programs for special needs. Individuals sent by the factories and communes for special training will return to their original organizations upon completion of the training. Otherwise, the state will decide upon the job assignments according to overall national plans.

No organization is free to hire someone without going through the official procedures. If an individual in organization X has proved to be highly capable, organization Y cannot buy him over with a higher salary. He can be transferred only with the approval of a higher level authority.[44] The total absence of occupational mobility is illustrated by Ross Terrill, an Australian-born professor at Harvard University. During his visit to a chemical fiber factory near Nanking in 1971, Terrill inquired about the possibility of an individual's changing his job. This was what he learned:

...the worker cannot decide that he'd like to work in another factory, or another trade, and simply seek and get a different job. I inquired of the spokesman of the factory Revolutionary Committee, "Can a worker transfer work by his own individual decision?" I might have asked if the leopard can change his spots. *"I ting pu-shih!"* ("Certainly not!") You must find your freedom in the collective; you cannot bid for it as an individual.[45]

Class Restrictions

Generally speaking, children of five Red classes—workers, peasants, Party cadres, Liberation Army members and those who died for the revolution—are given preferential considerations in both schooling and job assignment. Undesirable class backgrounds carry over even after more than twenty years. According to a former cadre of Ho Shan Commune, Yang Chiang County, Kwangtung Province, the undesirables in the villages are classified into five categories: ex-landlords, ex-rich peasants, counterrevolutionaries, rightists, and bad elements. They are usually assigned the more difficult work and allowed fewer work points. At the Ho Shan Commune, a person who belonged to any of the five classes was required to give up 20 percent of the work points he earned because he was not qualified to attend most of the village meetings, and therefore had more time for work. For this reason, he was required to contribute some free time to the commune. Children of the five undesirable classes in that commune were not allowed to go beyond elementary school.[46] Professor Terrill reported that up to 30 percent of the ex-landlords and ex-rich peasants were still not considered sound enough to be given the rights of ordinary commune members, and some "reactionary" ones were under supervision.[47]

College education, as a mechanism of recruitment of role performers, has been drastically changed since the Cultural Revolution to follow a more rigid policy of class restrictions. The old system, under which high school graduates were admitted into college through competitive entrance examinations, was pronounced bourgeois. The new procedures, which require students to spend time in the communes or the army in order to qualify for college education, tend to favor those with the correct class background, that is, peasant, worker, soldier, and Party cadre. For instance, at the Fu Tan University in Shanghai, where only 25 percent of the students were in those categories in 1956, the figure was 98 percent in 1971. At the Sun Yat-sen University in Canton, the corresponding figure was 97 percent.[48] "The new policy," according to American journalist Barbara W. Tuchman, who visited China in 1972, "presumes that working-class experience of actual jobs in various fields fits these young men and women to make better use of an education for purposes of serving the revolution."[49] Achievement as a basis for recruitment of role performers is not ignored, but is taken into consideration only after the primary criterion of ascribed class background has been fulfilled.

Rural vs. Urban Division

In the early years of the industrialization movement, there was a constant flow of rural manpower into the cities because of higher wages in factories. As a result, urban population more than doubled in the first ten years, increasing from about forty million in 1950 to almost one hundred million in 1959.[50] The exodus of rural manpower to the cities was so serious that the central government had to impose a special restriction. According to a resolution passed at a cabinet meeting with the prime minister on December 13, 1957, no government organizations, state enterprises, or military units would be allowed to recruit workers in the villages, or to employ any individuals who had moved from rural to urban areas, without state approval. Agricultural cooperatives and government organizations in the villages were specifically instructed not to recommend peasants for work in urban factories and mining districts.[51]

Such administrative measures were apparently not effective enough to relieve the population pressure on the cities. Through strict food rationing, the state prohibits the issuance of food coupons to anyone who has moved from a village to a city without approval by a responsible government office. In recent years, the Party has been trying to reduce urban population by sending students to the villages for permanent settlement under the slogan "Go up to the mountains and down to the villages."

Group Contexts of Cooperation and Competition
The Extended Family

During the past, the extended family provided the most important group context for cooperation and competition in China. A rural village generally consisted of one extended family or more, each including a number of nuclear families bearing the same last name. Within each extended family, a clear network of kinship relations could be established to include every member. Some members owned land, while those who were less well off worked as hired hands for their cousins or uncles or even nephews. Even when an outsider was hired, he would tend to be treated as one of the extended family. If the landlord happened to be the fourth son of the family, the outside hired hand would call him "Fourth Uncle" *(Szu Yieh)* in the same way that his own nephews would address him.

In towns and cities, the same general pattern prevailed. A storekeeper would hire his own relatives and treat his nonrelated employees as kin. In skilled trades, a relationship of master and apprentices was established to simulate kinship relations. Apprentices were bound to their masters as sons were bound to their fathers. Even persons outside any of these networks would attempt to cast their relations in the kinship framework by addressing the other person as "brother" or "uncle" or "granduncle," depending on age difference and parallelism to kinship. For instance, a friend of one's father became an "uncle" while an acquaintance of one's grandfather would be a "granduncle."

Cooperative efforts tended to be confined within the kinship network where mutual trust could be established on common ties to ancestors. Where cooperation had to be extended beyond the kinship circle, simulated kin relationships were created. Competition did not exist to any great extent in the villages, where the peasants tilled their portions of land year after year and maintained the same level of living, barring natural calamities. Within the same kinship group, competition was particularly to be avoided, lest it disrupt internal relations. The same general patterns were followed in business and trade, where a traditionally stable pace rather than intense competition dictated the manner of operation. For instance, the Chinese in the past used practically no advertising, except through word of mouth and a store sign which might say "Third Generation Old Store of the Wang Family."

The importance of the extended family was largely due to the fact that it controlled the major means of production, land. The Chinese found both economic subsistence and psychological security within the same network of kinship ties. These functions of the extended family would be incompatible with competition inside the group.

Breaking the Old

Viewed in this light, the steps the Party took to eliminate the landlords and nationalize business and industry became comprehensible. As long as the old economic basis of the social structure existed it would be difficult if not impossible to establish a new social order under Communism. Under rural land reform the land that belonged to the landlords and rich peasants was confiscated and redistributed to the poor peasants and tenants. Later, through the collective farm movement, the state took over the land. Private ownership has virtually ceased to exist in agriculture, except for small private plots. All business and industrial establishments have become state operated since 1956. Deprived of its economic foundation, the kinship system has been seriously impaired. No one has the material means to support anyone other than his own nuclear family.

These programs of structural change not only neutralized the kinship system as a barrier to the new patterns of cooperation and competition. They are also significant because they broke the Chinese cultural tradition of noninvolvement. This tradition is exemplified by an old saying: "Let's each sweep the snow in front of his own door, and never mind the frost on other people's roof." Because of this kind of deep-seated attitude, cooperation and competition in a group setting seldom took place. The rural land reform and the purge of industrialists and businessmen forced the peasants and workers to become involved. Once they took part in mass movements, continued participation in other campaigns, whether for production or otherwise, became a necessity.

New group contexts of cooperation and competition have formed accordingly. In agriculture, cooperation now takes place in ascending order in production teams, production brigades, and communes. Competition can be undertaken both within a group and between groups. Thus, in a production campaign, a commune will compete against other communes. But within each commune, the production brigades will compete against each other and within each brigade, the production teams will compete against each other. Competition within a production team, when the Party desires it, is supposed to take place on the basis of individuals as commune members, not as parts of families. In this spirit, the title of Model Peasant for instance is awarded to an individual peasant whether male or female—not to his family.

Nuclear Family

The story of Kuo Lien-tsai, a member of the First Production Team, Pung Tao Commune, Nan An County, Fukien, suggests, however, that the nuclear family may still be a cohesive informal unit of task cooperation in rural villages.[52] Kuo was a poor peasant of forty-one when he fled to Hongkong in late 1964. His wife was then thirty-eight. They had five children, aged four to seventeen. Except for their four-year-old girl and eight-year-old boy, who was going to the village school, the children all worked to help the parents. Here is Kuo's story about work in his family.

Take 1964 for instance. I myself, my wife, and our seventeen-year-old son, the three of us, every day started early in the morning and didn't stop till after dark. By the end of the year, we had earned 512 work points. For the second season, we got 144 catties of grains through our work points, plus 37 catties as compensation for the manure we had contributed, and 330 catties of free ration for our family of seven. This made a total of about 510 catties. Because we almost worked our heads off on our private plot both before and after commune work, cultivating waste land, planting sweet potatoes and sugarcane, we harvested 400 catties of sweet potatoes, about 80 catties of sugar, and 40 catties of beans. These got us an income about 40 percent of what we made from the commune. . . . [All this was not enough to feed a family of seven. So Kuo butchered a pig, sold it on the free market and used the money to buy rice on the black market.] We had 32 ducks, and I told our second son to look after them carefully. He took the ducks to the fields to feed themselves, so we didn't have to use much of our own food to feed them. . . .[53]

It may be noted that in his account, presented unedited, Kuo described how he, his wife, and his children toiled together, but mentioned nothing about his work relations with other members of his production team. It seems that he belonged to a peer group of older peasants outside the circle of what he called the "progressive elements" and the cadres. Because Kuo was classified as a poor peasant with a large family, he had been given an extra quota of free grain ration every year since 1959. But in 1964, during the Socialist Education movement, the village cadres skipped him when they distributed the extra rations. While Kuo was wondering why, some of his friends secretly told him that the cadres and some of the progressive elements were complaining because he was working too hard on his private plot and neglecting commune work. This behavior, which had been tolerated for some time, was now considered a manifestation of capitalistic self-interest. Kuo did not say who these friends were. From his account, they seemed to include the leader of his production team, of whom Kuo spoke rather fondly and who was later accused of protecting capitalist elements in the village.

Whoever were in Kuo's group, they apparently talked among themselves, often behind the backs of the cadres.

In May (1964), after a brief period of quietness (in which the production team leader was subject to criticism), we were required to learn Anti-Revisionism. . . . [Here he gave a brief, somewhat confused account, of what the cadres said about capitalism and Marxism.] We were told that the imperialists were our enemies from outside who used guns, and the revisionists were our enemies from inside who used pens. They attacked our Party and our leader Chairman Mao, they distorted facts. They said the revolution had succeeded for more than ten years, but people's life was still poor. They said people were still sharing pants and wearing sandals. I don't understand all the theories the cadres told us. About the last few things they said, we talked among ourselves behind their backs, and we all felt that was true.[54]

When the temperature of the campaign kept rising, and when Kuo realized that it might soon be his turn to receive the kind of severe criticism the others had been given, and to repay the damage caused by his ducks to the commune's crops in the amount of 630 catties of grain, he and several of his friends talked things over. There was no way he could repay the damage. Although Kuo did not say so, his friends were probably liable to similar charges. They decided to leave their families behind, and they fled to Hong Kong.

Young Peer Groups

From accounts in the official press, we see a different kind of work-oriented peer group among the young people that also suggests considerable cohesion. The following story is about a group of sixteen teenage girls at Hsiao Chin Chuang Production Brigade, Pao Ti County, Tientsin. Led by Chou Ke-chou, young chairwoman of the brigade's women's association, they had been carrying water for more than forty days to irrigate plants during a drought.

One day, they discovered that two rows of young plants had not lived. The girls talked about it. Chou Ke-chou looked at the two rows of withered plants and felt sad. She knew two girls were hurrying for speed and paying no attention to the quality of work. Give them a criticism right there? No. They tried hard too. Leave the matter alone? That won't do either. Thinking it over and over, this young girl got an idea. Making up her mind, she said to the others:

"Comrades, let's stop carrying water, and go for a site tour."

"A site tour?" The girls were perplexed. The fight against drought was so urgent, how could they have time for a site tour?

"Let's go see the land we irrigated." Having said that, Chou led the girls through the rows one by one. After the site tour, she called the girls together. They sat down and seriously summarized their experience.

A site tour is education. The two girls engaged in self-criticism, promising that they would learn from the others and work diligently. Taking this opportunity, Chou praised the girls for their spirit of self-criticism, and reminded the others to pay attention to the quality of their work. She encouraged them to continue their hard work, and strive for greater contribution to the revolution. A vivid, lively, on-the-spot conference was thus concluded, and the girls happily took up their heavy load again.[55]

It may be noted that both male and female peasants compete on equal basis, as sex is no longer a basis for role differentiation. At the Hsu Hsin Commune near Shanghai, for instance, of the 11,675 laborers, 55 percent were women, who accounted for 50 percent of the work.[56] They worked in the fields, operated tractors, and engaged in fishing, animal husbandry, handicrafts, and weaving, and manufacturing of farm equipment, farm chemicals, and electric bulbs. Some worked as nurses and barefoot doctors.

Urban Workers

In urban centers, cooperation and competition take place in factories, where the laborers work in shifts, and in state-operated enterprises. Factory workers cooperate among themselves within their own teams and compete with other teams. This can be illustrated by a recent campaign at the Paochi electric locomotive works.[57] During a meeting for criticism of Lin Piao and Confucius, workers in the No. 3 Repair Team proposed that seven old locomotives that had been idle for years be repaired because they were the products of the 1958 Great Leap Forward under Chairman Mao's call for self-reliance. Their recommendation was approved by the leadership cadres and the necessary parts were procured. Three repair teams, Nos. 2, 3, and 4, started a competition and restored six of the idle locomotives to working conditions. The cadres were prepared to conclude the competition because the remaining locomotive was practically beyond repair. But the workers would not quit. The job was finally given to the No. 3 Repair Team, which had started the campaign. In eleven days, working day and night, the team did what would normally take a month and a half, and produced a locomotive that looked like new.

Norms in Groups

The three cases—refugee Kuo Lien-tsai, the teenage girls, and the factory workers at Paochi—suggest three different group contexts having important bearings on patterns of cooperation and competition. For Kuo and other older peasants of Pung Tao Commune, the primary group for task cooperation was the nuclear family. In Kuo's family there was considerable cohesion and unity as the parents and children toiled together for survival. They did not seem to be greatly concerned about the collective welfare of the commune, however, as Kuo showed no hesitation or regret about sending his ducks to feed in the commune's fields. He and his family simply tried their best to make a living out of whatever they could get from the commune, and perhaps more importantly to them, from their private plot. Kuo belonged to an informal group of older peasants, but they were important to him only as sources of information and opinion, not as work partners or as a reference group for measuring his own achievement in a competitive sense.

The teenage girls in Chou Ke-chou's production brigade represent a different kind of group. It may be noted that while Kuo's seventeen-year-old son worked in the family, the girls worked in a group of their own. Whether this reflects a regional difference or a change since the Cultural Revolution, we do not know. Chou's story suggests, however, that the girls were more actively concerned with the collective performance of their group than were peasant Kuo and his older friends. For one thing, the girls had no families that they had to support. The manner in which Chou handled her two careless co-workers indicates a degree of cohesion in the group that would be conducive to the kind of cooperation and competition desired by the Party.

As a group, the workers at the Paochi repair shop appear to be closer to the teenage girls than to the older peasants in Kuo's commune. The repair team, not the family, was the primary group context in which they cooperated among themselves in competition with other teams. At least during that campaign, work spirit seemed to be high; the workers refused to quit even though the cadres had been satisfied with the initial results. The speedy, tireless pace of their work during the competition would again suggest considerable cohesion. The fact that the Paochi workers and the teenage girls were publicized and praised by the official press makes it apparent that their behavior is what the Party would like to see.

Of the three groups, that of the older peasants in Kuo Lien-tsai's commune is the only one in which some deeply entrenched norms stand in the way of the new patterns of cooperation and competition being promoted by the Party. In the other two groups, the family-based old norms do not seem to operate noticeably. The residual influence of the old behavioral norms among some of the peasants apparently weakens the unity of such formal groups as production teams and production brigades. This is evident from the conflict between the older peasants and the progressive elements. However, Party authorities have shown a tendency toward limited tolerance, perhaps because the productive efforts of the older peasants are indispensable to the economy. It is quite clear that the compromise is not meant to be long lasting, as the Party has been making periodic attempts to replace the old norms. Both the Cultural Revolution and the recent campaign launched in the name of criticizing Lin Piao and Confucius are examples.

Communication, Cooperation and Competition

The lack of clear role relations and the diverse backgrounds of technical knowledge and ideological consciousness among the role performers have necessitated constant flows of communication, partly informational and partly normative, to maintain the pace of cooperation and competition. We shall analyze the patterns of communication employed for identifying the task of cooperation or competition, for setting the desired level of performance once the task is identified, for searching and finding ways of implementation, for motivating the workers to achieve the desired level of performance, and for evaluating their performance.

Identifying the Task

A cooperative task is often identified not as a result of technical assessment by qualified specialists, but rather, on the basis of folk wisdom derived from diffuse, extensive communication among the mass of people. This process can be illustrated by a reservoir construction project of the Hsiang Huan County government. When the project was first brought up for discussion at the standing committee of the county, two proposals were advanced: to build a new reservoir for the entire county, or to improve an existing reservoir that would better serve an area where water was in short supply. No decision could be reached after prolonged discussion. At this point, the party secretary, Yang Chi-lo, said, "We really cannot come up with any good ideas while sitting in our office. Why don't we use our old method and go to the mass of people. Let's listen to what the poor and lower-middle peasants have to say. Then we can decide."[58]

Thus, instead of consulting engineers or irrigation specialists, the committee members went to visit four production brigades in different locations and talked to the peasants. The consensus was in favor of improving the existing reservoir.

While the communication that led to a decision on the reservoir was both informational and normative—what the peasants said and what the majority opinion was—the identification of a task of competition often follows the process of normative communication through pressure and challenge. One example is the use of tatzepao criticism to stimulate competition within a group. At the Harbin rolling stock plant, one day the workers in the steel-casting shop posted a tatzepao, "Why is our plant lagging behind?" It criticized some of the leaders for their conservative thinking and for their failure to fully arouse the mass of workers and renovate the plant's equipment. Once the problem was identified, a heated discussion followed, in which workers throughout the plant took part. This resulted in a mass competition movement to rebuild the old equipment.[59]

The group competition to repair seven idle locomotives at Paochi repair shop mentioned earlier was initiated by a tatzepao, in which the workers condemned some "slaves of imperialism" for "declaring a death penalty" for the China-made locomotives. Ever since the locomotives were shipped to Paochi in 1971, they had been abandoned in the shop. By exposing a slack performance, which would otherwise go unnoticed, and by invoking the cause of revolution, the tatzepao made a production race inevitable. Even the factory in Hunan that made those locomotives got a copy of that tatzepao and reproduced three thousand copies for distribution to its workers. They promised to supply all the necessary parts so that the locomotives could be rebuilt.[60]

Setting Performance Goals

How informational and normative communications are employed by Chinese workers to set cooperative production goals has been reported by Maria Antonietta Macciocchi, a member of the Italian Communist party, who visited the Tientsin Textile Factory No. 2 in 1970. The process typifies diffuse role relations. In the words of the Chinese worker with whom Macciocchi talked:

To avoid any confusion from the start because of the differences in our respective countries, remember that production goals in China are fixed by a state plan because this is a socialist system. The plan for the factory is drafted by the Ministry of Textile Industries and lasts for a year. Monthly work plans are drawn up at the factory itself by a production team from the revolutionary committee, which includes technicians, workers, and administrators. This is how the pace of work is defined.

An obvious aspect of capitalist exploitation is the pace of work, sometimes, fixed to a tenth of a second. Even the total manufacturing time for a product is calculated.

When we get a copy of the year's plan, we discuss it with the workers and then we prepare our own internal plan for the factory according to what we can accomplish. We do not automatically commit ourselves to follow our own plan 100 percent when we send it in for approval. Our estimates are based on a discussion of last year's production figures, our personal experiences, and our needs for machinery replacement and repair, which will be presented to the revolutionary committee on the next level. The plan is thereby worked out in detail and everyone understands it better. If we try hard, we can exceed the goals of the plan by using our productive resources—but only on the initiative of the masses. . . .[61]

It may be noted that information was shared widely among technicians, workers and administrators at different levels in drawing up production plans. The actual implementation of the plans and the pace of production, however, appear to be worked out largely through normative communication among the masses.

How mass media can be used to transmit information instantly and to apply group pressure for a goal-setting competition campaign is illustrated by the "radio broadcast race," which creates a framework for group comparison. The one staged by the mechanical industry in 1959 provides an example.[62] The race headquarters were located at the People's Central Broadcasting Station in Peking. Representatives from more than thirty mechanical factories were present when Deputy Prime Minister Po I-po opened the race with a call for higher productivity and better quality. Each representative made a brief report on what his factory had achieved and what it planned to do in future. Then the telephone lines were opened to receive calls from various factories as mechanical workers all over the country listened. Those who called pledged to support the race with a specific performance and challenged others to do the same. For instance, three factories in Shanghai pledged to increase their production goals by 30 to 44 percent and to reduce costs by 10 to 15 percent. This was accepted as a challenge by other factories in

Shanghai, Taiyuan, Changsha, and Peking. Each outlined the specific steps it was prepared to take in order to meet the challenge.

Finding Ways of Implementation

The Party relies heavily on communication within the group to find ways of implementation once a task of cooperation or competition has been accepted. For instance, after the decision had been made to build the Peking petroleum chemical plant, the problem was how to work out a design that would be economical in cost and time. Instead of assigning the design job to the engineers, the Party sent cadres, workers, and technicians to canvas the mass of workers and ask for their suggestions. The workers were challenged to think hard and speak out. Numerous suggestions were collected. The result of this campaign was described as a union of mass experience and scientific findings. The traditional methods were discarded in favor of an innovative approach.[63] Because of the technical nature of the designing, the communication in this case appears to be largely informational.

In other cases, it is primarily normative communication within the group that regulates task cooperation of a nontechnical nature. For instance, at the Hsuanwu hardware store in Peking, a peasant from a commune outside the city came in one day to order two hundred huge jars for soaking seeds and storing grain. The store soon got enough jars to fill the order. The question was: Should the store wait for the peasant to come for the jars or should it deliver them to the commune? The sales staff discussed the question at their study meeting and decided to deliver the jars. "So twenty-eight salesmen and sixteen saleswomen, each riding a pedicab with jars on it, started out the next day for the countryside." Many such discussions were regularly held by the sales staff on how to operate the store.[64]

A unique communication activity for seeking ways of practical implementation is known as the "Chuko Liang meeting." The name comes from an old Chinese saying, "When three stinky cobblers put their heads together, they can be as wise as Chuko Liang." The latter was reputed to be China's most brilliant statesman and military strategist during the Three Kingdom period (A. D. 220–280). "Thus during the war years," the *China Reconstructs* reports, "before every campaign it had been the custom to hold such a meeting in the trenches and pool the wisdom of the ordinary soldiers."[65] The Chuko Liang meeting exemplifies the diffuse role relations in Chinese Communist organizations.

The Chuko Liang meetings are not limited to military circles but have become a common practice when cadres want to seek suggestions from the grassroots level on problem solving. At the Lanchou petroleum chemical factory, for instance, the sand filter was once stuck, causing a slow-down in the operation. The *People's Daily* tells this story:

> The leadership cadres of the factory called a Chuko Liang meeting with the workers. Many comrades said the repair work was of questionable quality and should be done all over. However, old worker Wang Shou-yi, who has had many years of experience, did not express any opinions. After the meeting, the vice chairman of the factory's revolutionary committee, Hsia Chin-lin, specifically asked for his advice.
> Wang said: "I don't think the problem is with the repair. The sand tube is probably blocked by the hot sand. Perhaps we should try to blow it through." Hsia studied the problem with the Three-in-One Union team. Although Wang's was a minority opinion, they felt he was right. Finally, after trying for several days, they succeeded in blowing through the sand tube. It proved that Wang's opinion was correct.[66]

This particular example shows that the majority opinions coming out of Chuko Liang meetings may not always be valid. However, the norm of going to the masses, as exemplified by these meetings, can help locate the correct advice that eventually solves the problem. It may be noted that during such a meeting, not only is information shared, but also a consensus of objectives can be reached through the process of normative communication, as in the trench meetings.

Motivating Performance

Normative communication has been employed in essentially two different ways to motivate a high level of performance in either cooperation or competition. One is to create a framework of social comparison to encourage emulation. The other is to apply social pressure to prevent slack performance.

The mass media often publicize cases of success as a basis of social comparison. By emphasizing the normative goal of achievement and by supplying information regarding the superior performance of some individuals or units, the media under the Party's direction seek to initiate movements in which the role performers will endeavor to better each other's records. One example is the movement to "Learn from Tachai." Formerly a poverty area in the mountainous region of Shansi Province, with a labor force of only 106, the Tachai Brigade became nationally known when it achieved a record of production despite repeated natural calamities.[67] Mao was so impressed when he visited Tachai in 1964 that he declared, "In agriculture, learn from Tachai." Mao's endorsement set off a nationwide emulation campaign, in which the experience of Tachai was reported in newspapers, books, radio, television, and even film. All over the country, the communes called together their members to discuss the success of Tachai. Peasants from different locations were brought to visit Tachai, and by 1972 an estimated total of two million persons had come to this remote village to learn from the experience of its peasants.[68] Tachai thus became a national pace-setter.

Another example of nationwide media publicity to spur performance and competition is that about the Taching oil field in Manchuria. When oil was first discovered there in 1959, Taching was a barren land plagued by swamp in the summer and severe snow storms in the winter. The first group of workers and engineers to arrive had to sleep in the open, and had barely enough time to set up their makeshift huts before the heavy snow started. By 1964, Taching had become a bustling town of oil wells and huge machines. When the movement of "Learn from Taching" was launched in 1964, the newspapers and radio broadcasts were full of stories telling about the heroic deeds of its workers. For instance, Chu Hung-chang, an engineer, used his hands to plug a leaking water main when a welder was working to patch the leak next to his hands. Chi Hau-ting, a repair team leader, jumped into a fire and used his cotton jacket to put out the flame. Two linesmen, Mao Hsiao-tung and Hsiao Chuan-fa, used their bodies to connect a severed telephone line.[69] There was Oil Well Drilling Team No. 1202 that worked night and day to achieve a superior record.[70] These cases were praised as models.

While the Tachai and Taching movements were directed at two broad target groups—the peasants and workers in general—the same process has sometimes been employed to initiate competition among specific groups. At the Capital iron and steel company outside Peking, for instance, during a company-wide meeting for studying Mao Tse-tung's thought in August 1969, some of the workers suggested that they challenge steel workers in four industrial

centers—Wuhan, Paotow, Taiyuan, and Chungking—to a production contest. The suggestion was discussed at the meeting and
adopted. The challenge was publicized in the mass media, and was
promptly accepted by the workers of the four iron and steel companies. Through the mass media, the campaign made it necessary
for the five iron works to compare one another's performance constantly in order not to be left behind. Later, workers in all kinds of
companies and organizations across the country joined. "This
sparked off a countrywide competition in all organizations to equal
and excel each other in working and producing for the revolution."[71]

The method of social comparison is frequently applied at the
small-group level to stimulate competition. This can be illustrated
by the experience of a female medical student who had been sent to
help construction work during the Great Leap Forward:

> Well, we were supposed to work eight hours a day but there were so
> many "challenges" and "counter-challenges" between the various units
> that we were frequently told to work extra hours. There were three
> eight-hour shifts but those with "high political consciousness" refused
> to stop work when their time was up—and their display of enthusiasm
> spurred on the less active students, because no one wanted to be
> criticized as ideologically backward.[72]

That social comparison as a positive motivation sometimes fails
to achieve the desired performance is suggested by the experience
of Tachai. According to a report in the *People's Daily* on August
10, 1974, there seemed to be some resistance against the movement
of "Learn from Tachai" in spite of the publicized enthusiasm. The
report noted the existence of a "counter wind" among some people in Hsiyang County, the home of the Tachai Brigade, who refused to support the movement. They contended that Hsiyang County
had gone too far in recent years in following the footsteps of
Tachai.[73]

Because positive motivation is not totally efficacious, negative
sanctions have had to be enforced in a variety of ways to discourage
nonconformity. The primary remedy is the application of social
pressure, either through informal talk or by bringing the individual
to his peers for group criticism and reeducation. If no satisfactory
progress is evident, then the person's wage would be withheld. If
that should fail, the person would be demoted to a lower wage

grade. Meanwhile, group pressure is continuously applied.[74] It was not mentioned what the Party would do in a case a person should still refuse to be reformed. Perhaps the intense group pressure and withholding of wages would suffice in most cases. If everything should fail, the term "labor reform" as used by the Communist party would probably suggest that it be used as a last recourse.

How informal social pressure works to prevent slack performance is illustrated by a story told by Chen Yung-kuei, leader of the model Tachai Production Brigade.

In our Tachai Brigade we had a member who could join our labor, but who did not work hard. Since the liberation he had been depending on relief. During the autumn harvest of 1960, he owed our collective 60 JMP, and did not have money to pay for his grain. His woman said: "Hey, it's getting cold. How come they haven't given out relief cotton jackets?" It just happened that the few relief cotton jackets from the state had been given to the old bachelors. So none was left for him. So he talked to me: "How come I didn't get any relief?" I said: "You can work, so from now on I am not going to give you any relief. Relief won't do you any good."
In 1960, he worked only some 260 days, and his woman worked 14 days. The two of them thus got about 270 days. Because we didn't give him relief, we overcame his dependent thinking. In 1961, he worked even during the winter, and his woman went to the field whenever she had time. He got 361 days and his woman got 140 days. He not only did not lack food, but got some surplus and saved more than 200 JMP. He had 500 catties of grains stored in his home.[75]

Generally, the more formal group sanctions take the form of revolutionary mass criticism. For instance, when the Lungchiao Production Brigade of Changchiao Commune in Kiangsu decided to follow the experience of the model Tachai Brigade and grow two crops of rice a year instead of one, there was opposition within the group.

Now the small number of unreformed landlords, rich peasants, counter-revolutionaries and bad elements tried to sabotage this growth. "Grow two rice crops a year?" they whispered around. "You'll freeze in the winter and roast in the summer. Why look for trouble?"
The poor and lower-middle peasants dragged these persons out into the limelight and, using them as "live targets," launched a revolutionary mass criticism of them right in the fields, denouncing them for oppressing the people in the old days.[76]

The following gives a picture of what happened at the mass

criticism in Lungchiao Brigade's No. 3 Production Team, which had the largest number of poor and lower-middle peasants.

These peasants told the criticism meetings, "We poor people toiled from the first cock's crow to the last dog's bark. Our sweat irrigated the landlord's fields and we ended up with empty hands. Then Chairman Mao and the Communist party came and led us, we stood up and became our own masters. Now when we work more, sweat more, and grow more grain, we do it for the revolution." Pointing to the accused, they shouted, "Before liberation you and your kind rode on our backs and sucked our blood. Now you and Liu Shao-chi and his gang don't want us to learn from Tachai. You want us to go back to the old way and suffer a second time. Nothing doing!"[77]

It may be noted that the criticism was not made with regard to the technical feasibility of growing two crops of rice instead of one. It was phrased in terms of the ideological dispute with Liu Shao-chi, and reinforced by affective communication, that is, by discussion of the peasants' past grievances. The fact that those individuals were dragged out as live targets would suggest the presence of others who were also opposed to the idea. The ex-landlords and ex-rich peasants just provided a convenient group to criticize. Eventually, the opposition was silenced.

The same kind of tactics of criticism have been applied to such deviant behavior as cheating on the job. In a factory in Shanghai it was revealed in 1965 that eight workers had been found to be playing poker during their work hours. In two years and three months, from June 1963 when they started playing to September 1965, they wasted a total of 5,320 hours, equivalent to 665 man-days that should have been devoted to production. These workers were brought to a severe criticism session.[78]

Group Evaluation

We have seen that different wage levels are employed in the communes according to such criteria as ideological consciousness, work attitudes, productive proficiency, and physical strength. These are not clear-cut, operationalized criteria that would enable the commune director or whoever is responsible to decide which individual is entitled to what wage level. The Party's solution is to work out the distribution of wages through normative communication within the group. First, each production team evaluates all its peasants, men and women, in group discussions in which all commune members are allowed to participate. The group sets its own standards. The recommendations of each production team are then sent to the production brigade to which they belong. These recommendations are reviewed by the cadres at the brigade level and compiled into a brigade recommendation. The recommendations from the several production brigades are forwarded to the commune, where the cadres work out an overall wage distribution for the whole commune. The wage level for each worker is posted by the production team to which he belongs so that everyone knows the wage of everyone else.[79]

Before the Cultural Revolution, the peasants in some areas used to have long discussions every day about who should get how many work points for his work. Such daily discussions are no longer practiced since the Cultural Revolution. Two different methods of evaluation have been used, both originating from the Tachai model brigade.[80] One is known as the method of "Self-report and public evalutation according to a guide post." A record is kept of the number of days a peasant has worked and the kinds of work he has done during each month. At the end of the month, all members of the production brigade get together and agree on a person as a "guide post" through extensive discussion. This is a pace-setter in the brigade with the best political behavior and most outstanding work achievement. After the guide post is chosen, each member evaluates himself or herself in comparison with the guide post and submits a self-evaluation for group discussion and approval. The other method, which appears to be more widely practiced today, does away with the guide post, perhaps to avoid the internal tension and possible divisive effects this procedure would likely produce. At the end of the month, the members work out a set of criteria through public review and discussion. Each peasant will say how many work points he or she deserves on the basis of his or her contribution, according to those criteria. The self-assessments are then publicly evaluated by the group. At the Evergreen Commune thirty miles from Peking, for instance, the peasants apparently follow these procedures.[81] Three major criteria are used for evaluation: political behavior, attitude toward work, and the quantity and quality of the work. The popular adoption of this method seems to reflect the Party's active concern with the necessity of maintaining congenial internal relations in the production groups.[82]

Communication and Indoctrination
Study of Philosophy

Value-oriented communication is used extensively to reinforce the desirable behavioral norms and cultivate the correct ideological attitudes so that competition and cooperation will not become matters of expediency, but be undertaken as a moral duty. Even though the Party has found it necessary to apply group pressure and offer limited material incentives in order to maintain an optimal level of task performance, its ultimate objective is to have the workers and peasants engage in productive cooperation and competition for the sake of the proletarian dictatorship.

Much of the indoctrinating communication takes the form of a "study of philosophy," that is, discussion of materialist dialectics as interpreted by Chairman Mao. Viewed in an official perspective, "Materialist dialectics is an invincible weapon. China's workers, peasants, and soldiers are using it to criticize the bourgeois class, revisionism and different metaphysical fallacies which block the people's advance. They use it to analyze and solve contradictions in revolution and production, to educate themselves, unite comrades and attack the enemy."[83]

The program for the "study of philosophy" has had its ups and downs. The idea was apparently first introduced by Mao himself in 1956 when a tour of several industrial workshops at the Tientsin Textile Factory No. 2 convinced him the ideological level of workers was dangerously low. "Workers were turning into robots, as in capitalist countries, and were an easy prey for revisionism."[84] Mao suggested that a course of materialist dialectics be set up, but the director of the factory considered it a waste of the workers' time. It took more than two years before the course was established in 1958. Even then the director "sabotaged the program to the point where it became ineffective."[85]

The programs for the study of philosophy have been restored since the Cultural Revolution. At the Tientsin Textile Factory No. 2, for instance, according to Macciocchi, in each of the 127 factory work teams a group of workers stayed behind after work to study Mao's philosophy for an hour or two. Each group had its own room.[86] The American journalist Tuchman reported that at the steel smelting plant in Taiyuan, which employed fifty thousand workers, the study groups met four times a week after work for one and one-half hours. One session was devoted to technical subjects, and three to ideological matters and current events. These sessions were occasionally varied by recreation and sports.[87] More recently, if we take the Nanping textile factory as an example, the workers were organized into small classes to study word by word Chairman Mao's instructions on Communist ideology, and the writings of Marx, Engels, and Lenin on proletarian dictatorship. Actual cases collected from among the workers were cited to refute the revisionist thinkings of Liu Shao-chi and Lin Piao.[88]

What takes place in these study sessions seems to depend on the ideological mood of the observer as well as the observed. Macciocchi, herself a Communist, described it in such phrases as "a philosophical air," and "intellectual development."[89] To Ross Terrill of Harvard University, the scene reminded him of an Evangelical Bible class:

> Political meetings take a certain amount of the workers' time. Few seem either gripped or repelled by them. In hotels or factories I once or twice peered into a study meeting that reminded me, in its tight-lipped zeal, of an Evangelical Bible class. More often the ambience seemed languid; books dropped from the wrists, eyes far away—even once at Canton's Tung Fang Hotel, a card game going on simultaneously.[90]

The personal experience of former commune member Kuo Lientsai sounded similar. During the meetings for criticizing revisionism and building up work spirit in 1964, only a few progressive elements spoke up. The other peasants were either smoking or napping in the back of the room. A few slipped out.[91]

How political ideology functions to motivate workers can be illustrated by the experience we have cited before of the female medical student during the Great Leap Forward. Challenged by those students with "high political consciousness," she recalled, "we all worked like mad because we wanted to prove our political soundness." After they had returned from work following an exhausting day, the students sought to reassure themselves by saying: "It's tough, but nothing is insurmountable in the socialist society, and nothing is difficult for one with noble ambition. . . ."[92] It is the same political consciousness that was credited with the superior industrial productions achieved by factories in Shanghai in the first half of 1975.[93]

Correct ideological consciousness is sometimes invoked to rectify erroneous work attitudes, as illustrated by the case of Shanghai's direct current motor plant. Because of its production record, the plant had just been accorded the status of an "advanced unit." According to an official account, "A few workers felt conceited and boasted to people, 'You'll hear our plant now whenever you switch on the radio.' Others were over-cautious, 'From now on,' they said, 'we should be more steady in our work and more careful in speaking. If we make errors it will have a bad effect.' "[94]

Both attitudes were criticized in the study sessions. Boastful thinking was wrong, because those "workers who were conceited were resting on their laurels and did not want to progress further." However, those who suggested caution were considered to be contented with the past. "In essence, both ideas were based on the metaphysical idea that the world could stand still. They were the same." As a result of the ideological discussion, in which everybody took part, the workers decided that the plant should continue to advance through hard work.

Tatzepao and the Mass Media

As part of the indoctrination program, the workers are constantly reminded, by the unique medium of tatzepao, of the virtues of ideological commitment and hard work. According to Macciocchi:

Chinese factories are incredible places. Their large workshops are full of colorful tatzepao hanging from the ceiling to the floor. Some are glued to the wall, others are suspended by strings, and some are even put on the machines. The tatzepao are used in the factories to express opinions, to discuss political and philosophical matters, to protest any waste or errors, and to criticize small theft and negligence.[95]

In big cities like Shanghai, she saw tatzepao plastered on street walls for miles. Macciocchi was convinced that hundreds of thousands of individuals were involved in making these posters. The ideological experience of writing a tatzepao was told by a peasant during a discussion of the Tachai model brigade:

"Have you heard about the Tachai Brigade?" (Macciocchi asked.)
"Indeed," the peasant replies, "I also wrote a tatzepao against Liu Shao-chi, and I pasted it up in the village. Liu would have brought

back the division between rich and poor in the countryside. For the old people today there are five guarantees: food, clothing, a house, medical care, and burial. Who had that in the past?''

"But what did you write in your tatzepao? And did you really write it yourself?''

"Only partly. My daughters helped me. I wrote that Liu wanted to revive the principle of working the land for gain and not for the revolution. This principle would have corrupted the peasants and would have again formed a class of exploiters and a class of exploited people. The Red Guards came here, to the village, and they carried out great criticisms and helped us understand. We spoke a great deal of the Tachai Brigade then."[96]

Other than the study sessions and tatzepao, mass media are extensively employed to support and publicize the new norms of competition and cooperation advocated by the Party even when no production campaign is going on. We have already seen, in the example of Shanghai's direct current motor plant, how radio is used to give publicity to model units. The official Party newspaper, the *People's Daily*, features a parade of articles in which the virtues of serving the people, self-reliance, and innovativeness are praised. A few examples will suffice:

"How Communist Party Member Wang Chih Wholeheartedly Serves the People" - *People's Daily*, November 26, 1972.
"He Is Endlessly Progressing—The Story of Model Worker-Engineer Su Ching-ming" - *People's Daily*, November 18, 1972.
"Following the Tracks of Chairman Mao's Revolutionary Line—How Trains No. 21 and No. 2 Serve the People" - *People's Daily*, September 16, 1972.
"Use Materialist Dialectics to Overcome Difficulties in Coal Production—How the Workers at Pataohao Coal Mines, Chinchou City, Study Philosophy" - *People's Daily*, November 25, 1972.
"The Masters of Socialist Mines in Our Motherland—The Accomplishments of Tunghua Copper Mines Working for the Revolution" - *People's Daily*, September 22, 1972.
"Victory of Self-Reliance—The Achievement of Lead-Zinc Mines in Hengtung, Hunan" - *People's Daily*, July 16, 1975.
"Self-Reliance Has Boundless Power—How the People in Lung Nan Mountainous Region Fight Hard to Build Their Highway" - *People's Daily*, July 21, 1975.
"Fight for the Great Objective of Communism—The Story of Party Member Tien Hsin-chin" - *People's Daily*, July 24, 1975.
"If We Abandon the Interest of the Majority People, What Do We Hold in Our Heart?—The Story of Party Member and Production Team Leader Chang Chou-erh" - *People's Daily*, July 24, 1975.

Stories like these are apparently widely read; Macciocchi found that workers in China put the *People's Daily* beside their machines and look at it from time to time.[97]

Problem of Effectiveness

How effectively does the system of symbolic reward and social pressure operate as a substitute for material incentive? While no definitive answer is possible, we can gain some clues from the mass media in mainland China. A tatzepao written by three poor peasants in Liaoning Province in April 1974 tells a revealing story:

> In the fall of 1973 when the (Nanfang) production brigade began to dig production ditches, the cadres and commune members decided after a discussion to give remuneration according to a fixed quota by counting one work point for each meter of ditch dug. After a few days, when the cadres felt that the work was going too slowly, they changed the remuneration by counting one and one-half work points for each meter. Later, just before the advent of winter, the cadres again raised it to three work points per meter because they feared the commune members might not be able to finish the job on time. In so doing, they changed the remuneration for the fixed quota to counting work points. Is this not material incentive practiced by putting work points in command?[98]

The initial fixed quota of one work point per meter dug was a case of minimum material reward. It was apparently insufficient reward because the work was going slowly. At this point, the cadres did not try to generate social pressure or start a competition campaign within the brigade. As it happened, apparently pressed for time, the cadres decided to increase the material reward, raising the remuneration twice. We shall let the three peasants finish their story:

> The result was that the production ditch was completed, but the quality of the work was inadequate. Parts of the ditch not only failed to help production, but adversely affected production in mountainous areas. The most serious thing was that people were concerned with their individual work points and forgot about farming for the revolution. . . . We are members of the people's commune who farm for the revolution, not slaves who put work points in command.[99]

If the experience of Nanfang Production Brigade should be representative of situations elsewhere, then the system would appear to face a dilemma. Insufficient material reward did not seem to work too well in this case and there seemed to be reluctance on the part of cadres to apply social pressure. Yet when the material reward was amplified, the result was completion of work of a poor quality. Why is it that the Nanfang Brigade peasants not only failed to respond to Chairman Mao's call for selfless service but didn't even put in a good day's work for a good day's pay? That particular tatzepao blamed Lin Piao and Confucius. This might be true. But it is also possible to seek an answer by examining the overall reward system.

Three types of work for which the reward system is relevant can be distinguished. First, there is the routine work. In the commune, for instance, a peasant puts in a given amount of work per day for his production team, and by the end of a season he is rewarded with free rations and work point grains. If he slackens off, his work points will suffer, but other peasants who have worked hard will suffer with him because he is in effect taking away some of their free rations. In other words, he would be affecting the *individual* welfare of other commune members. The informal social pressure within his group most probably prevents him from loafing on the job.

Next, we can think of the periodic production campaigns, when the communes or factories are required to compete with each other. With the mass media publicizing cases of superb performance and urging every group to surpass its competitors, the peasants and workers probably feel they are placed under a spotlight. They cannot afford to let their own group down. Social pressure of a more formal nature can be generated by the mass media and by communication within the group to ensure a high level of performance.

It is the kind of work that is more than routine and yet not intensive enough to be part of a national or regional competition that seems to lie beyond the reach of social pressure. The ditch digging at Nanfang is an example. The peasants probably failed to see a clear connection between digging a ditch and their individual welfare, and thus the spontaneous processes of informal social pressure might not be operative. So why hurry? On the other hand, the task does not seem important enough for the cadres to justify the organization of formal social pressure through criticism meetings. After all, the cadres would have to consider the amount of time the criticism meetings would take up. They probably wanted to save the pressure tactics for the more important tasks. If so, this could explain why the cadres at Nanfang resorted to material incentives.

The somewhat puzzling part is the rather poor quality of work induced by material incentive. The spirit of Yu Kung (the foolish Old Man) who removed the mountain was not in evidence. If the years of indoctrination had any appreciable effect, it was not clearly demonstrated by the Nanfang peasants. The fact that this error was brought to public attention on a state radio would suggest that it was not an isolated case. Is it possible that the peasants have been so conditioned to the system that they can perform well only under the prodding of social pressure, be it formal or informal? Is it possible that when social pressure is not applied, they will take whatever material reward is available without bothering about the quality of work? These are rather disturbing questions for which our scanty data do not provide a clear answer.[100]

Competition, Cooperation, and Social Structure

From our analysis, one gets the impression that the predominant current theme in China is competition, rather than cooperation. Regardless of their roles, the people of China are urged to compete among themselves within their respective groups, as well as between different groups, in order to achieve the objective of socialist construction. Cooperation, where necessary, seems to be only a secondary means to facilitate the fulfillment of this ultimate end. When the contest is cast within the group, as is often the case, each person is on his own. Cooperation within a group becomes necessary often in the framework of competition between groups, now bound by a tight network of communication. If the national objective should ever shift, the patterns of competition and cooperation may change. For the last two and a half decades, the emphasis in China has been on competition and will most probably remain so in the foreseeable future.

The desired norms of competition, as aptly summarized by the general line of socialist construction, are to "go all out and aim high." Under that policy, diligence, hard struggle, persistence, and self-reliance are among the highly valued personal attributes. All this is manifest in Chairman Mao's often cited parable, "Yung Kung (the Foolish Old Man) Removed the Mountains." That is, nothing is impossible. The end product of the hard work should be "greater, faster, better, and more economical results." Popular support of such competition seems to be less than overwhelming in view of the resentment and evasion reported from time to time. For cooperation, the officially encouraged norms are selfless service and subordination of individual benefit under national interests. Any pursuit of individual gains, whether material or symbolic, has thus far been denounced.

It should hardly be surprising that the stated objectives of competition and cooperation are collectively rather than individually oriented. For a quarter century the Party has been urging the mass of people to work only for the collective goals of the state. Competition and cooperation within a predominantly individual framework are not allowed. Ever since the early 1950s the Party has been waging a campaign to denounce what is referred to as the evils of capitalist individualism. Judging by the intensity of language and persistence of criticism, it is inconceivable that the indoctrination campaign has not had some effect on attitudes. Perhaps more effective than the indoctrination campaign are the structural constraints imposed on the behavioral patterns of cooperation and competition. Since the state controls all the material resources and, through the mechanism of group dynamics, social sanctions as well, competitive and cooperative behavior within an individual framework is generally not rewarded.

In this regard, the group context takes on enormous importance. In the past, the extended family was both an economic unit for subsistence and a political unit for decision-making. Thus we found the cooperative and competitive behavior of that era to be oriented primarily toward the extended family. With the change of social structure in China, the extended family is no longer a functioning group, since it has lost its resource basis. In the rural countryside, the nuclear family still appears to be a residual unit of task cooperation centered around the private plot, even though much of the regular work takes place in the production team and the production brigade. In urban areas, competition and cooperation occur almost entirely outside the family context, as the family-owned business has completely disappeared. Nearly all who are gainfully employed work for the state, either in factories or in government enterprises or offices.[101] An occupational structure of this nature leaves very little room for alternative, nonstate-controlled groups to operate and, except for the private plot, virtually eliminates the economic basis for individually oriented behavior of competition and cooperation.[102]

The existence of the private plot, along with the still tolerated supportive mechanism of the rural free market, allows some minimal leeway for the peasants to work on a family basis after commune hours to supplement their meager incomes. This loophole in the system made it possible for deviant groups, like peasant Kuo Lien-tsai and his friends, to carry on and function in a limited manner in the villages. From an ideological point of view, there seems to be little doubt that the Party authorities would have liked to abolish the private plots and thus close the gap in the rural economic struture. Apparently reminded of the practical need for production and the enormous difficulties during the commune movement, the Party has finally given in and officially allowed private plots for commune members.[103]

While informal deviant groups probably exist in the villages, for most peasants the production teams would have to be the major group context in which they can advance their welfare individually as well as collectively. Wage earners in urban areas have no choice other than to stay where they are and make the best of it.

One may wonder why group pressure can be so effective in China. At least two aspects of the Chinese groups may be noted. One is a high degree of permanence. Whether one works for a commune or a factory, one has no chance of voluntary occupational mobility. Only the Party can move an individual from one post to another, and this is apparently not done frequently, particularly in the communes. Thus, when a person joins a commune or factory, he expects to stay with it until he is told otherwise. The other feature of the group in China is its comprehensiveness and dominance. An individual belongs essentially to one formal group. Every aspect of one's interactions—economic, political, social, and cultural—takes place within the same group context, whether it is a commune or factory. One has no alternative, since his group dominates his total life. Because of the heavy dependence of the people on their groups, it would be only natural that they should seek primarily to promote the interests of the group, and thus indirectly advance their own welfare. In this sense, the phenomenon known as the Peng Wei (groupism) principle would seem to be almost inevitable. By manipulating group dynamics to achieve its objective of socialist construction, the Party may have inadvertently magnified the importance of the group to the extent of overshadowing the national goals.

It may be noted that, as far as major characteristics are concerned, considerable similarity exists between the formal group in

China today and the kinship structure of the past. Like the group today, the kinship structure, in which membership could not be changed at will, had a high degree of permanence. In fact, in a relational sense, one could never leave one's extended family. The close intermarriages made it highly unlikely for a stranger to enter into any kinship network. The kinship structure also dominated one's life—economic, political, social, and cultural—much as the group does today, though perhaps to a lesser extent. Within the range of similarity, important differences should be noted. While the kinship group of the past functioned largely as an autonomous unit, the group today is only a small component of a closely supervised overall structure. The cultural values that supported the kinship structure evolved within the group itself. The ideological beliefs that direct life in the group today are given by the Party hierarchy. In a kinship context, reverence for the ancestors and concern for the extended family motivated the members to advance their welfare, a portion of which would be shared with less successful relatives so that the extended family could be maintained as an entity. In China today, it is the necessity for survival, combined perhaps with some measure of national purpose, that prompts the people to advance the interests of their respective groups, because their groups provide the only means for fulfilling their basic needs. The extended family as a group was important for symbolic as well as economic reasons. The groups today are important largely for practical reasons.

The formal group context in China today makes it possible to enforce the new normative patterns of competitive and cooperative behavior, largely through the process of face-to-face communication. We shall first review the roles of normative communication in connection with the minimal use of material incentives. Material rewards, when used properly, can be an effective mechanism to reinforce conformity and prevent deviance, and to ensure the desired patterns of competition and cooperation at the individual level. The differential distribution of material rewards can thus be regarded as one of the structural alternatives supporting the functional prerequistites of cooperation and competition. For this reason, as we have seen, the Chinese Communist party has found it necessary to retain some form of minimal material rewards as incentives.

However, a social system does not rely entirely on material incentives for regulating cooperative and competitive behavior. Individuals can be sufficiently motivated to engage in such behavior by internally accepted values, such as the Protestant ethic, or by externally applied pressure. Both can be achieved through communication. We have seen that the Party has been using a variety of channels—the study sessions, the tatzepao, and the mass media—in an attempt to lay a firm ideological foundation through value-oriented communication. If and when that is achieved, then the Chinese will be completely selfless and work only for the socialist construction as envisioned by Mao. *They will want to do what they have to do.* For the time being, however, the Party seems to be counting more on social pressure than on ideological consciousness as the major instrument to maintain the desired patterns of competition and cooperation.

Two kinds of social pressure, functioning through different communication channels, make it possible to minimize the reliance on material incentives. For the more or less routine task, informal social pressure operating within peer groups most likely keeps the level of performance above a minimum level. This is because the reward system makes it difficult for any one to loaf on the job without adversely affecting the welfare of his peers. For production races and campaigns, it is the more formal social pressure generated through the mass media and group meetings that helps maintain the pace of competition. The excessive need of the people to depend on the group would seem to lend weight to social pressure. However, there is some evidence to suggest that because of the Party's heavy reliance on social pressure, the Chinese peasants do not perform well once the pressure is withdrawn. This inadequacy does not seem to be corrected by the promise of temporary material reward.

Normative communication not only applies social pressure but also provides motivational support for group competition in China's production races. In an economic system built upon private ownership, competition and cooperation at the group level are maintained largely through a delicate structure of responsive prices, that is, if we assume the absence of exclusive domination and monopoly. The factors of supply and demand will regulate cooperation and competition between groups. In China, these mechanisms are not fully operative. Cooperation, and to some extent competition, are partly built into the overall economic planning of the state and carried out in terms of production goals. Work merely to fulfill production quotas, however, can be a lusterless undertaking, particularly when material rewards are held at a minimum. Perhaps this is why normative communication has to be extensively employed to organize and maintain production races between groups, as we have seen among the steelworkers, in order to add an element of stimulation and excitement. In that sense, communication appears to fill a gap left open due to the absence of free market competition.

Normative communication is also employed to regulate the use of minimal material incentives. The basis of evaluation is partly ideological and partly task oriented. The standards do not seem to be universally applied, as some of the offspring of ex-landlords and ex-rich peasants are denied the rights of ordinary commune members. However, the fact that evaluation of individuals and distribution of material rewards are worked out through internal communication within the group would tend to minimize the feelings of inequity and resentment, if any.

Our findings further suggest that communication combining information, social pressure, and ideology helps maintain the particular role relations of cooperation in China. Due to its unwillingness to grant the technicians and specialists a privileged status and authority in its social system, the Party has come to rely on the mass of people—workers and peasants—for much of the cooperative task performance. This approach of mass involvement has necessitated a diffuse relationship despite the need for role differentiation and specification in the country's industrialization programs. Individuals engaged in a cooperative endeavor do not have their specific roles spelled out, but rather are supposed collectively to pool their labor and wisdom. Using diffuse role relations, the Party has been trying to keep technical specialty subordinate to political ideology.

To make up for the incompatibility between the demands of technological specialization and the preference for diffuse role relations, the Party has had to rely upon the use of face-to-face communication on a massive scale. In task performance, workers, political cadres, and technicians are brought to participate in a continuous interchange of communication known as a "three-in-one" union, in which each plays no roles that are specifically his own, but shares with the others whatever he can contribute. In the process of information sharing, the technical expertness of the specialists becomes potentially utilizable in coordination with the practical experience of the workers. Pressure generated through the discussion of goals and means among the various role performers contributes to keeping their work up to a functional level. With the cadres' participation in guiding value-oriented communication, ideological soundness can be maintained.[104]

In sum, it seems that a structural imbalance has been created by the demands of industrialization and increased productivity on the one hand, and the Party's reluctance to rely on material incentives and institutionalized specific role relations on the other. Due to its ideological commitment, the Party leadership has chosen diffuse patterns of role relations and minimal use of material rewards even though these choices may have slowed down the initial pace of development. In order to minimize, if not to eliminate, the structural imbalance, communication has been used extensively with considerable effect. The Chinese case seems to suggest a new dimension for the roles of communication in national development, not so much to raise aspirations or induce deferred gratification as to help maintain task-oriented structural integration under conditions of internal stress.

V
Communication and Change in Manpower Training Institutions

When young Mao Tse-tung first went to school, he was already sixteen years old. His father had voiced objection because he would lose one laborer from his farm. He agreed only when young Mao gave him twelve silver dollars to hire someone in his place. When Mao arrived at Tung Shan School, in a city fifteen miles up river from his village, with luggage on his shoulders, he was almost turned away because he was too old and because his handwriting was too clumsy. The headmaster finally admitted him on a probational basis. At that time, Mao had read at home the Confucian *Analects* and the Four Classics, but did not understand much of the content. He did not learn much more in school, where the masters lectured on language, mathematics, history, and geography. Formal education at that time was apparently not meant for peasant children like Mao, as most of his fellow students came from urban families. Many of the richer students despised him because of his ragged jacket and trousers.[1]

The Chinese school system had made many physical improvements by 1949, but the general social orientations toward education were not too much different from those in Mao's day. It was a system staffed primarily by an urban elite for educating the children of the urban elite, not the sons and daughters of peasants. Most college graduates were hired as government employees or as school teachers. Those who had connections went to industry and business. Education was not meant for training manpower, and thus contributed relatively little to development.

The transformation of that system into what China has today, one in which children of peasants and workers are given preferential access to schooling, has been a long and arduous course. Instead of training an urban elite, the objective now is to prepare manpower for consolidating proletarian rule and carrying out the task of development. In the process, many of the old traditional values have been challenged, and the hierarchy of social status has been reversed. Students and teachers have had to undergo continuous ideological reform. The administrative structures of schools and universities have been overhauled, and the procedures for enroll- ment and evaluation of students revised. Perhaps even more signifi- cant in the long-range perspective is the attempt to change the basic attitudes of Chinese intellectuals toward education and labor, to alter the social structure through differential occupational assignments, and, in coordination with the proletarian-oriented manpower training programs, to create an ideological foundation for the New Socialist Chinese State. In all these processes of change, which we shall briefly describe, communication has played a major role. We shall illustrate the Party's use of communication in bring- ing about these changes, evaluate the effectiveness of the current system, and speculate about some of its latent functions.

Schools in China
School Systems

The public school systems the Chinese Communists inherited in 1949 consisted of six years of elementary school, divided into four years of lower division and two years of upper division, three years of junior high school, and three years of senior high school. Beyond that, the universities offered four-year baccalaureate degrees, while the vocational schools awarded certificates for two and three year programs. The People's Republic government largely retained these programs with relatively few changes until the Cultural Revolution in 1966.[2]

To understand the development of school systems in China one needs to examine the sayings of Chairman Mao Tse-tung and the waxing and waning of his influence in China during the last two and a half decades. One of the few occasions Mao spoke on education was his much quoted talk on handling contradictions among the people, delivered prior to the Hundred Flowers movement in early 1957, "Our education policy must enable everyone who gets an education to develop morally, intellectually, and physcially and become a cultured, socialist-minded worker."[3]

Education, as Mao pointed out, must serve the politics of the proletarian class and must be united with productive labor. It was perhaps a measure of the degree of his influence that this objective was pursued with less than whole-hearted vigor before the Great Leap Forward movement in 1958. After Liu Shao-chi had gained power in 1959 in the wake of the commune failures, Mao's ideas on education appeared to be given even less emphasis.

The Cultural Revolution reversed the trend and put Mao's thinking on education into prominence again. His much cited May 7, 1966, directive, contained in a letter to the then Marshal Lin Piao, spells out the new directions for China's school systems:

> Students should acquire knowledge; but they should also learn something else. They should learn to be not only scholars, but also workers, peasants, and soldiers. They should learn to criticize the capitalist class. The number of years in school should be reduced. Education should be revolutionary. The present situation where intellectuals of the capitalist class rule our schools, must not be allowed to continue.[4]

On another occasion, Mao was quoted as remarking on the curricula in schools before the Cultural Revolution, "There are at present too many curricula that drive people to death. Students at primary and middle schools and colleges are living in a tense environment everyday. . . . Curricula may be reduced by half."[5]

The major changes introduced to schools during and after the Cultural Revolution closely reflected Mao's thinking. The new systems have reduced the number of years students are required to stay in school, simplified the curricula, and given the students more time for direct contact with peasants and workers through actual labor. The curriculum changes and manual labor will be discussed in detail later. As figure 4 shows, children now start elementary school at age five instead of six as in the past, and finish elementary school in five instead of six years.[6] They can go on for three years of junior high school and graduate at the age of thirteen. After that, they cannot directly proceed to senior high school as they could in

AGE	GRADE	BEFORE	AFTER	GRADE
23		Graduate School		
22	5	University and College	University and College	3
21	4			2
20	3			1
19	2		Labor & Practice	
18	1			
17	3	Senior High School	Senior High School	3
16	2			2
15	1			1
14	3	Junior High School	Labor & Practice	
13	2			
12	1		Junior High School	3
11	6	Elementary School (upper division)		2
10	5			1
9	4		Elementary School	5
8	3	Elementary School (lower division)		4
7	2			3
6	1			2
5	3	Kindergarten		1
4	2		Kindergarten	2
3	1			1

Figure 4. School Systems of the People's Republic of China before and after the Cultural Revolution (From Koide Yoshio, "New Direction of Reform for College Education in Communist China," translated by Chung Huan-wen, *China Monthly*, December 1970, p. 592).

the past. Instead, they must go for at least two years of labor, mostly in a commune under the supervision of peasants. For those who gain permission for further education after their labor duties, there are three years of senior high school, after that at least two more years of labor, and then three instead of four years of college if they are chosen again. Senior high school is apparently not a necessary step toward college education, as peasants, workers, and soldiers with junior high school education have been admitted.

Admission Procedures

The new system has been experimented with since 1970 when universities and colleges reopened for enrollment. While it is still too early to tell whether the changes are transient or will remain in effect for a long time, we can note the major differences between the old and new systems, primarily in the admission of students and the job assignments for trained individuals. Under the old system, promotion from one school grade to another depended largely on academic achievement. This was revealed in an investigation report by the Kuangtung Province revolutionary committee during the Cultural Revolution.[7] Although no statistics were given, the rate of elimination was reported to be high from elementary school to junior high school, and even higher from junior to senior high school. The proportion of peasant children became progressively less in the higher grades. A main reason for this phenomenon, according to a report published in the *Liaoning Daily* and released by Hsinhua, was not the inferior intelligence of peasant children, but rather the class-related difference in motivation for achievement.

In the past people used to say that children of poor and lower-middle class peasants were not as smart as children of landlords and rich peasants. This is sheer nonsense. When the son of a landlord comes home, his father tells him: "Son, you have got to bury yourself in books and study hard. Our class background is not good, and we have no future in this society unless you study hard and get a good position." When the children of poor and lower-middle class peasants get home, scarcely have they put down their books when they are ordered by their parents to go to work in the fields.[8]

College entrance examinations before the Cultural Revolution were so competitive that only the best qualified stood a reasonable chance. In 1964, for instance, the subjects in which applicants were to be examined included the Chinese language, a foreign language, either Russian or English, mathematics, physics, and chemistry. Biology had previously been dropped from the list.[9] For all practical purposes, one's chance of going to college seemed pretty much determined by junior high school, if not earlier. If one did not get into a good junior high school, the chances of getting admitted into a good senior high school would be rather slim. Consequently, one could hardly expect to pass the highly competitive college-entrance examinations. Prior to the Cultural Revolution, most college students could expect to be assigned cadre positions upon their graduation unless they had committed serious political offenses.[10]

The new system has largely eliminated achievement-oriented competition. As mentioned earlier, junior high school graduates are required to perform at least two years of manual labor, mostly in a commune. Only those who receive favorable evaluation by the peasants will be recommended for senior high school. The others are expected to settle permanently in the communes. The same process applies to high school graduates. When Chinese universities first resumed classes in 1970, the high school graduates were not allowed personally to apply for admission. Only the units in which the students were working such as a commune, could recommend candidates. The main criteria were class backgrounds, political consciousness, and work performance. At first, only children of workers, peasants, and soldiers were eligible. The class background requirement was somewhat relaxed in 1971, apparently because some of the students admitted by that requirement were of uneven academic quality. Recent instructions by the Party seem to allow the admission of a small number of students who have demonstrated a firm ideological conviction and superior work performance even though their class backgrounds leave something to be desired.[11]

Students are now allowed to submit applications on their own for college admission. An application is first reviewed by the unit in which the student is working. The evaluation and recommendation by the peasants or workers are of crucial importance. If the application clears this first hurdle, it will then be submitted for approval by the district and the county (or the city). The university does the final screening.[12] An examination is required of those who have passed the local reviews, but this is no longer the major basis of acceptance or rejection. One student, Chang Tieh-sheng, became a national hero in 1973 when he failed to answer questions on physics and chemistry but instead wrote a letter condemning the college entrance examination.[13] Chang, a production team leader of Chaoshan Brigade, Paita Commune, Hsincheng County, Liaoning Province, made the following points in his letter:

1. Ever since he was sent to Paita Commune on graduating from junior high school in 1968, he had been busy with agricultural production, working almost 18 hours a day. He could not and would not put aside production simply because he needed time to prepare for the ex-

amination. "To do that," Chang said, "would be too much concerned with my own self interest."

2. He resented those students who did not have to work and had all the time for studying. If he had had just two days' time for reviewing, he would have been able to answer all the questions. He felt it was unfair that his chance for higher education should be determined by such an examination system.

3. He pointed out that his family background, political consciousness, and social relations were all good and clear. Furthermore, during the five years he had worked on the commune, he had made significant progress. He deserved the trust of the poor peasants and commune cadres.

This protest letter apparently received serious attention by the provincial authorities, in that it was published later in the *Liaoning Daily* on July 19, 1973. The editor commented that although Chang failed the physics and chemistry examination, he provided a thought-provoking answer to the problems of college admission. The case was given national publicity when the *People's Daily* reprinted Chang's letter on August 10, 1973, and praised him for his revolutionary spirit in an editorial on August 16, 1973.[14] Chang was awarded a place in the Liaoning Agricultural College, majoring in animal husbandry. Later he was chosen to be a member of the Chinese youth goodwill mission to Japan. In July 1974, the New China News Agency released a special feature to mark the anniversary of Chang's college education. He was described as an active revolutionary who had played a leadership role in reforming teaching methods at the college.[15]

Examinations in School

While in school, students are no longer evaluated by the conventional closed-book examinations as in the past. As early as 1956, the Marxism seminar of the People's University in Peking experimented with open-book examinations. A number of other universities began to apply this method to other subjects in 1964 with results described as encouraging. At Szechuan University, for instance, open-book examinations were employed in 44 out of 144 courses that year.[16] However, it was not until the Cultural Revolution, after Chairman Mao had given it his personal blessing, that this method of examinations became a nationwide practice. Mao was quoted as saying:

> The current examination methods contain many surprises, unusual questions and difficult problems. They are designed to deal with the

enemy, not the people. These types of examinations were used in the old days in the writing of the eight-legged essays. I do not approve of them and think that they should be completely remolded. I suggest taking some sample examination problems and having them published. Let the students study and do them with open books.[17]

In an open-book examination, the students now have two options. In the oral exam, the students are given the problems beforehand. They are allowed to discuss the problems among themselves and use the laboratory facilities whenever necessary. Each student is then examined orally by the teacher. In the written version, the students can either write the exam during the class, using whatever resources are available, or take it home. Students are permitted not only to talk with each other, but also to consult the teachers.

Closed-book examinations are still employed, primarily for subject matters that require rote memory, such as foreign languages. Grades are not always assigned. For instance, grades are considered improper for papers on Mao Tse-tung's thought. Instead, the instructors are asked to give comments only or discuss the papers with the students. Sometimes, the students first evaluate their papers among themselves before submitting them for evaluation by the teachers.[18]

These methods were followed for those who made up the first graduating class from China's universities after the Cultural Revolution. Students at Peking University, for instance, did not write final exams, but instead fulfilled graduation requirements by lecturing to workers or producing reports on their experiences while working on farms, or in mines, factories, and research institutes. A group of twelve students who lectured on Communist political economy at An Yuan coal mine near Peking were favorably evaluated by the miners. The reports prepared by the students on their practical experiences were officially described as better than the old-style examination papers based primarily on book research.[19]

These changes in the Chinese school system have been brought about according to a uniform pattern of procedure. A policy decision is first reached at the top Party hierarchy. The mass media, mostly the official *People's Daily*, the radio, the New China News Agency, and the Party publication *Red Flag*, play the role of announcing the thinking of Chairman Mao, either on the number of years of schooling, or the examination system, or manual labor.

The different schools and universities take up Mao's instructions for discussion among the students and teachers. Eventually the schools work out ways of implementing the instructions, often with minor variations to suit the local situation. The processes of change will be discussed later.

Curricula and Teaching Methods
Before the Cultural Revolution

In the first years after the Party came to power, curriculum changes were relatively few. Dr. Sun Yat-sen's Three Principles, which were taught in high schools and colleges under the Nationalist rule, were replaced with Marxism, Leninism, and the New Democratic Principles of Mao Tse-tung. Military training, commonly practiced in senior high schools and colleges during World War II, were resumed and intensified. Russian was taught instead of English. Weekly manual labor was required of all students. Otherwise, the old curricula were retained largely in their conventional form. During the Great Leap Forward movement, Mao made an attempt to reduce the academic requirements by increasing the demand for student labor. His efforts were largely nullified after Liu Shao-chi gained power in the early 1960s.

Liu's policy, as later revealed during the Cultural Revolution, emphasized the development of advanced academic expertise for a few, and a broad basis of practical knowledge for nearly everyone. This policy was referred to as the "sharp pagoda" approach. That is, while all eligible students were given the opportunity of basic education to acquire a functional literacy, only the academically qualified would be privileged to pursue higher education. Lu Tingyi, minister of culture who was later purged in the Cultural Revolution, was quoted as saying, "Difference in intelligence, just like difference in physical strength, is an undeniable fact. Some individuals will be able to learn more and we must not hold them down."[20]

Generally considered Liu Shao-chi's spokesman on education and cultural matters, Lu agreed to include some ideological education, but not to the extent of overriding the importance of other academic subjects. Knowledge was assigned top priority. Language arts, mathematics, physics, and chemistry were emphasized in high schools. Those who had a solid foundation in these subjects eventually went to college. Under this policy, relatively few children of peasants, workers, and revolutionary soldiers were able to receive college educations. For instance, at Taiping Lin Brigade, Lung An County, Kirin Province, there was only one high school student and no college student in the 194 poor and lower-middle peasant families in 1968. In the 41 families that belonged to the class of ex-landlords and ex-rich peasants, there were three high school students and two college students.[21] Similarly, at Sungshu Kou Brigade, Ai Hui County, Heilungkiang Province, the 54 poor and lower-middle peasant families had one student in high school and none in college. The 12 ex-landlord and ex-rich peasant families had six students in high school and four in college.[22]

Liu's academic-oriented policy also led to a proliferation of courses. Take the Lanchou May 7 High School as an example. Before the Cultural Revolution, it offered 17 courses: political studies, language arts, history, geography, foreign language, mathematics, physics, chemistry, biology, agriculture, labor, music, fine arts, physical education, military drills, handicrafts, and technology. Students were expected to take all of them. There were eleven courses required in a typical elementary school curriculum and thirteen courses in a junior high school curriculum.[23] The same emphasis was found in universities. Of approximately one million college students enrolled in 1965, 56 percent were in science and engineering, 25 percent in education, and the remaining 19 percent in humanities and the arts.[24] The dream of many college students was to be accepted for advanced graduate studies. In 1964, for instance, out of some twelve thousand applications, only twelve hundred were admitted into 180 institutions that offered graduate work and research programs. The largest single group, 105 graduate students, went to Peking University to do research in 70 different fields under the supervision of 80 professors.[25]

Since the Cultural Revolution

The Cultural Revolution changed China's basic educational policy. Practically all schools were closed during its initial stages. When most elementary schools and some high schools resumed classes in the spring of 1967, teachers faced the task of rewriting their curricula out of a nearly total vacuum. For several years, lasting till 1972, disorder and chaos prevailed in many schools as the teachers groped for some direction in which they could safely proceed. The various supervisory teams sent to schools from factories, communes, and the military apparently did little to ease the confusion.

For a while, the schools that had resumed classes operated without any clearly defined curricula. Some of the students were still "exchanging revolutionary experiences" in other parts of the country and had not returned to school yet.[26] In elementary schools, the students were primarily engaged in studying the writings of Mao Tse-tung, particularly his three old essays, "To Serve the People," "In Memory of Dr. Norman Bethune," and "The Foolish Old Man Who Removed a Mountain." Much time was devoted to singing revolutionary songs. While smaller children learned to read, older children had some lessons in arithmetic and science. Many high schools were not ready for class in the spring of 1967. For those that were, the curricula largely consisted of reading Mao's sayings, his sixteen instructions on the Cultural Revolution, and performing manual labor.[27] Meanwhile, fights among rival groups of Red Guards continued to break out in many high schools.

Following a call by the Party authorities, most elementary and high schools soon began their search for a set of new curricula that would be consistent with the spirit of the proletarian Cultural Revolution. Students and teachers were sent out to consult peasants and workers in lengthy discussion for advice on curriculum reform. A few pilot curricula that met the approval of the Party were published in the official mass media for nationwide dissemination. At the elementary school level, the pilot curriculum worked out by the May 7 Elementary School of Hung Shih Commune, Taichang County, Kiangsu Province, was nationally publicized. This curriculum had only six courses: Mao Tse-tung thought, proletarian class-conscious education, manual labor, language arts, arithmetic, and painting.[28] The widely acclaimed Shih Chin Shan High School of Peking adopted the following program: Mao Tse-tung thought, struggle against self and criticism of revisionism, proletarian class conscious education, language arts, foreign language, mathematics, chemistry, and physics, in addition to military training and manual labor.[29] The seventeen courses at the Lanchou May 7 High School were reduced to only five: Mao Tse-tung thought, industrial knowledge, agricultural knowledge, revolutionary literature, and military training/physical education. Manual labor was extra.[30] Mao Tse-tung thought, military training, and manual labor appeared to be the common core in these somewhat different curricula. The amount of time assigned to the study of Mao Tse-tung thought and related subjects varied from 75 percent of the whole program for the Lanchou May 7 School to one period a day at Peking No. 23 High School.[31]

The first comprehensive plan for educational reform adopted by the Party was announced in May 1969. This was a plan proposed by the revolutionary committee of Lishu County, Kirin Province, for elementary and high schools in the rural areas.[32] An editor's note that accompanied the announcement in the *People's Daily* asked all teachers and students in rural communes to review the plan and adapt it to their local conditions. This plan suggested five courses for elementary schools: Political studies and language arts, arithmetic, revolutionary literature, military training/physical education, and labor. For high schools, the plan also recommended five subjects: Mao Tse-tung thought, agricultural knowledge, revolutionary literature, military training/physical education, and labor. The more conventional subjects of mathematics, chemistry, physics, and geography were to be incorporated into agricultural knowledge wherever relevant. Depending on the local needs, the schools could have the option of setting up separate courses in mathematics, physics, chemistry, and geography. Although no overall plan was proposed for schools in cities, the general trend was to reduce the number of course offerings along the line set by the Party for rural areas. The major difference seemed to be in the teaching of foreign language, primarily English, in the cities. In large cities like Peking and Shanghai, English was taught in some elementary schools in 1971 on an experimental basis.[33]

New Textbooks

Because the old textbooks were considered to reflect Liu Shao-chi's revisionism, they had to be completely rewritten, a task that proved to be more difficult than the reorganization of curricula. Revolutionary literature seemed to present the thorniest problem since nearly all the established writers had been denounced during the Cultural Revolution. The solution was for teachers to talk to peasants and Party cadres and record their bitter histories. The peasants would recall their own experiences of the past, and the teachers would write them down verbatim for approval by the cadres.

The work of Wutai Commune, Shan Cheng, Honan Province, provided an example. The commune's cadres, teachers, and poor and lower-middle-class peasants, working as a team of a three-in-one union, prepared a new primer consisting of thirty lessons. Their first task was to destroy the old, following Mao principle *pu po, pu li,* that is, "if you don't destroy (the old), you don't establish (the new)." For instance, the first lesson in the old primer states:

School has started, school has started.
Let's carry our bags and go to school.
When you see your teacher, make a bow.
When you see your friends, say "how are you."[34]

This was found undesirable because it showed no proletarian political consciousness at all. The primer also included the Aesop fable about a crow which keeps dropping pebbles into a half-filled jar until it can reach and drink the water inside, Retold also was the familiar story about young Ssu-ma Kuang (A. D. 1019–1086). A playmate had fallen into a big water jar. While all other children panicked and fled, Ssu-ma Kuang picked up a stone and broke the jar to save the boy. These lessons had been part of the Chinese primers for decades. The peasants considered them nonsense. Another lesson advises:

"In front of the house and behind the shed, plant some cucumbers and plant some beans." This was strongly denounced because it encouraged people to work on their private plots.

The first lesson of the new primer says: "Long Live Chairman Mao." Another lesson says: "The revolutionary committee is wonderful." A poem contributed by the members of Chou Lou brigade states in part:

Standing in Chou Lou and looking toward Peking,
We have boundless loyalty to Chairman Mao.
Let's sweep away all evils that harm us,
And fight to the death to defend Mao Tse-tung.[35]

In preparing the primer, the mass line was strictly followed. According to the *People's Daily* report, "among the poor and lower-middle peasants, you suggest one lesson, and I suggest one lesson, and there we have our textbook.'' The primer was constantly revised to keep abreast with current developments. For instance, after Chairman Mao had given his latest instruction of ''carefully carry out *tou* (struggle), *pi* (criticism), and *kai* (reform),'' this was incorporated into the textbook.

Two examples will illustrate the infusion of ideology into nonideological subject matter. In a mathematics class at the May 7 Junior High School of Hsuan Hua mechanical factory, master worker Tung was invited to deliver his first lecture. He gave the following problem:

> When Tung (himself) was six years old, his whole family was suffering from hunger. His father borrowed 5 *tou* (approximately 180 pounds) of corn from a landlord, at the ''donkey rolling'' (that is, compound) interest rate of 5 percent a year. After three years, how much did the landlord demand from the Tung family?
>
> When the three-year term was due, Tung's father could not make the payment and had to mortgage all his four *mu* of land to the landlord. [One *mu* is approximately one-sixth acre.] The landlord then leased the land to the Tung family at 180 catties of grain per *mu* per year. How much profit did the landlord make on Tung's own land in four years?[36]

A simpler problem of addition, using the same ideological approach, was given to smaller children in the Shanghai area:

> Chairman Mao is the most, most red sun in our hearts. It is a great blessing to be received by Chairman Mao. On the National Day of 1968, Chairman Mao received at the Tienanmen Square 150 representatives from the capital's workers, the Liberation Army and peasants, and 67 representatives from the Red Guards and the revolutionary mass of people. How many representatives did Chairman Mao receive altogether that day?[37]

Higher Education

After all universities and colleges in China had been suspended for nearly two years, the official *People's Daily* revealed in 1968, in the form of an editor's note appended to a feature story on technical training in the Shanghai machine tools plant, that Chairman Mao favored the reopening of universities, particularly for science and engineering. Mao was quoted as saying:

> After all we still need universities. Here I mean primarily universities for science and engineering. But the number of years in college should be reduced; the education must be revolutionary. Proletarian politics

should assume command. Follow the road of engineering and technical training adopted for workers at the Shanghai machine tools plant. The students should be selected from among workers and peasants who have had practical experience. After they have been in school for a few years, they will return to their productive work.[38]

It is on the basis of these instructions that China's higher education is being rebuilt. Shortly after the official announcement, all universities began drawing up plans that would put the Shanghai machine tools plant experience into practice. Many of these plans, published in the *People's Daily* in the spring and summer of 1969, seemed to be paraphrasing what Mao had already said. The Tsinghua University plan was one of the few that proposed concrete steps. It called for technical education in two stages, first the practical aspects of technology and operation, to be followed in the second stage by more theoretical analysis and designing.

Mao's instruction made it implicit that he did not completely rule out college education in humanities, although his preference for science and engineering was clear. The officially approved thinking on humanities seemed to be reflected in the plan proposed by Peking University.[39] According to that plan, the focus of college programs in humanities should be loyalty to Chairman Mao. All courses in literature, history, philosophy, political science, and law should be built on a core of materials consisting of Mao Tse-tung thought. The entire college program was to be reduced to three years, during which at least two-thirds of the time should be spent in factories, communes, and military units, so that the students could learn to be workers, peasants, and soldiers as well as scholars. Furthermore, workers, peasants, and soldiers should be invited to lecture in universities.

The overriding principles for college education are thus adherence to the thought of Mao Tse-tung and reliance on practical experience. These principles were closely followed when the universities began to reopen and admit students in the fall of 1970. Futan University of Shanghai, one of the major Chinese universities with an established program on humanities, developed an entirely new curriculum from the writings of Chairman Mao to fill the vacuum of teaching materials. The curriculum, said to be adopted through prolonged debates and exchange of practical experience among students, teachers, peasants, and workers, consisted almost entirely of Mao Tse-tung's theories on philosophy, government economics, literature, education, history, and journalism. These were offered as basic textbooks for the humanities.[40]

In science and technology, the same emphasis on Mao Tse-tung's thoughts and practical experience prevailed in the preparation of teaching materials. The process generally involved the following steps: (1) screening of the old teaching materials through discussion and criticism by students, teachers, and workers to eliminate the influence of revisionism; (2) interaction with workers and peasants, both through actual manual labor and through sharing of experience, so that their practical knowledge could be incorporated into the textbooks; and (3) testing the teaching materials and textbooks on workers and peasants, through pilot lectures and discussion, for revision and improvement.

Two examples will illustrate this process. At Chiaotung University, noted for its academic achievements in engineering and mining, professors were sent to work in factories and mines to learn from the experience of workers. Some of the professors worked on railway construction. They surveyed the routes during the day and came back in the evening to consult the railway workers. They prepared their teaching materials with the workers' guidance, and gave pilot lectures for criticism by the workers.[41] The Kuangsi Medical College applied the thought of Mao Tse-tung to textbook preparation by sending a team of professors to seek the advice of some 700 "barefoot" doctors in military units, factories, and communes. They collected more than nine hundred suggestions for incorporation into the new textbooks. After the textbooks had been prepared, the team went back to the barefoot doctors for their criticism and suggestions for revision.[42]

The reliance on practical experience of the mass of people may have corrected what had been the traditional tendency in Chinese education to place blind dependence on textbooks. However, if the acceptance or rejection of what the books contain was based not on empirical evidence alone, but on political ideology as well, then the result could be counterproductive. The new textbooks had been in use for hardly two years before a tendency of passive compliance was noticed among college professors. This was known as "wearing new shoes, but walking old ways," that is, lack of initiative and total dependence on textbooks again—except that these were new textbooks.[43]

In a sense, this reaction by college professors should not have been totally unexpected. For a few years before the Cultural Revolution, they had been given some encouragement for the pursuit of academic activities and research. For these activities they were severely criticized during the Cultural Revolution. Most of the books they had read, and indeed a good part of the knowledge they had acquired over the years, had become dysfunctional because of the change of political atmosphere. Now that they had developed a set of new textbooks bearing the approval of peasants and workers, the safest approach would be for them to follow these textbooks faithfully. In fact, this technique of survival appeared to be carried to an extreme by some professors, who did nothing but let the students copy the textbooks in class.[44] Some professors were afraid of giving difficult assignments lest they be accused of mistreating those students who came from among peasants, workers, or the military.

Learning Through Manual Labor
Labor Performance

An effective way to acquire a sound proletarian ideology, according to the Chinese Communist leadership, is to engage in manual labor. This principle was applied to high schools and universities both before and after the Cultural Revolution. In Shanghai, for example, during the busy summer season of 1965, more than sixty thousand students and teachers in the universities and high schools were sent to nearby communes to help out with farm work. They were reinforced by some one hundred thousand others during the harvest season that fall. While in the communes, the students and teachers lived and worked with the peasants, staying anywhere from a few weeks to six months, depending on the demand for labor.[45] Through active participation in manual labor and close interactions with the peasants, the students are expected to gain a deeper understanding of life in a commune and to share the proletarian class orientations of the peasants.

Students in engineering and industrial schools are now sent to factories for practical experience under a system known as *chang hsiao kua kou,* meaning "factory and school hookup."[46] The idea of sending college students to factories to practice what they have learned is not new. Before the Cultural Revolution, many college students went to the factories, but more or less for a brief tour instead of to do actual work. They often caused interference and were not welcomed by the factory workers. Under the hookup system, high school and college students are now assigned to factories as regular workers for the entire duration of their practical training program.

The Lanchou May 7 High School, which was hooked up with the Lanchou iron works, offered an example of this labor-education system. The students operated in two shifts six days a week, one shift laboring in the morning and studying in the afternoon, the other shift doing the opposite. Later, the amount of labor was reduced to four half days a week. During the labor hours, the students were organized into fixed teams, each assigned to learn from a "master" who was an experienced worker at the iron works. In a way, it was similar to the master-apprentice arrangement in old China. During the busy farm season, all students in school were sent to help the peasants on a full-day basis.[47]

In addition to periodic labor performance in communes and factories, Chinese students and teachers are required to engage in manual labor at least one day a week on a regular basis. They do all kinds of work; in Peking, for instance, students were organized to collect manure. This apparently started a movement, as students in Canton soon followed their example.[48] The collection of manure for use as fertilizer appeared to be widely practiced by students. Elementary school students in Teh Hui County, Kirin Province, for instance, were asked each to carry a waste bag so that they could pick up manure on their way to school.[49] By requiring students to perform what was considered in the past to be the most lowly task, the Party apparently intended to discourage the traditional disdain of manual labor by Chinese intellectuals.

That the young people did not take to manual labor too well is illustrated by the tenderfoot son of Chen Yung-kuei, who is leader of the Tachai Production Brigade and who is a national labor hero. This is how Chen described the boy:

> I have a son. He was a junior high school student. His mother wanted him to go on in school and become a cadre in future. I wanted him to come home to do labor and learn to be a man on the farm. The two of us could not agree. We had different ideas. Finally, I persisted and got him back to our village. I had suffered a great deal when I was a kid. But he grew up in the age of Mao Tse-tung. He ate well, dressed well, and spent well. Everything was plentiful. I told him, "You grew up in a lucky home. You have got to work hard and learn to suffer." He was quite willing to work, but he just did not look like a laborer.

When the others go to work in the field, they take off their socks and shoes. They don't feel hurt. He was different. He had never walked barefoot before. After he took off his socks and shoes, his feet were so tender and he could not walk. I wanted to criticize him, but then I thought: "Well, let's wait till we get home." When I had just gotten home and begun to talk to him, my old woman said: "We have only this son, and you won't spare him. Doesn't your heart hurt for him?" I said: "I want to teach him because I love him." Later whenever I criticized him, my old woman would get mad. So I took him to the field to criticize him. One day in the field, I just had to make him take off his shoes and socks. It was a hot summer day, and the ground was boiling hot. After a day of labor, his feet had blisters. When he got home, his mother saw them and started crying, saying my heart was too hard. I said: "What of it! That's good for him. We want him to know that the fruits of labor are not gained without hard work."[50]

Other forms of manual labor have been combined with schooling. Since 1958, the Chinese Communist authorities have been advocating a "half-work and half-study" school system. Most of the schools in that system are converted from regular vocational schools in agriculture, forestry, or animal husbandry. For instance, of the 307 agricultural schools operating in 1965, 220 were converted to half-work and half-study schools that year. So were 37 of the 66 agricultural colleges.[51] Students in these schools spend approximately half the time working in the fields, similar to those enrolled in schools hooked up with factories.

In the communes, the Communist authorities since 1964 have established a country school system known as the *Keng Tu* elementary school. *Keng Tu* means "till and study." These schools follow a highly flexible schedule, so that the children can work on the farm whenever required, and come to school when they are not busy. By 1965, a year after the system was put on a trial basis, some seventeen million children were enrolled in these *Keng Tu* schools.[52]

Rural Resettlement

A unique form of manual labor now incorporated into the Chinese manpower training programs is the Rural Resettlement movement, known as *Shang Shan Hsia Hsiang*—"Go up to the mountain and down to the village." This movement requires high school and college students to work in communes and uncultivated outlying areas upon their graduation. The idea of sending students to the farms was first proposed by Chairman Mao in 1955 during the height of the agricultural collectivization movement. The original idea was for high school and even elementary school graduates to return to their native villages and work on the collective farms.[53] However, Mao's idea was apparently not taken seriously until the aftermath of the Great Leap Forward, when the commune experiment temporarily set back agricultural production and aggravated the shortage of rural manpower. In 1963, plans were drawn up for systematically sending students from the cities to the villages. By early 1964, an estimated total of forty million students had been sent "up to the mountains and down to the villages."[54]

The flow of young urban intellectuals to rural areas was reversed during the Cultural Revolution, when many students took advantage of the confusion to come back to the cities in the name of joining the revolution. By mid-1968, after the group loyal to Mao had consolidated its control, the Rural Resettlement movement was reactivated to become perhaps the most significant population migration in China during the twentieth century. This movement seemed to be partly motivated by the Party's desire to redisperse the concentration of students in urban areas once their roles in the Cultural Revolution had been performed. The movement was also intended to provide young Chinese intellectuals, after they had been in schools for several years, with a continual reinforcement of proletarian ideology through close interactions with the peasants. The official announcements gave no indications of a serious shortage of rural manpower to justify the reactivation of the movement in 1968 from an economic point of view.

Beginning in the summer of 1968, a campaign was started in the mass media calling on millions of students in the cities to take the advice of Chairman Mao and go to the communes, mines, and uncultivated areas.[55] From the tone of an editor's note published in the *People's Daily,* most students appeared reluctant to go. The editor condemned those students "who looked down upon the peasants and workers, and considered themselves to be somebody." The students were told to get rid of their arrogance and join the ranks of the revolutionary mass of people.[56]

By December that year, when the students were apparently not moved by the feature articles and editorials in the newspapers, an extensive campaign of interpersonal communication was started in order to pressure them into compliance. First, the workers' propaganda teams, the military propaganda teams, and the revolutionary committees in the schools called the students together. In group sessions, the students were asked to study the writings of Chairman Mao and to acknowledge their indebtedness to the Party leader for the privilege of education. They were also asked to criticize Liu Shao-chi's mistakes, particularly his attempt to sabotage the Rural Resettlement movement.[57] The implication was clear: refusal to join the movement would amount to a self-identification with Liu Shao-chi. Meanwhile, small discussion meetings were held by cadres in those families in which either the students or the parents were still reluctant to join. In prolonged meetings in which the cadres set an example by promising to send their children to villages, the students and parents engaged in self-criticism and mutual criticism until everybody agreed to support the movement.[58]

The experience in Tientsin furnished an illustration of Party tactics.[59] The revolutionary committees in Tientsin's various organizations, and the workers and military propaganda teams in the city's 230 high schools and colleges, sent work teams to visit every family with eligible students. They went street by street until the whole city was covered. For each street, the families were organized into discussion meetings to study the thought of Mao Tse-tung, and to criticize Liu Shao-chi. As a result, the city was said to be overwhelmed by students who volunteered to go to the mountains and the villages.

On the whole, these mass persuasion campaigns were apparently successful in enrolling the students for labor in the communes and in border regions. Take Hsi Hsiang County of Shansi Province for instance. Of the 670 students who were in city schools at that time, 648, or about 95 percent, agreed to go to work in the villages.[60] According to an official report, by early May 1969, millions of students from high schools and colleges had answered Chairman Mao's call and gone to the villages. The total number, though unspecified, was said to exceed the combined total of the previous ten years.[61]

The Rural Resettlement movement for graduates is different from the performance of labor required of those students still registered in school. Students who join the movement upon graduation do so with the understanding that they may have to stay in the villages for good. The Chinese term employed during the movement is *cha tui lo hu,* meaning "joining the line and settling in a home.'' In other words, join the ranks of the peasants for permanent settlement. High school graduates who have gone to the villages will have a slight chance of being recommended for college education after two or three years. For college graduates from the new system, the future is somewhat unclear, as the Party has not yet announced its policy regarding their employment.

Effects of the Movement

While the students are in the communes for settlement, they work under the supervision of the commune cadres and the peasants. It is the peasants who, under the cadres' direction, are responsible for the students' work assignment, ideological indoctrination, and everyday life. If we can assign credibility to reports in Red Guard publications during the Cultural Revolution, friction between students and peasants seemed to be not uncommon. In a few cases, coeds were said to have been assaulted by cadres in the villages. Some students were underpaid by the communes for their work.[62]

The stated objective of the Rural Resettlement movement was to inspire educated young people with a sound ideological enthusiasm for manual labor. The initial reaction by the students and parents, however, seemed to be one of disappointment and frustration. The feeling of parents was exemplified by this remark: ''You have been to school for nine years, but you still come back to till the land. Just like using a bamboo basket to hold water—all for nothing.''[63] Among the students, the popular saying was, ''School is useless.'' This trend appeared to be so widespread that the official Party publication *Red Flag* published a special article refuting it.[64] The sentiment of purposelessness was apparently shared even by the peasants. When they saw students coming from the cities to work under their supervision, their reaction was: ''Why bother sending our own children to school?'' It is quite possible that the children of peasants have perceived such attitudes in their parents. Some peasant children do not carry books to school. They take no notes and pay little attention to what is going on in class.[65]

Leadership by Workers and Peasants
Initial Role of Red Guards

The Cultural Revolution, aside from its political goals, was in part intended to correct the lack of enthusiasm among teachers as well as students in pursuing ideological education. Before 1966 most universities and schools were administered by representatives of teachers who sat on the executive committees under the direction of Party cadres. As long as the teachers remained in their positions of authority, the Chinese Communist leadership recognized, the new beliefs and values would be difficult to establish. By allowing the Red Guards to take over the schools temporarily during the Cultural Revolution, the Party leadership under Mao succeeded in removing the old intellectuals from their positions in the educational system. However, the Red Guards were unable and perhaps not expected to provide leadership and restore order in the schools once they had torn down the old structure. Furthermore, some of the Red Guards soon demonstrated the same kind of bourgeois thinking that they had professed to eradicate from teachers. There was a rapid decline of interest in the movement for struggle and criticism. One thinking prevalent among some Red Guard groups even considered it disadvantageous to study the philosophy of Mao Tse-tung. These tendencies were revealed in a denunciation by Yao Wen-yuan, the Party's major spokesman for the Cultural Revolution.[66]

The Party authorities under Mao's leadership responded to these tendencies by sending teams of revolutionary workers to take over the schools from the Red Guards. The official announcement came in an article by Yao published in both the *Red Flag* and the *People's Daily* in August 1968. The instructions of Chairman Mao, according to Yao, were:

> In order to achieve the proletarian educational revolution, the workers class must assume leadership. The mass of workers must take an active part. A three-in-one union must be formed for workers, the Liberation Army, and the progressive elements among those students, teachers, and workers in schools who are determined to pursue the proletarian educational revolution to the end. The workers' propaganda teams will stay in schools indefinitely to participate in the entire work of struggle, criticism, and reform, and will assume permanent leadership. In the villages, the poor and lower-middle class peasants, who are the most loyal allies of the workers class, will operate the schools.[67]

Following this announcement, propaganda teams were organized out of factory workers who were considered ideologically progressive, and sent to take over universities, high schools and elementary schools in the cities. Sporadic feeble resistance was noted by the *People's Daily,* which acknowledged the existence of capitalist remnants in schools who refused to take orders from the proletarian headquarters led by Chairman Mao Tse-tung and the then Marshal Lin Piao.[68] At the Tsinghua University, for instance, some professors and students felt that even though workers were highly capable of operating a factory, they hardly knew a thing about administering a university.[69] Red Guards at the Futan University in Shanghai took an attitude of antagonism toward the workers who moved into their campus. Some of them begin to hide their weapons, instead of surrendering them as ordered.[70] However, the transition from the Red Guards to the workers teams was eventually accomplished with the support of the Liberation Army within a few months.

The Process of Takeover

After a workers' propaganda team had moved into a school, the first thing it did was to seize the media of communication. All broadcasting facilities, including loudspeakers, were impounded. So were the bulletin boards. All the tatzepao were stripped from the walls. Then the team started an intensive indoctrination campaign of its own, using the loudspeakers, tatzepao, small-group discussions, and even individual *tan hsin*, meaning "heart-to-heart" talks. At the Tsinghua University, the workers team organized more than a hundred subteams to carry out its struggle and criticism against those teachers and students who showed signs of following the revisionist line of education.[71]

The workers' propaganda teams also sought to quiet the disorder then prevalent in most schools by taking over the administration. In each school, delegates from the workers' propaganda team served on the revolutionary committee that assumed overall responsibility for the operation of the school. In Peking's No. 23 High School, for example, the revolutionary committee in early 1970 consisted of three workers' delegates, two military members, two Party cadres, three teachers, one staff member, and four Red Guards.[72] Decisions were reached through discussion by the committee. Initially, the workers and the military delegates appeared to exert more influence than the cadres and other members of the revolutionary committee. By late 1971, after the Party had consolidated its control over the country, the Party cadres on the revolutionary committees began to regain their power in schools and universities. Complaints soon began to be heard from the workers because they had little to do in the schools. Some workers wanted to return to their factories to rejoin their own crews. The Party's response, to take the Chiaotung University as an example, was to keep the workers in the schools and allow them somewhat greater participation in the decision-making process under the guidance of the Party cadres. The workers were consulted more on all major decisions and invited to attended administrative meetings at the university.[73] Relatively little has been heard about the military teams in schools and universities since the Party regained its control in late 1971.

Supervision by Peasants

In the rural communes, Mao's instruction was to place the schools under the supervision of poor and lower-middle class peasants. The peasants were instructed to gain firm control of four aspects of school education. The first was power. They must solidly hold the power of decision-making in their hands because the previous system was considered to discriminate against children of peasants. The second was loyalty. Above everything, they must make sure that the students would be forever loyal to Chairman Mao from generation to generation. The third was educational revolution. The peasants were asked to select from among themselves those who were competent to teach revolutionary lessons, that is, tell about the sufferings of the past. At the same time, they were required to supervise the educational reform of the old teachers through criticism. The fourth was continuity of proletarian leadership. During the past, children from peasant families were described as looking down upon peasant life once they had been through junior high school. Some did not even want to sit with peasants. Such attitudes must be corrected by turning the schools into a training ground for future proletarian leaders "who could till the land with their hoes, criticize the capitalist class with their pens, and defend socialism with their guns."[74]

These objectives were to be accomplished through constant communication between the peasants on the one hand, and the students and teachers on the other. A special report on the educational reform in three communes in Lao Shan County, Shantung Province, provides an example. Before the Cultural Revolution, all regular schools were supervised by the Bureau of Cultural Affairs of the county. This system, which gave the peasants practically no voice in the operation of the schools, was changed by placing the high schools under the supervision of the communes, and the elementary schools under the direction of the production brigades. In each school a revolutionary committee was formed out of representatives of peasants, Party cadres in the respective commune or production brigades, and representatives of students and teachers in a three-in-one union. At the beginning of each month the committee met to review the school's activities in the previous month and to plan for the coming month. The peasants examined the progress of learning and assigned labor duties for students and teachers according to the brigade's production plans. During the middle of each month, the peasant representatives met with the students and teachers again to review their study of Mao Tse-tung thought. Students and teachers were regularly required to attend meetings with the peasants to "struggle against self interest and criticize revisionism." Some of the brigades organized students into surveillance teams to watch over former landlords, rich peasants, and individuals identified as rightists and counterrevolutionaries. They were required to report their findings to the Party cadres in the brigades.[75]

Class-Oriented Indoctrination
Six Strategies

The Chinese Communist authorities consider the proletarian class-oriented indoctrination an important basis of their manpower training, a means of creating the New Chinese Man as a foundation of the New Socialist Chinese State. This philosophy was clearly enunciated in an editorial in the *People's Daily,* "Education for the class struggle should be pursued constantly, year after year, month after month, and day after day, from generation to generation."[76]

This objective is not be be achieved through a philosophical comparison between the Communist ideology and the capitalist system. Such a comparison would necessarily be couched in abstract terms which most children and young people would find difficult to understand. Instead, the Party has chosen to instill in the younger generation an antagonsim against the old and a love for the new. This is to be achieved by bringing back the past through living examples, following six related strategies.[77] The first strategy is "to tell," meaning to tell bitter stories of the past. The tellers of stories are usually the "four olds,"—old Red Army soldiers, old cadres, old poor peasants, and old workers, who suffered poverty and hardship in the past. They tell different kinds of personal experiences: the history of one's village, of one's factory, of a particular battle during the revolution, of the development of a cooperative farm, and so on. Regardless of the particulars, the main theme is generally the same, known in Chinese as *yi ku, ssu tien.* That is, "remember the bitter experience of the past and appreciate the sweet life of the present." Stories of this nature are told in all schools, usually at the beginning of a semester. At Tung Shih Commune, Lung Hai County, Fukien Province, for instance, the first lesson the children received was called a "meal of bitter remembrance," that is, bitter stories told by poor peasants.[78] When the Shui Yuan Commune of Ying Kou County asked peasants to run its elementary schools, among the first things the peasants did was to share their bitter stories with the students.[79]

The second strategy is "to exhibit." Many exhibitions have been organized to contrast the new with the old. Some are simply called yi ku ssu tien exhibitions. Each county usually has a permanent type exhibition, while itinerant ones travel from commune to commune. Items on display include old lease contracts with the landlords, sticks presumably used by landlords to beat the tenants, broken rice bowls used by beggars, and ragged old clothes. School children visit these exhibitions on weekends.

One unique exhibition is the Rental Collection Hall, an array of 114 sculptures depicting the oppression of peasants by landlords in the past.[80] The exhibition is based on the story of Liu Wen-chai, a big landlord in Szechwan who once owned more than twelve thousand *mu* (about two thousand acres) of land and collected 5,600,000 catties of grains a year from his tenants (one catty is about 1.1 pounds). In 1958, Liu's former residence at Jen An, Szechwan, was transformed by the Party into a landlord's home exhibition. In 1965, the Party authorities in Szechwan decided to recreate the life of Liu's tenants in clay sculptures vividly arranged in six scenes: tenants delivering grains, landlord's agents checking grains, weighing grains, preparing overdue accounts, landlord's agents arresting tenants, and tenants revolting. These scenes present a picture of the helpless tenants and their families suffering under the oppression of the landlord's agents that eventually led to a rebellion. The sculptures were first exhibited in Liu's home and later moved to Peking for permanent display. In the first two months following its public opening in Peking in May 1966, the exhibition attracted more than one million visitors.

The third strategy is "to search." Because some young people may not believe the bitter stories told, the Party has been organizing students into teams to "dig bitter roots," that is, to search for convincing stories. As a form of behavioral involvement the search is usually done while the students are performing their labor duties on the farms. They go around asking peasants to tell them their stories.

The fourth strategy is "to discuss." The stories are not to be listened to passively, but must be discussed actively. Some of the discussion takes place within the students' own group, in which each student is required to express his impressions and comments. Sometimes the students are asked to write down the lesson they have learned from a particular story or exhibition. Such comments usually end with a statement of rededication to the cause of proletarian revolution.

The fifth strategy is "to record." This is related to the third strategy. Individuals as well as organizations are required to keep a record of the bitter stories they have come across, either through their own experience or as a result of the search. The record is written into a relevant case history—family history, village history, production team history, and the like. It should tell the process of transformation from the bitter past to the sweet present. In organizations, these histories are kept in a file. The contents are sometimes written into folk songs or short musicals for popular entertainment.

The sixth strategy is "to transmit." While all the strategies involve transmission, this one refers to permanent display of the written form so that it can be securely transmitted from generation to generation. For instance, the Hsia Ho Production Brigade of Fu Tung County, Hopei Province, recorded the history of its class struggle in big characters on the display walls of all its production teams. A brief version of that history was engraved on a stone monument erected at the center of the brigade.[81]

These same tactics have apparently been followed ever since. A recent report in the *People's Daily* says that at the Chih Lo Commune not far from Yenan, the Party branch has been regularly organizing discussion sessions in which poor peasants from the old society share their personal histories with children who belong to the group of Little Red Soldiers. "Remembering the past" meals are often served. The children take periodic excursions to visit exhibitions of the class struggle.[82]

A variety of other forms are utilized to impress upon the younger generation a clear class consciousness. While students are working on the farms for their labor duties, they sometimes receive what is known as a "rice paddy education."[83] The peasant in charge takes the students to the rice paddies, and while there, leads the students in a group discussion criticizing the bourgeois-oriented agricultural policy of Liu Shao-chi. The peasants tell the students that they work in the rice paddies for the sole purpose of revolution. Only after the discussion was concluded would the peasant teach the students how to plant rice.

Indoctrination for Children

Political indoctrination for children starts in the nursery school so that the thought of Mao Tse-tung can be imprinted early in the young minds. The nursery school at the celebrated Tachai Commune in Shansi Province offers an example. To teacher Chia Chun-soh, the most fundamental objective of preschool education was to instill in the children a profound love for Chairman Mao. One day Chia asked the children: "Who made these clothes for you?" A child said "My Mom sewed them." Upon this, Chia began to tell a story of the miserable life of peasants in the old society—how they did not even have clothes to wear, and how Chairman Mao gave them their clothes. After he had finished the story, the children came to believe that it was Chairman Mao who gave them their clothing. The same process was repeated to convince the children that the food they ate, and the houses they lived in, were not provided by Mom and Dad, but given to them by Chairman Mao. When it came time to eat, the children were told to remember the bitterness of the past.[84]

The Chinese Communist party has in recent years begun to pay more attention to preschool children. These young children, aged from three to five, are referred to as the "three don't care" groups. That is, the schools don't care for them, the street committees don't care for them, and even the parents don't care for them because they do not have the time. The dilemma was stated by the *People's Daily* when discussing them, "Should these small children be organized so that they can be brought up in the environment of Chairman Mao's thought when they are very young, or should we leave them alone, let the nonproletarian class ideology invade their young hearts, and wait till they have reached an appropriate age to receive education in school?"[85]

The answer has been the former. The Party has been organizing the preschool children into "little red classes." At the Kailuan coal mine district some fifteen hundred preschool children were organized into little red classes, according to their residential area. The children met regularly under the supervision of elementary school children of the upper grades, who were in turn supervised by members of the street committees. Children in the little red classes learned Mao Tse-tung thought and engaged in play activities intended to help them remember the bitter past and appreciate the sweet present. The preschool children soon learned to write "Long Live Chairman Mao" and "Long Live the Chinese Communist party." Many learned to cite some twenty or thirty Mao quotations.[86]

When the Communist authorities say parents don't care for their children because they are too busy, they are referring to the parents' failure to provide proper indoctrination rather than to their negligence in looking after the children's physical welfare. Chinese parents seem to take good care of their children, but perhaps not in a way that meets the approval of the Party. This can be inferred from official pronouncements that condemn the parents for their traditional, family-oriented attitudes toward child rearing.[87] In a sense, the traditional Chinese attitudes are partly oriented toward the parents themselves, because children are regarded as a form of insurance against old age. This can be seen in the first half of an old Chinese saying: "Raise children to guard against old age." But the traditional Chinese attitudes also reflect the parents' care and concern, as expressed in the second part of the same saying: "Expect sons to become dragons," that is, to acquire success and fame that will bring honor to the family. The Chinese Communist authorities have stated that parents must first cleanse their minds of old traditions before they can teach their children to be good citizens. The Party has proposed a new version of the saying, that is: "Raise children to guard against revisionism (instead of old age); teach sons to become guardians of power (instead of dragons).'' Power, in this connection, refers to power of the proletarian class.

The *People's Daily* argued in this manner:

> If we raise children from a selfish point of view, then we will be teaching our children according to the interests of our own family. If we raise children by following the thought of Chairman Mao, then we will be teaching them according to the interests of the people, and of the nation. If we retain the private "self," then we would raise children to protect against old age. But if we follow the "public" spirit, then we can raise children to protect ourselves against revisionism.[88]

Effects of Indoctrination

How effective is proletarian, class-oriented indoctrination? Is the New Chinese Man emerging? In the absence of clear evidence from a representative segment of the younger generation, a definitive answer is not possible. The fragmentary information available to us, however, would suggest that the degree of effectiveness is, in all probability, negatively related to age. When the children in the Taichai Commune nursery say that their clothes, their food, and their houses are all given to them by Chairman Mao, they most probably believe what they say. Children at the age of three or four have only a limited experience of their own. They depend heavily on mediated experience, on what is told them, particularly, by a trustworthy source. When their teacher, someone they have come to like and trust, tells them that Chairman Mao gives them everything, they will most probably take his word.

Indeed, some of the young children have taken this word so seriously that they apply what they have learned in school to their parents. Chinese children today have been repeatedly told in school:

"Parents are dear to you, but Chairman Mao is even dearer. Obey your parents if they follow Chairman Mao's instruction. Otherwise, do not obey them. But always obey Chairman Mao."[89] These instructions were faithfully followed by Tung Yi-chang, an eleven-year-old Little Red Guard. Tung's mother was raising pigs, which often wandered to eat the rice plants that belonged to the production team. When this was brought to her attention, she refused to admit her negligence. Little Tung considered her attitudes to reflect the self-interest condemned by Chairman Mao. He confronted his mother with a criticism. His mother finally admitted her error.[90]

With older children, however, the indoctrination seems to work somewhat less well. Take the students of Shih Chin Shan High School in Peking as an example. When they were sent to the Peking capital steel works for labor duties, they received a lecture from old worker Chao Teh-yih on Mao Tse-tung thought. Chao told about his own selfless service—how he always volunteered to stay in the factory on Saturday evenings, how he used his leisure time to give free haircuts to other workers, how he organized classes in his home to study Mao Tse-tung thought, and how he required his children to clean public latrines. After he had finished his story, some students were heard to comment: "This master worker doesn't know how to play it right." When another worker came and talked about his bitter family history and accused the evil old society, some students laughed.[91]

College students, who face the reality of finding a job and making a living, are perhaps too old to laugh. According to the *Wen Hui Pao* of Shanghai, some intellectuals were frustrated, dejected, and disheartened because they lacked the confidence and determination to be reeducated. "They are afraid of revolution, and are trying to escape criticism and struggle. Their behavior is shameful."[92] While some college students have shown manifest signs of dissatisfaction, most of the others seem to be taking a more cautious attitude, known as *shui ta liu* or "follow the main current." According to an analysis by the *Red Flag:*

> Some people do not seriously use Mao Tse-tung thought to analyze and differentiate what is right and what is wrong. They do not resolutely defend the proletarian policy of Chairman Mao. Instead, they simply "follow the main current." You say you want to be stern, I'll support you. You say you want to be lenient, I also agree. You want to struggle against someone, I'll follow. You want to liberate him, I'll also come along. Some of them have doubts about some of the erroneous tendencies, or are aware of the mistakes made by others. But "since this is none of my business, let's keep quiet. The best way of self-preservation is not to look for trouble. All I need is to be blameless myself." Some of these people even consider their non-proletarian erroneous behavior to be a case of "following the majority opinion."[93]

Influence of the Old Culture

A main obstacle to the ideological conversion is the rather tenacious influence of the old culture, some of which seems to have survived the many rectification campaigns. Part of the old Chinese culture is manifest, existing in the customs, habits, rituals, and ceremonies. The Party has been trying hard to replace these habits. But there is the other part, which is latent and almost invisible. It is part of the Chinese language, being embodied in the many old sayings that have profound influence on the people because they use them in their daily lives.

Several factors suggest why the old sayings are so pervasive and influential. Many of them are crystalizations of folk wisdom and have a validity of sorts. For instance, one saying that particularly bothers the Party authorities is, "Leave a way out when handling a problem, so that you can see each other again someday."[94] This is a folk expression of the Confucian principle of the Golden Mean, contrary to the Chinese Communist tactics of unreserved criticism. Most sayings, like the one cited above, rhyme in Chinese. Because they are easy to say, they acquire popularity. One rhymed saying, said to echo the fatalism of Confucius, is, "If your destiny gives you five bushels, you don't have to get up at five o'clock."[95] Another rhymed popular saying is, "When you plant flowers, the fragrance spreads a thousand miles; when you plant thorns, you sting yourself." The moral is, say nice things about others and don't criticize them.[96] Other sayings depend for effect on a smooth repetition of words. For instance: "Dragon's eyes see pearls, phoenix' eyes see treasure, but cow's eyes see only hay." This saying is denounced because it contradicts the proletarian policy of education and reflects Lin Piao's genius principle. A similar example is, "If you are blessed, other people serve you; if you are not blessed you serve other people." Because of this saying, the *People's Daily* contends, people in the old society accepted the exploitation of capitalists and landlords without question.[97]

The Party authorities apparently know that to remove the influence of the old sayings will be no easy task. One reason is that some sayings simply defy logic but are accepted as true because the Chinese have been saying them for ages. The following provides an example, although much of the original flavor is lost in translation. There is a Chinese plant known as *huang lien*, which has a strong bitter taste. The Chinese character for bitter is *ku*, which can also mean "miserable." The double meaning of ku is manipulated in this saying, "A wooden doll carved out of *huang lien* plant—is a miserable (ku) little fellow." It is true that a doll carved out of huang lien tastes bitter (ku). But because this is true, says the *People's Daily,* people in the past were convinced that their miserable (ku) life should be accepted as an unchangeable fact.[98]

In the current campaign against Lin Piao and Confucius, some of the criticisms are directed at what the Party calls the "reactionary, old sayings." The strategy is to collect all the reactionary sayings so that they can be criticized and refuted. This was done, for instance, at Peking's handicrafts and arts factory.[99] Each of the sayings was examined in the light of Marxism, Leninism, and Mao Tse-tung thought. Not all old sayings are condemned. A few that are in favor of collective labor have been retained and publicized. For instance, one old saying is, "When three stinky cobblers put their heads together, they can be as wise as Chuko Liang." The Party has dropped the word "stinky," probably because it reflects unfavorably on laborers. The revised saying goes like this, "When three shoe repairmen put their heads together, they can be as wise as Chuko Liang."[100] Somehow, in Chinese it does not sound quite so crisp as the original saying did.

The Party has been trying to popularize a number of new revolutionary sayings to take the place of the reactionary ones. For instance, "Heart holds the motherland, eyes set on the world." Or, "Tell mountains to lower their heads, order rivers to yield the way." These, however, sound like political slogans and lack the folksy touch of the old sayings. The efforts to eradicate the old sayings are most likely going to be difficult because one would almost have to change the spoken language.

Besides the sayings, some of the old philosophy—undesirable from the Party's viewpoint—lurks behind the traditional stories and novels that have been popular among the Chinese for ages. The young people apparently find them appealing, as these stories are surreptitiously read and told despite an official ban.[101] One such occasion was reported by the Chih Lo Commune in 1974. An unidentified person, described simply as a bad element, was one day caught in his home telling stories from the traditional past that were considered poisonous. The circumstances were not clearly described, but the report in the *People's Daily* left the impression that he was attracting quite an audience of young people. He was confronted by the Little Red Soldiers and brought to a face-to-face struggle.[102]

The concerted efforts by the Party to cultivate a proletarian class-consciousness and a selfless dedication to the cause of revolution have succeeded in bringing about massive overt conformity. The extent of internal conviction and true belief, however, still remains to be tested by time.

Reeducation of Teachers
Teachers as Models

While teachers assume an important position in any society, the specific nature of their roles varies according to the predominant cultural values. In old China, teachers were charged with the responsibility not only of the transmission of knowledge but also with the inculcation of moral principles in the pupils. The latter function was to be fulfilled not so much through enunciation as through behavioral exemplification. This can be seen in the almost synonymous use of "teacher" and "model" in a frequently quoted Chinese saying: *wei jen* (to become) *shih* (teacher) *piao* (model).

This tradition appears to have been inherited by the Chinese Communists, who would like the teachers in China to be both a source of technical knowledge and a model of proletarian ideology and behavior. These assignments, however, have placed the Chinese teachers in a predicament. Because most of them have a bourgeois background, they are hardly in a position to provide the kind of ideologically correct examples that would please the Communist leadership. It is therefore no accident that teachers in mainland China have had to undergo an assortment of ideological reforms from time to time.

Among the first actions the Party took after 1949 was the indoctrination of intellectuals and teachers. By late 1950, some half million high school and elementary school teachers and about four hundred fifty thousand intellectuals, including college professors, had gone through crash courses of political training.[103] Lasting from one to three months, these courses emphasized Marxism and Leninism, as well as Mao Tse-tung's new democratic principles. Through group discussion and self criticism, the initial campaign of thought reform sought to pave the way for the acceptance of the new ideology by launching a severe attack on the old beliefs and values of Chinese culture. The climax of training was reached when each trainee wrote an autobiography in which every aspect of the self was bared.[104]

The initial ideological training was augmented by action programs in which the teachers had to participate. During the Land Reform movement of 1951, for instance, many college professors were sent to the villages in northern and central China to observe the actual struggle against the landlords. The experience of Professor Li Yu-yi of Peking University illustrates the feelings of the participants: "Only when we went to the villages to engage in the work of land reform did we begin to clearly understand the concept of class struggle. Now we know revolution means violence. It involves the violent action of one class to overthrow the power of another class. In this life-and-death struggle, there is only one side we can take. There can never be another alternative."[105]

From 1951 till the eve of the Hundred Flowers movement of 1957, the intellectuals of China, particularly those teaching in colleges and high schools, were required to make searching self-examinations in almost every major campaign. Many who spoke up against the Communist authorities during the Hundred Flowers movement were later severely criticized during the Anti-Rightist movement that followed. Here is a partial list of some of the mass campaigns involving the intellectuals during that period:[106]

1950 1. Land reform
      2. Resist-America, Aid-Korea
      3. Ideological reform of teachers of institutions of higher education
      4. Signing of peace movement documents

1951 1. Land reform (continued)
      2. Resist-America, Aid-Korea (continued)
      3. Signing of peace movement documents (continued)
      4. Suppression of counterrevolutionaries
      5. Three-Anti movement (anticorruption, antiwaste, and antibureaucracy)

1952 1. Thought reform
      2. Land reform (continued)
      3. Resist-America, Aid-Korea (continued)
      4. Study of Wu Hsun (a campaign against the bourgeois mentality of intellectuals, particularly writers and film producers)
      5. Five-Anti movement (antibribery, antitax evasion, antifraud, antitheft of state secrets, antileakage of state economic assets)
      6. Study of Mao Tse-tung's *On Contradiction*

1953 1. Sino-Soviet friendship
      2. Resist-America, Aid-Korea (ending this year)
      3. General line of transition to socialism

1954 1. Study of the constitution of the Chinese Communist party
      2. Red chamber dream incident (thought reform for writers and intellectuals)

1955 1. Hu Feng incident (thought reform campaign)
      2. Suppression of counterrevolutionaries (second major campaign)
      3. Movement of opposing the use of nuclear weapons

1956 1. Study of Mao's works
      2. Hundred Flowers movement

1957 1. Hundred Flowers movement (reaching a climax that spring)
      2. Ideological rectification
      3. Study of Mao's *On the Internal Contradictions Among People*
      4. Anti-rightist movement

1958 1. Great Leap Forward
      2. General line in socialist construction
      3. Debate on being red and expert
      4. Thought reform (antiwaste, anticonservatism)
      5. Tatzepao
      6. Turn over the heart to the party
      7. Communes
      8. Integration of education and labor

Trend toward Pragmatism

In the aftermath of the commune movement, when Liu Shao-chi was exerting more influence over the direction of China's development, the ideological indoctrination of teachers began to slow down, though it was not abandoned. The study of Marx, Lenin, and Mao Tse-tung was still pursued. In the name of integration of education and labor, teachers were required to participate in manual labor in villages and factories in the early 1960s in order to set a good example for students. But the harsh criticism that had often confronted teachers in the previous few years was much less evident. Instead, various kinds of positive inducements were offered Chinese teachers, in terms of Party membership, greater responsibility in the schools, promotion and salary increments, and for a relatively select few, even advanced studies in socialist countries abroad. Young scholars who made significant progress in scientific discoveries quickly earned national distinctions.

One such example was Luan Chi-cheng. With only a primary school education, Luan started as an apprentice in a factory at the age of sixteen. He finished the junior high school courses on his own in less than six months while carrying a full-time job. In another eight months, he mastered the mathematics, chemistry, and physics for senior high school. Then he began teaching mathematics in the technical school of his factory. After he had learned advanced mathematics by himself, Luan was assigned to teach college level mathematics for his fellow workers. He was given much national publicity.[107]

The emphasis during that period seemed to accentuate the expert more than the red aspect of the "red and expert" controversy. Without officially discontinuing their study of Communist doctrines, college professors were encouraged to participate in academically oriented seminars in order to improve their level of learning. Teachers at South China Agricultural College, for instance, visited each other's classes to broaden the scope of their technical knowledge. In Peking, 170 outstanding teachers in high schools and elementary schools were chosen to share their knowledge and teaching experience with less qualified teachers in the city. Senior professors at Wuhan University who were authorities in their respective fields were asked to take on younger, junior faculty members as apprentices so that their expertise could be transmitted to the next generation.[108]

Criticism and Reinstatement

This trend toward pragmatism was put to an end by the Cultural Revolution in the summer of 1966. With Red Guards roaming over the country in a frantic movement to destroy the "four olds"—old culture, old beliefs, old customs, and old habits—all universities and most schools were closed. Some teachers joined the Red Guards, but most went through an agonizing ordeal of criticism and struggle. Those who had occupied responsible positions were removed when propaganda teams from the army and factories took over the schools.

As we have cited earlier, it did not take the Party long to recognize that the workers and the military teams lacked the qualifications to operate the schools and universities all by themselves. Thus, the Party had to "liberate" most of the teachers who had been suspended during the Cultural Revolution. Although the workers and the military were still given the leadership position, beginning in the fall of 1968 teachers were allowed to join the workers, the military, and the students in a three-in-one union to work out educational reform following the instructions of Chairman Mao.[109] By the spring of 1969, many college professors who had special qualifications had been recruited to join education reform groups in factories or take part in planning for a new education system. By 1972, most of the old teachers had been restored because of the need of qualified personnel. At the Tungchi University, for instance, of the 140 teachers who joined the three-in-one union, 117 had been with the university since before the Cultural Revolution.[110]

Meanwhile, a nationwide program was initiated to reform the teachers. Five steps were followed for their screening and reform: (1) Teachers who were considered "class enemies" were to be singled out in struggle meetings. Those who made acceptable confessions were "allowed a way out," meaning to be kept for educational reform. Those who were stubborn were to be "stricken down," meaning dismissed. (2) Teachers who were not class enemies but who had committed serious errors were to be treated with patience and reeducated through self-criticism and mutual criticism. (3) Those who were not class enemies but whose family backgrounds were questionable had to clear up all questions before they would be allowed to "proceed ahead lightly," that is, resume their teaching duties. (4) The few who were not qualified to teach were to be sent away for labor resettlement. (5) Those teachers who were progressive were to be recruited into leadership positions. In group discussions supervised by the workers' teams and Party cadres, the teachers were required to resolve among themselves the nature of treatment for each of them.[111]

In each school, those teachers who were retained were generally organized into three groups: one group was sent to villages for labor reform for a period of time, another group received lectures on the class struggle from peasants who had come to the school for that purpose, and a third group learned to give lectures on Communist ideology under the supervision of peasants. The three groups rotated after a period. This system, practiced by the San Chang Commune, Tung Tai County, Kiangsu Province, was officially recommended for general adoption by all schools.[112] A similar rotation system was followed by universities. College teachers who had been retained through screening were organized into three teams. According to an officially approved plan, one team was to stay in school and prepare teaching materials, another was to study plans of revolutionary education with workers and peasants, and a third team was to go to villages for labor reform.[113] At the same time, many workers and peasants were recruited to teach ideology courses in high schools and elementary schools.

In addition to being assigned to labor reform, Chinese teachers were organized for a thorough study of Mao Tse-tung thought. At Peking University, more than 120 such classes were conducted for its professors under the guidance of workers and peasants. Some of the workers and peasants visited the professors in their homes for individual discussion. More than 100 sayings by Chairman Mao, considered most relevant to the reform of teachers, were selected for careful study. During the study sessions, the teachers were asked to conduct a complete review of their family and class backgrounds in order to locate the roots of their erroneous thinking. They were asked to remember the bitter past and appreciate the sweet present, in a manner we have previously discussed.[114]

The reinstatement of old teachers was not accomplished without resistance from within the Party. As acknowledged by the *People's Daily,* there were those in the Party who were strongly opposed to restoring some of the teachers to their original positions because of their "deep contamination by the thinking of feudalism, capitalism, and revisionism."[115] In view of the repeated campaigns of criticism and struggle in the past, it is not surprising that Chinese teachers would manifest worry and apprehension in the face of the new opposition from within the Party. Some teachers were described as so unsure of themselves that they were reluctant to take any initiative on anything. They demonstrated the same "follow the main current" attitude that was found among college students.[116]

Chinese teachers today no longer command the respect they once did from their students, and the erosion of their position of authority seems to have accelerated since the Cultural Revolution. College professors are afraid to give knowledge top priority. Nor are they considered trustworthy sources of knowledge, since they themselves have had to consult peasants and workers on a wide variety of subject matter. In elementary schools in the past, children used to say "How are you, teacher" when they arrived in school. Now the first thing they say is "Long Live Chairman Mao." In the past they saluted their teacher. Now they salute only Chairman Mao.[117] Teachers are now openly criticized by students. A twelve-year-old girl became a hero recently for criticizing her elementary school teacher. The case of Huang Shuai, a fifth-grade pupil, was given front page coverage in the *People's Daily* because of her courage to stand up against an unidentified teacher in Chung Kuang Chun Elementary School in Peking and assert her rights of criticism as a student in Mao Tse-tung's era.[118]

Persistence of the Old

How the old educational institution dies hard is suggested by some of the criticisms raised during the campaign against Confucius and Lin Piao. To illustrate, we shall cite the case of a Hunan dialect opera, *A Song of Gardeners*. Produced in 1972 as a model vernacular for the Hunan special professional art performance and sung in Chairman Mao's native dialect, this opera praised the work of two teachers, Yu Yin and Fang Chueh, who reformed an undisciplined fourth-grade pupil. At the time this opera was introduced, the two teachers were presented as models. During the current campaign against Confucius and Lin Piao, however, they are denounced as villains for taking the road of Confucius.

According to a severe criticism published in the *People's Daily*, the opera committed the error of totally ignoring Party leadership in education.[119] Both Yu and Fang are presented as Party members. But, said the review, throughout the play one does not see the existence of Party organization, nor can anyone tell what relations, if any, exist between the two teachers and the Party. Instead of acknowledging the leadership of the Party, the opera glorified the individual achievements of the two teachers as "gardeners."

In their songs and dialogues, said the review, the two gardeners treated the pupils as their personal disciples. For instance, Yu, the female teacher, was singing: "See tomorrow, the peaches will be red and the plums ripe, presenting a scene of plentiful harvest." The reference to peaches and plums is considered reactionary because in the old Confucian tradition, a master having many disciples is said to have planted peaches and plums all over the land. Calling teachers "gardeners" and students "peaches and plums" thus became a serious distortion of the new student-teacher relations under socialism.

The two teachers were further criticized for overly emphasizing knowledge and neglecting ideology, the same errors that prevailed before the Cultural Revolution. For instance, when the curtain rises, the male teacher, Fang, is seen as unable to hide his joy while marking a perfect examination. He is exclaiming: "Correct (making a check mark), all correct." On the other hand, Fang looks down on Tao Li, the son of a locomotive worker, calling him "good for nothing," an uncontrollable "wild bull." Tao hardly studies at all and spends his time playing with a toy locomotive.

"What is studying for?" asked teacher Fang.
"For revolution," answered the boy.
"And playing with a toy locomotive?"
"Also for revolution."

In a fury, Fang seized the toy locomotive and flung it across the stage. He started severely scolding the boy. Yu, the female teacher, intervened, suggesting that they use persuasion rather than coercion. "Only patience and care can produce good students," she said, meaning students with superior knowledge. But, according to the review, both teachers committed the error of placing knowledge first, even though they use different approaches. The review further condemned the opera because it creates a model pupil, Hsiao Lin, a girl who cares about nothing except studying. She not only gives no support to the boy in his fight against revisionist education, but helps the two teachers pull Tao backward to the road of revisionism. The review concludes: "The appearance of *A Song of Gardeners* in this day in the aftermath of the Great Proletarian Cultural Revolution is no accident. It shows that in the entire process of socialist revolution, we face a long, recurring class struggle and line struggle in the superstructures, including arts and education."[120]

Changes in Educational Institutions

We have witnessed phenomenal changes in the institutions for manpower training in mainland China during the past quarter century. Characterizing these institutional changes is a shift in the emphasis of manpower training from technology to ideology, from building the nation's economy to laying a foundation for the socialist transformation of twentieth-century China. As we have seen, these changes have come about with many twists and turns.

In the initial period, approximately from 1949 to 1957, the Party leadership tried to remodel China's educational institutions by reforming the teachers as well as the students, while keeping the institutional structure relatively untouched. The first attempt at drastic change came with the Great Leap Forward. Manual labor was increased; ideological indoctrination was intensified. Mao spoke of sending millions of students to the mountains and the villages. When the Great Leap Forward collapsed, the educational institutions also moved back to their pre-Leap status. The years between 1960 and 1966 represented perhaps the peak of academic development in China along the conventional path. This was a period where the expert seemed to take precedence over the red. The Cultural Revolution changed all this.

Structural Change

Mao had probably long realized that even though an ultimate ideological conversion is crucial, attempts to change ideology, in the manner the Party had been pursuing, would be largely futile as long as the institutions of education remained in their old structure. What people say in self-criticism and mutual criticism may have some impact on their value and belief structure, but it is quite likely that the enthusiastic verbal pronouncements may not have gone far toward the stage of overt performance. If the old structure of administration and decision-making should remain relatively unchanged in the schools, if the teachers who were educated in the old traditions should be allowed to remain unchallenged in their positions, the Party could not expect any fundamental changes in the emphasis and methods of education. The old value of knowledge would be upheld, and the old norm of teachers lecturing to students would be followed. Students, often with a bourgeois background, who were produced under this system would readily find their way to cadre positions because they were the ones who possessed the qualifications and valued knowledge to function in these positions. Mao apparently realized that in order to build a new system, he must first tear down the old system. In order to establish an institution of education that would produce laborers with a socialist class consciousnesss, the old institution had to go.

The Red Guards, rampaging over the country in 1966 and 1967, performed for Mao the function of destroying the old institution of education in China. Teachers all over the country were effectively removed from their positions in the schools and universities, and made to go through an ordeal of self-examination and criticism. Old curricula and textbooks were thrown out. The high school and college admission procedures that the Party had inherited from the past were abandoned. Lecturing as a method of teaching was denounced.

Almost immediately, the Party leadership under Mao moved to build a new institution in place of the old, first for the elementary schools, then for the high schools, and after a long lag of four years, for the universities. What Mao did closely followed an old Chinese saying: *"pu po, pu li,"* meaning "if you do not destroy (the old), you do not build (the new)."

Building the new, however, turned out to be more difficult than destroying the old. After the teachers had been removed, and after the Red Guards had served their purposes and moved along, who was there to fill the vacuum? Partly following his ideological conviction and partly out of necessity, Mao turned to the peasants and workers. With the transitional support of the military—in the days when Lin Piao was an heir apparent to Mao—the peasants and workers took over the schools and universities. The general course of action had already been set for them by the Party, and thus it would be misleading to say that the peasants and workers had a major voice in deciding the future direction of China's educational institutions. But within the general purview of Party policy, the peasants and workers had much to contribute regarding the contents of the new curricula, the methods of teaching and evaluation, the daily administration of schools, and the admission procedures and standards. For a while, representatives of peasants and workers even carried on some of the actual teaching, by telling their own case histories and criticizing the revisionism of Liu Shao-chi. By the time the old teachers were allowed to rejoin the schools, China's institutions of education had already been radically changed, in structure and in content, as well as in norms, values, and goals. It was no longer the teachers' executive committee, but the entirely new revolutionary committee consisting mainly of peasants, workers, military representatives, and Party cadres, that administered the schools. The old content of the curricula, which leaned toward the more abstract and theoretical side of knowledge, was replaced with practical experience suitable for immediate application. The norms of lecturing and memorizing gave way to discussion and sharing of experience. Knowledge somewhat lost its value for its own sake.

Education in China today is no longer a means of achieving the goal of individual advancement. Rather, if one has made some achievement by demonstrating a strong ideological conviction and a superb labor performance, then one is rewarded with further education. The additional education does not guarantee a higher position, as it usually did before the Cultural Revolution. It does seem to mean a kind of recognition given to a person by his peers and the Party leadership. It makes further recognition and eventual advancement easier, provided one continues to engage in the same behavior that has earned him the privilege of higher education in the first place, that is, ideological consciousness and hard work. In other words, education is no longer a major social mechanism for making differential job assignments. Other social mechanisms, primarily peer-group evaluations by peasants or workers, depending on where one is performing one's labor duties after junior or senior high school, selectively assign different individuals to different routes of occupational careers, including additional schooling.

The change of job assignment standards and procedures, as it climaxed in the Rural Resettlement movement, will perhaps have far-reaching and long-ranging effects on the social structure in China. By sending all students to the villages upon graduation from junior high school, this movement has effectively blocked the traditional route whereby children of ex-landlords, ex-rich peasants and bourgeoisie could hope to advance academically and occupationally. We suspect many of these children do not possess the physical strength and work habits which would be highly regarded by the peasants. Since the peasants now perform the first round of evaluation, it is quite likely that a large proportion of these children will end in the communes when they are in their teens and will stay there. If so, this will reverse the past trend by which a disproportionately large percentage of peasant children remained in the communes for good.

Communication and Institutional Change

We have seen how communication, both through mass media and interpersonal channels, has played an essential role in changing the institutions of manpower training in China. In the initial period up to the eve of the Great Leap Forward, the Party primarily relied on value-oriented communication to foster an ideological reform of individuals. In almost every movement, attempts were made to strengthen the ideological commitment of the participants, including teachers and students. The mass media generally played the role of setting the course of its general direction. At the interpersonal level, the individuals took part in whatever activities were required of them, whether to study the thought of Mao Tsetung, or to engage in self-examination, or to criticize reactionary thinking. These value-oriented communication activities were supplemented by labor duties. Through their own experience in labor and through their close interactions with the peasants, both teachers and students were expected to acquire a personal understanding of life beyond their academic environment and to develop the kinds of values and attitudes favorable to manual labor.

These attempts at ideological change were scaled down following the unsuccessful Great Leap Forward. It was not until the Cultural Revolution that the Party leadership under Mao revived the communication activities for change. The new strategies of communication were different from the old in that they were directed at institutional change more than at individual change. A number of differences can be noted. Again, as in the past, the mass media assumed the role of the crier for the Party. However, the important directives of Chairman Mao were not delivered in official statements, but came secondhand either in the words of a subordinate spokesman (for example, Yao Wen-yuan) or in the form of an editor's note in the *People's Daily*. It appeared that Mao was not sure how the country would react to his new instruction, and therefore was using the secondhand approach as a buffer device, almost like a trial balloon. Most of his instructions were vague, and sometimes seemingly irrelevant, for instance, proposing the Shanghai machine tools plant training program as a model for science and engineering education in universities. It looked as if he were reserving for himself some flexibility in case the nation should turn out to be not yet ready to follow him.

At this point, the Party would make no move. It simply waited. Meanwhile, a mass movement of normative communication slowly took shape to create a new perception of social reality. How quickly and extensively the schools and universities in China actually responded to Mao's instruction could not be ascertained. In the official *People's Daily* as well as the provincial newspapers, feature articles would soon appear one after another, describing how different schools in various localities were discussing Chairman Mao's ideas and coming up with concrete proposals for implementation. These feature articles were written either in the name of the "revolutionary teachers and students" of a particular school, or by a correspondent of the official newspaper. It was not known what standards of selection, if any, were employed by the editors. At any rate, all the articles invariably voiced support for Chairman Mao's ideas, although their specific proposals might vary somewhat. Using the official media of communication as a forum, a chorus of public opinion thus appeared to emerge. Through this façade of nearly unanimous public opinion, new norms and values and new directions of education gradually took shape. Schools and universities across the country joined in the discussion through their own small groups. They too wanted to change the curricula, to revise teaching methods, to adopt new procedures for admission and examination, and to reorganize the administrative structures of their schools. To the individual teachers and students observing the event, their perception would be that of a whole country proceeding to adopt a new system of education that developed out of open discussion and wide participation by themselves. It was they themselves who rewrote the textbooks, modified the curricula, changed the methods of teaching, and adopted the new procedures for admission and evaluation of students.

When this moment arrived, the Party issued its official directive to put a final touch to the institutional change. This involved a complete reorganization of the administrative structures of the schools and universities. Actions were taken by sending workers and military propaganda teams to take over the day-to-day administration. If there were forces who would resist this move, they had already lost their first round in the contest of perceived public opinions. With the military backing the workers, the takeover was accomplished with little resistance.

It is important to note that the combined use of normative communication and coercion was successful because of two crucial elements. We can see the necessity for the Party to have total control of the mass media of communication, so that a forum of favorable public opinion could be generated and maintained. Not even the slightest dissension was allowed on major policy issues, although methods of implementation could be openly discussed and sometimes questioned. In this regard one is reminded of the experiments by Asch concerning the effects of social pressure on perception. The misperception of reality was found to be the most pronounced when social pressure was applied with a force of unanimity. As long as a single manifestation of disagreement was allowed, the effectiveness of social pressure became greatly attenuated.[121] The full awareness of the importance of gaining total control of all communication media was indicated by the actions of the workers' propaganda teams previously mentioned; when they moved into a campus, they first seized all broadcasting facilities and bulletin boards, and stripped the walls of tatzepao.

Of equal importance is the existence of a social mechanism by which people can be quickly brought together so that pressure can be applied and group support mobilized. Such a social mechanism exists in China in the form of small study groups. In every village, and on every street, the Chinese have been organized into study groups with a set of professed values and established norms of behavior. When an idea is handed down by the Party, the members of the group get together to discuss the idea, express their endorsement, and take appropriate action whenever called for. Without either of these social mechanisms, the Party's strategy of normative communication could not have been so effective in bringing about the intended results.

The effectiveness and limitations of this communication strategy were most vividly illustrated during the movement called "go up to the mountains and down to the villages." Initially, the Party seemed to depend primarily on the mass media of communication, by urging students to take the advice of Chairman Mao and go where their services were most urgently needed. It was quite possible that the Party was using the mass media merely to prepare the way for the subsequent campaign of interpersonal communication. At any rate, the campaign of persuasion through the mass media alone had very little effect. It was not until after normative communication had been organized at the interpersonal level, in group meetings and even individual visits, where the idea was discussed and group pressure applied, that popular endorsement was obtained. Then the students began to volunteer.

Effects and Latent Functions

To what extent has the Chinese Communist leadership under Mao succeeded in achieving its objectives of reforming China's institutions of manpower training? From appearances, many of the objectives seem to have been achieved. Indeed, one cannot recall any other case in modern history in which such drastic changes have been introduced to a system of education within a few years. Both the curricula and textbooks have been completely revised, from elementary school to university. The school systems have been changed to incorporate manual labor as an intrinsic part of manpower training. A unique admission procedure, hitherto unheard of, has been established. Evaluation of students is done in a variety of ways that would shock many a traditional educator. Administrative decision-making is now in the hands of peasants, workers, Party cadres, students, and teachers in what is peculiarly known as a three-in-one union. The time-honored method of lecturing has given way to discussion and criticism. Learning is no longer a matter of memorizing or understanding what is in the books, but is a process of acquiring and sharing experience by living it.

These changes, however, have not been achieved without considerable cost. The overall objective of the Chinese Communist manpower training programs is the ideological, intellectual, and physical development of the people to assume the role of laborers with socialist class consciousness. Although we do not have much direct evidence, it seems the manual labor now required during and between periods of schooling has contributed to the physical development of the Chinese younger generation. The Chinese young men and women we see on television today are no longer the stereotype of traditional scholars who are described as ''not having enough strength to grasp a struggling chicken.'' They appear to be physically well developed. But intellectual and ideological development seems to be a different matter.

Even though China's new educational system provides the students with ample practical experience, it is difficult to see how intellectual development can be pursued to a high level when knowledge for its own sake is decried. It is true that Chinese scholars in the past tended to apply their time to the kind of esoteric academic exercise that seemed to have no immediate relevance. In a strict utilitarian sense, their efforts could be a waste, an investment of manpower with uncertain returns. But if a whole country tackles practical problems only, if no basic research is undertaken, then the result could be intellectual stagnation. There are already indications that such a trend is developing among high school and university students, who believe that education is useless. Furthermore, if we assume that what one learns is largely predetermined by how one is going to be evaluated, then additional questions can be raised about the nature of education in China today. The peasants and the workers may be down to earth and wise in a practical sense, and their input into the learning process may help to take the students out of their ivory tower. But if the peasants and workers have a major voice in the evaluation of students, as they seem to now, then it becomes questionable whether a very high standard of intellectual development can be achieved. Another factor that would likely slow down the pace of intellectual development is the infusion of ideology into learning. It is true that most disciplines have their biases and blinders and are thus not entirely free of ideological constraints. But if every discipline has to be cast in the uniform confines of one ideology, or rather one particular interpretation of that ideology, one would begin to doubt how it is possible to have the kind of exchange of ideas that is so crucial to intellectual growth.

It is interesting to note that, in their stated objective of manpower training, the Chinese Communist leaders have placed ideological development ahead of intellectual and physical development. Under the new system, an enormous emphasis is focused on the ideological aspects of education, on the creation of the New Chinese Man. When one is reminded of the virtues of the proletarian ideology day in and day out—by teachers, by fellow students, by workers and peasants—it would be difficult to see how the barrage of indoctrination could fail to have some effect. Indeed, the fragmentary evidence we have would suggest rather profound effect on children. The ideological communication employed by the Party does seem to have created a generation of children whose beliefs and values are different from those of the previous generation. However, the positive effects seem to wear off as the children grow older. By the time they reach college age, for many if not most, their strong ideological convictions seem to have been diluted by exposure to the old adult culture and by frustration and worry because of the uncertainty that surrounds their lives.

Although its stated ultimate goal is the ideological conversion of the mass of people, for the immediate present, the Chinese Communist party seems to be relying more on changing the structural constraints as a means of bringing about a transformation of Chinese society. One example is the movement of ''go up to the mountains and down to the villages." This is the pivotal feature in China's manpower training programs, perhaps far more important than changes in the curricula and school system. Without the Rural Resettlement movement, all other changes would be peripheral. Essentially the same type of students would be enrolled as before, and when they graduated, they would be absorbed into the same upper-level occupational strata. The children of peasants would have relatively little chance of moving out of the villages into non-agricultural jobs. The Rural Resettlement movement reversed this pattern by changing the procedures of admission and job assignments upon graduation. Now, as previously mentioned, when students graduate from junior high school, they are assigned to two years of manual labor, mostly in the communes. Only those who are favorably evaluated by the peasants and workers are allowed to proceed to senior high schools. The same process is followed in selecting high school graduates who are to have a chance at college education. Thus, the routes of educational and occupational mobility are entirely changed. Most students in colleges today are children of peasants, workers, and members of the Liberation Army. From both Communist publications and visitors' accounts, the Rural Resettlement movement seems to be a major source of frustration for city children. But if this movement should persist for many more years, the frustration would probably become more widely accepted. In time, a fundamental social transformation may take place through a massive migration of urban residents to rural areas. Many students from the cities will find it necessary to lower or modify their aspirations and to adapt to life in the villages where they must settle permanently. At the same time, the Party's official policy of proletarian class preference and evaluation procedures can be expected to produce in future a new crop of elite individuals from peasant and worker families. Because of their experience in manual labor and a higher level of education, these individuals would be the ones to hold key positions in different strata of the social organization. They would have both the desirable class backgrounds and the task-related qualifications to move up the social ladder when opportunities arise. If and when this happens, a new social order will come to China as a consequence of the changes in educational institutions.

Until then, one wonders how long China's new institution of manpower training will last. By "institution" here we mean not just a university or a bureaucratic office, but an entire system, with its organized patterns of interactions. The life of an institution is largely dependent on its functional relations with other institutions, on whether it serves some useful purposes for a significantly large group of individuals or for a society as a whole. In a societal perspective, China's manpower training programs should be functional to the overall economic development of the country. From all indications, the programs seem to be producing various kinds of trained manpower for the tasks of development, even though there might be more efficient ways of achieving the same ends. However, for an institution to carry on, it must also fulfill some individually oriented functions, by satisfying a minimum of individual needs. At least for the time being, China's new institution of manpower training does not appear to be fulfilling the objectives of those individuals who previously had better access to scarce goods and services. These individuals have temporarily lost control of the power of decision-making, which led to the institutional changes. Events in mainland China in early 1976 suggest that they have not entirely given up, and that a struggle for power is still going on.[122] If in the future these individuals should regain some of their lost power, one may expect to see a reinstitution of some of the old practices in China's system of education. If that does not happen, say in the next fifteen or twenty years, then China's new institution of education may very well acquire a life of its own.

VI
Communication and
Decision-Making Processes

On August 9, 1958, following his inspection in Honan and Hopeh, Chairman Mao Tse-tung came to Shantung for a meeting with a group of Party leaders and high-level provincial cadres. After listening to their reports on agricultural organizations, he commented in his usual low-key manner; "(I'd) rather think the commune would be better. It has the advantages of putting the workers, peasants, traders, students, and soldiers together, and makes it easier to lead them."[1]

Thus started the most unusual social experiment in China's history, the Commune movement. The year 1958 was an eventful milestone for mainland Chinese. That spring, the Great Leap Forward had been launched, leaving a lasting impact on Chinese society.[2] In August, the Liberation Army started the offshore island war against Quemoy. Shortly after Mao's pronouncement, the millions of Chinese peasants learned that they were going to begin a new life in what was known as the People's Commune. That the Chinese people were unprepared for this new life was indicated by a feature story in the *People's Daily* in early September, in which three reporters professed that they knew absolutely nothing about the commune.[3]

We shall examine the Commune movement because it provides a

case study of the decision-making process within China's leadership structure. By *decision-making,* we are referring to the process of evaluating alternative courses of policy actions, and finally selecting one to pursue. In a traditional society in which life had few choices for most people, the occasion for this kind of decision-making was infrequent. Because of the static social-economic structure, a routine life generally prevailed for both private citizens and public administration. An old Chinese saying puts it in a perhaps simplified way, "The men till and the women weave; they start to work at sunrise and retire to rest at sunset." Unless the system was disturbed either by internal calamities or by external pressure, the government rarely found itself in a position of having to choose from among several alternatives for a new policy action.

The needs of development force the status quo to change. By its very nature, development necessitates a departure from the old way of life and requires continuous explorations into the untried world for new means of utilizing material and human resources. The policymakers are compelled to assess alternative possibilities with respect to the allocation of resources as well as the organization of manpower. Important decisions will have to be made, presumably in a rational manner on the basis of an objective evaluation of the best available information. The process of decision-making has far-reaching implications because huge resources are likely to be committed. The pace and direction of development may hinge on the kinds of decisions the government makes. It is for these reasons that the decision-making process becomes an important aspect of development.

A number of factors recommend the People's Commune as a relevant case for studying the decision-making process in China. It is perhaps the single most important decision the Chinese Communist party has made since it came into power in 1949. It involved nearly the entire population of the mainland in an unprecedented manner. The course of events that developed during the Commune movement necessitated a rather drastic change in the original decision, thus allowing us to observe not only the process of original decision-making, but also the process of modification. There is another advantage in studying this case: most of the important decisions involved in the Commune movement have been officially recorded.

Primarily using official Chinese publications, we shall first present a brief account of the major events leading up to the People's Commune. We shall examine how the Communist leadership gathered information on the feasibility of the commune experiment, how the original decision was reached, and how communication was used to pave the way for the official announcement of the decision and to generate popular support. We shall further demonstrate how communication helped maintain a flow of feedback information for assessing the progress of the movement. Finally, we shall review the roles of communication which enabled the Party leadership to size up the rapidly aggravating situation and to modify its original decision.

Prelude and Feasibility Testing

From all indications, the Commune movement seemed to have developed with some degree of haste. Agricultural production in China had barely moved to the advanced cooperative stage in 1956 after a succession of reorganizations that began with the Land Reform movement. The change from traditional tenant farming to collective agricultural production had been so fast and the mood of the peasants so unsettled that even Mao himself, speaking in early 1957, estimated that it would take at least five more years before the Party could consolidate the agricultural cooperatives and take a step forward.[4] In the *Plans for Rural Development in Twelve Years (1956-1967)* approved by the Party's Central Committee in May 1958, there was not the slightest hint of the commune.[5]

The enigma as to why the Commune movement was decided upon still remains unsolved. Nevertheless, we can gain some clues from the circumstances that led to the Commune movement, particularly from the events since the winter of 1957. In November that year, Mao went to Moscow to meet with Nikita Khrushchev and to negotiate the renewal of Russian economic aid. He returned without a commitment. From December 1957 to March 1958, Mao took off on extensive tours across the country, apparently looking for ways of further developing China's economy without additional Russian aid. During his trip, Mao held three important conferences with the Party's regional leaders in Hangchow, Chekiang Province (December 1957), Nanning, Kwangsi Province (January 1958), and Chengtu, Szechuan Province (March 1958). If any records were kept of these meetings, few have yet been released. It is safe to assume that the Great Leap Forward movement, which was subsequently proclaimed in May 1958, had been discussed and approved during one of those secret conferences. It is also safe to assume, judging by later events, that the Party leaders examined alternative ways of boosting agricultural production but failed to reach a conclusion. But the trend seemed to be clear. Both Chairman Mao and the Party appeared to be leaning toward massive mobilization of China's only major resource, manpower, in their search for a way of continued development.

Essentially, the Party had two options: to keep the agricultural cooperatives in their original sizes, about two hundred to three hundred families each, or to move toward larger production units by merging the current small cooperatives.[6] As later events revealed, the Party leadership was split over this issue, and heated debates went on for some time. Mao was represented as basically in favor of the larger cooperatives. Although it was not disclosed who were opposed, Liu Shao-chi was probably one. Significantly, Liu was the one who officially announced the Great Leap Forward, but he said almost nothing about the commune during the height of the movement. The fact that the Party eventually chose Liu to pick up the pieces after the initial commune failure would strongly suggest that he had not favored the experiment.

Nevertheless, the arguments supporting the large cooperative concept—thus far without an official name—appeared to be rather overwhelming, as it was subsequently revealed. With a large cooperative of over a thousand families, it would be possible to adopt mechanized farming and cut down the cost of management. A more efficient division of labor could be worked out in order to engage not only in agriculture but also in handicrafts and small industries. Convincing data were cited to support these arguments by contrasting the financial conditions of large and small cooperatives.[7] The Anfeng Cooperative of Honan, which had more the one thousand families, increased its total production by 170 percent from 1956 to 1957 and set aside 160,000 JMP for capital investment. It was able to acquire 960 modern farm tools, 1,604 sprayers, 47 power pumps, 39 sewing machines, three tractors, one diesel generator, and eight small lathes. It also built a kiln for making tiles. Its bonus for 1957 amounted to 150 JMP for each person. Its neighboring Hanchiato Cooperative had only 185 families. With its meager public funds, it bought only a few modern farm tools and no power equipment at all. Its bonus for 1957 was 41 JMP for each person.

Although no definite decision was made at the conferences, those who favored the large cooperatives seemed to have gained some ground as a result of the debates. Immediately after the Chengtu conference, unpublicized work proceeded at Chayashan, Juiping County, Honan Province, in April that year to combine a number of small cooperatives into a single production organization on an experimental basis. This experiment was apparently intended to test feasibility of combining and to provide more information as a basis for future decision-making. Eventually, 27 agricultural cooperatives in the neighborhood were reorganized into a big cooperative having a total membership of 9,360 families.[8] Shortly afterwards, similar experiments went unpublicized in several other locations, including Pingyu, Chiliying and Shangchen, Honan Province; Hsushui, Hopeh Province; Shangchih, Heilungkiang Province; Chi-hsien, Shansi Province; Kaiping, Liaoning Province. These experiments were revealed later during the Commune movement in the fall of 1958.[9] The news blackout was such that the mass media played no part during the stage when the Party leadership was collecting information on the commune's feasibility. All the activities of information gathering went on through the Party's closely supervised internal channels of communication. A tight control of information was probably imposed even within the Party; the groups engaged in those experiments did not seem to know what other groups were doing. For instance, the name "People's Commune" was not uniformly employed for all the experiments. In Shansi Province, the merged cooperatives were called *Lao Tung Ta Chun*, or "huge labor army."[10] In Liaoning Province, they were simply referred to as *Ta She*, or "large cooperative."[11] There was no indication during the subsequent commune campaign in August and September as to whether any of those experimental communes had ever consulted one another.

A number of developments suggested that the focus of the initial experiment seemed to be on Chayashan in Honan. The Chayashan big cooperative was the first one to develop and adopt the commune organization. The fact that it did not call itself Chayashan Commune, but instead assumed the rather dignified title of Wei-hsin (Sputnik) Commune would further speak for its importance.

When work began in April to merge the small cooperatives at Chayashan, problems were almost inevitable. By late July, most of the difficulties had probably been ironed out. It was at Chayashan that a regional conference was called from July 29 to August 5, 1958, to take a final look at the feasibility of the commune experiment.[12] Apparently, detailed regulations about the organization and operation of the commune had been drafted and presented to the conference. They were approved at the conference and adopted by the Sputnik Commune on August 7, 1958, although the public announcement was withheld till early September. These were the only commune regulations publicized and editorially praised by the official *People's Daily*.[13]

Significantly, the formal approval of the Sputnik Commune regulations coincided with Mao's inspection trips. On August 4, 1958, Mao visited Tachikuo cooperative in Hsushui County, Honan Province. This was apparently one of the rural districts chosen by the Party for testing the commune concept. A report in the *People's Daily* gave a glowing account of the warm reception the villagers gave for Mao and the impressive statistics the village cadres had prepared. Wearing grey pants and a white shirt, Mao engaged in a jovial conversation with Li Chiang-sheng, the chief of the village cooperative, and village Party secretary Yen Yu-ju:

"How is this year's wheat harvest?"

"Very good, better than any year before," replied Li Chiang-sheng.

"How many catties per *mu?*" Chairman Mao asked. [One *mu* is about one-sixth acre.]

"754 catties!" said Party secretary Yen Yu-ju.

"Ah!" Chairman Mao exclaimed in approval. "That's a lot."

After listening to a brief report, the *People's Daily* account continued, Chairman Mao widened his eyes, looked around the room smiling, and said:

"This summer you reaped more than 90,000,000 catties of grains. Now you are going to have an autumn harvest of 1,100,000,000 catties. What are you going to do with your food?"

Everybody was stunned by Chairman Mao's question. Finally,

Chang Kuo-chung (the first secretary of Hsushui County) said: "We'll use our grains to exchange for machinery."

Chairman Mao said, "It's not just your county that's having a food surplus. Every county is having a food surplus. You want machinery, but other people don't want your grains."

"We can use the sweet potatoes to make alcohol," said Li Chiang-sheng.

Chairman Mao said, "Then every county will be making alcohol. How can we use up all the alcohol?"

Chairman Mao laughed, looking around him. Then everybody laughed. Chang Kuo-chung said, smiling, "We were concerned only with producing more food."

Chairman Mao said, "Now you'd better be concerned with how to eat the food."

Many people were whispering in private: "See how far in advance Chairman Mao sees a problem, and how careful he is!"[14]

It was amid such high spirits and optimism that Mao conducted his personal inspection tours of the several experimental cooperatives. At the Tachikuo Cooperative, he visited the mess halls, the nurseries, the lucky homes for the aged, and was greatly impressed. Everywhere he went, he kept asking: "What are you going to do with all this food?" He even told the cadres in the rural district and the cooperative, "Since you have so much food, you can plant less in future. Work half a day, and during the other half, do something cultural, learn science, have some cultural entertainment, start a university and a high school. What do you think?"[15] Someone told him the cooperative already had its red-and-expert university.

According to the same *People's Daily* account, Tachikuo Cooperative had been preparing to establish a commune. After Mao left, the cooperative's cadres called a meeting that very night, and decided to reorganize it into a commune.

Two days later Mao visited Chiliying, in Hsinhsiang County, Honan, where, according to the *People's Daily,* the peasants had "already established the Chiliying People's Commune on the basis of agricultural cooperatives following the instructions of Chairman Mao."[16] This was the only specific reference suggesting that Mao had provided instructions on the organization of the commune. Accompanied by Honan Governor Wu Chih-pu and other high-

ranking Party officials, Mao toured the village and received similarly encouraging reports. He was highly impressed. One local cadre
even promised to bring the good news of a bumper autumn harvest
to Chairman Mao personally in Peking.

The records did not show that Mao ever visited the Chayashan
Sputnik Commune during his tour. Whether he did or not, Mao
was almost certainly kept informed of the progress at Chayashan,
which seemed to be the key experimental commune. Mao was on
his way from Hsushui, Hopeh Province, to Chiliying, Honan Province when the regional conference at Chayashan was concluded. It
was inconceivable that the Sputnik Commune regulations could
have been adopted without his knowledge and blessing. Indeed,
the language and content of the Sputnik Commune regulations
sounded so much like a formal statement of national policy rather
than the working rules of a local cooperative that one wonders
whether these regulations were not penned by someone in the top
hierarchy of the Party. Comparing the Sputnik Commune regulations and the Party's Peitaiho resolutions on the People's Commune later passed on August 29, one sees a striking similarity except for the operational details contained in the former.

In all probability, when Mao left Honan and proceeded to Shantung on August 9, he had already made up his mind. He must have
felt he had enough information to make a decision. If so, he had
apparently confided his thinking to few aides. The first secretary of
Shantung Province, Tan Chi-lung, obviously failed to read Chairman Mao's mind when he reported during a briefing that the province was ready to experiment with a large collective farm in Pei-
yuan Rural District, Licheng County.[17] This was when Mao made
his much quoted remark: ''(I'd) rather think the commune would
be better.'' This mild rebuff caused Tan Chi-lung to write a special
article in the Party publication *Red Flag* in praise of the People's
Commune.[18] Chairman Mao's words, Tan said, clarified many of
his tangled confusions.

The tone of Mao's remarks, however, suggested some reservations. We suspect that even at the last moment there was opposition from within the Party. Whereas the proponents had a strong
case in the Sputnik Commune and other experimental showcases,
the skeptics had nothing concrete to present except doubts and hesitations. The total absence of public communication under which
the experiments were conducted had prevented any genuine input

from the peasants and lower-level cadres into the decision-making process. The only input Mao received from the grassroots level came during his personal tours, on which an atmosphere of festivity made an objective evaluation all but impossible. Quite possibly Mao himself was swayed by the high spirits and optimism which his subordinates had generated to please him. As a result, Mao and the Party moved into a major decision without obtaining full information on its feasibility.

Involving the People

It is noteworthy that the Party did not immediately give its official approval after Mao had pronounced his blessing. In fact, Mao's comment that he'd "rather think the commune would be better" was never formally announced, but was obliquely cited by others when reporting on the commune movement. What the Party did was to withhold any official proclamation and to launch a synchronized publicity campaign through the mass media and interpersonal channels to promote the People's Commune. Thus, in late August, without much prior notice, the people of China came to learn that the high tide of the People's Commune movement had arrived. The *Red Flag* declared in its editorial unofficially inaugurating the commune movement:

Following the great victories in agricultural production this summer and autumn, the peasants in our vast territories are taking another step to organize themselves. They are merging the small agricultural producers' cooperatives into big ones, turning the agricultural cooperatives into people's communes that incorporate workers, peasants, traders, students, and soldiers into a single organization. The establishment of the people's communes within the boundaries of the entire country is developing into a new, irresistible tide of mass movement.[19]

The mass of people were represented in the editorial as receiving the movement with enthusiasm. The agricultural cooperative, it was suggested, were no longer suitable for the increasing demand of productivity. The commune system, with its pooled manpower and large organization, would be ideal for efficient use of land, construction of irrigation works, mechanized farming, and development of forestry, animal husbandry, fishing, and small industry. The editorial also provided some hints as to the kind of life people could expect in the commune. Not only would the commune produce efficiently, but life would also be collectivized. Women would find it possible to engage fully in productive work in the field, because the commune kitchens would provide food services to all, the nursery schools would take care of babies and children, and the sewing groups would make clothes, and so on. Because of the growing demand for collective labor, because the commune kitchens would feed everybody, the small private garden plots and hog raising by individual peasants would be both infeasible and unnecessary. In short, the commune would represent a transition from collective ownership by the agricultural cooperatives to ownership by the whole people, under which everything would belong to the state.

Meanwhile, the *People's Daily* and the provincial newspapers were filled with stories describing the warm response by the peasants. At the Sputnik Commune in Honan, it was disclosed, the peasants had posted thousands of tatzepao praising the commune and affirming their determination to join. Each family filled out an application form along with a statement of resolute decision. Altogether more the forty-one thousand tatzepao, application forms, and statements of resolution were tallied.[20] At the Chaoying Commune, also in Honan, many cadres and peasants feared that they might not be able to join. Agricultural cooperatives located as far as 20 kilometers away sent representatives carrying loads of applications and statements of resolution to Chaoying Commune to ask for acceptance. When that commune started, it had 13,000 families. The number rose to 15,000 in just one day, and went further to 18,000 overnight. By the time it held its inaugural ceremony two days later, the commune had accepted 20,457 peasant families with a total population of more than 94,000.[21]

A holiday mood was created for the event. The peasants put on their best clothes and paraded in groups to deliver their applications. The parade was preceded by drums and gongs, and decorated by lanterns and banners, as if for a wedding. When the peasants arrived at the commune headquarters, they submitted their applications and then went home to post a "happy tidings" tatzepao. At the Chaoying Commune, 275 such happy tatzepao were posted during the inauguration ceremony.[22]

The inauguration, however, was generally not brought about without some arguments and persuasion. All over the country, the peasants were asked to engage in a *tapienlun* ("big debate") on whether they should establish the commune, what were the advantages of the commune, and whether they could effectively operate the commune. A general pattern was discernible from newspaper reports. In Kuanghua County, Hupeh Province, for instance, establishing the commune was acknowledged to be a major change, to which different class groups would react differently. The poor and lower-middle-class peasants, who were considered generally in favor of the movement, were called together first by the cadres in each agricultural cooperative to exchange views. After they had been convinced, they went to talk to the better-off middle-class peasants, often individually, to clear up their doubts.[23] The open debates, which followed, appeared to be more like a mechanism for promoting favorable public opinions and involving the peasants emotionally than a forum for expressing serious dissent.

At the open debates, the peasants were urged to express their opinions and offer suggestions on the practical implementation of the commune. This was referred to as "blooming and blossoming." An incomplete tally at the Chaoying Commune found some twenty-seven thousand suggestions and opinions blossomed by the peasants.[24] Tatzepao were used extensively as a local medium of communication for the expressed views. More than 10,500 such tatzepao were posted throughout the Chaoying Commune during the opening phase of the movement.[25] In Kuanghua County, Hupeh, which had an agricultural population of 250,000, more than 300,000 tatzepao and statements of resolutions were written and posted. Almost everybody expressed his or her views.[26]

One tatzepao posted by the Hsinlien Production Brigade in Kuanghua County provides an example of what was said in the posters. The original Chinese version was rhymed.

Communist Party
Provides good leadership,
The road of collectivization is so nice.
Mutual aid we got soon after liberation,
Sharing with each other boosted production.
In 1954 we had elementary cooperatives,
Which were even better than mutual aid.
In 1956 toward advanced cooperatives we moved,
Abolishing the system of private land ownership.
Collective production had many virtues,

Co-op members improved their livelihood,
Except the land lots were too small,
Limiting the sizes of waterworks;
Use of machines was inconvenient;
Division of labor fared not so well.
If we want to live still better,
The People's Commune must be started.
All five groups are joined in one,
All five groups are closely united.
A commune is large and manpower is strong,
Industry and agriculture can both surge on.
Technology and culture all will thrive,
To further improve people's livelihood.
Communist leadership is so sure,
Leading us to run to the fore,
With the powerful mass backing us.
The People's Commune will be a success,
The People's Commune will be a success![27]

The commune campaign represented an ingenius combination of informational, normative, and affective communications. Information regarding the commune was disseminated selectively to create a favorable perception of the movement. Group support was carefully organized. At the same time, the peasants were brought to a mood of excitement and gaiety to greet this new venture. In general, it was not until a sufficient base of public support had been generated through discussions within the groups, and not until the sentiments of the peasants had been aroused to a high pitch, that they were asked to write their statements of resolution and fill out the applications.[28]

Normative communication was used effectively not only to mobilize public support, but also to solve practical problems that would affect the peasants directly. This process enabled the peasants to bring their problems to public attention and, through group discussions, to seek a feasible solution. One common problem was that of combining rich and poor cooperatives in the same commune. In Ankuo County, Honan Province, for instance, some of the cadres in the richer cooperatives were reluctant to pool their huge public funds and mechanized equipment into a commune with poorer cooperatives that had little to contribute. This problem came up in several areas within the county and was resolved only through an "open heart" big debate among cadres and peasants. The richer cooperatives realized that they, as the more advanced units, had the responsibility to help the less advanced ones.[29] A similar problem had to do with the responsibility for debts and loan repayments. Some of the small cooperatives had large outstanding debts, which they were eager to unload onto the commune they were about to join. Other members felt it was unfair for them to assume the debts of someone else. After much discussion, it was decided that debts incurred for the purchase of capital investment should be assumed by the commune, while production loans acquired for seeds, fertilizer, and chemicals should be repaid by the cooperatives themselves out of their crops.[30] Another much-debated issue centered on the distribution of rewards, whether "to each according to his needs," or "to each according to his work." At the Hungchi (Red Flag) Commune in Tsinghai Province, some members were in favor of the former. Citing this principle, commune member Chang Ping-kui demanded a fur jacket and a pair of cotton-padded slacks because those were his needs. The Hungchi Commune, like all others, adopted the principle of "to each according to his work" after lengthy discussion.[31]

When the Party unofficially initiated the Commune movement through the mass media, it apparently intended to see how the people would respond before it took an official, final position. If Chairman Mao and his top aides were reading only the reports in the press, they could not help getting the impression that the whole country warmly endorsed the communes. Other than the lanterns and banners and happy tidings parades, there were reports about peasants who were so enthusiastic that they begged for permission to submit all their personal properties to the commune. At the Hsushui Commune, it was reported, some peasants submitted all their private plots, fruit trees, and even their cattle and push carts. They were described as pleading with the commune cadres, "Please let us submit our things. This is the source of our sickness. Once we submit them, our sickness will be cured."[32]

In the midst of such publicized optimism, the Party's Central Committee met at Peitaiho in Hopeh Province, and approved on August 29 a resolution officially endorsing the popular demand for communes.[33] The Peitaiho resolution began by describing the commune movement as inevitable, and predicted an irresistible tide in the near future. However, there were indications that some of the Party's top leaders still had reservations about the communes.

Although the commune resolution was approved on August 29, it was not released until September 10. Apparently, some Party leaders wanted an additional period of waiting. The first official release after the Peitaiho Conference was a statement published in the *People's Daily* on September 1, in which the Party reaffirmed the Great Leap Forward in both agriculture and industry. Almost in passing, the statement said the conference had had a "heated discussion of the problem of establishing the People's Communes in the rural villages of the entire country." The statement did not use the term "resolved," but said it was "pointed out" that the commune was an inevitable trend, and must be established on the basis of the peasants' own volition through blooming, blossoming, and debates by the masses.[34]

Nine days later, the Peitaiho resolution itself was announced. While officially endorsing the Commune movement and laying the general guidelines, the resolution was rather vague about operational details. It set no target date for the completion of the movement, but left it to the local districts to proceed at a pace suited to their own situations. It provided no clear-cut directions on allocating public funds. It saw no need for written stipulations regarding the handling of private plots but suggested that, in general, private plots could probably be collectively managed by the communes, while things like scattered fruit trees could be privately kept for the time being, to be settled later. As for the distribution of rewards, the resolution considered it necessary to stay with the principle of "to each according to his work," but left open the possibility that at a future date, when everything is ready, the communes might distribute the rewards "to each according to his needs."

When the Peitaiho resolution was finally announced on September 10, the Party had irretrievably committed itself to the policy of the People's Commune. The Party pushed through the Commune movement with unusual speed. By October 1, 1958, 90.4 percent of the peasants had been reorganized into 23,397 communes, with an average size of 5,538 families.[35]

Assessing the Progress

In view of the rather serious difficulties the Commune movement eventually encountered, it is inconceivable that these problems did not manifest some symptoms during the initial period before the Party announced its official endorsement. Yet the mass media during those weeks contained nothing but highly favorable reactions. Perhaps the official media had been instructed by the Party not to publish any unfavorable comments. More likely, the local cadres were so overwhelmed by the impressive achievements of the Sputnik Commune and other early experiments that they felt compelled to present a rosy picture. The possibility cannot be ruled out that the Party leaders were pushed into the Commune movement by the tide of public communication which they themselves helped generate.

Soon after the official endorsement in early September, it was noticed that things were not going quite well. A report in the *People's Daily* on September 18 indicated that the conflict of interest between rich cooperatives and poor cooperatives in the communes was far more serious than anticipated. At Chianghuai Commune in Anhui Province, according to that report, there was a mood called "let's eat up till we all become poor."[36] This mood, serious enough to be severely denounced by the official newspaper, seemed to reflect the reactions of the better-off peasants against the commune's collectivization of properties. The following day, a report in the *People's Daily* revealed that in Honan Province, where the Commune movement had been first initiated, steps were being taken to "consolidate" the communes. The report noted the existence of three groups that were not supporting the communes: those who took a wait-and-see attitude, those who were pessimistic about the movement, and a more militant group who prepared "to settle all acounts after the autumn harvest." In Chinese, "to settle accounts" means "to get even." Among the steps taken by the Party authorities in Honan to ease the situation was one to readjust the distribution of commune income for public funds and individual wages, recommended at a 70/30 percent split.[37] The report also mentioned the need for improving the food services, the first indication of complaints about the commune kitchens. Another report in the *People's Daily,* on September 22, noted that certain ex-landlords, rich peasants, counterrevolutionaries, and rightists were taking advantage of the situation to spread rumors and stir up trouble, and attempting to wreck the communes. Although no details were revealed, the public admission itself suggests that the problem was not a minor one. The same report commented on some "disturbances" among local cadres who were afraid of either losing their positions or cutting their salaries when the small agricultural cooperatives were reorganized into a commune. The Party newspaper reassured them by promising to maintain the pay schedules for most cadres and relocate those cadres whose positions might be eliminated.[38]

The Party's Central Committee must have become aware of the adverse reactions by this time. On September 11, immediately after the official announcement of the commune resolution, the Party sent out an inspection team, headed by Li Hsien-nien, a member of the Central Committee and minister of finance, to size up the situation. The group returned to Peking on September 30 after visiting communes in Hopeh, Honan, and Hupeh. What the group actually saw and reported to the Central Committee was never published. But barely enough was revealed in a letter written by Li while on the road, and later published in the official Party magazine the *Red Flag,* to suggest that what he found was not at all reassuring.[39]

Li began by praising the enthusiasm and confidence of the people in the communes and their faith in the Party and Chairman Mao. After these brief introductory remarks, he addressed himself to the practical problems he had observed. One was the distribution of wages. Some cooperatives previously had high wage scales while others had low ones. After they had been reorganized into a single commune, what uniform wage scales should they adopt? A related problem was food and other free services. Some communes provided seven free services: food, clothes, medical care, birth, education, housing, and weddings and funerals. Other communes provided six, five or just one, that is, food. How far should the commune go? This question had practical importance because it implied the degree of collectivization of life. More free services would mean lower cash wages, and less leeway for the peasants to allocate their spending. Providing many services, Li noted, would be even more difficult in urban areas. "What are we going to do in the cities? What are we going to do with factory workers and employees of the state? As seen (by us), the situation is pressing, and we must give timely consideration to this problem."[40]

Party cadres in the communes had their concerns. Li noted that some cadres were worried about having nothing to do after their agricultural cooperatives were reorganized into communes. However, Li offered no solution. This seemed to suggest that the Party had difficulty in carrying out its plan of relocating those cadres who had lost jobs. Another major concern among the cadres had to do with finance, management, and taxation. According to the Party policy, each commune was expected to take over all the properties and employees of the state in its respective area (for examples, banks and state-operated stores), assume the overall financial and managerial responsibility, and submit to the state a designated total of taxes after meeting all expenses. This policy apparently caused so much alarm among the cadres that Li felt the communes should not be required to follow this policy in a rigid, uniform pattern. Rather, each commune should be allowed to work out its own pace and schedule according to the local situation.[41]

The letter itself was written while Li was in Chengchow, Honan Province. Perhaps more significant than the letter was the brief postscript, written after Li had proceeded from Chengchow to Hupeh Province.

> From what we have seen in Hupeh, they seem to be taking even more cautious steps. They have set up the frames of the communes, but for the time being have not touched the lower level organizations. Nor have they adopted the practice of eating without pay (a reference to free food service). They are of the opinion that retail commerce had better not be assigned to the communes. I think this approach is acceptable too. Different places have different situations. We should not force them to follow the same uniform methods of implementation.[42]

Li's counsel for caution contrasted with the earlier mood of enthusiasm and haste presented by the official press. Its publication gave the first indication of a possible readjustment. Meanwhile, reports on unfavorable peasant reactions began to appear in the press. At the Hsushui Commune, one of the early models visited by Chairman Mao, attempts at poisoning the commune food were discovered. These attempts were attributed to ex-landlords, rich peasants, and counterrevolutionaries.[43] Similar attempts were reported in various unidentified places. At the Juiping Sputnik Commune, someone dumped poison into a number of fish ponds, killing millions of fish.[44] Passive resistance appeared to be not uncommon. In some places, no one took care of public grain storage. At the Wuchiatze Warehouse, in Chuangcheng, Heilungkiang Province, for instance, huge quantities of grains were left unattended in the fields. According to incomplete statistics, grain spoilage exceeded three million tan (50 kilograms to 1 tan) in Shansi and Hupeh.[45] In Honan Province, severe loss was noted in packing, transporting, and storing grains, cotton, and tobacco. In one place, more than a dozen bales of cotton were discarded on the roadside for days and ignored.[46] The Party magazine *Red Flag* admitted that many peasants were simply dragging their feet since what one did had little to do with what one would get. The peasants even composed a new folk song:

> Commune work,
> Drag your feet.
> When noon time comes,
> Let's go and eat.[47]

By late October, the Party openly admitted that the commune kitchens were not providing adequate services. An editorial in the *People's Daily* pointed out the error of treating the common kitchens as a small matter. Something that would affect the livelihood of five hundred million peasants, it stated, had to be handled very carefully.[48] Apparently, when the Party instructed the peasants to dismantle their stoves and join the mess halls, it overlooked the importance of stoves as a necessary heating device in northern China. The editorial now suggested that stoves be restored during the coming winter, and that families in northern China be temporarily allowed to cook at home so that they didn't have to walk back and forth in the snow. Soon afterwards more articles appeared in the press to offer practical experiences in managing commune kitchens.[49]

Another editorial in the *People's Daily* dropped the hint that the peasants were not getting enough rest. The editorial praised them for their high spirits in working endlessly day and night, often exceeding their production quota by 200 or 300 percent. The leadership, it said, must look after their health. Citing the experience in Shansi and Hopeh, the official newspaper suggested that the peasants be allowed at least eight hours of sleep on any regular work day, and at least six hours of sleep when performing emergency labor duties. Extra hours of rest were recommended for teenagers and pregnant women workers.[50]

At about the same time, reports appeared in the press on how to combine free supply and wage distribution into an equitable reward system. It was acknowledged that the free supply system put those families with many labor hands at a disadvantage. But they were asked to support the system for the benefit of others who had large families to feed but not enough labor hands of their own. The division of commune income between public funds and individual distribution was also extensively discussed.[51]

The mass media had popularized the communes during the initial phase of the movement; now they provided a mechanism for feedback throughout the country. The official editorials on commune food services and adequate rest indicated to the peasants that their needs were not being neglected. To the cadres, the media pointed out the problems that called for immediate attention. Reports on passive resistance and sabotage suggested that the Party was rather realistic in assessing the situation, once the commune policy had been adopted. These reports could have given the peasants as well as the cadres a hint that perhaps some change was forthcoming. In that sense, they prepared for the subsequent modification of the commune policy.

Revamping the Decision

Although the original decision to establish the communes was reached by the Party leadership without much input from the mass of people, the decision to modify the communes seemed to be made by taking the grassroots reactions into account. The mass media, by reporting on some of the serious difficulties encountered, impressed on the Party leaders the need for reassessment.

Although unfavorable reports did not begin to appear until the second half of September, it is safe to assume that the Party had been aware of the adverse situation much earlier. Quite possibly it was some of the initial symptoms of trouble that held up the official announcement of the Peitaiho resolution for more than ten days. By early November the situation had apparently become so serious that Mao found it necessary to call a special meeting in Chengchow to review the Commune movement, a meeting attended by some of the leading members of the Central Committee as well as prominent provincial leaders. Although the agenda of the Chengchow meeting was not announced, the commune was most probably the center of the discussion. The Chengchow meeting lasted from November 2 to 10, but reached no conclusion. Later events suggested that the pro-commune group within the Party's leadership acquired a breathing period, apparently hoping that in time most of the problems would take care of themselves. Significantly, the closing of the unpublicized Chengchow meeting coincided with a second editorial in the *People's Daily* on the commune food services, in which the official newspaper asked the commune kitchens to provide not only rice, but also vegetables and meat.[52]

The situation, however, continued to worsen. Mao called a second meeting, this time in Wuchang. From November 21 to 27, Chairman Mao and a number of the top leaders of the Central Committee as well as the first secretaries of the Party in the various provinces, municipalities, and autonomous regions met in a caucus. Immediately afterwards, from November 28 to December 10, Mao convened the sixth plenary session of the Eighth Central Committee, attended by 84 members and 82 alternate members. Both the Chengchow meeting and the Wuchang meeting prepared for the plenary session, as it was later officially announced.[53] That the Party's top leaders met for a total of 29 days in three lengthy meetings within a month and a half would fully speak of the enormousness and urgency of the problems.

The outcome was no less startling. The Party decided to back down from its original position regarding the communes. Chairman Mao asked that he not be nominated as candidate for chairman of the People's Republic of China for the next term, although he would remain as chairman of the Party's Central Committee. The Party accepted his request. The full text of the Party's communique was as follows:

> In the past few years, Comrade Mao Tse-tung has more than once expressed to the Central Committee of the Party the wish that he should not continue to hold the post of Chairman of the People's Republic of China. Following full and all-round consideration, the Plenary Session of the Central Committee has decided to approve this proposal of Comrade Mao Tse-tung's, and not to nominate him again as candidate for Chairman of the People's Republic of China at the First Session of the Second National People's Congress. The Plenary Session of the Central Committee deems this to be a completely positive proposal, because, relinquishing his duties as Chairman of the state and working solely as Chairman of the Central Committee of the Party, Comrade Mao Tse-tung will be enabled all the better to concentrate his energies on dealing with questions of the direction, policy, and line of the Party and the state; he may also be enabled to set aside more time for Marxist-Leninist theoretical work, without affecting his continued leading role in the work of the state. This will be in the better interests of the whole Party and of all the people of the country. Comrade Mao Tse-tung is the sincerely beloved and long-tested leader of the people of various nationalities of the whole country. He will remain leader of the entire

people of various nationalities even when he no longer holds the post of Chairman of the state. If some special situation arises in the future which should require him to take up this work again, he can still be nominated again to assume the duties of the Chairman of the state in compliance with the opinion of the people and the decision of the Party. Party committees at all levels should, in accordance with these reasons, give full explanations to the cadres and masses both inside and outside the Party at appropriate meetings of the Party, sessions of the people's congresses of various levels, meetings of workers in industrial and mining enterprises, and meetings in people's communes, offices, schools and armed units, so that the reasons for this may be understood by all and that there may be no misunderstanding.[54]

Although the Party's decision approving Chairman Mao's request was made on December 10, the communique was not issued until December 17. It appeared in the *People's Daily* on December 18 under the banner headline "Chairman Mao Always Leads Us." The one-week postponement in publicizing the communique was apparently necessary to prepare the Party cadres for this event and to enable them to give full explanations to the masses of people. When the news was announced, many papers carried headlines in red above the communique, along with charts showing the figures of major industrial and agricultural output in 1957, the rocketing figures of estimated production in 1958, and the targets for 1959.[55]

The Party's Wuhan resolution on the commune, issued at the same time as the communique on Chairman Mao, began on a similarly optimistic note:

In 1958 a new social organization appeared, fresh as the morning sun, above the broad horizon of East Asia. This was the large-scale people's communes in the rural areas of our country which combines industry, agriculture, trade, education, and military affairs and in which government administration and commune management are integrated. Since their first appearance the people's communes with their immense vitality have attracted widespread attention.

The movement to set up people's communes has grown very rapidly. Within a few months starting in the summer of 1958, all of the more than 740,000 agricultural producers' cooperatives in the country, in response to the enthusiastic demand of the mass of peasants, reorganized themselves into over 26,000 people's communes. Over 120 million households, or more than 99 percent of all China's peasant households of various nationalities, have joined the people's communes. This shows that the emergence of the people's communes is not fortuitous; it is the outcome of the economic and political development of our country, the outcome of the socialist rectification campaign conducted by the Party, of the Party's general line for socialist construction and the great leap forward of socialist construction in 1958.[56]

In essence, however, the Wuhan resolution made a number of important revisions. First, it acknowledged that city conditions were more complex than those in the countryside, and noted that the Party should not be in a hurry to set up people's communes on a large scale in the cities. In the rural countryside, the resolution noted, there was not enough experience in running and developing the communes. The urgent tasks were to consolidate the communes, define their working systems, and improve the organization of production and life. The resolution reaffirmed the principle of distribution "to each according to his work" and stated that "the wage paid according to work done must occupy an important place over a long period and will, in certain periods, take first place." On the controversy between accumulation of public funds and distribution of individual wages, the resolution advised that the portion of a commune's income used to meet the individual and collective expenses of the members should be increased annually in order to improve the livelihood of the people year by year. The scope of free supply should not be too wide. Commune kitchens should be well run. The resolution ruled out the redistribution of personal property, and made clear that houses, clothing, bedding, and furniture, as well as bank deposits would remain with individual members, and would always belong to them. When necessary, the commune might borrow the surplus housing space of members with their consent, but ownership would still rest with the owners. Members could retain odd trees around their houses, small farm tools, small instruments, small domestic animals, and poultry. They could also continue to engage in some small domestic side-line occupations if these did not hamper their collective labor. The resolution asked Party cadres "to make earnest self-criticism and listen with modesty to the masses' opinions." The mass of people were to be mobilized "with great daring to air their views freely and frankly, to carry out debates and post tatzepao, to commend good persons and deeds, to criticize wrong ideas and bad styles of work, to sum up experiences, to clarify the line of work, and to develop a thorough going socialist and communist ideological education movement."[57]

Thus concluded the initial phase of the commune movement. Five months later, on April 27, 1959, the second National People's

Congress elected Liu Shao-chi chairman of the People's Republic of China. Liu's policy, known as *San Chih I Pao,* reverted close to the advanced cooperatives. The commune members were allowed to retain and cultivate the small private plots around their houses, and to sell the products at open markets. While a commune consisted of a number of production brigades, and under each of those a number of production teams, the actual labor of production was organized around small consortiums of a few families each. The families in a consortium took care of the cattle and farm tools they used. Although they could be organized into a larger labor force whenever needed, they normally worked in the same designated field, for which they assumed responsibility.[58] Agricultural production quotas were set on the individual families, not on the collective. This practice was intended to provide the flexibility of efficient use of rural manpower while minimizing foot-dragging. The communes had to pledge to deliver to the state their share of taxes and grains. Beyond that, the communes were free to dispose of their profit, or assume responsibility for any loss, in ways that they saw fit.

Liu's policy of *San Chih I Pao* came under severe criticism in theory during the Cultural Revolution. In practice, however, the Party leadership under Mao did not take strong steps to abolish it, except for the restoration of collective production quotas. Perhaps the enormous difficulties caused by the hasty Commune movement in 1958 had made the Party somewhat wary about changing the structure of agricultural production. Compared to the cities, the rural communes were relatively undisturbed during the Cultural Revolution, despite sporadic reports of violence. In 1970, the Party revived its earlier movement of "in agriculture, learn from Tachai."[59] While the Tachai Brigade was praised for its ideological dedication and highly efficient collective farming, the movement apparently tried to convince the peasants that they could increase their overall production and live well, as Tachai did, by doing away with private plots and an open market. The learn from Tachai movement, however, seemed to have produced indifferent results. Recent visitors to China found that commune members still retained their private plots and were able to sell their surplus products on the open market.[60] The new constitution adopted on January 17, 1975 has now given official approval to small private plots and family sideline productions, provided they do not threaten the supremacy of the commune's collective economy.[61]

The Decision-Making Process

It seems that the decision-making process in the case of the People's Commune was, by and large, not open, but confined within a relatively small circle of top-level Party leaders. The impetus for the Commune movement came from the Party leadership in its attempt to seek new ways of economic development. The movement did not originate from popular demands of the people. In fact, the mass of people were not informed until after the decision had been made.

However, the commune decision was certainly not made by one man, even though the influence of Chairman Mao was strong. Within the top hierarchy of the Party there had been prolonged discussions of the commune as one of the alternatives. Before the decision was made, the Party went through a phase of information gathering to test the feasibility of the commune by conducting a number of unannounced experiments. It is entirely possible that the Party leadership ordered these experiments with an open mind. Subsequent events, however, suggest that the local cadres who carried out the experiments did so with a predetermined mind to succeed, rather than to evaluate feasibility. If this had been the case, then the eagerness of the local cadres to succeed and please the top leadership, even to the extent of ignoring some aspects of reality, appears to be a major weakness in the system. It would tend to deprive the Party of an objective basis of decision-making.

Although we do not know what data were presented to Mao during his inspection tour of Honan, Hopeh, and Shantung in early August 1958, later events suggest that he most probably got a highly favorable picture. From Mao's comment, it seems that he approved the Commune movement with some slight misgivings. One might wonder whether his and the Party's decision would have been different had Mao been presented with an objective assessment.

Up to this point, all the information concerning the commune was restricted within the organizational channels of the Party. Once the decision was made, but before it was officially announced, a massive communication campaign using all media and interpersonal channels was launched to involve the peasants and to generate their support. The course had already been set for them, so that they did not have the option not to join the communes. But the peasants were given some choice regarding minor practical details in implementing the movement. While the mass media were presenting a uniform picture of popular support, group pressure was brought to bear on the individual peasants to enroll them in the communes. Not until the media had created the appearance of popular demand, and not until the forces of group pressure had been fully set in motion, did the Party officially announce the Commune movement.

The mass media played the role of generating popular support up to this point. After the official announcement was made, the media began to take on the role of assessing the reality and carrying feedback information from the grassroots level up to the Party hierarchy, while maintaining their former role of support. Once the Party had made a public commitment to the commune, it had an interest in being informed of its progress.

The rather spotty but nevertheless objective assessment of reality by the mass media, which one could gather through a façade of enthusiastic public response, seemed to have a number of important functions. First, it signaled to the masses of peasants that their problems were not being ignored, and that they could count on the official media to air some of their grievances and gain the attention of the Party hierarchy. It also indicated to the local cadres what problems should be attended to immediately, and in what manner. These signals were essential in order to hold the popular sentiments of the peasants within manageable bounds. Second, it paved the way for a policy change if such a change should become necessary. It gave the Party leadership some room for flexibility. But perhaps more significantly, these signals brought the peasants' problems from the confines of private complaints to the domain of public attention, and created an atmosphere in which divergent views could be more readily expressed and discussed within the Party leadership. Not that the reports in the media eventually convinced the Party to change its course of action. The Party obviously had other sources of information, for instance, the visits made by Finance Minister Li Hsien-nien, which told the top leaders much more than was ever revealed in the media. The media reports, it seems, lent some weight, whether intentionally or unintentionally, to the counterarguments that eventually prevailed.

Much has happened since the Commune movement of 1958, and one wonders whether the decision-making process in China has remained essentially the same. From what we know about educational reform in the aftermath of the Cultural Revolution, the answer would seem to be affirmative. There is no evidence to suggest that the impetus of the school reform came from teachers and students. The initial decision was made by the group of Party leaders who were loyal to Mao, and communication played very much the same roles as it did in the commune movement—informing the people, generating their support, and assessing the progress. But we note one major difference which would suggest that the Party leadership had gained more experience since the commune setback in 1958. Instead of conducting experiments in a shroud of secrecy, as it did for the communes, the Party let the schools and universities conduct their own experiments. The mass media acted as a carrier of information, providing general guidelines from the Party and picking up the more successful cases of experiments to serve as models for others. In this manner, the Party avoided its earlier mistake of imposing on the mass of people a system which did not work and from which it had to retreat. In the case of the recent educational reform, the initial policy decision was still made within a small circle, but, within limits set by the Party, most of the implementational details were worked out through extensive communication among students and teachers as well as peasants, workers, and military representatives.

As far as decision-making is concerned, the social system in China may be characterized by a closed, small network of Party leaders at the top, and a vast network of people at the bottom (figure 5). There are lines of communication linking up these two networks, partly through the mass media of communication and partly through the organizational channels of the Party apparatus. The relations between the small network at the top and the large network at the bottom are rather unique. All important decisions at a national level are made within the top circle, to which the people in the bottom circle have practically no access without special allowances. Before a major decision is made, the top circle depends primarily on the Party's own organizational channels to obtain information relevant to the decision-making, partly from the people.

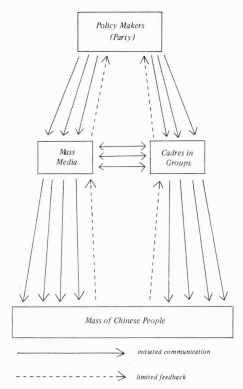

Figure 5. Communication in the Decision-Making Process in China

The initiation of communication comes primarily from the top. The people in the bottom circle may be the source of information, but they are generally kept in the dark as to what the information might be used for. Indeed they may not even know they are engaged in providing information. Nevertheless, information obtained in this manner plays an essential role in the decision-making process. There appears to be no assurance, however, that the Party can count on the internal channels alone for adequate and valid information it would need for making decisions. The information the Party received through such channels during the initial phase of the commune experiment was evidently inadequate. The quality of such information may have improved since then.

The top and bottom circles are further linked through the mass media channels, which come into full play after an initial decision is made. Communications through the mass media proceed from both top and bottom. The mass media carry guidelines for the policy implementation to the peasants and workers, and send feedback information regarding obstacles and difficulties to the Party leadership. If information within the Party that has led to the initial decision should prove to be inadequate, the inadequacy would be caught at this point through mass media communication. The Party apparatus would be operating to provide information throughout, except that it would be aided by mass media communication after the initial decision has been made. It is important to note that the people in the bottom circle cannot directly tell the leaders in the top circle what they do or do not want. They cannot initiate a decision. They can only hope that their expectations will somehow be taken into consideration in the decision-making process. But when a decision is made, presumably after taking into account some of their expectations, the people in the bottom circle can influence the implementation of the decision by pointing out its impractical features, provided that they do not challenge the policy decision itself.

VII
Communication and Conflict Resolution

Conflict, according to Maoist ideology, is the source of energy for development and progress.[1] It is through the conflict between the exploited class and the exploiters, this ideology contends, that the productive forces of labor can be released from the old relationships governing production in order to support socialist construction.

A fundamental class conflict is assumed to characterize the relationships between control of the means of production and the forces of production:

> When at a certain stage the relations of production seriously interfere with the development of the forces of production, the conflict and struggle will sharpen between the reactionary class that represents the old relations of production and the revolutionary class that demands new relations of production. Such conflict and struggle will basically end when the reactionary class is overthrown and the new relations of production are established.[2]

Chairman Mao Tse-tung refers to conflicts of this kind as "contradictions between the people and the enemies."[3] Such conflicts are considered antagonistic in nature, and have been handled as such. The landlord-tenant relations were regarded as "contradictory" to (that is, limiting) the full growth of agricultural productivity, and were abolished in the Land Reform movement. After several stages of transition, new patterns of agricultural production have been institutionalized in the communes. The Communist party saw similar conflicts between owners and workers in industry and business, and took steps to liquidate private ownership. Now, all manufacturing industries and trades are under state ownership and operation. The roles of communication in these tortuous moves of social transformation have already been discussed.

With the removal of landlords and business owners from their control of capital production materials, the "contradictions" between the people and the class enemies were considered largely resolved. However, Mao recognized a different variety of conflicts, that is, conflicts among the people. In Mao's thinking, "people" has the specific meaning that ". . . all classes, strata, and social groups which approve, support and work for the cause of socialist construction belong to the category of the people, while those social forces and groups which resist the socialist revolution, and are hostile to and try to wreck socialist construction, are enemies of the people."[4]

In practice, peasants, workers, and those intellectuals who are not opposed to the Communist government are included in the category of "the people." Conflicts among the people, Mao has acknowledged, exist between collective interests and individual interests, between democracy and what he calls centralism, and between those in leadership positions and the led, largely arising from the bureaucratic practices of certain state functionaries in their relationships with the masses. Such conflicts, Mao has declared, are nonantagonistic, and should be resolved on the basis of unity, not division. The formula Mao has proposed for resolving conflicts among the people is: "unity—criticism—unity." "To elaborate, this means to start off with a desire for unity and resolve contradictions through criticism or struggle so as to achieve a new unity on a new basis."[5]

Mao and his Party have been actively concerned with the "nonantagonistic" conflict apparently for a number of reasons. *Conflict* in this sense refers to the contention over decision-making regarding the use of scarce material resources and the award of status. According to the German sociologist Georg Simmel, conflicts of this nature are inherent in any society, so that no group can be completely harmonious.[6] In a traditional society, like old China, social relations, with their commensurate distribution of rewards, were highly stabilized so that conflicts tended to lie dormant, but were not nonexistent. In a society undergoing rapid change, when the old social relations are disrupted but the new social relations have not been firmly established, people tend to jockey more intensively for positions and access to decision-making. Conflicts will likely be aggravated. The pace of development will undoubtedly depend on how such conflicts are resolved, and on whether human and material resources are concentrated on constructive enterprise or diverted to internecine warfare. In other words, the process of development inevitably generates conflicts, which need to be resolved in a way conducive to, not destructive of, the release of energy. Thus, conflict resolution becomes an important issue to China, as it is to any other developing country.

There is a second reason why Mao's China is so much concerned about conflict resolution among her people. While in other countries conflict is an inevitable by-product of development, China has chosen to employ conflict as an active instrument of development. Through the Party-directed class struggles, the Chinese people have learned to confront their erstwhile superiors as a way of correcting inequitable distribution of rewards and status. Their participation in the class struggles has been essential in hastening the downfall of the landlords and urban owners and in bringing about major changes in the social structure. However, through class struggles the Chinese people have also learned to assert themselves, albeit mildly, and to raise demands in a way their ancestors never dreamed of. Since the state has now assumed overall responsibility for the use of material resources and the award of status, it has inadvertently become the ultimate recipient of these demands. In a sense, the state has inherited the latent conflicts that previously existed between the mass of people and the old elite. Finding effective means of resolving such conflicts therefore becomes vital, not only to the promotion of China's development, but also to the maintenance and integration of the new social system.

In this chapter we shall discuss the source and nature of such conflicts among the people, and the manner in which the Party has sought to resolve them, primarily through communication. The general theme behind the Party's strategy is: By bringing conflicts to the open for public discussion and by examining them in perspectives that are consistent with Communist ideology, the Party will be able to prevent an undue accumulation of tension among the people and to minimize their feelings of frustration toward the state. In other words, the Party counts on the extensive use of communication—the sharing of objectives and sentiments—as a means of resolving conflicts that may arise during the course of drastic social change and development. In examining the Party's communication strategies, we shall give special attention to three media, tatzepao (big character posters), letters to the editor, and *tapienlun* (big debates). These media, as we shall illustrate, are the major mechanisms of conflict exposure and resolution in the social system of mainland China.

Collective versus Individual Interests

The conflict between collective and individual interests is primarily economic in nature. This conflict seems to have presented the most pervasive and difficult problem for the Party over the past two decades. As followers of Marxism, the Chinese Communists regard the control of the means and the fruits of production to be the basis of all social relations. By abolishing private ownership of land and industrial equipment, the Party has succeeded in changing the relationships governing production. No individuals in China are allowed to own any major means of production, and thus no exploiters can exist. In theory, what remains to be done is to distribute the fruits of labor among the peasants and workers equitably, first, to each according to his work, and eventually, to each according to his need. In practice, this is easier said than done. In all these years, through many trials and errors, the Chinese Communist leadership has yet to find a system of distribution that proves to be satisfactory to the mass of people and consistent with Maoist ideology at the same time. The unresolved problems of distribution are reflected in the conflict between collective interests and individual interests, and have caused strains in the relations between the people and the Party cadres. The peasants and workers are inclined to think that since they are the producers of all material goods, they should be entitled to share increasingly in the benefits. The state leadership, thinking primarily in terms of long-range collective goals of socialist construction, has been slow in permitting an improvement of material well-being for the people. The nature of this conflict was well illustrated in an editorial in the *People's Daily:*

> The mass of people are directly engaged in productive labor, primarily manual labor, and generally do not have direct access to adminis-

trative power. Because of their roles, they are apt to observe a problem in their local perspective. They are apt to emphasize the immediate interests in their own locality, and find it difficult to understand the overall situation and problems of socialist construction. On the other hand, those in positions of leadership are directly engaged in exercising administrative power, and generally do not participate in manual labor. They are apt to see the long range and collective interests, and overlook the practical situation and individual needs of the mass of people.[7]

The current practices of allowing representatives of peasants and workers to sit on revolutionary committees and of requiring the Party's administrative cadres to engage in manual labor in the May 7 cadre schools can be seen as attempts to minimize the difference in role-related perspectives. These practices may have some long range effects, but they cannot resolve the more imminent conflict as reflected in the rising demands for better wages and improved individual welfare. We shall cite a few examples from Communist publications to illustrate.

Urban Conflict

One common problem reflecting the collective-individual conflict concerned wages and fringe benefits. At Peking's first lathe factory, this conflict was brought into the open when a number of apprentices took advantage of the "blossoming" campaign in 1957 and posted tatzepao to complain about their low wages.[8] Many posters were written in the name of "poor little apprentices," or "miserable little apprentices." In their tatzepao they wrote: "Prolonging our apprenticeship is to waste our youthful years"; "The future of apprentices is miserable"; "Our life is poor."

A couple of weeks later, one worker, Niu Che-jen, posted a tatzepao under the headline of "Little apprentices are not miserable." He said the apprentices were receiving safety training, learning special techniques from their master workers, and getting paid above the average standard for peasants and the people in general. The following day about a hundred tatzepao appeared in the factory, mostly criticizing Niu: "The wages for apprentices are earned by days and nights of hard labor. They are not high at all. Some apprentices think they are too low." "The standard of living in the whole country is going up, and yet Niu Che-jen wants to lower apprentices' wages. This is simply turning back the wheels of history." "We are the youth of the Mao Tse-tung generation; we de-

serve to enjoy the standard of living of the Mao Tse-tung generation." "Socialist construction is meant to provide good food and
clothes. Does Niu Che-jen want to impose the miserable apprentice life of the old society on us?"

A number of older workers, however, spoke in support of Niu.
Their opinions aroused even greater antagonism among the apprentices and more tatzepao were posted, finally covering the entire
outside walls of the auditorium. Many tatzepao demanded an open
debate. Under the sponsorship of the factory's administrative offices, the debate went on for several evenings in the packed political
classroom. From the account given in the *Worker's Daily*, the debate could be described as heated, with the apprentices un-
yieldingly pressing their demand for higher wages and the older
workers pleading with them to be content with what they had. The
older workers cited statistics to prove that the apprentices already
earned more than the peasants, but the apprentices contended that
they deserved more for their skills. What finally seemed to have
convinced the apprentices was the emotion-laden, personal testimony of a worker about his miserable life as an apprentice in the
old society. It was apparently something the apprentices never experienced and thus could not understand until personally revealed
by a fellow worker. This testimony changed the mood of the debate, which became gradually more favorable to the older workers.
In the end, according to the *Worker's Daily*, the apprentices realized it was wrong to raise these demands with the state. A consensus was reached. This case illustrates the use of affective communication to trigger favorable normative processes that eventually led
to conflict resolution. Only then did the apprentices accept the
standards suggested by the older workers.

The collective-individual conflict for the apprentices was resolved
by deemphasizing individual interests, by suggesting that it was
improper for the apprentices to ask for more. The case of the
Shanghai fountain pen factory illustrates how the same conflict was
resolved by emphasizing collective interests.[9] Workers of the factory, also taking advantage of the "blossoming" campaign of
1957, complained that the leadership in the factory was "too
stingy" and often took advantage of the workers regarding their
fringe benefits. The administrative cadres held a big debate to answer the complaints. The workers asked for an in increase of fringe
benefits of two to four JMP a month, a request they considered to

be highly reasonable in view of the huge profits they produced for the state. Unlike the case of Peking's apprentices, there appeared to be no dissenting voice among the workers. At the debate, the administrative cadres made public the factory's accounts to show that the workers were already receiving the maximum fringe benefits permitted by the state's regulations. To increase the fringe benefits by two JMP would require a change of regulations so that all the twenty-four million factory workers in the nation would be equally treated. This would mean additional expenditures enough to build eight Yangtze River Bridges. Many workers said: "We didn't realize that if we each spend two JMP less, our country can do so many things." Others said: "With two JMP extra, we get four haircuts, or go to restaurant once, or see two Yueh opera shows. Then it's gone. But the state can use them to push ahead with socialist construction." The presentation of information in a value-oriented perspective, that is, patriotism, helped resolve the conflict.

Rural Conflicts

In the villages, the conflict between collective and individual interests manifested itself in the consumption of grains, a problem that was particularly significant in a country that depended on grain export for the purchase of industrial materials. Following the establishment of cooperative farms, private ownership of production materials virtually disappeared in the Chinese villages. Except for small, scattered private plots, no avenues were left open by which the peasants could pursue the advancement of individual welfare. In this context, many peasants felt that since they worked for the cooperative, they had a legitimate claim to as much food as they needed. This thinking was deplored by the Party, as reflected in an editorial in the *People's Daily:*

> During the past, secondary labor hands and children in the family often ate liquid food; now they all want to eat solid food. During the past, the peasants ate less during the non-busy season, now they want to eat just as much whether in busy or non-busy seasons. They complain and fuss if their cooperative does not give them what they want to eat. They feel that you gain if you eat more, and you lose if you eat less. . . . This is an attitude of individual concern that cares only for oneself and not for our nation. If this attitude is not overcome, the socialist construction of our nation will suffer serious losses.[10]

Similar to the individual concern among peasants was the *Peng*

Wei principle (groupism) among rural cadres. The following was printed by the *People's Daily* in the same editorial:

> These cadres are concerned only with some petty gains of their own cooperative or village, and do not see the long-range benefits of the peasantry and the basic objectives of our nation. Acting as a group, they hide their production figures by reporting low crop and high loss, so that their village can get by with selling a small amount of surplus grains and keeping the extra supply for themselves.[11]

Because of these tendencies among the peasants and rural cadres, the editorial noted, the compulsory sales of grains to the government in that year dropped by 3,900,000,000 catties from the year before. This drop was not caused by a decrease in agricultural production, because sales of surplus grains on the open market increased by 12,700,000,000 catties that year.[12] To resolve this conflict between collective and individual interests, the Party employed the technique of normative group communication known as "democratic evaluation." According to the practices in Shang Kao Village, Tai An County, Shantung Province, which were publicized in the *People's Daily,* the peasants were called together by the village cadres and told why it was necessary to cut down grain consumption for the sake of socialist construction. A few peasants would speak up to voice their support. Once a favorable group environment was established, then each family was asked to declare the amount of grain it would need. Whatever then remained was to be submitted to the government for compulsory sale. By setting everything on record, this technique had the dual effect of cutting down grain consumption by the peasants and restraining the village cadres from hiding production figures. Through this kind of group communication, Shang Kao Village was able to exceed its quota of compulsory grain sale by nearly 9 percent during 1957.[13]

Democracy versus Centralism

In the early summer of 1957, the intellectuals of China were presented with the spectacle of the Chinese Communist party severely attacking three prominent statesmen-scholars. In the following months the verbal assaults were to extend to many scholars of lesser prestige all over the country in what has become known as the Anti-rightist campaign.[14] We shall analyze the communication techniques employed by the Party because, unlike land reform, the *Wu Fan* movement, and the suppression of counterrevolutionaries, this campaign was not directed at class enemies, but reflected, in Mao's terms, a "contradiction among the people." The conflict was between democracy and what Mao calls centralism. Essentially it was a contest between the Party leadership and the non-Party intellectuals over the direction of China's economic development as well as the process of decision-making.

The campaign took the Chinese intellectuals by surprise because it came at an unlikely moment and condemned unlikely targets. Only a few months before, following an unpublished but widely known address in February in which Chairman Mao went out of his way to invite criticism of the Party, the nation had just begun to indulge in an outburst of expression hitherto unknown in China. At first most Chinese intellectuals received Mao's call for criticism with caution. When the Party actually encouraged criticism by sponsoring open discussion sessions in April, many began to respond seriously. The brief weeks of April and May saw the blooming and blossoming of the Hundred Flowers. The clamp-down in the aftermath of such raised expectations and indulgence was thus particularly hard to take.

The targets of verbal attacks chosen by the Party were no less surprising. While many well-known scholars were not spared, the vituperation zeroed in on three men: Chang Po-chun, Lo Lung-chi, and Chang Nai-chi. All three were accomplished scholars. Moreover, though not Party members, they had been treated with favor by the Party and given cabinet posts in the central government. Chang Po-chun, first vice chairman of the Democratic League and chairman of the China Peasants and Workers Democratic party, was minister of Communication. Lo Lung-chi, second vice chairman of the Democratic League, was minister of the Timber Industry. Chang Nai-chi, vice chairman of the Democratic National Reconstruction Association, and vice chairman of the National Federation of Industry and Commerce, was minister of Food Supply. All three had been active supporters of the Chinese Communists during the civil war preceding 1949.

Like many other non-Communist scholars, they had spoken up during the Hundred Flowers movement of April and May. But unlike others who had merely voiced complaints of one kind or another, Chang Po-chun, Lo Lung-chi, and Chang Nai-chi had taken actions that set themselves on a course of collision with the Peking authorities. Though too easily drowned out by the ambiguous invectives against the "rightists," the significance of this collision can be seen in the perspective of the nation's policy of economic development. Two basic issues were at stake: What should be the direction of China's development? And who should participate in the process of decision-making regarding development? Although no full records are available on what the three leaders of the rightist groups said and did, enough can be gathered from the subsequent criticisms directed against them to provide a broad outline of the nature of the conflict.

Rightist Contentions

Chang Po-chun, leader of the China Peasants and Workers Democratic party, seemed to be much concerned about the agricultural policy. He had supported the Land Reform movement which redistributed land to peasants, but was opposed to collectivization of agricultural production.[15] Chang's feeling toward the life of peasants was revealed during a forum discussion at his own China Peasants and Workers Democratic party, in which he described what he had seen at the poverty-stricken Wuchin Village one day on his way back from Tientsin to Peking, "There, only 40 *li* from Peking, people have to get ready the night before, bringing their cotton blankets, to line up for three days of ration of mixed grains, some pickled turnip, or a piece of bean cake. Whereas here, [we have] tall buildings, and butter and bread."[16]

Chang took two actions that became intolerable to the Chinese Communist party leadership. He took advantage of the period of relaxed control in the months following the Hungarian Revolution and sent his top organizers to Manchuria, Shantung, Tientsin, and Shanghai to recruit members for his China Peasants and Workers Democratic party. The method he employed was described as not one of "fishing," but one of "casting a big net." In Tientsin, for instance, Chang's party recruited more than two hundred new members within one month.[17] He was quoted by a senior member of his own party as saying that he planned to contest with the Communist party for leadership in the country.[18]

What irritated the Communist authorities more was perhaps Chang's call for setting up a "Political Planning Council" which would have ended the Communist party's monopoly in decision-making. Chang, and likewise Lo Lung-chi, had been complaining about being totally powerless even though they were both cabinet ministers. "Is there anything we can decide on our own? Not only can we not, but we are not even supposed to talk too much," Chang was quoted as saying.[19] The Political Planning Council, as proposed, would take the power of decision-making away from the Communist party and vest it in the council consisting of members from all parties. Chang was quoted as saying: "If you [the Chinese Communists] can't do it, let us give it a try."[20]

A close colleague of Chang Po-chun, Lo Lung-chi incurred the wrath of the Communist party because, like Chang, he opposed radical socialism and favored retaining some form of private enterprise. Lo endorsed Chang's proposal for a Political Planning Council. Even before the council could be established, Lo wanted to set up a "Committee of Mutual Supervision" which would in effect challenge the Communist party's monopoly of executive power.[21] At the same time, Lo was pushing hard for instituting a redress committee, which would set right all the mistrials and grievances caused by the Communist party during the *San Fan* (Three Anti) movement and the Suppression of Counter-Revolutionaries movement. What seemed to have particularly angered the Peking authorities was his suggestion that no members of the Chinese Communist party be allowed to participate in the redress committee, on the ground that a fair investigation would otherwise be jeopardized.[22] Lo, who had lived in Chungking during the war and had many connections there, was apparently working to develop a network of grassroots supporters for the Democratic League in Szechuan Province. He was quoted as having said that the "small intellectuals" of the proletarian class were not qualified to lead the "big intellectuals" of the petite bourgeoise. This remark was considered an insult to the Chinese Communist party.[23]

The concern of Chang Nai-chi, then minister of Food Supply, was primarily for industry and business. Once the owners of factories and commercial establishments had surrendered their assets to the state, Chang argued, the basic differences between the former capitalists and workers disappeared. Now they both worked for the state. The former owners and management staff should be employed and utilized just like any other technicians, and therefore Chang saw no particular need for their ideological reform.[24] Chang did not favor the exclusive predominance of the working class in industry and business, and wanted to restore an equilibrium of checks and balances between the workers and the industrialists. Following the nationalization of private industries and business in 1956, the central government had agreed to pay the former owners interest on their surrendered assets for seven years. There were suggestions from workers groups that the interest payments represented exploitation of the working class and should be discontinued. Chang defended the interest payments, which he defined as "gain without labor" due to the contribution by industrialists, but not exploitation, which would be intentional. He even supported a proposal that the interest payments be extended to twenty years.[25] As vice chairman of the National Federation of Industry and Commerce, Chang had a strong following among industrialists and businessmen. He also spoke out against certain bureaucratic practices of Party officials, which he said were dogmatic and unrealistic, and thus worse than capitalism:

Why is it that the working efficiency of some socialist enterprises and even some of our government organizations is inferior to that of modern, capitalist enterprises? Why is it that modern, capitalist enterprises have high working efficiency? The reason is simple. Capitalists are oriented toward profit, but they also have a spirit of entrepreneurship. In order to make a profit, they have to manage their enterprise well. Naturally, they will want to use talent. In the current Anti-rightist Campaign, we have discovered that some enterprises and government organizations demonstrate in their personnel management a tendency of "seniority substituting for virtue, and virtue taking precedence over talent." Such a tendency of confusing the right with the wrong could not have existed in a modern, capitalist enterprise.[26]

Party Tactics

From April to early June, the leaders of the Chinese Communist party listened to these blunt remarks without making any response. The silence was broken on June 8 by an editorial in the *People's Daily* entitled: "What Is This All About?" In unmistakably strong language, the Party official newspaper noted that a small group of rightists was challenging the leadership of the Communist party and openly demanding its "ouster."

They are attempting to take advantage of this moment and to overthrow the Communist party and the working class. They are attempting to overthrow the great undertaking of socialism and to drag history back to the days of capitalist dictatorship, in fact, to the days of semi-colonialism before the victory of the Revolution. They want to place the Chinese people under the reactionary rule of the imperialists and their running dogs.[27]

The editorial declared that the Party's position would not be shaken, and that the pursuit of class struggle would continue. Apparently, the Party's decision to strike back was made some time after May 25 when the pro-Party remarks of a member of the rightist group were denounced by his colleagues as a "shameful example of aiding the tiger." If someone who defended socialism and the Communist party was considered to be aiding the tiger, said the *People's Daily* editorial, then the Communist party must be the tiger.[28] The editorial made it clear that such insinuation was not to be tolerated. Synchronizing with the appearance of the June 8 editorial, workers in Peking, Shanghai, Tientsin, Shenyang, and Anshan held mass meetings in which they denounced the statements of the rightist leaders.[29]

From the middle of June till early July, under pressure from the Communist party, a number of criticism meetings were held in which Chang Po-chun, Lo Lung-chi, and Chang Nai-chi were attacked by their close associates and erstwhile followers. Each of the three rightist leaders was criticized by members of his own political organization. Many of their critics, like sociologist Fei Hsiao-tung, were well-known scholars, and had themselves voiced similar complaints during the Hundred Flowers blooming in April and May. Their choice appeared to be: Either cooperate with the Party, or themselves be held responsible for what they had earlier said. They chose to cooperate. It was through their testimony that the confidential remarks and organizational maneuvers by the three leaders became publicly known. Eager to clear themselves, the critics made many damaging allegations, which the three rightist leaders were unable to refute. All these criticisms and allegations were published in the *People's Daily* and nationally circulated. After these initial rounds of denunciation, each of the three rightist leaders was brought to face more severe criticisms in his own respective ministry in an official manner.[30] More charges were leveled against them. Meanwhile, at the National Congress of People's Delegates then convening in Peking in July, speaker after speaker mounted the rostrum to denounce the three rightist leaders. In the end, each of them made a number of public confessions until the Party was satisfied.

The techniques of conflict resolution using both mass media and communication within the group had a number of salient features. During the blooming and blossoming in April and May, the impetus of conflict had originated primarily from the rightist groups. Because of the Party's silence, its own members and outside supporters did not know how to respond. The June 8 editorial in the *People's Daily* signalled the beginning of the Party's counterattack, and defined the Party's positions regarding the major direction of socialist construction. From there on, the outcome of the confrontation between the Party and the rightist groups was never in doubt. The Party was not going to yield any ground.

The rightist groups made a number of tactical errors. Although Chang Po-chun and his followers in the China Peasants and Worker Democratic party expressed their concern for the welfare of the peasants, they had no organizational support at the grassroots level. Thus they had little communication with or response from the peasants. Chang Nai-chi was speaking for the benefit of industrialists and businessmen, and in so doing alienated the large working class. Lo Lung-chi's demand for a redress committee, judging from the number of letters he received from across the country,[31] seemed to reflect a popular sentiment current among the intellectuals. But without the expressed support of the peasants and workers, he had no solid backing.

It is in the context of these circumstances that we can understand the counterattack tactics employed by the Communist leaders. Since the only support for the rightist leaders came from their own associates and colleagues in the Democratic Leagues and other minority political organizations, they could be effectively defused if their associates could be persuaded to denounce them publicly. This, in essence, was what the Communsist leaders did. By immediately staging mass meetings and demonstrations in Peking and several major industrial cities, the Party served the rightist groups with a reminder of what had happened during the San Fan and Wu Fan movements. These mass demonstrations, plus individually applied pressure, were sufficient to secure the cooperation of sociologist Fei Hsiao-tung and other prominent members of the rightist groups. Their public accusations effectively deprived the three rightist leaders of any social support, and placed them in virtual isolation. The psychological effects of being deserted and denounced by one's close supporters must be staggering. Here we are reminded of the experiments by psychologist Asch, which showed that first providing and then withdrawing support could have devastating effects on naïve subjects.[32] Furthermore, having the three rightist leaders attacked by their own associates tended to create an impression among the mass of people that the ideas they had proposed were indeed erroneous. This impression subsequently appeared to be confirmed when the three rightist leaders themselves made public confessions of their misdeeds and pleaded forgiveness. The Party's tactics, representing an optimal combination of coercion and persuasion, relied on the creation of group pressure through normative communication to neutralize the influence of the rightists and resolve the conflict in its own favor.

The significance of the Anti-rightist campaign lies in the fact that it ended the challenge to the Communist party's leadership by non-Communist political elements, particularly with regard to the process of decision-making and the direction of China's economic development. The Hundred Flowers movement brought a latent conflict into the open, and the Anti-rightist campaign resolved that conflict. It was in the aftermath of the latter campaign, when the residual dissenting voices outside the Party had been effectively muted, that the Party launched its Great Leap Forward in the spring of 1958, and later that fall, started the Commune movement.

Leaders Versus The Led

When Mao mentioned the conflict between leaders and the led, he did not clarify its nature other than by saying it was due to the bureaucratic practices of certain state functionaries in their relations with the masses.[33] Bureaucratic practices were nothing new in China. In old China, and no doubt elsewhere too, ordinary people simply avoided bureaucrats wherever they could. Even though the roles of the bureaucrats were not supportive of the roles of the ordinary citizens, no serious conflict arose except when one occasionally had to deal with the other beyond such routine interactions as the collection of taxes and levies. The low frequency of interactions made it easier to compartmentalize two otherwise incompatible roles and to minimize their role conflict.

This uneasy equilibrium between the people and the state functionaries was changed under the Chinese Communist system when the latter were assigned new duties that brought them into close interaction with the masses. The Party cadres now assume roles that are vastly different from the old roles of bureaucrats. Instead of sitting in their offices and issuing orders, they are required to lead and organize the mass of people in perpetual action programs designed to achieve the Communist objectives of socialist construction. They are not only required to play the role of taskmaster, which is usually unpopular, but also have become the state's agents in constantly demanding change: from land reform to the mutual aid team, to the agricultural cooperative, and finally to the commune. Each change necessitated abandoning a former routine and adjusting to something new, unfamiliar, and therefore threatening.

Ten Too Many, Ten Too Few

Even if the cadres knew how to play their new roles properly, some conflict with the mass of people would appear to be inevitable. The situation was much aggravated due to the fact that the cadres tended to adopt some of the age-old bureaucratic practices. While the peasants were being pushed to carry forward an unprecedented social transformation, many cadres who were supposed to lead the peasants were simply sitting on their hands. The cadres issued orders and expected them to be carried out. Their practices were described by the people, and acknowledged by the Party, as "ten too many and ten too few":

> Too many are sitting in their offices; too few are taking part in labor;
> Too many are talking, and too few are doing anything;
> Too many are setting objectives, and too few are providing concrete measures;
> Too many see their own merits, and too few see the merits of others;
> Too many are complaining, and too few are examining themselves;
> Too many are dictatorial, and too few are democratic;
> Too many are blaming others, and too few are solving problems;
> Too many use coercion, and too few use persuasion;
> Too many are subjective, and too few listen to the people.[34]

Given the tasks the peasants were required to accomplish, and given the bureaucratic practices by the cadres, it would hardly be surprising that conflict would arise between the masses and the cadres. With private ownership already abolished, the relations between the masses and the cadres were acknowledged to be a major determinant of the continued development of productivity.[35] Only after the resolution of any conflict between them, only when the masses and the cadres have developed "one heart," meaning a consensus of means and objectives, can the task of socialist construction proceed. The Communist party leadership is clearly aware of this problem, and over the last two decades has been making various attempts to resolve the mass-cadre conflict. There is no clear evidence as to whether and to what extent the Party has succeeded.

Communication and Labor

The Party has relied essentially on two mechanisms for resolving conflicts of this nature. One is the use of communication, both informational and normative. It is through such communication, the Party leadership believes, that conflict can be brought into the open for public examination and eventual resolution. The Party authorities consider conflict resolution of this nature not as a one-time undertaking, but as an ongoing process. Because the situation is forever changing, the needs of the masses and their task demands are changing.[36] Therefore, as an old conflict is resolved, new conflicts will arise to require attention. Through such continuous conflict discovery and resolution, the Party authorities believe, the revolution will move forward.[37]

Because conflict resolution is considered an ongoing process, communication has been employed on a continuous basis, typically in waves. When a particular campaign is on, the waves are high. In between campaigns, the waves lie low, but nevertheless keep moving. Because the mass-cadre conflict is located in a group situation, normative communication within the group assumes primary significance while the mass media play the general role of initiating and supporting the campaign. The major means of communication for bringing group conflict into the open is the tatzepao. For instance, in the Yangchow District, during a campaign from August 20 to September 4, 1958, intended to discover conflicts among the peasants and the cadres, more than fifty thousand tatzepao were posted, in which the peasants voiced complaints and criticisms of their cadres.[38] The two major sources of conflict were "commandism," and favoritism by some of the cadres. For resolving conflict, the major means of communication is tapienlun (big debate). During the campaign in the Yangchow District, more than one hundred tapienlun and discussion sessions were held to seek solutions of the problems.[39] Another medium is the letters to the editor columns, in which minor conflicts and petty grievances are aired. These means of communication will be further discussed.

Other than by means of communication, the Party has been

seeking to minimize conflict between the masses and cadres by requiring the latter to engage in manual labor. If the cadres can work alongside the peasants, the Party authorities hope, then they will understand the practical difficulties involved and will not depend on commands and orders. They will not be called "pale-face scholars" by the peasants, but will earn more respect.[40] As early as 1957, the Party was beginning to send its cadres to the villages in the first up to the mountains and down to the villages movement. The current May 7 cadre schools, where middle and upper level provincial cadres are enrolled for manual labor, represent a similar attempt. There is some evidence to suggest that cadres who performed manual labor were better received by the peasants.[41]

The difficulty of getting the Party cadres to engage in manual labor was illustrated by a recent report in the *New York Times.* The May 7 schools are supposed to cultivate the cadres' stamina in manual labor, but according to the *New York Times,* "foreign visitors who have visited the schools in recent years have generally reported that they were surprisingly cheerful places. . . . A letter in *Nanfang Jih Pao,* the official newspaper in Canton, said that many officials on communes had not met specified minimum requirements of cadres' participation in labor. Apparently, many officials are evading their labor duties on the farms."[42]

Tatzepao

Chairman Mao has been quoted as saying, "Tatzepao is a highly useful new weapon. . . . It has been widely used, and should continue to be used forever."[43] Tatzepao were not invented by the Chinese Communists. In fact, posters of various kinds have been part of the Chinese culture for ages. The official edicts of the emperor used to be written on paper and posted at the entrance gate of a city wall. The arrival of an operatic troupe in a village was usually announced by posters. A fascinating example of Chinese peasants using anonymous posters during the old days as a means of conflict arousal was provided by Siao Yu, a well-known scholar who was a schoolmate of Mao Tse-tung. In his personal memoir, Siao wrote about a case during his boyhood when someone in his village put up anonymous posters accusing a tenant of cheating Siao's landlord grandfather. This was intended to stir up a quarrel between the tenant and the landlord. Such posters were called *hsi kuang yueh,* meaning "west shining moon." According to Siao's interpretation, the term probably meant an exposure in the darkness, as the west side of the moon shines before dawn. The content was generally written in the form of a folk song. The posters were put up during the night, often on a roadside tree, on the railings of a bridge, or in front of a store, so that people could readily see them.[44] In this particular case, the anonymous posters brought the tenant, the landlord, and other interested parties together, so that the misunderstanding was eventually clarified.

The basic continuity between *hsi kuang yueh* and the Communist tatzepao is rather striking despite many technical differences. A tatzepao is also written on paper and posted in a public place. As remarked by the *People's Daily* during the Anti-rightist campaign:

> There are now so many tatzepao in the government agencies that sharply colored "no smoking" signs have had to be put up. Indeed, tatzepao are plentiful. You see them from one floor to another, on all walls, on windows, at staircases and inside offices. In corridors, strings or ropes were stretched from one wall to another to hang the reams and reams of tatzepao.[45]

Many different formats are followed in tatzepao: satirical prose, verse, accusatory letters, folk songs, comic strips, and cartoons. Colors are extensively used. During the Anti-rightist campaign, so many posters were put up that they had to be replaced daily, and sometimes several times a day.[46] While many tatzepao were signed, particularly those following the Party line in a current campaign, apparently a considerable number were anonymous, like those complaining of low wages for apprentices.

Varying Effects

The tatzepao is primarily a means of normative communication for airing divergent views and, like *hsi kuang yueh,* for bringing a conflict into the open for public examination and discussion. The effects are sometimes immediate. At Peking's Shih Ching Shan iron and steel works, a water pipe for a charcoal stove had needed repair for several years. The workers had made more than a hundred requests, but got no results. During the Anti-rightist campaign, someone posted a tatzepao, which was followed by more than a dozen others. Within half a day, the pipe was repaired.[47] At the Ministry of Hydraulic Power Supply, a proposal for a new profit-sharing system had been made, but shelved. Six officials fin-

ally wrote a tatzepao demanding a reply. The proposal was promptly accepted.[48] Engineer Wu Shih-cheh, an American-trained technician, did not get along well with his colleagues and resented their
criticisms. During the Anti-rightist campaign, he became the object of more than a hundred tatzepao that criticized him for failing
to surrender his heart to the people. According to the *Peking Daily,*
Wu was finally convinced and wrote more than 170 tatzepao himself to confess his errors. The conflict in this case appeared to be one
between collectivism and individualism, as told by Wu himself in
one tatzepao:

> I am a person with a serious problem of individualism. In the eight
> years since the liberation, the way I do my job and view a problem has
> always been based on individualism. I have no class consciousness, no
> mass viewpoint, and therefore I have made numerous errors and
> achieved nothing. From now on, I shall boost up my spirit, warmly love
> my work, and do everything possible to accomplish the task my
> superiors will assign to me. I shall go to the lower levels to examine
> their work, and get involved. I shall not just stand aside and make ir-
> relevant remarks. I shall resoltutely join the mass of people in a Big
> Leap Forward.[49]

The tatzepao Wu wrote had the effect of securing for him public
acceptance. After he had written those tatzepao, the attitudes of his
colleagues changed. Writing tatzepao also seemed to have some
cathartic effects on Wu himself, because after he had written them,
"he suddenly felt the distance between him and the mass and the
Party had been shortened."[50]

Not all tatzepao, however, were equally effective. Especially during the initial phase of the Anti-rightist campaign, when tatzepao
began to be extensively used for exposing conflict, there were individuals who wrote tatzepao because it was a required performance.
Before they posted a tatzepao to criticize a colleague, they would
first tell him in private that they did not mean what they said.[51]
Such lack of enthusiasm was said to be gradually overcome as the
campaign proceeded. Still, many tatzepao were acknowledged to
be just platitudes and without specific content.[52] Nor were all accusations in the tatzepao accepted as true. Some contained half
truths, while others were proved to be completely false.

The *Peking Daily* offered these comments:

> Of course, some of the criticisms written in tatzepao are not com-
> pletely true, and some are even completely false. Under these circum-

stances, we need to exercise caution and to make a careful analysis. If the criticisms are basically correct, but contain minor discrepancies, or if the wording is not entirely proper, then we should receive such criticisms with an attitude of welcome. If the content is untrue, or if the viewpoint is incorrect, then we can proceed to explain or correct it at an appropriate time. The more important points can be brought to the mass for discussion. We must trust the majority of the mass of people, and believe that after we have collectively analyzed the situation, the truth will emerge, and the right and wrong can be distinguished.[53]

The point is, unless a conflict is brought to public attention, its validity or falsehood simply cannot be ascertained. But after it is so brought to attention, then through open discussion the truth will eventually emerge. In this instance, "truth" seems to be defined in a way acceptable to the Party. During the initial phase of the Antirightist campaign, the rightist groups had posted many tatzepao criticizing the Party and socialism. What emerged was officially described as "temporary confusion," rather than "truth." But once the tatzepao was adoped by the Party, it then became a "sharp weapon" of "exposing and refuting the rightists," and of "reasoning and struggling."[54]

Why Effective?

Why are tatzepao so effective? In part, the effectiveness of the tatzepao is due to its ability to focus localized peer-group pressure directly on an individual. Engineer Wu Shi-cheh provides an example. Wu had been verbally criticized before, but he had been able to ignore the criticisms. When tens of tatzepao focused public attention on him, they simply could not be ignored. He tried to explain his position to his colleagues, but the more he explained, the more tatzepao were posted against him. It is important to note that in Wu's case, he had no supporters who would help defend him. Finally Wu had to bow to the concerted pressure from his peers.[55]

Tatzepao are effective also becasue they can bring a conflict from latent neglect to open attention for *both* the leadership and the mass of people. The faulty pipe at the Shih Ching Shan iron and steel works and the profit-sharing system at the Ministry of Hydraulic Water Supply are examples. As stated by Lo Keh-ming, a district first secretary of Kuangtung Province,

When a problem arises, particularly a new problem, each person tends to have his particular view and particular way of handling it. Through tatzepao, these divergent views can be publicly compared and examined, and different ways of handling the problem can be fully exposed and coordinated, so that through subsequent debates, any ideological differences can be resolved.[56]

Without the aid of tatzepao, it was believed, the conflict would remain at the verbal level in the staff conference, and could not be fully resolved because it lacked a sufficient basis of public consensus and commitment.

Tatzepao have been used as a means of exposing conflict because of their snowballing effect. Once a tatzepao is posted, others tend to follow, reinforcing and supporting each other, until a public mood is created.[57] How the snowballing effect works is illustrated by the case of Shen Chin-yin, a 68-year-old engineer who was originally opposed to the idea of posting tatzepao but eventually became an enthusiast. At first Shen had viewed them with contempt, and did not want to read them, thinking: "What's so great about tatzepao? What can a few big characters do?" Nevertheless, he read a few and his attention was caught by the wasteful practices and bureaucratic shortcomings exposed in them. He became interested and read many more. His attitude changed. He was soon actively writing many tatzepao himself.[58]

The tatzepao device is different from small-group criticisms not only because of the wider attention it can attract, but also because it can provide an impersonal buffer when close personal relations tend to make face-to-face criticism difficult. Once the norms of tatzepao were established, brothers, and even husbands and wives were able to criticize each other without any qualms.[59] This can be illustrated by a tatzepao written by a woman student in a political training school for industrial and business personnel in Shanghai. Addressing her husband, she wrote:

> While you were studying in the political school, you copied some of the [rightist] poisonous-weed, vulgar poems that were posted during the period of blooming and blossoming, and brought them home for your personal enjoyment. You particularly liked one verse which says, "All around us are Fa Hai Monks, and so have mercy on Lady Pai Shu-cheng." Let me ask you: "How many Fa Hai Monks are around you? (And whom do you imply?) Do you consider yourself to be Lady Pai Shu-cheng?"[60]

The effects of tatzepao in applying peer-group pressure are sometimes augmented by the psychological mechanism of shame, as illustrated by the practices in Ching Ho District in Szechuan Province. An inspection team visiting the district found much neglect and waste among the local cadres and had posted tatzepao to ridicule these practices. One was as follows:

> Cooperative 51, don't go to sleep,
> If you sleep people will laugh,
> The rice plants in your fields are sparse and few,
> But the weeds are thick and full,
> Taller even than a foot high,
> So that Fat Soul Wang can lie on them and sleep.[61]

One cooperative posted satiric tatzepao in its office and recited them during every meeting. Only when a problem referred to by a satiric tatzepao had been taken care of, would it be omitted from the recitation. The members of the cooperatives were so ashamed that they swore, "People live by face. Trees live by skin. Now that our mistakes have been told us, we must correct them. We'll do better in the next inspection."[62]

Recent Campaigns

Popularized during the rectification campaign and extensively utilized during the Cultural Revolution,[63] the tatzepao has found its place among the major social institutions in mainland China. The campaign against Lin Piao and Confucius provides the latest demonstration of the power of tatzepao.

Much has been reported in the wire services about the tatzepao campaign in Peking in the summer of 1974.[64] Most of the posters were displayed in front of government offices. The targets of criticism included such high-ranking military commanders as Li Teh-sheng, as well as lower-level cadres. The nature of conflicts brought to public attention seemed to cover a wide range, from demands for political reform to attacks on unidentified officials for the unjust positions they held. Some poster writers, including a worker at Peking's No. 2 mechanical factory who used the pseudonym "Golden Monkey," were apparently using the anti-Lin Piao and anti-Confucius campaign as a cover to raise questions embarrassing to the government. Those posters were later removed. It was not revealed whether any actions were taken by the government in response to the tatzepao criticisms.

When a tatzepao airs a conflict over a minor issue, conflict resolution most probably follows. We shall cite two recent reports in the *People's Daily* to illustrate. During the campaign against Lin Piao and Confucius, the workers at Shanghai's No. 6 construction company posted a tatzepao that criticized the cadres for treating themselves as the "rulers" of workers. This was because the cadres had introduced a time-check form for registering those workers who arrived late or left early. What the cadres should have done but failed to do, the tatzepao said, was to raise the political consciousness of the workers so that they would work hard according to the instructions of Chairman Mao. For the cadres to impose the time-register form would be to place themselves above the workers. This was considered a manifestation of revisionism. Because of the tatzepao, the report said, the cadres could no longer sit in their offices, but must go to the work teams to learn from the workers and receive their criticism. The time-register form was soon abolished.[65]

At Chiang Chun Village, which was described as covered with tatzepao in August 1974, the posters brought the peasants and the cadres to a minor confrontation. Located next to a river, the village had more than three hundred *mu* (about fifty acres) of sandy beach. The peasants had been working to remove the sandy top and replace it with fertile soil. The cadres, however, found that the brigade could make more money by selling the sand to a nearby construction project than by developing the land for agricultural production. This was severely criticized in a tatzepao written by the Third Production Team. The peasants working on the sandy beach supported that tatzepao. The brigade's cadres finally agreed to use the sandy land for agriculture.[66]

As acknowledged by the Communist authorities themselves, by bringing up conflicts for resolution, the tatzepao has become an important social mechanism for regulating the relations between the mass of people and the cadres, and for stimulating productive activities.[67]

Letters to the Editor

The tatzepao has been an effective means of normative communication because, among other factors, it can give individuals a sense of personal involvement and commitment. People do not just *read* tatzepao; they are aroused to write and post some of their own. Through the posters, the peasants and workers can tackle in a timely manner local problems that the mass media of communication generally cannot match. But there is one limitation. Tatzepao cannot reach a huge, heterogenous audience.

For this reason, the Party has been actively using the media, primarily the newspapers, as a means of exposing conflicts and airing grievances that are not restricted to particular localities, but are of general public concern. This is done through the letters to the editor columns in the *People's Daily* and the provincial newspapers.

Early attempts at soliciting letters from the people were not highly successful, as many letters remained unopened in the "complaint letter boxes."[68] The situation apparently improved somewhat after the San Fan movement. From the very beginning, the *People's Daily* has followed a policy of publishing letters that point out mismanagement or deviation from Party policies by cadres. Even though the provincial newspapers are not accessible to the outside world, they appear to reserve more space for letters. Emmett Dedmon, an American journalist who visited China in 1972, was not allowed to look at any provincial newspapers, but learned from his Chinese guides that the center two pages of the usual four-page edition are devoted to letters from readers. Most letters criticized local cadres for not putting Chairman Mao's instructions into practice and for avoiding manual labor.[69]

An analysis of the letters published in 1967 and 1968 in the *People's Daily* produced some interesting findings.[70] The letters appeared in a special column called "Letters from Revolutionary Masses," usually on page two or three of a six-page edition. There was no apparent time sequence in which this column appeared. Sometimes, a whole month passed without a single letter being published, but occasionally this column appeared several times a week. The number of letters published on any day varied from one to four.

Some of the letters seemed to serve the function of tension release, in the sense that they provided the letter writers with a means to vent some of their petty grievances.[71] Generally, the individual was frustrated in some manner, and wanted to bring his case to public attention. For instance, one peasant wrote to describe how he had walked several miles to buy a hoe, but found the co-op store closed well beyond 9 A.M.[72] Another reader complained because a loud-speaker kept him awake all night.[73] Of the 182 letters published during these two years, 10 were of this nature.

Nature of Conflicts

Far more numerous than letters airing minor grievances were those that exposed a conflict, that is, expressed rival claims to scarce resources and status as well as differences of ideology. Of the total, 126 letters were classified under the conflict category. Slightly less than half of those letters expressed complaint over the use of human resources, for example, too many meetings, poor management, and wasteful policies of education. For instance, two members of Chuan Shui Commune, Peng Chi County, Liaoning Province, protested the numerous meetings. In March 1968, of the commune's twenty-three cadres, only two were working in the commune. The others spent most of their time attending meetings.[74] A letter from two bank clerks revealed that in one government organization, the two opposing factions had each set up an account in the bank but refused to let the national bank audit their acounts.[75] A young worker at Peking's steel mill No. 3 complained that the things he learned from the books had no relevance whatsoever to his work.[76]

About one-fourth of the conflict-related letters had to do with allocation of material resources, primarily criticism of wasteful practices and objection to bonus distribution. A reader in Anhui Province wrote that some production units used funds from collective crops for big feasts.[77] Two readers in Honan Province wrote separate letters opposing the demand of their cadres that each family hoist a red flag in front of its house, because to do so would cost the commune both money and cloth rations to comply.[78] All the letters that discussed the bonus expressed objection.

Contention over high status and style of leadership was voiced in about one-third of the letters. In one incident at a Peking shirt factory, prolonged disputes occurred among the workers over the appointment of a deputy director.[79] In other cases, the positions of cadres were challenged because they failed to provide leadership in production, or in economizing on the use of material resources.[80] About one-fifth of the letters revealed conflicts of an ideological nature, in which the writers either admitted their erroneous thinking of the past, or attacked the ideological errors of unidentified class enemies.[81]

That two-thirds of the letters published in that period were related to exposure of conflicts, though of a minor nature, suggests a degree of social approval both by the Party and by the readers, for bringing matters of disagreement to a forum of public attention. In more than half the cases the conflict mentioned in the letters had already been resolved, primarily through relatively open discussion between the parties concerned, but in some cases over a lengthy period of time. In all the cases in which the conflict was resolved, the thought of Mao Tse-tung was given credit as the guiding principle that led the parties involved to reach a compromise. Even in those letters that only presented a situation of conflict, some quotations of Mao were cited to indicate the preferred manner for resolution.

Social Functions

The availability of the letters column would seem to give individuals—readers as well as writers—a sense of involvement and participation. From a group perspective, the timely airing of a common minor conflict would alert the mass of people to seek some form of conflict resolution before a serious division could develop. In this sense, by giving the individuals a sense of participation and by prompting the mass of people to resolve the conflict in time, the letters would seem to have the function of helping maintain the unity of a group.

From the Party's viewpoint, the letters provide a means of checking on the performance of its local level cadres.[82] Knowing that their misdeeds could be given a public hearing in the provincial or national media, the local cadres would be expected to exercise caution and restraint. It seems that the Party is clearly aware of the control function of the letters, because they provide a direct channel of feedback to the Party regarding local situations. This awareness was indicated in a special article in the *Red Flag:*

> Letters written by the people are the best research materials. They provide information you don't hear around the conference table, nor do you get in written reports. They are important sources of references for leaders at the various levels to enable them to grasp the overall situation and coordinate their work.[83]

The Party apparently recognized the importance of the letters not only as a medium of communication between the Party and the people, but also as a mechanism for promoting group solidarity, because they bring conflict to public attention. The same article in the *Red Flag* states:

> Handling the letters and visits by the people is an important task of mass coordination and ideological indoctrination. Party committee members and revolutionary committees at the various levels must do the job seriously and do it well, because the letters provide a close link be-

tween the mass of people and the Party and government, and contribute to the solidarity of the proletarian rule.[84]

The letters to the editor column, however, does not seem to be open to everybody. An analysis of the letter writers revealed that they were predominantly workers, peasants, soldiers, and cadres. Apparently, ex-landlords and rich peasants either are not allowed to write or do not consider themselves fit to write letters to the *People's Daily*.[85]

Tapienlun

The letters column is a mass medium for exposing minor conflicts and petty grievances that are of general concern to the public. The tatzepao serve a similar function at the local level. However, neither letters nor tatzepao alone could effectively bring the parties in conflict to reach a consensus.[86] From some of the letters we have seen that minor conflicts, once they are exposed, are resolved through a relatively open discussion between the parties concerned. For conflicts of a somewhat more serious nature and involving more individuals, the Party has come to rely on a form of public communication known as tapienlun, or "big debate."

The analogy between the Party's debate strategy and the age-old Chinese practices reported by Mao's schoolmate Siao Yu merits a brief examination.[87] After the *hsi kuang yueh* (west shining moon) posters had anonymously accused a tenant of cheating his landlord, Siao recalled, the tenant came to Siao's grandfather, the landlord, to plead innocence. Even though Siao's grandfather told him not to worry, the tenant did not feel reassured. The misunderstanding that had caused the anonymous posters still remained, at least in the minds of other villagers. Finally, Siao's grandfather agreed to call a meeting, which was attended by himself, the tenant, and a number of others who might be in one way or another involved. While wine and food were being served, the tenant publicly pleaded his innocence and Siao's grandfather announced his satisfaction and continued confidence in the tenant. A conflict had been perceived by the village public—whether or not it actually existed was immaterial—and it had to be resolved in the presence of the village public. The tapienlun aims to perform the same function.

A tapienlun, of course, is far more complex than the village meeting called by Siao's grandfather and the tenant. The purpose of the big debate is to examine all sides of a controversy involving conflicting interests, and to seek a resolution through public discussion in a manner acceptable to both the Party and the mass of people. We shall cite two examples, one from an urban factory and one from a rural village, to illustrate the communication processes in the tapienlun.

Debates in Factories

The case of the Chi Yeh Yen motor vehicle repair factory was an example of conflict between collective and individual interests.[88] It was started by a tatzepao written and signed by two workers, Hsu Kuo-liang and Teng Ping-chang, entitled: "Production records are improving everyday, but fringe benefits are diminishing every day." In the tatzepao, the two workers complained that while the working efficiency in the factory had increased by more than ten times, many fringe benefits had been discontinued. They mentioned in particular the factory's decision to abolish the year-end bonus, the cash reimbursement for unused leave, merit raises, free tickets for train trips, the supply of cotton towels, and work uniforms for mechanics. The Party leadership in the factory felt that other workers in the factory more or less shared some of the views expressed in that tatzepao. The thinking was considered to be both popular and representative to some extent. The conflict was therefore serious and deserved to be clarified and resolved through a big debate.

A tapienlun is not simply an act of calling the workers together for an exchange of views and thoughts. In this instance, it involved a series of carefully planned, and well-synchronized communication events. Once a big debate was decided upon, the cadres at the factory began interviewing and collecting relevant information that they could use to support their arguments. Four Party cadres and the factory's correspondent visited the homes of the two workers who had written the tatzepao, and found that both families had improved their standard of living since 1949. The cadres also prepared statistics to show that the average wage for workers in the factory had increased from 57.94 JMP in 1950 to 71.30 JMP in 1957. In 1952, the factory's workers had a total savings deposit of 46,200 JMP. In 1957, the total savings had increased to 326,991 JMP. Other statistics were prepared and distributed to all workers.

The next step was to select and train a core of debaters who could present the Party's side during the debate. More than a hundred such core debaters were chosen, including the small group leaders of the Party, of the Communist Youth Corps, and of the labor union, foremen, old workers, and some younger members of the factory. They were given a brief course by the factory's Party secretary on the objectives of the debate and the strategy to be followed, that is, "unity—criticism—unity." During the training course, the whole group went through all the arguments that they were going to use to refute the tatzepao posted by the two workers.

When the core debaters felt ready, the Party leadership moved to the most critical stage, the debate itself. The debate came in three phases: first in small groups, then in combined larger groups, and finally for the whole factory. The purpose was to develop a favorite climate in the small groups before all the workers were brought together to reach a consensus. As it turned out, the small-group debates proved to be less than successful. The Party could assign only a few core debaters to each small group of workers. Facing numerical odds, the core debaters were unable to prevail upon the workers, who, as members of the same shift, apparently had considerable cohesiveness among themselves. At the end of the small-group debates, the counterarguments represented in the tatzepao had gained the upper hand.

The Party maneuvered by combining a number of small groups. The situation changed immediately. Now a sufficient number of core debaters were brought together so that they could adequately support each other. On the other hand, when workers from different shifts were brought together, they lost the advantage of group cohesiveness. At the combined group debates, the demands contained in the tatzepao began to be criticized and the arguments for the Party gained more and more support. During this phase, the role of the old workers was crucial. They were able to use their own bitter personal experience to compare life in the past with what the workers had at that time. Apparently, while the workers were not convinced by the statistics the Party leadership had compiled, they listened to their old colleagues. Only when a generally favorable mood had been created in the combined groups, did the Party leadership consider the time to be ripe for calling all the workers together for a final session. While in the small groups and the combined groups the workers were allowed free time to express themselves, at the final whole factory session only seven old workers were chosen to speak. They all criticized the tatzepao. The whole factory session concluded by hearing a self-criticism by Hsu Kuo-liang and

Teng Ping-chang, the two workers who had started the conflict. While the debates were going on, the Party leadership also organized its own movement of tatzepao to attack Hsu and Teng. Satirical prose and cartoons were posted to present a picture of two workers who were enjoying a comfortable life but ungrateful for what they had received.

After the debates had been concluded to the satisfaction of the Party leadership, the factory's Party secretary made a summary report to the workers, in which he attributed the erroneous thinking to the capitalist individualism still entertained by some workers. The debates were apparently not wholly successful in stamping out capitalist individualism, because the *Workers Daily* estimated that although upwards of 90 percent of the workers were convinced, the remainder presumably were still unreconciled.

Debates in Villages

The case of Pai Chuan Village, Ho Hsun, Shansi Province, covered a whole range of conflicts between individual and collective interests, between the peasants and the cadres, and between socialism and private ownership.[89] According to the *People's Daily,* of the 227 families in the Chin Hua Agricultural Producers Cooperative of Pai Chuan Village, 56.3 percent were genuinely supporting the cooperative movement, 37.4 percent had divergent views, and the remaining 6.2 percent showed a serious tendency toward antagonism and passive resistance. At all levels, the *People's Daily* acknowledged, there were peasants who had different degrees of dissatisfaction toward the state, toward socialism, toward their cooperative, and toward the Party cadres in their midst.

Among the complaints by the peasants were: The state had set the prices of agricultural products too low, so that the peasants did not earn enough and thus their living scale was poor. The low standard of living was partly the result of exploitation by cadres, because the cadres earned higher wages and lived better than the cooperative members. Cadres in the cooperative kept larger private plots than the cooperative members. The agricultural cooperative allowed its members not enough freedom. For instance, cooperative members did not have any pocket money to spend. The life of a hired hand in the old society was said to be better, for at least one got to spend the money he earned.

These complaints were aired after a Party's rectification work team had arrived in the village and assured the peasants that the village's cadres would not retaliate after the team's departure. Among the first things the work team did after its arrival was to recruit a group of core debaters from among members of the Party and the Communist Youth League, and from among the more progressive peasants. These individuals were organized to visit each family and talk to men and women, young and old, to learn about their complaints. In a few days, a total of 105 problems were discovered touching upon conflicts of the various kinds. At this point, the general mood in the village was unfavorable to the Party. The sentiments of the peasants were described to be: "Now that you know our problems, what are you going to do about them?" Some of the village cadres were so pessimistic that they were ready to quit.

Upon careful analysis, the work team found that two-thirds of the problems reflected an ideological misconception or a lack of understanding of socialism on the part of the mass of people. Only one-third involved conflicts with the village cadres that would call for immediate action. At a meeting called by the work team and attended by the local cadres, it was decided to resolve the ideological conflicts through a tapienlun. The local cadres, for their part, agreed to take care of the more immediate problems that had caused a strain in their relations with the peasants, particularly the large sizes of their private plots.

Three topics were chosen for the big debate: Was the life of peasants really poor? Were agricultural cooperatives good or not good? Did the village need the leadership of the cadres, and if so, why did the peasants complain so much about the cadres? The debate took place in the production teams. About the life of peasants, many considered it to be poor, and those peasants who disagreed could not present a convincing case. The younger peasants were among those who complained most, particularly about lack of pocket money and poor food. Again it was the old peasants who through their own experience finally convinced the others that though life in the cooperative might not be as good as it should be, it was better than in the past. About the cooperative, many peasants felt the system was too restrictive and provided too little freedom. Then someone asked: What was too restrictive and what was not free enough? The debate concluded that the cooperative was highly restrictive if the members wanted to pursue individual profit without regard to the collective welfare. The cooperative allowed the members no freedom "to do something wicked and bad," meaning to wreck the cooperative system. The members did not have the choice to withdraw. These restrictions were considered desirable.

The most heated debate was centered on the relations with the cadres. Many peasants were described as indignant and emotional during the debate. Some peasants said, "Under the leadership [of the cadres] we have no democracy. We can do without this kind of leadership. In the old society nobody oversaw us, and we managed all the same."[90]

This viewpoint was eventually rejected. It was pointed out that if there should be a head for a family—a proposition all peasants would accept—then there should also be some kind of leadership for a cooperative. While most peasants were ready to go along with that, some were still not convinced. "If the cadres are meant to serve the people," these peasants asked, "how come we don't feel comfortable with them?" The answer was: Because the cadres were looking after the collective interests, while the peasants were more concerned with their individual interests. "But if the cadres are indeed concerned only with the collective interests, why should they be allowed to keep larger private plots?" The work team was prepared. It promised that the cadres would cut the sizes of their private plots. The local cadres admitted that they had not been democratic enough in managing the cooperative and pledged to follow the mass line and to listen to the peasants more. According to the *People's Daily,* most peasants were satisfied. As a result of the tapienlun, the conflicts involving the peasants and cadres were resolved. Morale improved. In Production Brigade No. 4, women workers who had refused to go to the field now joined readily. Some cooperative members even used their leisure time and holidays to cut weeds.[91]

Processes of Tapienlun

The processes of a tapienlun can be characterized as a series of communication events designed to create for the people a highly structured perception of their situation. As a result of this new perception, the peasants and workers are expected to modify their relations with the cadres and the state. Some of the communication events, for example, interviewing persons and collecting facts, are informational and are intended to change the way the peasants and workers perceive the physical reality of their situation. For instance, the two complaining workers were shown actually to have improved their livelihood, or, the proposed increased in fringe benefits for workers was shown to be the equivalent of eight Yangtze River bridges a year. Other communication events, for example, the sentimental testimonials of old workers and old peasants, are partly affective and partly normative, designed to change the perception of the social reality of the situation. Apparently, information regarding the physical reality, even though selected and presented in favor of the Party line, is not always sufficient to convince the mass of people, as the experience of the Chi Yeh Yen motor repair factory illustrated. It took the personal tear-jerking experience of the old workers, with whom the others could identify, to interpret the physical reality for them. The acceptance of their interpretation was further assured by the normative process of allowing only old workers to speak at the whole factory meeting, where their views could generate a perception of unanimous support. All the discussions and debates, it may be noted, took place within the framework of Communist ideology.

A tapienlun is therefore a series of well-coordinated and well-controlled communication events, in which the peasants and workers are allowed considerable, but not unrestrained participation. It is this participation which makes it easier for the peasants and workers to perceive their situation in a way conducive to the resolution of conflict.

The term tapienlun was used less often during the years after the Cultural Revolution until it emerged again in the anti-Lin Piao and anti-Confucius campaigns of 1974 and 1975, and most recently, in the campaign to criticize rightist education in 1976. While the tapienlun generally takes place in the face-to-face context of factory work groups or production teams, the rapidly expanding facilities of wired loudspeakers have now given the debates a new format. A release by the New China News Agency on September 19, 1974, showed that most communes now have their own transmitting stations, and that more than 90 percent of the production brigades and production teams are connected to the wired broadcasting system. A total of 63 percent of peasant families have had broadcast speakers installed in their homes.[92] These facilities have been used to support the debates, as illustrated at a meeting for criticizing Lin Piao and Confucius at the Chiang Chun Brigade, Shensi Province.

Early in the morning of February 14, 1974, when the transmitting station at the brigade had just finished broadcasting a few critical speeches written by the members of the Communist Youth Corps, many peasants arrived at the station and asked to speak over the wired broadcasting system. Other peasants listened in the field from speakers installed on trees. From time to time, they sent representatives to the station to respond to what had been said. The opinions expressed were one-sided, as all those who spoke condemned Lin Piao and Confucius. However, it was revealed during the broadcast meeting that there were "class enemies" in the brigade who were "attempting in vain" to "change the sky," that is, seeking to alter the socialist system. Some confusion seemed to have existed among the peasants until several members of a study group wrote a convincing refutation and broadcast it over the station.[93] It was again the use of normative communication, within the framework of approved value orientations, that averted a potential conflict among the peasants.

Conflict and Development

Conflict has always existed in China, as indeed in any society, because the old social structure tended to maintain an uneven and inequitable distribution of material goods and statuses. The old Chinese traditions of authoritarian submission and the fatalism of the peasantry tended to suppress the conflict. Once in a while, when life conditions became unbearable in the midst of natural calamities, the latent conflict would erupt into a peasant uprising. As a Chinese saying goes, the peasants "stand up to take a course of high risk." Such uprisings, however, resulted in temporary disruption, but not permanent resolution of conflict in the social structure. After an uprising was put down, the old relationships again prevailed, and the conflict were suspended until the next flare-up.

The Chinese Communist leaders undoubtedly capitalized on the latent, unresolved conflicts in China's old society in bringing their revolution to a military success. When the Communist regime was established in 1949, the task of resolving the social conflicts and instituting new social relations had barely begun. The steps the Communist leadership initially took—through a series of arousals and resolutions of conflict—resulted in the abolition of private ownership in agricultural and industrial production. By 1957, with the establishment of advanced agricultural cooperatives and the state takeover of all industry and business, the old social structure had lost its economic base and was on the verge of collapse. But new social relations were yet to be established. What Mao referred to in his celebrated talk in February 1957—in his terminology, the contradictions among the people—reflected the unstable new social relations that were then beginning to take shape.

Since the state has taken over all production materials, the previous conflicts between the mass and the ownership class have become conflicts between the mass and the state. Mao refers to this conflict as one between collective interests and individual interests. It involves a conflict in the relationship between the people and the state with regard to the distribution of the fruits of labor. The peasants and workers apparently want an increasing share of individual benefits, while the state, mindful of the needs of capital investment and military outlays, has been reluctant to meet their demands fully. This is perhaps the most fundamental conflict in Communist China, and it remains not fully resolved even today.

The conflict involving what Mao called democracy and centralism was a contest in 1957 between the Communist party and the bourgeois intellectuals who had previously supported the Communist revolution. At stake was China's direction of development. The intellectuals wanted to retain some form of private enterprise, and demanded more representation in the decision-making process. This conflict, though resolved almost entirely in favor of the Party at that time, seemed to have left considerable residue. The recurring battle right up to the present between Maoist Communism and revisionism can be viewed as a different version of the same conflict that pitted the bourgeois intellectuals against the Communists during the Hundred Flowers movement. The anti-Confucius campaign and the purge of Teng Hsiao-ping would seem to indicate that this conflict, like the one between collective and individual interests, is far from being fully resolved.

In comparison, the conflict between the cadres and the mass of the people may be the least thorny of all, even though it has practical significance in the day-to-day operation of the social system in mainland China. When the peasants and workers feel that their individual needs are not being adequately fulfilled, and when they have to work under a social system for which they have yet to develop wholehearted support, it is not surprising that they would take out some of their frustration against their immediate supervisors. This tendency would be further strengthened, as it was during the Anti-rightist campaign, when the cadres appeared to be living a life considerably better than the common lot of the peasants and workers. The practice of commandism by some of the cadres, as exemplified in the "ten too many and ten too few" incidents, certainly did not help alleviate the conflict. The Anti-rightist campaign was intended to resolve the cadre-mass conflict, and apparently succeeded to some extent. The Cultural Revolution, aside from the power struggle at the top, represented another such attempt, as did the May 7 cadre schools in its aftermath. There are indications that some of the earlier practices that alienated the people have been modified and corrected. However, the cadre-mass conflict is expected to linger on because the strains in their relations are not entirely caused by the practices of the cadres themselves. The cadre-mass conflict appears to be only a manifestation of the deeper conflict between the individual and the state, and between individual interests and collective interests. As long as the cadres act as the agents of the state's policy of collectivism, and as long as this policy is not fully accepted by the people, the cadre-mass conflict cannot be resolved.

The reliance by the Party on communication as a means of conflict resolution points to the difficult situation facing the leadership. The Communist leaders correctly diagnosed the conflicts in the social structure of old China and successfully manipulated those conflicts in achieving their revolution. They also capitalized on the conflicts over the means and fruits of production to remove the landlords and industrial owners from their superior positions in the social structure. In so doing, the Party leadership succeeded in resolving what they called the "contradictions between the people and the class enemy." They then had to deal only with "contradictions among the people." The new conflicts, it may be noted, are inherent in the social relations which the Communist leadership has been trying to establish in place of the old. These conflicts can most probably be mitigated, if not totally resolved, by modifying the new social relations; for instance, by providing more individual benefits and allowing more small, private ownership. The new constitution, by approving limited private plots for villagers and minor individual labor for workers, could be a step in this direction.[94] However, to help resolve the basic conflict inherent in social relations, the Party has had to rely on massive use of communication. The strategy seems to be: If the conflict can be brought into the open at an opportune moment, by tatzepao or letters in the print media, then at least a temporary resolution can be achieved through public discussion, such as tapienlun. It may be noted that both tatzepao and tapienlun have been incorporated into the new constitution of the People's Republic as legitimate means by which the mass of people can express their views.[95]

The processes of conflict exposure and resolution are not completely open, as the dispute is permitted to touch only on minor problems of implementation, not basic matters of policy and ideology. Only those individuals who belong to the category of the people—primarily workers, peasants, soldiers, cadres, and revolution-minded intellectuals—are encouraged to express criticisms and disagreements. The public discussion following exposure of minor conflict has to stay within the bounds of the thought of Chairman Mao. Major conflicts within the Party hierarchy, when they occur, seem to have been resolved primarily through political infighting, as during the Cultural Revolution, rather than through open discussion.

Nevertheless, the processes of communication we have analyzed have important social functions. By bringing matters of discontent and disagreemnt to public attention, these processes help alleviate the accumulation of frustration. They give the individuals some sense of participation and keep the level of tension within manageable bounds, thus contributing to the maintenance of social integration at a time of change and instability. In a more constructive perspective, the continuous processes of conflict exposure and resolution have helped the Party in its attempt to restructure the perception of the peasants and workers, so that they would see their situation of material inadequacy as a necessary, intermediate step toward future collective achievement. To the extent this has been partly successful, the Party has been able to mobilize enough energy for development programs. In this sense, the communication processes we have analyzed are essential for maintaining the viability of the Chinese Communist social system and for generating the energy it needs for economic development.

VIII
Communication, Social Structure, and Development

Structural Change and Development

Development, in any form, requires the unlocking of human energy and creativity in order to utilize available material resources. Indeed, the history of mankind reflects the diverse human inputs that have either facilitated or impeded this progress. Whether in the West or the East, traditions of human relations over the centuries have been prominent among the major stumbling blocks. The lack of physical mobility bound the medieval man to his immediate environs, restricting his knowledge and vision. His empathy or psychic mobility—that is, his ability to visualize any roles beyond his direct personal experience—was highly limited. Traditions, therefore, remained largely unchallenged.

Daniel Lerner, surveying the course of events in Western Europe, sees empathy as a key element that can free mankind from the bondage of traditions and set the wheel of development turning. The accelerating expansion of communication in the West during the last few centuries has widened man's vision and contributed to his empathy.[1] Since traditions are in fact man's own creation, by expanding his empathy, man actually sets his future self free from his past self. He will dare to explore the unknown and try the impossible. Thus, new technology is discovered, new goals are set, and new ways of organizing human efforts are tried and adapted. Material resources hitherto untapped are drawn on to create affluence and provide a higher standard of living. Development, in this approach, rests on the individual man as cornerstone. His creativity and energy are assumed to function at their best when man is set free, both phsically, socially, and psychologically.

The approach by Mao, tried out in China during the last quarter century, shares the same emphasis on breaking the hold of tradition. All the Maoist campaigns—whether the Great Leap Forward, the Cultural Revolution, or the criticism of Confucius—deliver one message loud and clear: man has been locked in by traditions, which must be done away with if development is to move forward apace. But the method advocated by Mao to bring about the downfall of traditions is radically different from Western theory and practices. In the Maoist approach, it is not the individual man, but the collective man, that is considered capable of breaking the shackles of human bondage. It is not the cultivation of individual empathy, but the affirmation of collective will, that can achieve the full development of human energy and creativity.[2]

Mao's basic premise is the inability of the individual to free himself from the traditions, which are manifested in the old values and beliefs. These, deeply rooted in the old social structure, in Mao's thinking, control both human relations and their material base. It is only by destroying the old social structure and by changing its material base, according to the Maoists, that the collective man can proceed to initiate a set of new goals, values and beliefs, and thereby develop full human potentials. Man must strive for development in the collectivity, not seek it as an individual.

Development in China during the past quarter century thus exemplifies drastic structural transformation through collective will rather than evolutionary change as engendered by individual empathy.

The Party began by changing the structure of rural China through the Land Reform movement. Communciations—informational, normative, and affective—were used effectively, primarily through interpersonal channels with the support of the mass media, to activate latent dissatisfaction among the peasants, to build a basis of common identity for them, and to commit them to a class struggle against the landlords. After the removal of the landlords, a period of interim confusion followed, during which some of the Party's rural cadres misused their newly acquired power for personal gain. The Party then brought to bear the tactics of self-criticism and mutual criticism in group sessions to rectify the behavior of the cadres, and forced them to communicate with the peasants.

With the power of cadres curtailed and channels of communication opened to the peasants, the Party began to organize the rural population into new groups, progressing in stages from mutual aid teams to people's communes. The result has been a radical change in the traditional Chinese social structure. The kinship system in which the landlords held both social influence and economic power, has been greatly weakened. In its place, the Party has institutionalized the new groups in which the members together labor and study the thought of Mao Tse-tung. These groups are given their own resources as well as the responsibility to make the best use of them within the Party's guidelines. The burden is on the local groups to carry out their share of the state's development programs. Having laid down these structural constraints, the Party has been able to apply group pressure on the Chinese people for performing the necessary tasks.

Whatever the issue—whether to participate in a production campaign, to practice economy in consumption, to criticize Lin Piao and Confucius, or to assign birth quotas—the group takes the directives from above and works out a way to carry them out. To use an analogy suggested by Wilbur Schramm, the groups in China have become local engines that run on their own fuel, as it were. The fuel is the social pressure the members themselves generate by normative communication within the group setting.[3]

Two important features have made it possible for the Chinese groups to function effectively in this manner. One is the catalytic role of cadres. As agents of the Party and the state, the cadres see to it that directives are carried out. They have a responsibility to make sure that the Party's basic policies, that is, curtailment of individual interests and prevention of revisionism, are strictly followed. They play an important part in the group's activities by suggesting general courses of action. But they do not have the authority to tell the peasants exactly how to implement the programs. This limitation leaves room for the peasants to participate by expressing their views and sometimes criticizing the conduct of the cadres. For instance, when the cadres of Sun Wa Commune failed to work out overall plans of agricultural construction, they were criticized by two peasants for waste of manpower and resources.[4]

The second factor derives from the group ownership of the means of production and material resources. In general, a commune is required to manage the use of its own resources and, except in emergency, receives no help from the state. In this way, the Party has made it both *necessary* and *feasible* for the commune members to rely on themselves. They either swim or sink. Besides, since the collective ownership system makes it unlikely that individuals can realize appreciable personal gains, the group can plan the use of the resources at its disposal primarily for achieving the objectives of the development programs, instead of being overly concerned with protecting vested interests. Because the distribution of rewards is also made on a group basis, the members cannot afford to permit slack individual performance. Strictly speaking, it is not the group, as an entity, that exerts social pressure. Rather, it is the members in the group who bring pressure to bear on their peers lest their half-hearted effort adversely affect the group's collective well-being. This is how the micro and macro aspects of human interactions are integrated in China under Maoist communism.

To sum up, it was primarily through skillful communication, reinforced by coercion when necessary, that the Party authorities were initially able to involve the Chinese people—the peasants and workers—in changing the traditional social structure and its material base. Once the new social structure is embodied in the Party-controlled groups, it has the function of generating those processes of communication and group pressure that bind the Chinese people to the tasks of development as an intrinsic part of their own survival. While the old social structure conserved the traditions, the new social structure now impinges on the Chinese people in such a way that they must pool their labor and resources, largely at the dictate of the collectivity.

Characteristics of the Chinese System

Several characteristics may be noted about the Chinese social system. While there is intensive communication proceeding both vertically and horizontally, this does not mean that the people are free to say what they want. No one can challenge with impunity the basic premises of the system, that is, the subordination of individual interests to collective interests, the supremacy of the proletarian dictatorship, and the sagacity and wisdom attributed to Chairman Mao. In fact, once they are publicly proclaimed, one must only support, not dispute, the basic decisions of the Party. For instance, ever since Lin Piao was declared an ardent supporter of Confucius, the Chinese people have been diligently studying the official *People's Daily* for correct clues to guide them in their criticism of the former marshal.

Family planning provides another example. In the years of the Great Leap Forward when birth control was taboo, no one could see any benefit in limiting the number of children. People were thought to be primarily producers, not consumers. Now that the Party's policy has changed, it is recognized as a virtue to delay marriage and to observe childbirth quotas. Indeed, the intensive communication that permeates one's life is intended to mobilize the maximum public support for the Party's decisions, and to work out the most practical implementation. It is not intended to encourage skepticism and dissension.

A problem often encountered in other developing countries is the lack of communication between the planners and the people at the grassroots level. Sometimes, elaborately planned development projects have inadvertently caused near disasters to the intended beneficiaries because both the planners and even the change agents are outsiders, who do not understand the local social-ecological conditions and generally make no attempt to seek input from the villagers. This shortcoming seems to be minimized under the Chinese system. While policy decisions are centrally controlled, the Party allows extensive communication at the local level through the practice of the three-in-one union. By bringing administrative cadres, technicians, and peasants together to discuss ways of carrying out a project, this practice tends to reduce the likelihood of enforcing something that is locally infeasible.

In some developing countries, one goal is to raise individual aspirations as a requisite for development. Chinese Communist leaders seem to be doing just the opposite. Urban teenagers have been urged to "go up to the mountains and down to the villages" for permanent settlement in largely undeveloped rural areas. Cadres are required to perform manual labor as well as administrative desk work, to be reinforced by periodic journeys to the May 7 cadre school for intensive labor. The message is quite clear: do not entertain high individual aspirations; sacrifice personal gain for the good of the state. On the other hand, the mass of people, particularly the peasants, have been encouraged to raise their *collective* aspirations—for their communes, for the factories, and for the country as a whole. The collective goals are to be set high and achieved by daring to challenge the traditional social barriers and the traditional culture.

The emphasis of collective goals instead of individual aspirations has created problems of motivation for cooperation and competition. With personal gains held at a bare minimum, the Chinese seem to be following a pattern that approaches what the British sociologist Herbert Spencer called "compulsory cooperation," in which the will of the citizen in all transactions, private and public, is subordinated to that of the government.[5] The Chinese still retain some form of private life within the family. But much of what they do in cooperation with others, whether in communes or factories or schools, is overshadowed by a public will that is created and maintained by communications, value-oriented as well as normative, partly through the mass media but primarily within the group setting. The same social pressure generated through normative communication keeps up the pace of competition in the absence of strong individual incentives. The scanty evidence that occasionally leaks through the official media would suggest that the public will is not completely effective, and that individual incentives still exist within the constraints set by the Party. Nevertheless, it is clear that without the prodding of social pressure, without the push of public will, the minimum individual incentives could not have maintained the level of performance that has enabled China to achieve her present status of self-sufficiency. It may be noted that such a system of task-oriented cooperation and competition would be feasible only if job mobility is denied, as it is in China.

The processes of normative communication in the local groups have important functions for both the state and the people of China. For the state, group communication has become a vital mechanism of social control as well as a stimulant of task performance. Without the social pressure generated from group communication, the Party would have to rely either on administrative orders, which are recognized to be ineffective, or to resort to the unmitigated use of coercion, which is impracticable. With small groups, however, the Party simply sends the directives to the local cadres and lets the groups find their own ways of implementation.

The same social pressure keeps the group members away from the temptation of nonconformity and deviance. Thus, a population as large as that of China can be rigorously steered along a path designated by the Party.

For the majority of individuals, their groups can serve as a partial buffer between themselves and the state. The Party directives will have to be complied with in principle. But the groups have some leeway regarding specific implementation. Birth quotas assigned to a group, for instance, can occasionally be exchanged. Production goals are distributed among group members through discussion. Even in a criticism campaign, a group's leaders sometimes give limited shelter to some of the accused members while minimally trying to satisfy the demands of the authorities.[6] For those individuals whose class backgrounds are not contaminated, and who have worked compliantly within the overall social and economic framework, their group does provide a degree of security as well as of material subsistence. Furthermore, the group discussion of directives before implementation would give the members a sense of involvement, making the state's demands somewhat more tolerable. It is through such processes of normative communication that the local groups function as vital links between the state and the individuals.

Due to the fact that the Chinese social system decries profit-oriented "rationality," an important function, which in other societies is generally filfilled by the market mechanism, has come to be assumed by communication in China. This has to do with the information feedback function in economic decision-making. Even in this day of computerized data storage and analysis, major policy decisions in a capitalist society are usually based on no more than an educated guess. Because most economic matters are eventually settled in terms of monetary gains and losses, the marketplace with its more or less spontaneously regulated prices functions as a stabilizing force, as a kind of safety-valve. Grossly erroneous decisions are usually caught in time and corrected. In China, which practices a strictly planned economy, the feedback benefit of prices is lost. Major decisions are not always based on adequate information, which is difficult to assess anyway, but often depend on ideology and personal sentiments, as in the case of the Commune movement. In the absence of pricing mechanisms, the Party has had to rely on informational communication for essential feedback on the feasibilty and adequacy of policy decisions. It was this feedback that enabled the Party leadership to pull back from the brink of disaster in the Commune experiment.

The intensive communication in China, particularly at the grass-roots level, fulfills another function that is generally performed by public opinion polls and legislative debates in countries like the United States. Even though the Party leadership does not allow the open expression of pessimism and dissent, it is nevertheless interested in understanding the mood of the people. It wants to know their expectations and complaints. The Party is not likely to yield much ground if such expectations and complaints should run counter to the basic policy of proletarian dictatorship. However, it is in the Party's interest to minimize potential conflicts by making minor compromises. It is through communication, by sending the higher level cadres down to the villages to talk to the peasants, by encouraging the posting of tatzepao, and by allowing criticisms of a minor, practical nature in letters to the editor, that the Party keeps itself informed of public sentiments. In this way, minor conflicts can be exposed and given attention before serious tension accumulates to an unmanageable degree. Once the conflicts are presented to the public, the parties in conflict can be brought together in direct communication to seek a resolution.

Following Chairman Mao's instructions on "serving the people," the Party has been encouraging selfless service as a cardinal virtue. This is in some respects in keeping with the Chinese tradition of restraining the self in deference to the demands of authorities. Filial piety and loyalty to the emperor were virtues based on selfless dedication. Now Mao wants the Chinese to adopt a selfless spirit toward an ideologically oriented collectivity which he calls the "people." Over the years a number of heroes have been eulogized for sacrificing their lives for the people.[7] It is entirely possible that the Chinese today are more strongly motivated by a selfless concern than ever before. Of course, no society can expect its people to deny self-interest totally. The feasibility of selfless service, however, can be examined from the perspective of the reward system as it is currently practiced in China.

Because of the continuous emphasis on intergroup competition, a phenomenon known as the Peng Wei (groupism) principle has become widespread. This is reflected in an intensely eager concern for the welfare of one's own group, often achieved at the expense of other groups. When people are striving to promote their own group interest, selfless service is likely to take a back seat. Within the various groups a similar situation has been noted. During a production contest within a group, each person has to be on his own. One cannot afford to be totally selfless if he wants to maintain his standing in the competition.[8] Even when no campaign is on, the system of group evaluation of work points among the peasants, in which each person's performance is compared with that of everyone else, would tend to discourage selfless service because time spent in serving others would probably not help one's own production records. The reward system, therefore, does not seem to be conducive to selfless service despite the call of Chairman Mao.

In the beginning of this volume, we have hypothesized that value-oriented communication, though extensively employed for the long-range goal of changing the traditional Chinese values and beliefs and creating the New Chinese Man, has thus far been less vital than normative communication to the integration and functioning of the Chinese social system. We shall discuss our findings in the perspective of this hypothesis.

Mao's emphasis on value-oriented communication and ideology seems to reflect the age-old Chinese philosophy of man more than the Marxist theory. According to Marx, economic relations, particularly control over the means of production, determine social relations. Consciousness, that is, ideology, is not ignored but is regarded as a mediating factor between economic and social relations. In China, new economic relations have largely been institutionalized to the extent that the state controls all major means of production as well as the distribution of the fruits of labor. As long as the economic relations are maintained—and there seem to be few indications of any major internal challenge—the Marxists should be content to let new social relations emerge and become stabilized. Mao's insistence on continuous ideological reform, however, even after the new economic relations have been established for an entire generation, would seem to cast doubt on the validity of Marxist "inevitability." Instead, Mao's emphasis on ideology appears to lend support to the German sociologist Max Weber, who regards ideology as an independent variable in social and economic development.[9]

Indeed, Mao seems to have gone a step further than Weber because he considers ideology to be the most important factor. In this regard, he comes close to Confucius, whose teachings have now been criticized. To Mao, values and beliefs are not merely cognitive correlates of the social structure. Rather, the economic and social relations that have already been established in China are to serve as structural aids to help achieve the ultimate goal of total, voluntary acceptance of Maoist ideology by the Chinese people. If and when this goal is achieved, then the Chinese will behave not in order to fulfill self-interest, but to perform selfless service to the proletarian state according to Mao's vision—just as the Indian Brahmans chose a mystical and ascetic religious life and the medieval European aristocrats preferred a high-risk military career instead of lucrative trade.[10] The New Chinese Man will be born. No external behavioral restraints will be necessary. This emphasis on the creation of the New Chinese Man, reflecting somewhat the traditional Confucian concern for self-perfection, is a major difference between the Chinese approach and its Russian antecedent.

This kind of ideological conversion, however, is still a long-range objective for the future. The structural changes for development and the functioning and integration of the Chinese social system have thus far relied primarily on the application of social pressure through the processes of normative communication. Although value-oriented communication has played the necessary role of providing an ideological framework for social pressure, its contribution to China's development for the present seems to be secondary to that of normative communication, because *the process is more crucial than the specific content.* In other words, once the processes of normative communication have been institutionalized to generate and apply pressure, they would be adequate for getting the development tasks done even if a somewhat different ideological framework, for example, nationalism, happened to be employed.

Integration and Development

The patterns of China's development present an exception to the general trend of structural differentiation in most developed countries. Traditional societies typically are not highly differentiated. Old China, for instance, was a conglomeration of semiautonomous villages, in which the gentry class controlled the allocation of material resources, shaped the exercise of local political power, and dominated the ideology of the people through a combination of ancestor worship and Confucian ethics. The vast population was loosely held together, partly by a common culture and partly by a bureaucratic structure, whose major functions were to collect taxes and levies and to prevent serious breaches of law and order.

In a developed country, like the United States, a high level of technical specialization has been accompanied by a corresponding degree of structural differentiation in the social system. Political power, economic prowess, ideology, religion, and information dissemination have been anchored in differentiated structural bases. The political parties, big business, labor, the church, universities, voluntary associations, and mass media interact in a check-and-balance fashion. Because the locus of control is differentiated, no single interest group holds an exclusive and dominant position. Integration of such a society is achieved by what the French sociologist Emile Durkheim calls "organic solidarity," a system in which mutual interdependence makes it necessary for the different components to cooperate with and accommodate one another.[11] There is room for individual differences in thought as well as in behavior as long as the overall interdependence is not seriously threatened.

Since 1949, China has progressed a long way toward industrialization and development. A relatively high level of technical specialization has been achieved. However, China under Communism has thus far strongly resisted structural differentiation. This can be seen both at the level of broad institutions and the level of interactions in group settings. Instead of allowing the emergence of differentiated structures, the Party leadership has made an effort to merge political power, allocation of economic resources, and affirmation of ideology within one single structure. The same Party hierarchy, through its revolutionary committees, makes major policy decisions, determines the use of manpower and material resources, and sets the direction of rigid ideological conformity. All the people are guided to live within the same organized totality of beliefs and sentiments. Within the groups, instead of developing clearly delineated divisions of labor and specific role relations, the Party has fostered the three-in-one unions in which individuals in varying positions are required to work together in an undifferentiated manner. Technical specialization does not lead to role differentiations regarding rights and obligations.

Under this system, the various components are not held together primarily by interdependence, because the components have few specific functions that are exclusively their own, but rather, all depend on the Party structure for direction and guidance through its vast and efficient communication networks. Integration of the Chinese Communist social system approximates the "mechanical solidarity" Durkheim speaks of, in which individuals are subordinate to the undifferentiated collective conscience of society[12]—in this case, the Communist ideology as interpreted by Chairman Mao. It is a more or less homogeneous mass of people—peasants, workers, soldiers, students, teachers, and cadres—who should ideally be alike in dress, speech, behavior, and thought, all functioning properly under the direction of the Party organizations.

Durkheim uses the relation between a person and his possessions to illustrate the nature of mechanical solidarity, by which the people are united almost like "inanimate bodies."

What justifies this term (mechanical solidarity) is that the link which thus unites the individual to the society is wholly analogous to that which links a person and his possessions. In this light, the individual conscience is simply a reflection of the collective type and follows all of its movements as the possessed object follows those of its owner. In societies where this type of solidarity is highly developed, the individual does not belong to himself. . . . Society can literally do with him as it wishes.[13]

Seen in this light, continuous ideological indoctrination becomes necessary not only as a framework for social pressure, but also because it could eventually provide a unifying theme to bind the mass of people together. Through a constant flood of messages from the media as well as through interpersonal channels, the people of China are reminded continuously that there can be only one correct way of life, and that only in the success of proletarian revolution can they find collective security.

Social integration in this Chinese system is aided by the presence of a group of social and ideological outcasts. These are the offspring of ex-landlords, ex-rich peasants, and urban capitalists, the rightists, and those who are broadly categorized as "bad elements." They belong to the class of former oppressors. In the early years after the revolution, individuals with such class backgrounds enjoyed a brief period of benign neglect. Some of them were able to advance occupationally through academic achievements.[14] The Cultural Revolution cast them out of the social mainstream. Now they are referred to as class enemies. They have practically no access to higher education or responsible positions. Other persons apparently avoid associating with them, either in social interactions or in marriage, lest such association impair their own "social relations," which are important for schooling and occupational advancement. The presence of the "bad elements" has been maintained for a number of reasons. They are often singled out for criticism during mass campaigns. Numbering approximately 10 to 15 percent of the total population, they constitute a valuable source of labor.[15] Their social stigma serves as a constant reminder of the oppressor class in the old society. It gives the mass of people a sense of "we" against "them." They are a convenient scapegoat when something goes wrong. In short, their presence contributes to the integration of the rest of the population by serving as a negative reference group.

Toward the mass of people, on the other hand, the Party appears to show some tolerance of minor deviations, reflecting, as it were, a concern for integration. The Party is probably aware that not all behavior proceeds according to the rigid ideological reqirements it has set down. It apparently knows, as illustrated by refugee accounts, that peasants in some areas are working hard on their private plots.[16] It also knows, as acknowledged in the official media, that many people are "following the main current" and utter superficial platitudes in criticism sessions. It cannot be unaware of the bureaucratic practices of its cadres, as they have been bared in the campaign against Lin Piao and Confucius. The many wasteful practices that came to public attention during the Cultural Revolution were probably not characteristic of that period alone. The Party has directed constant attention to these problems in many campaigns. But it has stopped short of pushing the people and cadres too hard. Between campaigns there is ususally a period of respite. It may be called a case of "communication by silence," that is, a message communicated not by what one says but by what one does not say. It gives the mass of people some room for catching their breath, albeit rather narrow room.

A basic problem inherent in the Chinese Communist approach has to do with the prospect of sustained economic growth after the initial successes of specific development programs. Development, no matter how it is conceptualized, is an ongoing, continuous progress, not something that a nation can achieve by a set target date. It involves the continuous release and utilization of human and material resources. For this reason, the manner in which a country achieves its transition from underdevelopment to development—the so-called economic takeoff—is important not only in terms of immediate results, but also in its implications for continued self-sustaining growth.

It is conceivable that certain patterns of transition are more conducive than others to sustained future development, even though they may seem to have a lower rate of return in the present. Not knowing what all the possible patterns are, we can think of at least two general categories from the structural point of view. One we would call the assimilative pattern, in which the various elements of society are generally allowed to play some constructive roles even though their overall performance may not appear to be economically efficient. It is conceivable, however, that in the long run the various components of society would develop a kind of interdependence similar to Durkheim's organic solidarity. With such interdependence, rigid ideological conformity would not be necessary and there would be no need to divert an excessive amount of human energy to contesting one another. Given a favorable economic environment, a steady and sustained pace of development may follow even though initial progress is not impressive.

The other general category we shall call the conflict-generating pattern, for want of a better term. This pattern, as exemplified by Marxist teachings, seeks to generate human energy for development from the class struggle. Not all elements of society are allowed to play constructive roles in the course of development. Only those whose class backgrounds and ideological commitments are considered correct can have full participation. The others, presumably a minority, are treated as enemies to be struggled against. Within the participant mass of people, structural differentiation is not encouraged because it might foster interest-group autonomy and thereby weaken the overall monolithic unity. Ideological reinforcement and continuous class struggle are necessary in order to maintain a high degree of identity and motivation among the mass of people. Because huge manpower resources can be mobilized under this pattern, its initial rate of achievement may be quite impressive. The question is: how long can a society keep up an internal class struggle as a way of releasing human energy for development? An even graver risk lies in the possibility that once a society has established a pattern of conflict as a way of life, there may develop a tendency to engage in social conflict continuously even when the need for class struggle no longer exists.

Transferability of the Chinese Experience

In the beginning of this volume, we raised the question of whether, and to what extent, China's experience of development can be applied or adapted to other countries. We shall now return to this question.[17]

China has achieved notable results through her development efforts. Ever since agricultural production recovered in the aftermath of the commune experiment, China has generally been able to feed her population of some eight hundred million people. Medical care has improved as a result of the barefoot doctor system. The birthrate has been lowered substantially, particularly in the last few years. Unemployment, a plague in other developing countries, does not pose a serious problem in China since all who can work share in collective labor. With universal education for nearly all school-age children, the rate of literacy has increased. The foreign domination that was ushered in by the Opium War has come to an end at last with the departure of the most recent wave of outsiders, the Russians. While individual aspirations are held back, the system does seem to provide a degree of material security to a majority of the Chinese people. When a country like Ethiopia surveys the problems at home and then looks at these results of China's development, it would naturally be attracted by the Chinese model.

It appears that the Chinese authorities themselves have not been overly active in recommending their methods to other countries. Deputy Foreign Minister Chang Han-fu, for instance, refused to say that other nations should adopt the Chinese Communist approach, but suggested that it is "a matter entirely for decision by the people of the countries concerned."[18] Before discussing the question of transferability, however, we shall consider a basic issue that calls for a policy decision of a philosophical nature.

If we look at the experiences of Western European countries, particularly of Great Britain during the Industrial Revolution, we can see development as essentially a process of changes in the social organization, necessitated by advances in technology, in order to make optimal use of manpower and material resources. In Britain, it was primarily innovations in textile manufacturing that initiated a series of far-reaching changes in both the way of life of individuals and societal modes of organization, resulting in sustained development over nearly a century. There is a crucial element in this process, namely, the new technology that started the development was itself a product of the preexisting indigenous social-economic system. Therefore, even though the European development was not without its birth pains, the social organizational changes that took place to accommodate the new technological advancements came about largely through an evolutionary interplay of economic factors and social demands. It did not require a revolutionary social transformation.

Situations today are quite different for countries in the less-developed world. In order to develop, and indeed just to survive, there are no alternatives except to make a serious effort to adapt some of the new technology. China, for instance, did not reject modern technology, but rather, has prepared herself organizationally to make an efficient use of technology within the limits of her own resources and ideological framework. However, the cultural and structural foundations that enabled countries like Britain to move ahead in the early nineteenth century are generally absent in most of the developing countries. Britain was fortunate enough to have a largely literate population, a strong Protestant work ethic, an intellectual climate that encouraged innovations, a rigid structure of primogeniture that forced younger sons to seek occupational and social mobility elsewhere, a relatively well-developed transportation network of roads and canals to move materials and manufactured goods, and fairly efficient financial and marketing institutions, not to mention her natural resources and readily available colonial markets. Few developing countries today are so enviably endowed. Modern technology from the West just does not fit well into their social-economic systems, as the frustrating experiences of Manchu China demonstrated. The course of events that happened in Europe following its revolution in technology will not repeat itself in the less-developed world.

Thus, it seems that a key question facing the developing countries today is not whether they can afford to wait a hundred years, but whether merely "waiting" for a hundred years would do them any good. The question is not *when* they will become developed, but rather, whether development is *feasible,* given a country's existing social structure. The question is not whether a country should seek industrialization or urbanization, but rather, whether it is necessary to introduce certain changes in its social structure in order to make an optimal use of modern technology for development. This is a philosophical question to which each country must seek an answer of its own. To consider transferability of the Chinese experience without facing this basic issue would be like, to cite an old Chinese saying, trying to uproot a tree "by pulling its leaves instead of its roots."

If, as a result of policy determination, some changes in social structure are deemed necessary for development, then the leadership of a country needs to consider a second question. That is, how extensive the structural changes should be, and whether the changes are to be brought about primarily through a process of *stimulated evolution* following initial change programs by the government, or through a process of *radical change*, or a mixture of both. It is by no means clear that radical structural change is the only feasible road toward development. But if a country should prefer to go that route, then it can ask itself further questions regarding the feasibility of the Chinese approach. First, does it have complete control of the mass media as the Communist party does in China? To the extent that the media are not under complete control, then unanimity and a perceptual basis of legitimacy probably cannot readily be achieved for the actions the government may want to take.

Second, does it have an effective apparatus to organize and carry out massive campaigns of interpersonal communication at the group level? As the Chinese Communist party leaders themselves have acknowledged, none of the social structural changes could have been brought about by administrative orders. Social structure can be changed only at the grassroots level. If a government does not have control at that level, as Peking does through its Party cadres in local groups, attempting to change the social structure would most likely create confusion or even chaos.

Third, it must examine the nature of its existing social structure to see if a sufficient basis of genuine grievances can be found in order to exploit and expand interclass conflict. Without such a basis, the initial class struggle and the revolutionary structural change would be difficult to achieve.

Furthermore, does the government have complete control over the allocation of material resources and manpower to back up the application of group pressure? After all, the Chinese Communist system is able to function at its present level of efficiency because other than the group an individual is assigned to—whether a commune, a factory, or a mine—there are practically no alternative contexts in which he can expect to find the material support for his survival. Group pressure in China is effective because the individual cannot afford to leave the group.

At this point, one needs to note the delicate state of equilibrium that seems to exist in the new social structure of China. There have been periods of unrest and passive resistance in mainland China during the last two decades. But up until the industrial strikes in Chekiang Province in the summer of 1975, there have been few indications that the peasants and workers have actively sought to change their positions in the overall structure.[19] A number of explanations can be offered: the lack of organization, the tremendous odds against any attempt at change, the slowly improving standard of living, a sense of participation, and a feeling of national purpose. All these may be valid. However, one must not overlook an important characteristic of the Chinese people: a capacity for tolerance and patience even in situations of severe stress. These attributes seem to be a reflection of submission to authority that has been noted as part of the Chinese personality. Because of their traditional deference to authority figures, the Chinese thus far seem to be tolerant of what other peoples would regard as excessive demands by their government.[20] Furthermore, for centuries the Chinese have been accustomed to hard work as a way of compensating for their inadequate technology. Their low level of productivity and their inability to cope with natural calamities have created a habit of practicing economy.[21] These qualities of diligence and frugality would seem to make it easier for the Chinese to accept the Communist programs of production increase and consumption curtailment. One is tempted to speculate whether these attributes—submission to authority, frugality, and acceptance of hard work—might not be part of the reasons why violent reactions occurred in countries like Poland, Hungary, and East Germany, but not in China until the Tienanmen Square riots in April 1976.[22] Thus, another question for any nation considering the Chinese model: are the cultural characteristics such as to mitigate the mood of resistance and ease the process of turbulent change?

Finally, there is a question of value judgment: are the leaders and the people prepared to bear the enormous human cost that the

Chinese sustained, particularly during the initial period of the revolution? Is the Chinese Communist approach the only feasible one? It seems that all these questions would have to be answered before the Chinese Communist model of development could be given very serious consideration by other developing countries.

Whether or not the Chinese Communist approach lends itself to any specific country, it does suggest a number of general principles relevant to development. First, development programs must reach the people. They must involve the people in planning, implementation, and evaluation. An extensive amount of communication, both vertical and horizontal, is necessary in order to achieve this objective. If there are structural obstacles, the country must consider feasible ways of removing or minimizing them.

Second, development programs must seek to improve the life of peasants and workers as well as the more privileged segments of society. This objective probably cannot be achieved without a redistribution of wealth. The country would have to be prepared to sacrifice some vested interests in order to reallocate material resources and make development possible. It must be prepared to act, and not let plans merely sit on shelves. Communication can play a vital role by arousing the people to the need of development, by explaining the overall objectives and getting adequate feedback, and by mobilizing popular support in order to minimize resistance by those whose vested interests would be affected.

Third, development is an all-out effort, not confined to one or two aspects of productive activities. It has to be tackled in a holistic, not a piecemeal, manner. It generally requires change in cultural values as well as in economic behavior. It involves changes not only of individual attitudes and behavior, but also of patterns of interactions in a group setting. Group behavioral change may well be more important than individual behavioral change in some contexts. In short, development means the building of new social institutions, to be supported by new normative behavioral patterns—new values, new beliefs, and new actions. In this sense, development necessitates communication because it is only through the communication process that the new patterns of interactions can be depicted, elicited, and reinforced. It is also through communication that the validity of traditional values and beliefs can be reassessed and alternatives advocated. In the course of building new social institutions, it is usually necessary to modify or even to transform old institutions. Heavy reliance on coercion may be an expedient way, but may be counterproductive in the long run. Communication can act as a lubricant to smooth the process of change. It seems that the more the people are allowed to participate in the process of change—through extensive communication—the less likely the course of development will be disruptive to the society as a whole.

We shall close our discussion of development with a brief note on the role of ideology. Ideology is a powerful stimulant of human behavior. It has achieved many wonders in man's varied history. The validity of ideology, however, needs to be tested against reality, at least occasionally. The American Nobel laureate in economics, Simon Kuznets, expresses a concern which is perhaps shared by many who care about the future of the developing peoples.

For if any of the older theories concerning economic growth or social life in general are congealed into a doctrine and given the official blessing of immutability and perennial validity; if they become the basis, no matter how violated in practice, of a policy gospel that is above criticism; and if means of communication are barred to anyone who dares to review the doctrines in the light of new evidence, the consequences can easily be foreseen.[23]

Appendix A
Mao Tse-Tung:
Twenty Manifestations of Bureaucracy*

1. At the highest level there is very little knowledge; they do not understand the opinion of the masses; they do not investigate and study; they do not grasp specific policies; they do not conduct political and ideological work; they are divorced from reality, from the masses, and from the leadership of the party; they always issue orders, and the orders are usually wrong; they certainly mislead the country and the people; at the least they obstruct the consistent adherence to the party line and policies; and they cannot meet with the people.

2. They are conceited, complacent, and they aimlessly discuss politics. They do not grasp their work; they are subjective and one-sided; they are careless; they do not listen to people; they are truculent and arbitrary; they force orders; they do not care about reality; they maintain blind control. This is authoritarian bureaucracy.

3. They are very busy from morning until evening; they labor the whole year long; they do not examine people and they do not investigate matters; they do not study policies; they do not rely upon

---

*From Joint Publications Research Service (JPRS), U.S. Department of Commerce (49826) No. 90, February 12, 1970.

the masses; they do not prepare their statements; they do not plan their work. This is brainless, misdirected bureaucracy. In other words, it is routinism.

4. Their bureaucratic attitude is immense; they can not have any direction; they are egoistic; they beat their gongs to blaze the way; they cause people to become afraid just by looking at them; they repeatedly hurl all kinds of abuse at people; their work style is crude; they do not treat people equally. This is the bureaucracy of the overlords.

5. They are ignorant; they are ashamed to ask anything; they exaggerate and they lie; they are very false; they attribute errors to people; they attribute merit to themselves; they swindle the central government; they deceive those above them and fool those below them; they conceal faults and gloss over wrongs. This is the dishonest bureaucracy.

6. They do not understand politics; they do not do their work; they push things off onto others; they do not meet their responsibilities; they haggle; they put things off; they are insensitive; they lose their alertness. This is the irresponsible bureaucracy.

7. They are negligent about things; they subsist as best they can; they do not have anything to do with people; they always make mistakes; they offer themselves respectfully to those above them and are idle towards those below them; they are careful in every respect; they are eight-sided and slippery as eels. This is the bureaucracy of those who work as officials and barely make a living.

8. They do not completely learn politics; they do not advance in their work; their manner of speech is tasteless; they have no direction in their leadership; they neglect the duties of their office while taking the pay; they make up things for the sake of appearances. The idlers (for example, the landlord) do not begin any matters, but concentrate mainly upon their idleness; those who work hard are virtuous, and do not act like the officials are treated poorly. This is the deceitful, talentless bureaucracy.

9. They are stupid; they are confused; they do not have a mind of their own; they are rotten sensualists; they glut themselves for days on end; they are not diligent at all, they are inconstant and they are ignorant. This is the stupid, useless bureaucracy.

10. They want others to read documents; the others read and they sleep; they criticize without looking at things; they criticize mistakes and blame people; they have nothing to do with mistakes;

they do not discuss things; they put things aside and ignore it; they are yes men to those above them; they pretend to understand those below them, when they do not; they gesticulate; and they harbor disagreements with those on their same level. This is the lazy bureaucracy.

11. Government offices grow bigger and bigger; things are more confused; there are more people than there are jobs; they go around in circles; they quarrel and bicker; people are disinclined to do extra things; they do not fulfill their specific duties. This is the bureaucracy of government offices.

12. Documents are numerous; there is red tape; instructions proliferate; there are numerous unread reports that are not criticized; many tables and schedules are drawn up and are not used; meetings are numerous and nothing is passed on; and there are many close associations but nothing is learned. This is the bureaucracy of red tape and formalism.

13. They seek pleasure and fear hardships; they engage in backdoor deals; one person becomes an official and the entire family benefits; one person reaches nirvana and all his close associates rise up to heaven; there are parties and gifts are presented. . . . This is the bureaucracy for the exceptional.

14. The greater an official becomes, the worse his temperament gets; his demands for supporting himself become higher and higher; his home and its furnishings become more and more luxurious; and his access to things becomes better and better. The upper strata gets the larger share while the lower gets high prices; there is extravagance and waste; the upper and lower and the left and right raise their hands. This is the bureaucracy of putting on official airs.

15. They are egotistical; they satisfy private ends by public means; there is embezzlement and speculation; the more they devour, the more they want; and they never step back or give in. This is egotistical bureaucracy.

16. They fight among themselves for power and money; they extend their hands into the party; they want fame and fortune; they want positions, and if they do not get it they are not satisfied; they choose to be fat and to be lean; they pay a great deal of attention to wages; they are cozy when it comes to their comrades but they care nothing about the masses. This is the bureaucracy that is fighting for power and money.

17. A plural leadership cannot be harmoniously united; they ex-

ert themselves in many directions, and their work is in a state of chaos; they try to crowd each other out; the top is divorced from the bottom and there is no centralization, nor is there any democracy. This is the disunited bureaucracy.

18. There is no organization; they employ personal friends; they engage in factionalism; they maintain feudal relationships; they form cliques to further their own private interest; they protect each other; the individual stands above everything else; these petty officials harm the masses. This is sectarian bureaucracy.

19. Their revolutionary will is weak; their politics has degenerated and changed its character; they act as if they are highly qualified; they put on official airs; they do not exercise their minds or their hands. They eat their fill every day; they easily avoid hard work; they call a doctor when they are not sick; they go on excursions to the mountains and to the seashore; they do things superficially; they worry about their individual interests, but they do not worry whatsoever about the national interest. This is degenerate bureaucracy.

20. They promote erroneous tendencies and a spirit of reaction; they connive with bad persons and tolerate bad situations; they engage in villainy and transgress the law; they engage in speculation; they are a threat to the party and the state; they suppress democracy; they fight and take revenge; they violate laws and regulations; they protect the bad; they do not differentiate between the enemy and ourselves. This is the bureaucracy of erroneous tendencies and reaction.

Appendix B
Mao Tse-Tung:
Talks With Party Leaders
at the 1964 Spring Festival
on Educational Work (February 13, 1964) *

Today I want to talk to you about education. Today industry has made great progress and I believe that education should also have some reforms. However, education as it now is still leaves much to be desired.

The period of schooling may be shortened.

[The Government] may organize a women's militia or women's corps so that girls sixteen or seventeen years of age may experience a military life for six months to one year. I think those seventeen-year-olds may also serve in the army.

There are at present too many curricula that drive people to death. Students at primary and middle schools and colleges are living in a tense environment every day. Their eyes are getting more near-sighted day by day because the school facilities are bad; lighting conditions are poor.

Curricula may be reduced by half. It won't do to have students having no cultural recreation, such as swimming and sports.

Historically, the highest graduates of the Hanlin Academy were not very outstanding. Li Pai and Tu Fu were neither Chinshih nor Hanlin. Han Yu and Liu Chung-yuan were only second degree

*From *Current Background*, No. 891 (October 8, 1969), pp. 42–44.

Chinshih. Wang Shih-fu, Kuan Han-ching, Lo Kuan-chung, Pu Sung-ling and Chao Hsueh-chin were neither Chinshih nor Hanlin. Not all those who were awarded the degrees of Chinshih or Hanlin succeeded.

Among the emperors of the Ming dynasty, only Ming Tai Chu (accession A. D. 1368) and Ming Cheng Chu (accession A. D. 1403) were successful. One of them could not read and the other could read only a few words. Later in the reign of Chia Ching (A. D. 1522–1566), intellectuals came to power. This led to no good. The nation was badly ruled. Those who read more books could not make good emperors and were harmful to the welfare of the people. Liu Hsiu was only a grand secretary and Liu Pang a big bag of wind, yet both were excellent emperors of the Han Dynasty.

The current examination methods contain many surprises, unusual questions, and difficult problems. They are designed to deal with the enemy, not the people. These types of examinations were used in the old days in the writing of the eight-legged essays. I do not approve of them and think that they should be completely remolded. I suggest taking some sample examination problems and having them published. Let the students study and answer them with open books. For example, we might consider preparing twenty questions about *The Dream of the Red Chamber.* If a student can correctly answer questions and if some of the answers are good and creative, he may be given 100 points. If he answers all 20 questions and the answers are correct but are ordinary without creative thinking, he should be given 50 or 60 points. In examinations, students should be allowed to whisper to each other and to hire others to take the examinations for them. If your answer is right, I copy yours. Copying is good too. In the past, whispering and hiring of examinees were done on the sly. Now let them be open. When I cannot do what you have done, then let me copy. It should be allowed. We should experiment with this system.

Teachers giving lectures should allow the students to fall asleep. If the lecture is no good, it makes no sense to force others to listen. Listening to distasteful things with eyes opened wide is worse than sleeping in the class. Sleeping may help one to recover from fatigue. Students should be given the choice of not listening to monotonous lectures.

The present methods are detrimental to talented men and youths. I do not think that people should study so much. Examinations are designed for dealing with the enemy. They poison people to death and should be abolished.

Actors, actresses, poets, dramatists, and writers should be driven out of the cities and all of them should be sent down in groups to the rural areas and factories. They should not always stay in offices. If they do so, they can write nothing. Only when you go down to the rural areas should you be provided with rice.

Li Shih-chen of the Ming dynasty personally went to search for herbs in the countryside for a long time; Chu Chung-chih did not attend any middle school or college. Confucius was brought up in a poor peasant family. He was once a shepherd and never attended a college. At one time he was a trumpeter playing at funerals. He also practiced accounting, learned to play string instruments, shoot arrows, and drive carts. Since he came from the masses, he knew the pains of the masses. Later on, when he served as an official in the State of Lu, he became a great intellectual and was alienated from the activities of the masses. This was probably so because he employed as his bodyguard Tze Lu, who kept the masses away. Our policies are correct, but the methods are wrong. The current duration of schooling and curricula and the teaching and examination methods must all be reformed. All of them are very detrimental.

Gorky attended school for only two years; his knowledge was gained entirely through his own efforts. Benjamin Franklin of America sold newspapers when he was young. James Watt, the inventor of the steam engine, was a laborer.

We should not read too many books. We must read Marxist books but not too many of them. A few dozen of such books will suffice. Reading too many books will lead the readers to take opposing views and to become bookworms, dogmatists, or revisionists.

Confucian teachings do not contain any instruction on industry and agriculture. Therefore, students of Confucius exercise their limbs less and know no names for grains. We must do something about this problem.

The problem now is that there are too many courses and too many books that overload the students. It is not necessary that all subjects have to be tested. For instance, middle-school students should learn a little logic and grammar without being subjected to any test. They will comprehend these in time when they are engaged in practical work. It is enough for them to know what is grammar and what is logic.

Appendix C
A Note on Methodology and Structural Analysis

Sources of Material

A few words may be in order regarding the sources of material for this book. In discussing research on contemporary China, the American sinologist Michel Oksenberg lists five primary sources: (1) mainland Chinese press and monitored radio broadcasts; (2) former residents of the People's Republic; (3) visitors' accounts; (4) novels and short stories published by the People's Republic; and (5) secret Chinese Communist documents.[1] One more source can be mentioned now that the door to China is ajar: on-the-scene interviews and observation in China.

In preparing this book, I have relied heavily on mainland Chinese publications, particularly the *People's Daily,* which is most readily available. The Party official journal, *Red Flag,* has been cited frequently for much the same reason. Other Chinese mainland publications have been used to the extent that their contents are available. Radio broadcasts monitored from China, particularly in more recent years, have been scanned as another useful source.

No attempt has been made to conduct systematic interviews with former residents of the People's Republic, except as they were introduced to the writer through mutual acquaintances. The number of former residents thus interviewed was rather small, and the contents of the conversations were somewhat varied according to the circumstances under which they took place. Quantitative results would not be meaningful, and thus were not attempted. Nor were any parts of the conversations cited in this volume. These informal interviews, however, have been highly valuable in providing background information and occasional insights.

Over the years, a number of former residents have published accounts of their experiences in China, in either English or Chinese. These have been used rather frequently in this volume for purposes of illustration. Since the door to China was opened in 1972, some scholars and correspondents have been able to visit the country. Their accounts have been a rich source of information. China watchers and correspondents posted in Hong Kong are also useful sources.

No attempts have been made to use novels and short stories published in the People's Republic. Even though their contents are often highly revealing and should lend themselves to analysis of themes and styles, they are not immediately relevant to the research problems at hand.[2] The writer has no access to any secret Chinese documents that may have fallen into the hands of outside agencies.

The analysis of the processes of social structural change requires a historical perspective. The examination of Chinese publications and documents over the years is therefore necessary and useful. However, such an analysis would also call for a study of the social structure in its present form. For this purpose, on-the-scene interviews and observation would be highly relevant. When a team of American scholars was visiting China in 1973, an agreement was reached by which the government of the People's Republic permits researchers from the United States to undertake a number of projects in cooperation with Chinese scholars—for instance, plant studies, earthquake prediction, acupuncture, archaeology, and others.[3] The American visitors brought up the topic of research proposals in the social sciences and humanities, including China studies. Premier Chou En-lai, who talked to the delegation from the Social Science Research Council for two hours on May 27, 1973, explained with reference to these proposals, "I have found that we need a stage of preparation. I am still hopeful that they can be taken up in the future."[4]

The inability of a researcher to visit China and observe Chinese society first hand need not be a serious handicap, although it does temporarily result in the loss of a valuable source of information. The American anthropologist Francis L. K. Hsu, who visited China recently with his family, made the comment that ". . . each observer, native or foreign, can see only a segment of reality, inevitably colored by his or her background and previous experience. We can approach the truth only by observing the same event from different angles aided by observers of diverse backgrounds."[5]

As long as observers of differing backgrounds have been able to get into China and bring back their diverse impressions, it is relatively unimportant whether or not each researcher is able to visit the land himself. By objectively analyzing these sources, by methodically examining the contents of mainland Chinese publications (which usually present the official viewpoints of the Party), we hope it is possible to come up with a balanced assessment of the reality.

Analysis of Structural Changes

Social structural change is a broad concept. Following Radcliffe-Brown, social structure is conceptualized as a network of role relations that exist in and through communication.[6] The overall structure of a society like China consists of a system of structural components, that is, family, commune, street committee, school, and others, each of which is referred to as an institution. Identifiable within an institution are certain regulated and patterned social processes (interactions) that relate the participants to one another to form a structural unit.

Function as a concept refers to the manner in which the the social processes in an institution contribute to the operation of (a) the individual role players who participate in the institution, and/or (b) other structural components in the broad social system of which the institution is a part. Those functions that are considered necessary for the operation of a social system are referred to as functional requisites.[7] Socialization of a child is an example. The family is an institution in which the child interacts with his parents following some regulated patterns, and such patterns of interactions are said to be functional in the sense that they will help the child maintain his status within the family, get along with others outside the family as he grows up, and play other roles that are essential to the operation of the entire social system.

Even though both structure and function are conceptualized in behavioral, interactional terms, they are distinct concepts by virtue of the different perspectives employed. By structure, we refer to the patterns of interactions within an institution. By function, we refer to the relations (consequences) of such interactions (say, within the family) to other interactions (outside the family) in different institutions. Functions may be manifest or latent. The notion of structural alternatives implies that different social systems may have different patterns of interactions (structural alternatives) that can fulfill the same functional requisite, for example, socialization.

The structural components of a society are assumed to be interrelated in such a manner as to form a system, in the sense that change in one structural component is likely to be followed by changes in some other components. This interrelatedness therefore represents a moving, not a static equilibrium. By social structural change, we mean change in the patterns of interactions affecting the rights and obligations of the role participants.[8] For instance, the interaction patterns between landlords and tenants were changed and their rights and obligations redefined after the land reform. The structural change can be gradual and evolutionary, or drastic and revolutionary, as in China. It can happen due to internal structural strain, or as a result of external pressure, or both.

The process of development may be seen in terms of changes in the social structure in order to make the optimal use of manpower and materials with the latest advancement of technology. In analyzing China's process of development, we essentially ask: What specific social structural changes have taken place? It is recognized that development can take different routes, and that there can be different ways by which the full use of manpower, efficient division of labor, and application of technology can be achieved. In order to understand China's development in a more general framework, however, it would be desirable to cast the specific structural changes that have occurred in China in terms that would permit cross-cultural comparison. We have thus chosen to analyze our data under a number of functional requisites, that is, common problems that must be solved in order to facilitate development. These are: capital formation, establishment of a communication network, cooperation and competition, manpower training, responsive decision-making, and conflict resolution. These are by no means proposed as the only functional requisites for development. They are simply among the more salient features in the Chinese experience, reflecting perhaps part of the social structural fabric that is crucial to development.

In short, it is assumed that, for development to take place, certain functional requisites must be met, but each society may have its own ways, its own structural alternatives for fulfilling those functional requisites. Researchers interested in analyzing the development patterns in another country can examine the Chinese experience, and see how it may differ from that of the other country in terms of those functional requisites.

Appendix D
Plates

A demonstrator from the agricultural cooperative helps a mutual aid team test out its newly bought plough. (*China Pictorial,* April 1954, p. 23).

Factory director Yuan Yi-shen discusses cotton production with workers. (*Jen Min Hua Pao,* no. 6, 1966, p. 12).

Peasants working to reclaim an old riverbed under the direction of their leader. (*China Pictorial*, June 1958, p.28).

Peasants and their families at a criticism meeting shout slogans to condemn Liu Shao-chi's agricultural policy. (*Jen Min Hua Pao*, no. 12, 1967, p. 32).

Commune members building a reservoir. (*Jen Min Hua Pao,*
no. 4, 1966, p. 35).

Leadership cadres discuss production problems with workers in a factory.
(*Jen Min Hua Pao,* no. 3, 1966, p. 26).

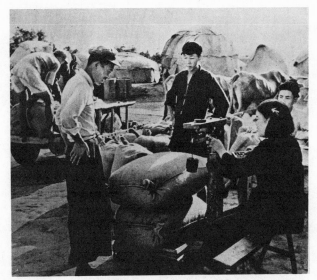

Members of an agricultural cooperative sold part of their grain to the state in the 1950s. (*China Pictorial,* August 1955, p. 33).

Agricultural cooperative members holding a discussion meeting with their team leader in the field. (*China Pic-torial,* October 1953, p.18).

Commune members holding small-group discussion to criticize anti-Party, anti-Socialism thinking and behavior. (*Jen Min Hua Pao,* no. 10, 1966, p. 9).

A mass criticism meeting in Tsing Tao. (*Jen Min Hua Pao,* no. 11, 1967, p. 18).

A "family criticism meeting" attended by workers and their families. (*Jen Min Hua Pao,* no. 12, 1967, p. 33).

Members of an agricultural cooperative working together during threshing. (*China Pictorial,* October 1958, p. 2).

Members of a youth shock brigade working on a farm. (*China Pictorial*, July 1955, p. 14).

Peasant representatives inspecting a model paddy field. (*China Pictorial*, September 1955, p. 14).

A peasant tells his story of the "bitterness of the past and the sweetness of the present" at a mass criticism rally. (*Jen Min Hua Pao*, no. 11, 1967, p.19).

Workers celebrate the completion of a production contest with banners and drums. Big character poster salutes Chairman Mao Tse-tung. (*Jen Min Hua Pao*, no. 4, 1967, p. 13).

Chairman Mao Tse-tung chatting with peasants during his cross-country tour in 1958. (*China Pictorial,* September 1958, p. 3).

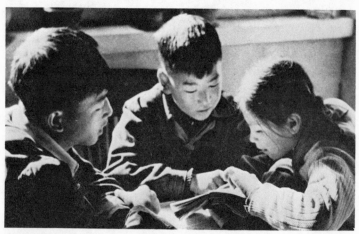

Children learn the ideology of collectivism in a small study group. (*Jen Min Hua Pao,* no. 6, 1966, p. 24).

Factory workers in Shanghai, organized into small groups, study the works of Chairman Mao Tse-tung. (*Jen Min Hua Pao,* no. 12, 1967, p.26).

Peasants and their families in an isolated mountain area study Chairman Mao's saying: "Never be selfish, always work for others." (*Jen Min Hua Pao,* no. 6, 1967, p. 7).

Writing tatzepao is often a group activity, as demonstrated by students at the Hunan First Teachers' College. (*Jen Min Hua Pao,* no. 9, 1966, p. 47).

Students at Peking University posting tatzepao. (*Jen Min Hua Pao,* no. 11, 1967, p. 7).

Big character posters cover street walls. (*Jen Min Hua Pao*, no. 4, 1967, p. 25).

Residents in Peking, organized into small groups, study the works of Chairman Mao Tse-tung. (*Jen Min Hua Pao*, no. 2, 1967, p. 17).

A wired loudspeaker is set up in a village to broadcast domestic and international news. (*Jen Min Hua Pao,* no. 5, 1972, p. 33).

Notes

CHAPTER I
1. This brief account is based on Chang Kuo-tao, *My Memoir*, vol. 1, chap. 6, "The First National Congress of the Chinese Communist Party" (Hong Kong: Ming Pao Publishers, 1971), pp. 133–148. Chang, then a student of Peking University, was the chairman of the meeting.

2. *Quotations from Chairman Mao Tse-tung* (Peking: Foreign Language Press, 1967), p. 118.

3. See Fei Hsiao-tung, *Peasant Life in China* (New York: Dutton, 1939); also Chung-li Chang, *The Chinese Gentry: Studies on Their Role in Nineteenth Century Chinese Society* (Seattle: University of Washington Press, 1955).

4. These estimates were made by Shu-ching Lee. See Lee, "The Heart of China's Problem, the Land Tenure System," *Journal of Farm Economics* 30(1948): 259–270.

5. Francis L. K. Hsu, *Under the Ancestors' Shadow* (London: Routledge & Kegan Paul, 1949); also Hsu, *Americans and Chinese: Two Ways of Life* (New York: Abelard-Schuman, 1953).

6. For concepts of economic development, see Simon Kuznets, *Economic Growth* (Glencoe, Ill.: Free Press, 1959); Kuznets, *Economic Growth and Structure* (New York: W. W. Norton, 1965); Kuznets, *Economic Growth of Nations: Total Output and Production Structure* (Cambridge: Harvard University Press, Belknap Press, 1971); for a non-American view of development, see Celso Furtado, *Development and Underdevelopment* (Berkeley: University of California Press, 1964).

7. Joseph A. Schumpeter, *The Theory of Economic Development: An Enquiry into Profits, Capital, Credit, Interest and the Business Cycle* (Cambridge: Harvard

University Press, 1934); John M. Keynes, *The General Theory of Employment, Interest and Money* (New York: Harcourt, Brace & World, 1936).

8. For instance, there must be tax inducements for investment, legal production of private property, a banking system to facilitate and protect savings, a stock exchange to adjust and relocate the flow of capital, corporate law to protect investors from management manipulation, and state regulation of money supply, etc.

9. Max Weber, *The Protestant Ethic and the Spirit of Capitalism* (New York: Scribner, 1958).

10. For a discussion of vicious circle and growth cycle, see Daniel Lerner, "Toward a Communication Theory of Modernization: A Set of Considerations," in Lucian W. Pye, ed., *Communications and Political Development* (Princeton, Princeton University Press, 1963), pp. 327–350.

11. For instance, the social structural background of the British industrial revolution is discussed by Neil J. Smelser, "Sociological History: The Industrial Revolution of the British Working-Class Family," in Smelser, *Essays in Sociological Explanation* (Englewood Cliffs: Prentice-Hall, Inc., 1968), pp. 76–91.

12. Karl Marx, *Capital: A Critique of Political Economy*, vol. 1, *The Process of Capitalist Production* (Chicago: Charles H. Kerr, 1919).

13. Sun Yat-sen, *The Three Principles of the People*, Frank W. Price, trans. (Shanghai: China Committee, Institute of Pacific Relations, 1927); also *Fundamentals of National Reconstruction* (Shanghai: Shanghai Commercial Press, 1930).

14. For the concept of social system as a network of role relations, see Talcott Parsons, *The Social System* (Glencoe, Ill.: Free Press, 1951). Also see A. R. Radcliffe-Brown, "On Social Structure," in *Structure and Function in Primitive Society* (New York: Free Press, 1956), pp. 188–204. Social change is discussed by Parsons, "The Processes of Change of Social Systems," in Parsons, *Social System*, pp. 480–535; and Neil J. Smelser, "Toward a General Theory of Social Change," in Smelser, *Essays*, pp. 192–280.

15. Herbert Spencer, *Principles of Sociology*, vol. 1 (London: Williams and Norgate, 1876), pp. 437–442; Charles Cooley, *Social Organization* (New York: Charles Scribner's Sons, 1909), p. 61; Edward Sapir, "Communication," in *Encyclopedia of the Social Sciences*, 1st edition (New York: MacMillan, 1935, vol. 4), p. 78; Robert E. Park, "Reflections on Communication and Culture," *American Journal of Sociology* 44 (1939): 191–205. Also John Dewey, *Human Nature and Conduct* (New York: Henry Holt & Co., 1922), pp. 58–63.

16. Daniel Lerner, *The Passing of Traditional Society: Modernizing the Middle East* (Glencoe, Ill.: Free Press, 1958).

17. Wilbur Schramm, *Men, Messages and Media* (New York: Harper & Row, 1973), pp. 3–4.

18. Harold D. Lasswell, "The Structure and Function of Communication in Society," in Wilbur Schramm, ed., *Mass Communication* (Urbana: University of Illinois Press, 1960), pp. 117–130.

19. Schramm, *Men, Messages*, pp. 30–31.

20. Lasswell, *Structure;* also Daniel Lerner, "Communication Systems and Social Systems," in Schramm, ed., *Mass Communication*, pp. 131–140.

21. Claude Levi-Strauss, "Social Structure," in Sol Tax, ed., *Anthropology Today* (Chicago: The University of Chicago Press, 1962), pp. 321–350; Lucian W. Pye, "Introduction," in Pye, ed., *Communications*, p. 4.

22. See Leon Festinger, "Informal Social Communication," in *Psychological Review* 57(1950): 271–282; Morton Deutsch and Harold B. Gerard, "A Study of Normative and Informational Social Influences Upon Individual Judgment," in *Journal of Abnormal and Social Psychology* 51(1955): 629–636; Talcott Parsons, *The Social System* (Glencoe, Ill.: Free Press, 1951); Talcott Parsons and Edward A. Shils, eds.,

Toward a General Theory of Action (Cambridge: Harvard University Press, 1951); also Wilbur Schramm, *Men, Messages.*

23. Clyde Kluckhohn, "Values and Value-Orientations in the Theory of Action: An Exploration in Definition and Classification," in Parsons and Shils eds., *General Theory,* pp. 388–433.

24. *Seppuku,* or *hara-kiri,* was the ceremonial act of self-disembowelment formerly practiced by Japanese samurai (military retainers) to redress a disgrace.

25. Festinger, "Informal Social Communication," pp. 271–282.

26. Pye, ed., *Communications.*

27. See Appendix C for a brief review of the structural-functional approach.

28. Lerner, *Traditional Society;* Wilbur Schramm, "Communication and Development and the Development Process," in Pye, ed., *Communications,* pp. 30–57.

29. The teachings of Confucius regarding man's relations with the physical and social environments embody eight phases: *Ke-wu* (distinction of things), *Chih-chih* (completion of knowledge), *Cheng-i* (veracity of intention), *Cheng-hsin* (rectification of the heart), *Hsiu-shen* (cultivation of the whole person), *Chi-chia* (management of the family), *Chih-kuo* (government of the state), *Ping-tien-hsia* (peace for the whole universe). See *A Systematical Digest of the Doctrines of Confucius, According to the Analects, Great Learning, and Doctrine of the Mean,* P. G. von Mollendorff, trans., (General Evangelical Protestant Missionary Society of Germany, 1873).

30. *Mo Tzu, Basic Writings,* Burton Watson, trans. (New York: Columbia University Press, 1963).

31. For a discussion of Lenin's tactics of agitation and propaganda, see Alex Inkeles, *Public Opinion in Soviet Russia* (Cambridge: Harvard University Press, 1962). While both refer to interpersonal communication, in Soviet Russia agitation is directed to the mass of people, while propaganda applies to the elites. For Lenin's thinking, see Vladimir I. Lenin, *What is to be Done? Burning Questions of Our Movement,* S. V. and Patricia Utechin, trans. (Oxford: Clarendon Press, 1963).

32. Franz Schurmann has analyzed the Chinese Communist ideology in depth. See Schurmann, *Ideology and Organization in Communist China* (Berkeley: University of California Press, 1971).

33. *Mencius,* W. A. C. H. Dobson, trans. (University of Toronto Press, 1963). The dates of Mencius are based on Dobson.

34. See for instance, Tang Hsiao-wen, "Why Do We Say Hsun Tzu Was a Legalist?" *Red Flag* 1 (1975): 50–56.

35. *Hsun Tze, Basic Writings,* Burton Watson, trans. (New York: Columbia University Press, 1963).

36. Han Fei Tzu has been regarded favorably by the Chinese Communist Party. See Liang Ling-yih, "A Great Synthesizer of Legalist Thinking in the Chin Dynasty—Han Fei Tzu Reviewed." *Red Flag* 9 (1974): 22–31. Also, "Han Fei—An Outstanding Exponent of Pre-Chin Legalist Ideas." *Peking Review,* November 15, 1974, pp. 15–21.

37. Mao Tse-tung has apparently drawn on the ideas of Confucius selectively. He says: "We should sum up our history from Confucius to Sun Yat-sen and take over this valuable legacy. This is important for guiding the great movement of today." *Selected Works of Mao Tse-tung,* vol. 2 (Peking: Foreign Language Press, 1966), p. 209.

38. Mao Tse-tung, "Get Organized!" (November 29, 1943). *Selected Works of Mao Tse-tung,* vol. 3 (Peking: Foreign Language Press, 1966), p. 158.

39. The first detailed analysis of the mass-media system of the People's Republic and, except for statistical data, still an authoritative source is Frederick T. C. Yu, *Mass Persuasion in Communist China* (New York: Frederick A. Praeger, 1964). The

chapter on tatzepao is the first known analysis of this unique Chinese medium in the literature. Other useful sources include Franklin W. Houn, *To Change a Nation: Propaganda and Indoctrination in Communist China* (Glencoe, Ill.: Free Press, 1961); Alan P. Liu, *The Press and Journals in Communist China* (Cambridge: Center for International Studies, MIT, 1966); Alan P. Liu, *Communications and National Integration in Communist China* (Berkeley: University of California Press, 1971).

40. For a discussion of the factors concerning the effects of communication in the Western perspective, see Schramm, *Men, Messages,* particularly chapters 11, 12, 13, pp. 189–262.

41. For a discussion of the two-step flow hypothesis, see Elihu Katz and Paul Lazarsfeld, *Personal Influence: The Part Played by People in the Flow of Mass Communication* (Glencoe, Ill.: Free Press, 1955).

42. The techniques of persuasion employed by the Chinese Communists have been analyzed. See Edgar H. Schein, *Coercive Persuasion: A Socio-Psychological Analysis of the Brainwashing of American Civilian Prisoners by the Chinese Communists* (New York: W. W. Norton, 1961); Robert J. Lifton, *Thought Reform and the Psychology of Totalism: A Study of Brainwashing in China* (New York: W. W. Norton, 1961). Also Yu, *Mass Persuasion.*

43. Personal communication from Wilbur Schramm.

44. Mao Tse-tung, "A Talk to the Editorial Staff of the Shansi-Suiyuan Daily," in *Selected Works of Mao Tse-tung,* vol. 4 (Peking: Foreign Language Press, 1966), p. 241.

45. For a discussion of the small study groups, see Franz Schurmann, "Organization and Response in Communist China," *Annals of the American Academy of Political and Social Sciences* 321 (January 1959): 51–66; also Paul J. Hiniker, "The Mass Media and Study Groups in Communist China," in David K. Berlo, ed., *Mass Communication and the Development of Nations,* chap. 6 (East Lansing, Michigan, International Communication Institute, Michigan State University, 1968, mimeographed).

46. A. T. Boisen, "Economic Distress and Religious Experience: A Study of the Holy Rollers," *Psychiatry* 2 (1939): 185–194.

47. Chiang Kui-lin, *Twelve Years with Hsinhua* (Taipei: Chengsheng Broadcasting Corp., 1962). Chiang joined Hsinhua as an apprentice and rose to the position of an overseas correspondent. While stationed in Cairo, Chiang sought political asylum at the Indian Embassy in Cairo in December 1959.

48. "A Journalist and His Paper," in Francis Harper, ed., *Out of China: A Collection of Interviews with Refugees from China* (Hong Kong: Dragonfly Books, 1964), pp. 219–220.

49. Ibid., pp. 222–225.

50. Emmett Dedmon, *China Journal* (Chicago: Rand McNally, 1973), p. 140. Also Chang Kuo-hsin, "World News Read Only by China's Selected Few," *IPI Report,* vol. 25, February 1976, No. 2, pp. 1–2.

51. Cheng Huan, "Television Gains Ground," *Far East Economic Review Yearbook—1973* (Hong Kong), p. 112. When television was first introduced in Peking in May 1958, the capital city had about 20,000 sets.

52. Dedmon, *China Journal,* p. 135, p. 140.

53. In Canton, for instance, there were about 250 such bulletin boards in 1962. See Harper, *Out of China,* p. 217.

54. For instance, the *Canton Evening News,* which circulated in the Canton area, had a peak circulation of about 330,000 copies before the newsprint shortage in the early 1960s. Ibid.

55. "We Must Carry the Voice of Chairman Mao to All Corners of the Land," *People's Daily,* January 20, 1967.

56. The October 12, 1974 issue of the *People's Daily*, chosen at random, illustrates this general trend.

> On page 1: Half the space is taken up by a feature story on the successful 32,000-mile voyage by a 10,000-ton cargo ship built in China: "A Victory Song of Self-Independence and Self-Reliance: The First Ocean Voyage of the SS Feng Ching." There is an editorial celebrating the independence of Laos. The remaining space, about one sixth of the page, is used for three news items: Foreign Minister Chi Peng-fei sending off the vice premier of Laos; the arrival of the Venezuelan congressional delegation; and the arrival of the Italian Communist delegation.
>
> Page 2: The entire page is taken up by a story with the following headline: "Praise to Chairman Mao for His Great Victory of the Proletarian Military Line; Penetratingly Criticize Lin Piao's Rightist Opportunism during the Battle of Shenyang, Liaoning."
>
> Page 3: Three features: "A Highly Promising Barefoot Doctor—the Model Behavior of Comrade Sun Li-cheh," more than half a page; "The New Face of Yao Minority People at Chuang Village," about one-fourth of a page; "Acupuncture Therapy Receives Wide Welcome in the Nation."
>
> Page 4: More than one-third of the page carries the story, continued from page 1, of the victorious voyage of the cargo ship. About one-fourth of a page is taken up by description of an Australian trade exhibition in Peking. In the remaining space are seven brevities, including two about the Australian trade mission. The others: a salute to the Polish Army; arrival of a Japanese press group; departure of a North Vietnamese friendship mission; departure of a Chinese music mission for Tokyo; and visit by an art group from Nepal.
>
> Page 5: Five stories: activities of foreign visitors who had come for the October 1 celebration; independence celebration by the Pathet Lao; antigovernment demonstration in Saigon; expulsion of the Taiwan Volleyball Association in favor of the People's Republic association by the International Volleyball Federation meeting in Mexico City; the work of the Chinese agricultural mission in Romania.
>
> Page 6: Five stories: the trade exhibition of the People's Republic in Tokyo; another feature on the same exhibition; a report on the UN General Assembly meeting; the government of Algeria condemning superpowers for threatening oil-producing countries; Deputy Foreign Minister Chiao Kuan-hua received by West German foreign minister. There was an announcement on page 6 regarding music, dance, and opera shows for celebrating the twenty-fifth anniversary of the People's Republic.

57. Yu, *Mass Persuasion,* p. 124. Estimated on the basis of 600 million people, 1.5 million radio sets represented 2.5 sets per 1,000 persons. This would be a slight increase from the United Nations' estimate of 2 sets per 1,000 persons for 1950. The number of radio sets per 1,000 persons increased to 10 by 1960, 16 by 1970, and 19 by 1973. The corresponding statistics for India, for instance, are 1 set per 1,000 persons in 1950, 5 sets in 1960, 21 sets in both 1970 and 1973. Because of the extensive use in China of wired-broadcasting for her rural population, the size of audience reached by radio would be many times what the UN statistics would indicate. For UN statistics, see the *United Nations Statistical Yearbook* for 1950, 1960, and 1970; figures for 1973 are from unpublished UNESCO survey data made available through Wilbur Schramm.

58. A Swiss delegation that visited China in August 1974 found the radio to be part of the standard equipment of every household, at least on the east coast. See Alphons Matt, "Press in China a Mystery Even to China Watchers," *IPI Report,* vol. 23, December 1974, No. 12, pp. 1–3.

59. Yu, *Mass Persuasion,* p. 127.

60. "Village Broadcasting Network in Our Country Is Getting Better and Better," *People's Daily,* September 21, 1974.

61. Ibid.

62. The following account and statistics are based on "Peasant Correspondents of Huang Lou Commune," *Wenhui Pao* (Shanghai), December 24, 1968.

63. The report on Huang Lou Commune, in *Wenhui Pao* (Shanghai), December 24, 1968, provides a few illustrations.

One night a peasant correspondent at Huang Lou Commune heard over the People's Central Broadcasting Station an article from the *People's Daily* on the barefoot doctor system. Although it was already past 10 P.M., she called together the poor and lower-middle peasants in her production team to discuss the article. Afterwards, she wrote an article expressing their support to be broadcast over the commune's line-broadcasting station the following day.

In another case, several commune members were carrying top soil for their private plots during the commune's working hours. One peasant correspondent learned about it, and got someone to write a letter. He then published the letter in the production brigade's news bulletin, with a sharply worded editor's note. This story was later broadcast on the commune's station.

Once a commune member was preparing to give a big birthday feast to celebrate the "longevity" of his grandmother according to old Chinese tradition. When a peasant correspondent learned about it, he did not write an article of criticism, but instead organized the poor and lower-middle peasants of the production team to talk to this person. Armed with the thought of Mao Tse-tung, said the *Wenhui Pao,* they finally convinced him to give up the feast and the birthday celebration. This person admitted: "I was wrong, because I did not learn Chairman Mao's thought well enough."

CHAPTER II

1. Chou En-lai has described China's manpower as the "most precious capital," not just as labor but as "creators of production equipment." See Chou En-lai, "The Great Ten Years," in *The Glorious Ten Years* (Hong Kong: San Lien Book Co., 1959), p. 41. A number of surveys of China's economic development are available. See Yuan-li Wu, *An Economic Survey of Communist China* (New York: Bookman Associates, 1956); Ygael Gluckstein, *Mao's China—An Economic and Political Survey* (Boston: Beacon Press, 1957); Choh-ming Li, *Economic Development of Communist China* (Berkeley: University of California Press, 1959); Trevor J. Hughes and D. E. T. Luard, *The Economic Development of Communist China—1949-1960* (London, Oxford University Press, 1961); Ta-ching Liu and Kung-chia Yeh, *The Economy of the Chinese Mainland: National Income and Economic Development, 1933-1959* (Princeton: Princeton University Press, 1965); Yuan-li Wu, *The Economy of Communist China* (New York: Frederick A. Praeger, 1965); Nai-Ruenn Chen and Walter Galenson, *The Chinese Economy Under Communism* (Chicago: Aldine Publishing Co., 1969).

2. Max Weber, *The Protestant Ethic and the Spirit of Capitalism* (New York: Scribner, 1958).

3. For the concept of deferred gratification, see Louis Schneider and Svenne Lysgaard, "The Deferred Gratification Pattern: A Preliminary Study," *American Sociological Review* 18 (1953): 142–149. For the role of deferred gratification and some empirical evidence, see Wilbur Schramm, "Communication Development and the Development Process," in Lucian W. Pye, ed., *Communication and Political Development* (Princeton: Princeton University Press), pp. 5–32, and Godwin C.

Chu, "Media Use and Deferred Gratification in Economic Development," paper presented at the Association for Education in Journalism, Boulder, Colorado, 1967. Mimeographed. University of Hawaii, Honolulu, Asia Collection, Sinclair Library, or Hamilton Library.

4. Richard D. Lambert and Bert F. Hoselitz, *The Role of Savings and Wealth in Southeast Asia and the West* (Paris: UNESCO, 1963). It may be argued that the cash with which a person buys jewelry or unproductive land holdings will still be in circulation. An essential aspect of capital formation, however, is not the accumulation and circulation of cash as such, which is only a medium for undefined purposes, but rather the allocation of resources for productive activities. If a culture values large holdings of unproductive land as a prestige symbol, the jeweler may use his profits also to acquire that prestige symbol. If a large portion of a society's resources should ultimately be tied up in such unproductive forms, overall capital formation for development will most likely suffer. In other words, a lot of cash may be circulating, but it may circulate in the forms of jewels and decorative land that do not contribute to higher productivity.

5. Marion J. Levy, Jr., "Contrasting Factors in the Modernization of China and Japan," *Economic Development and Cultural Change* 2 (1953): 161–197. For the concept of social structure, see A. R. Radcliffe-Brown, "On Social Structure," in *Structure and Function in Primitive Society* (New York: Free Press, 1965), pp. 188–204. Also, Claude Levi-Strauss, "Social Structure," in Sol Tax, ed., *Anthropology Today* (Chicago: University of Chicago Press, 1962), pp. 321–350.

6. Karl Marx, *Capital: A Critique of Political Economy,* vol. 1, *The Process of Capitalist Production* (Chicago: Charles H. Kerr and Co., 1919). Surplus value is defined as the difference between the "use value" of labor, i.e., the value-creating capacity of labor, and the "exchange value" of labor, i.e., the market price of labor expressed in wages. Labor is held to be the most crucial element in production.

7. Liao Lu-yen, "The Dazzling Achievements on the Agricultural Battle Front in Ten Years," in *The Glorious Ten Years* (Hong Kong: San Lien Book Co., 1959), p. 121. Liao was deputy secretary-general in charge of agriculture in the Office of the Prime Minister.

8. Liao Lu-yen, "The Great Victory in Three Years of Land Reform Movement," *Important Documents of the Chinese Communists,* vol. 5, compiled and published by Central Committee of Kuomintang, Sixth Division, Taipei, Taiwan, 1953, pp. 222–225.

9. Nieh Yung-cheng, "Summary Report on Land Reform in the Outskirts of Peking, approved by the Prime Minister's Office of the Central People's Government on November 21, 1950, reprinted in *Xin Hua Ban Yue Kan* 1 (1951): 539–542. Nieh was mayor of Peking.

10. Liao Lu-yen, "Great Victory," p. 224.

11. Nieh Yung-cheng, "Summary Report," p. 541.

12. Ibid., p. 542.

13. Ching-wen Chou, *Ten Years of Hurricane—The True Faces of the Red Regime* (Hong Kong: Shih Tai Critique Publishers, 1959), pp. 170–172.

14. Liao Lu-yen, "Great Victory," p. 224.

15. Nieh Yung-cheng, "Summary Report," p. 541.

16. Liao Lu-yen, "Great Victory," p. 224. One unofficial estimate put the number of individuals purged or killed in the Land Reform movement at approximately 20,000,000. See Cheng Chu-yuan, *Communist China—Its Situation and Prospect* (Hong Kong: Free Press, 1959), p. 177.

17. Nieh Yung-cheng, "Summary Report," p. 540.

18. Ibid., pp. 541–542.

19. Ibid., p. 541.

20. Liao Lu-yen, "Great Victory," pp. 224–225.

21. See Liao Lu-yen, "Dazzling Achievements," p. 120; also Liao Lu-yen, "Great Victory," p. 226.

22. For a definition of Five Anti, see Chou En-lai, "Great Ten Years," p. 35. According to Po I-po, then minister of finance in charge of the Five Anti movement in his capacity as chairman of the Central Economy Inspection Committee, a total of 450,000 private industrial and commercial establishments were investigated in nine major cities, including Peking, Shanghai, Tientsin, Wuhan, Canton, and Mukden. In Shanghai alone, some 163,400 private establishments were investigated. See Gluckstein, *Mao's China*, pp. 199–200.

23. The following account is based on Hua Ming, *An Analysis of San Fan (Three Anti) and Wu Fan (Five Anti)* (Hong Kong: Union Publication, 1952), pp. 48–73.

24. This was the *San Fan* (Three Anti) movement, which was directed against corruption, waste, and bureaucraticism among Party cadres. See Chou En-lai, "Great Ten Years," p. 35.

25. Hua Ming, *An Analysis*, p. 72.

26. See S. E. Asch, "The Effects of Group Pressure," in Alex Inkeles, ed., *Readings on Modern Sociology* (Englewood Cliffs: Prentice-Hall, 1966), pp. 206–215.

27. See Gluckstein, *Mao's China*, p. 200, and Walt W. Rostow, *The Prospects for Communist China* (New York: John Wiley & Sons, 1954), p. 80.

28. See Hsu Ti-hsin, "The Great and Penetrating Change in the Economy of Our Mother Land," in *The Bright Eight Years* (Hong Kong: New Democratic Publishing House, 1958), p. 9. Hsu was the deputy director of the eighth section, Office of the Prime Minister.

29. See Robert Loh, *Escape from Red China* (New York: Coward-McCann, 1962), pp. 178–188.

30. Ibid., p. 187.

31. For instance, the increase of industrial productivity was estimated at 15 percent for 1954, but the increase of wages averaged only 1.1 percent that year. In 1955, industrial productivity went up by 10 percent, but wages increased by an average of 0.3 percent. See Cheng Chu-yuan, *Communist China*, p. 181.

32. See Sung Shao-wu, "The Movement for Increased Production and Practicing Economy," *People's China* 7 (April 1, 1952): 9. Sung was director of the Planning Bureau, Committee of Financial and Economic Affairs.

33. According to Deputy Prime Minister Li Hsien-nien, foreign aid, mostly loans from Soviet Russia, made up only 2 percent of the total revenues of Communist China during the first ten years. See Li Hsien-nien, "The Great Achievements in Finance in the People's Republic of China During Ten Years," in *Ten Years of National Development*, vol. 1 (Hong Kong: Chiwen Publishing House, 1959), p. 234.

34. Mao Tse-tung, "On the New Democratic Principle," speech delivered in Yenan in January 1940, reprinted in Mao Tse-tung, *On the New Democratic Principle and Other Speeches* (Peking: People's Publishing House, 1966), p. 18.

35. Li Shu-cheng, "The Great Achievements in Agricultural Production in New China in the Last Three Years," in *Important Documents of the Chinese Communists*, vol. 5, p. 228. Li Shu-cheng was minister of agriculture.

36. The exploitation by rural cadres will be discussed in detail in chapter 3.

37. See Wang Chien, "The Mutual Aid and Co-operative Movement in North China," *People's China* 8 (April 16, 1953): 8–11. For a detailed analysis of the use of communication in the Mutual Aid movement, see Godwin C. Chu, "Communication and Group Transformation in the People's Republic of China—The Case of the Mutual Aid Teams," East-West Communication Institute, East-West Center, Honolulu, Hawaii, July 1975.

38. Wang Chien, "Mutual Aid," p.10.

39. Chou En-lai, "Great Ten Years," p. 38.

40. Wang Chien, "Mutual Aid," p. 10.

41. Ibid., p. 11.

42. Kurt Lewin, "Group Decision and Social Change," in Eleanor Maccoby, Theodore Newcomb, and Eugene Hartley, eds., *Readings in Social Psychology* (New York: Holt, Rinehart & Winston, 1958), pp. 197–211; also Kurt Lewin, "Frontiers in Group Dynamics," *Human Relations* 7 (1947): 5–41.

43. Liao Lu-yen, "Dazzling Achievements," p. 130. The Chinese terms were: *chua hsien chin, tai lo hou; chua lo hou, pi hsien chin*. Problems of competition are further discussed in chapter 4.

44. Chao Erh-lu, "Mechanical Industry in Ten Years," in *Ten Years of National Development*, vol. 1, pp. 81–82. Chao was minister of First Mechanical Industry.

45. Ibid., p. 82.

46. *Workers Daily*, September 30, 1959.

47. Chi Ling, "Collection and Distribution of Foodstuffs in Communist China in the Last Ten Years," in *Communist China's Ten Years* (Hong Kong: Union Publishers, 1960), pp. 414–416.

48. "Strengthen the Economic Work During the Food Purchase Program," *People's Daily* editorial, November 30, 1953.

49. Liu Chih-heng, "Report on Economic Work: Manage Well the Work of Rural Savings," *People's Daily*, October 10, 1954.

50. "Peasants in Shansi Province Actively Repay Loans That Are Due," *People's Daily*, November 28, 1953.

51. "Rural Savings Exceed 4,000,000,000,000 Yuan," *People's Daily*, February 26, 1954. This was the old currency convertible at the rate of 10,000 Yuan to 1 JMP.

52. "Big Victory in Our Nation's Food Purchase Program," *People's Daily*, March 1, 1954.

53. Chu Cheng, "How to Accomplish the Task of Savings Deposit and Withdrawal as Related to Grain Sales," *Ta Kung Pao* (Tientsin), April 12, 1954.

54. *Liberation Daily* (Shanghai), May 15, 1952.

55. "Peoples in Cities and Villages Have Saved 70,000,000,000 JMP," *People's Daily*, December 18, 1958.

56. John C. Pelzel, "Economic Management of a Production Brigade in Post-Leap China," in W. E. Willmott, ed., *Economic Organization in Chinese Society* (Stanford: Stanford University Press, 1972), p. 411.

57. "The Preliminary Formation of a Socialist Rural Credit System," *People's Daily*, November 22, 1974.

58. For instance, China was importing food and exporting raw materials in 1936, the year before the Sino-Japanese War, but exporting food and importing industrial materials during the nine-year period from 1950 to 1958. For details of comparison, see Lou Hua, "Communist China's Foreign Trade in Ten Years," in *Communist China's Ten Years*, pp. 161–203.

59. Li Hsien-nien, "Great Achievements," pp. 229-230.

60. Li Feng, "China's Industry Is Standing Up," in *Ten Years of National Development*, vol. 1, p. 59.

61. Wang Szu-hua, "Ten Years of Development Surpasses One Thousand Years," in *Ten Years of National Development*, vol. 1, p. 155.

62. For detailed estimates and analysis of trade in this period, see A. H. Usack and R. E. Batsavage, "The International Trade of the People's Republic of China," in *People's Republic of China: An Economic Assessment* (a compendium of papers submitted to the Joint Economic Committee, Congress of the United States, May 18, 1972), pp. 335–370.

63. The original idea that led to what is now known as the Thomas theorem in

sociology was first introduced in an almost casual manner by William I. Thomas and Florian Znaniecki in their discussion of the traditional attitudes of Polish peasants, in *The Polish Peasant in Europe and America* (New York: Knopf, 1927), p. 68. The theorem was restated in its current version by Thomas in a 1938 conference on Polish peasants. See Herbert Blumer, *An Appraisal of Thomas and Znaniecki's "The Polish Peasant in Europe and America"* (New York: Social Science Research Council, Bulletin 44, 1939), p. 85.

CHAPTER III

1. S. C. Dube, "Communication, Innovation, and Planned Change in India," in Daniel Lerner and Wilbur Schramm, eds., *Communication and Change in the Developing Countries* (Honolulu: East-West Center Press, 1967), pp. 129–167.

2. Wilbur Schramm, "Communication Development and the Development Process," in Lucian W. Pye, ed., *Communication and Political Development* (Princeton: Princeton University Press, 1963), pp. 30–57; also Daniel Lerner, "Toward a Communication Theory of Modernization," in Pye, *Communication*, pp. 327–350; Schramm, "Communication and Change," in Lerner and Schramm, *Communication and Change*, pp. 5–32.

3. For an analysis of China's population programs, see Pi-chao Chen, "China's Population Program at the Grassroots Level," *Studies in Family Planning* 4, no. 8 (August 1973): 219–277; also Pi-chao Chen, with Ann Elizabeth Miller, "Lessons from the Chinese Experience: China's Planned Birth Program and Its Transferability," *Studies in Family Planning* 6, no. 10 (October 1975): 354–366.

4. For an analysis of the roles of cadres in the Chinese Communist administrative structure, see A. Doak Barnett (with a contribution by Ezra Vogel), *Cadres, Bureaucracy, and Political Power in Communist China* (New York: Columbia University Press, 1967). Other publications dealing with Communist China's cadres include: John W. Lewis, *Leadership in Communist China* (Ithaca: Cornell University Press, 1963); Michel Oksenberg, "Paths to Leadership in Communist China," *Current Scene* 3 (August 1965): 1–11; Oksenberg, "Local Leaders in Rural China, 1962–1965," in A. Doak Barnett, ed., *Chinese Communist Politics in Action* (Seattle: University of Washington Press, 1969), pp. 155–215; Victor C. Funnel, "Bureaucracy and the Chinese Communist Party," *Current Scene* 9 (May 1971): 1–14; Ezra F. Vogel, "From Revolutionaries to Semi-Bureaucrats: The Regularization of Cadres," *China Quarterly* 29 (January-March 1967): 36–60.

5. The following is based on An Tze-wen, "Cadre Operation of the People's Republic of China during the Last Three Years," official report prepared by the Ministry of Personnel, Central Government of the People's Republic, published in *People's Daily*, September 20, 1952. According to estimates made by Funnel, the number of cadres rose to 5,270,000 by 1955 and 7,920,000 by 1958. See Funnel, "Bureaucracy," p. 6.

6. "An Important Key in the Close Coordination between the Party and the Mass of People," *People's Daily* editorial, January 3, 1951.

7. "Decision of the Central Committee of Chinese Communist party on the Establishment of a Propaganda Network for the Whole Party among the Masses of People," *People's Daily*, January 3, 1951. Also see Frederick T. C. Yu, *Mass Persuasion in Communist China* (New York: Frederick A. Praeger, 1964), pp. 78–89.

8. "An Important Key to Close Relations between the Party and the Mass of People," *People's Daily* editorial, January 3, 1951.

9. Li Lun, "The Conditions of the Party's Propaganda Networks in Various Places during the Past Year," *People's Daily*, January 4, 1951.

10. "Decision of the Central Committee of Chinese Communist Party," *People's Daily*. Also Yu, "Mass Persuasion," p. 79.

11. Li Lun, "Conditions."

12. An Tze-wen, "We Must Carry out a Resolute Struggle of the New Three-Anti Movement in Various Organizations in the Entire Country," official report presented at the First National Committee of the People's Political Consultative Conference on February 7, 1953. Released by New China News Agency on February 9, 1953.

13. Ibid.

14. An Tze-wen, "To Struggle for Eradication of the Passive Attitude and Unhealthy Conditions in Party Organizations," official report prepared by the Ministry of Personnel for the Study Session of the Central Government Cadres on January 7, 1953. Published in *People's Daily*, February 12, 1953.

15. Ibid.

16. An Tze-wen, "Resolute Struggle."

17. "A Report on how Party Secretaries in Various Regions are Correctly Carrying out the Rectification Policy of the Party," *People's Daily*, April 2, 1953.

18. "*New Hunan Daily* Discusses Li Ssu-hsi Thinking," *People's Daily*, September 26, 1951.

19. For a description of peasant passivity after the land reform, see Thomas F. Bernstein, "Keeping the Revolution Going: Problems of Village Leadership after Land Reform," in John W. Lewis, ed., *Party Leadership and Revolutionary Power in China* (London: Cambridge University Press, 1970), pp. 239–267.

20. "A Report on how Party Secretaries in Various Regions are Correctly Carrying out the Rectification Policy of the Party," *People's Daily*, April 2, 1953.

21. "How to Handle Rural Party Members who Hired Workers, Operated Loans, Set up a Business, or Leased Land," *Tientsin Daily News*, February 27, 1953. These provisions were announced by the Northern China Bureau of the Chinese Communist party Central Committee during the Rural Rectification campaign. Party members were allowed to hire only short-term helpers when there was a definite need. Loan operations were prohibited. Party members were allowed to run small businesses only if they hired no helpers. Leasing of farm land was allowed only if the Party member himself was sick and unable to work, or was away from home and there were no other adults in the family who could work.

22. *Shansi Daily*, August 22, 1951.

23. An Tze-wen, "Eradication."

24. Ibid.

25. Ibid.

26. Hua Ming, *An Analysis of San Fan (Three Anti) and Wu Fan (Five Anti)* (Hong Kong: Union Publication, 1952), p. 3.

27. "Severely Punish Corrupt Elements," *People's Daily* editorial, December 9, 1951. (The yuan was the old currency; 10,000 yuan equaled 1 JMP.)

28. Hua Ming, *An Analysis*, p. 36.

29. The following is based on an eyewitness account by a former resident of mainland China who participated in the Central Government of the People's Republic for nearly eight years before his departure in late 1956. See Chou Ching-wen, *Ten Years of Hurricane—The True Faces of the Red Regime* (Hong Kong: Shih Tai Critique Pulishers, 1959), pp. 211–225.

30. Han Yi-wei, *Three Years of Revolution* (Hong Kong: South Wind Publishing Company, 1955), pp. 67–68.

31. The following is based on An Tze-wen, "Resolute Struggle."

32. "Some Experiences from the Rural Rectification Campaign," *People's Daily*, April 2, 1953.

33. "Develop and Consolidate the Fruits of the Rural Rectification Campaign," *People's Daily*, June 6, 1953.

34. "Party Secretaries," *People's Daily*, April 2, 1953.

35. An Tze-wen, "Strengthen the Work of Party Reform and Party Expansion on the Foundation of Victory in the *San Fan* and *Wu Fan* Movements," *People's Daily*, July 1, 1952. The criteria are known as the eight standards of a Chinese Communist party member.

36. "Some Experiences from the Rural Rectification Campaign," *People's Daily*, April 2, 1953.

37. Ibid.

38. The following is based on the *People's Daily* article cited above.

39. Ibid.

40. Ibid.

41. "Develop and Consolidate the Fruits of the Rural Rectification Campaign," *People's Daily*, June 6, 1953.

42. Hsu Shih-chao, "The Criticism Sessions Educated Me," in Fei Hsiao-tung, et. al., *The Reform of Old Characters* (Canton: Popular Culture Publishers, 1950), pp. 64–66.

43. An Tze-wen, "Eradication."

44. For a brief discussion of the Anti-rightist campaign of 1957–1958, see chapter 7.

45. For a description of the operation of a commune, see John C. Pelzel, "Economic Management of a Production Brigade in Post-Leap China," in W. E. Willmott, ed., *Economic Organization in Chinese Society* (Stanford: Stanford University Press, 1972), pp. 387–414.

46. These secret military papers fell into the hands of Khamba guerrillas after they had overrun a Chinese regimental post in Tibet in the late summer of 1961. The papers were released by the U.S. Department of State on August 5, 1963. See John W. Lewis, "China's Secret Military Papers: 'Continuities' and 'Revelations,' " *China Quarterly*, April–June 1964, pp. 68–78.

47. For more detailed descriptions of the Socialist Education movement, see Chin Hua, "Four Clean-ups and Three Renewals," *China Monthly* 7 (1965): 32; Harold Munthe-Kaas, "China's Four Clean-ups," *Far Eastern Economic Review*, June 9, 1966, pp. 479–484; Parris H. Chang, "Struggle Between the Two Roads in China's Countryside," *Current Scene*, February 15, 1968; Richard Baum and Frederick C. Teiwes, *Ssu-Ching: The Socialist Education Movement of 1962-1966* (Berkeley: Center for Chinese Studies, University of California, 1968); Richard Baum, "Revolution and Reaction in the Chinese Countryside: The Socialist Education Movement in Cultural Revolutionary Perspectives," *China Quarterly*, April-June 1969, pp. 92–119; Jan S. Brybyla, *The Political Economy of Communist China* (Scranton: International Textbook, 1970), chap. 10, "The Socialist Education Campaign and the Sino-Soviet Dispute, 1963–1965," pp. 423–476.

48. "Let Mao Tse-tung Thought Lead Everything," *People's Daily* editorial, January 1, 1969; "A Timely Liberation for Those Cadres Who Have Admitted Their Mistakes," *People's Daily*, January 29, 1969; "Use Mao Tse-tung Thought to Lead the Work of Struggle, Criticism and Reform," *People's Daily*, April 10, 1969.

49. "Liuho May 7 School Provides New Experience for Revolutionizing Government Offices," *People's Daily*, October 5, 1968. Pfeffer, analyzing the May 7 Schools, considers them to be an attempt to create new leaders who do not place themselves above the masses. See Richard M. Pfeffer, "Leaders and Masses," in Michel Oksenberg, ed., *China's Developmental Experience* (New York: Praeger, 1973), pp. 157–174.

50. "Cultivate Revolutionary Warriors Through Labor," *People's Daily*, November 17, 1968.

51. *Nan Fang Daily*, January 10, 1969.

52. "From Unhappiness to Warm Enthusiasm," *People's Daily*, September 8, 1969.

53. "Sweep the 'Labor is Punishment' Idea into the Historical Garbage Can," *People's Daily*, December 16, 1969.

54. "Criticize 'Let Us Just Hang Around for One Year,' " *People's Daily*, October 17, 1969.

55. "From Big Relief to Heavy Responsibility," *People's Daily*, November 10, 1969.

56. "Thoroughly Criticize the Idea that Joining the Party is a Sure Way of Acquiring High Official Status," *People's Daily*, October 14, 1969.

57. Chi Kan-hsueh, "Fully Realize the Superiority of May 7 Cadre Schools," *People's Daily*, May 6, 1974.

58. Ibid.

59. Mao Tse-tung, "Chairman Mao Discusses Twenty Manifestations of Bureaucracy," Joint Publications Research Service (JPRS), U.S. Department of Commerce (49826) No. 90, February 12, 1970.

60. Fairbank regards *Pao-Chia* as a system of mutual guaranty and responsibility among the village households. See John K. Fairbank, "Synarchy Under the Treaties," in Fairbank, ed., *Chinese Thought and Institutions* (University of Chicago Press, 1957), p. 210.

61. Max Weber, *The Theory of Social Economic Organization*, A. M. Henderson and Talcott Parsons, trans. (New York: Oxford University Press, 1947), particularly pp. 329–340.

62. Whyte, in comparing the Weberian ideal type of rational bureaucracy with the Maoist conception of large-scale organization, considers the most important difference to be the reliance on the application of specialized knowledge of the officials in the Weberian bureaucracy versus the Chinese emphasis upon mass mobilization. See Martin K. Whyte, "Bureaucracy and Modernization in China: The Maoist Critique," *American Sociological Review* 38, no. 2 (April 1973): 149–165.

CHAPTER IV

1. See Fei Hsiao-tung, *Peasant Life in China* (New York: Dutton, 1939).

2. Sun Yat-sen, *The Three Principles of the People*, Frank W. Price, trans. (Shanghai: China Committee, Institute of Pacific Relations, 1927), p. 210.

3. For a discussion of the concepts of cooperation and competition, see Mark A. May and Leonard W. Doob, *Competition and Cooperation* (New York: Social Science Research Council, 1937); Margaret Mead, ed., *Cooperation and Competition Among Primitive Peoples* (New York and London: McGraw-Hill, 1937); and Morton Deutsch, "An Experimental Study of the Effects of Cooperation and Competition Upon Group Process," *Human Relations* 2 (1949): 199–232. Unlike conflict, competition is not aimed at the removal or destruction of the rival. The concept of conflict is analyzed in Georg Simmel, *Conflict*, Kurt H. Wolff, trans. (Glencoe, Ill.: Free Press, 1955).

4. For concepts of role and status, see Ralph Linton, *The Study of Man* (New York: Appleton-Century, 1936); and Robert K. Merton, *Social Theory and Social Structure* (New York: Free Press, 1968). The concepts of specific versus diffuse role relations are based on Talcott Parsons, *The Social System* (Glencoe, Ill.: Free Press, 1951).

5. For concepts of achievement versus ascription, see Parsons, *Social System*. These concepts are continuums rather than dichotomies.

6. The distinction between *Gemeinschaft* and *Gesellschaft* suggested by Toennies appears to characterize these two patterns of social process. See Ferdinand Toennies,

Community and Society (*Gemeinschaft* and *Gesellschaft*), Charles P. Loomis, trans. (East Lansing: Michigan State University Press, 1957).

7. See Lu Cheng-chao, "Railway's Ten Years," in *Ten Years of National Development,* vol. 2 (Hong Kong: Chiwen Publishing Co., 1959), p. 27. Lu was vice minister of railways of the People's Republic.

8. Lu Cheng-chao, "Railway's Ten Years," pp. 28–29.

9. Lu Cheng-chao, "Railway's Ten Years," p. 29.

10. I Fan, "The Movement of Increasing Production and Practicing Economy in Communist China," *China Monthly,* no. 77 (August 1970): 366–369.

11. "Peking Steelworkers Set Off Nationwide Emulation Drive," *China Reconstructs* 19, no. 1 (January 1970): 4.

12. Ibid., p. 7.

13. "The General Line for Socialist Construction," *China Reconstructs* 22, no. 4 (April 1973): 12–13.

14. Lu Cheng-chao, "Railway's Ten Years," pp. 25–26.

15. Liao Lu-yen, "The Dazzling Achievement on the Agricultural Battlefront in Ten Years," in *The Glorious Ten Years* (Hong Kong: San Lien Co., 1959), p. 128. Liao was deputy secretary-general in charge of agriculture in the Office of the Prime Minister.

16. "Veteran Worker Tireless in Building Socialism," *China Reconstructs* 22, no. 5 (May 1973): 35.

17. Ibid.

18. "Lu Yu-lan, A Country Party Secretary," *China Reconstructs* 22, no. 3 (March 1973): 2–6.

19. "Eradicate Anarchism and Properly Do Spring Planting," *People's Daily,* March 19, 1968.

20. "Firmly Grasp Two Roads of Struggle and Reform the Unreasonable Management System," *People's Daily,* November 24, 1968.

21. *People's Daily,* April 13, 1958.

22. "We Must Seek Correct Relations Between Revolution and Production," *People's Daily,* July 12, 1975.

23. Cheng Chu-yuan, *Communist China—Its Situation and Prospect* (Hong Kong: Free Press, 1959), pp. 159–160.

24. "An Interview with a Commune Member of Pung Tao Commune, Nan An County, Fukien," *China Monthly* 28 (June 1966): 30–32.

25. Ross Terrill, *800,000,000—The Real China* (New York: Dell Publishing Company, 1971), p. 101.

26. Cheng Chien, "Don't Fail to Appreciate Blessings," *Worker's Daily,* November 15, 1957.

27. "Deep and Thorough Debate on Problems of Livelihood at Shanghai's First Fountain Pen Factory," *People's Daily,* November 27, 1957.

28. Charles Hoffman, "Work Incentives in Chinese Industry and Agriculture," in *An Economic Profile of Mainland China,* vol. 2 (Washington: U.S. Government Printing Office, 1967), p. 475.

29. Liu Chien, "How to Organize *Tapienlun,*" *Worker's Daily,* December 26, 1957.

30. "The Economic Life of Two Textile Workers in Peking," China News Agency, Canton, April 16, 1965.

31. Liao Lu-yen "Dazzling Achievement," p. 129.

32. "Kansu Party Committee Solves 'Material Incentive' Problems," Lanchow, Kansu Provincial Broadcast, July 3, 1975. FBIS-CHI-74-132, p. M1–2.

33. "Help Organize Good Collective Kitchens for Educated Youth Sent Down to the Villages." *People's Daily,* August 18, 1974.

34. "New Socialist Ideology Flows Everywhere—The Lively Political Work at Hsiao Chin Chuang Brigade, Pao Ti County, Tientsin," *People's Daily*, August 6, 1974.

35. Feng Ting, "Conquering Individualism Is the Key to Being Both Red and Expert," concluding report delivered at the debate on being red and expert at Peking University, *China Youth Daily*, June 7, 1958. Reprinted in *March Toward Deeply Red and Thoroughly Expert* (Peking: People's Publishing Press, 1958), p. 77.

36. "The County Secretary Who Closely Communicates with the Mass," *Jen Min Hua Pao*, July 1972, pp. 10–13.

37. "Ho Chien-hsiu," *Jen Min Hua Pao*, August 1972, pp. 32–33.

38. "Revolutionizing Industrial Designing," *China Reconstructs* 22, no. 5 (May 1972): 36–38.

39. Maria Antonietta Macciocchi, *Daily Life in Revolutionary China*, Kathy Brown et al., trans. (New York and London: Monthly Review Press, 1972), p. 137.

40. Liao Lu-yen, "Dazzling Achievements," p. 129.

41. Liao Lu-yen, "Dazzling Achievements," p. 130.

42. Ma Wen-hui, "Ten Years of Struggle for High Speed Development of Productivity and Better Livelihood of Workers," in *Ten Years of National Development*, vol. 2 (Hong Kong: Chiwen Publishing Co., 1959), pp. 137–151. Ma was minister of labor of the People's Republic.

43. "Lanchou May 7 High School—Factory Runs School, Both Hooked Up," *Red Flag* 2 (1969): 30–35.

44. Ma Wen-hui, "Ten Years of Struggle," p. 142.

45. Terrill, *800,000,000*, p. 100.

46. "Rural Class Policy In Yang Chiang County,"*China Monthly*, no. 31, October 1966, p. 972.

47. Terrill, *800,000,000*, p. 101.

48. Terrill, ibid., p. 121.

49. Barbara Tuchman, *Notes from China* (New York: Collier Books, 1972), p. 53.

50. Liu Hsiu-feng, "High Speed Progress of Reconstruction," in *Ten Years of National Development*, vol. 1 (Hong Kong: Chiwen Publishing Co., 1959), p. 167. Liu was minister of civil engineering.

51. "Regulations on the Employment of Rural Residents in Urban Areas," *People's Handbook 1958* (compiled by *Takung Pao* and published by Hsinhua Book Store, Peking), p. 595.

52. "Interview with a Commune Member," *China Monthly* 28 (June 1966): 30–32.

53. Ibid.

54. Ibid.

55. "New Socialist Ideology Flows Everywhere," *People's Daily*, August 18, 1974.

56. "The Women Members in Our Communes," *Jen Min Hua Pao*, March 1972, pp. 24-27.

57. "A Happy Achievement of the 'Criticize Lin Piao, Criticize Confucius' Movement—Paochi Electric Locomotive Workers Repair Seven Dismantled Locomotives," *People's Daily*, August 8, 1974.

58. "The County Secretary," *Jen Min Hua Pao*, July 1972, pp. 10–13.

59. "Old Factory Faces New Tasks," *China Reconstructs* 22, no. 5 (May 1973): 38–41.

60. "A Happy Achievement," *People's Daily*, August 8, 1974.

61. Macciocchi, *Daily Life*, pp. 138-139.

62. "Mechanical Workers in the Nation Quickly and Economically Accomplish the Radio Broadcast Race," *People's Daily*, April 17, 1959.

63. "A Petroleum Chemical Base Under Construction," *Jen Min Hua Pao,* January 1972, pp. 22–27.

64. "Stores and Salesmen in Peking," *China Reconstructs* 21, no. 3 (March 1972): 46.

65. "Between Officers and Men," *China Reconstructs* 22, no. 4 (April 1973): 14–16.

66. "Leadership Stands in the Front Line to Grasp Revolution and Promote Production," *People's Daily,* August 12, 1974.

67. "Learn from Tachai," *People's Daily* editorial, February 10, 1964. "The Road of Tachai," *People's Daily,* February 10, 1964.

68. Macciocchi, *Daily Life,* p. 200.

69. "Learn from Taching—The Spirit and People of Taching," *People's Daily,* April 20, 1964.

70. "The Knife that Never Dulls, the Story of Oil Well Drilling Team No. 1202," *People's Daily,* April 25, 1964.

71. "Peking Steelworkers," *China Reconstructs,* p. 2.

72. Francis Harper, ed., *Out of China—A Collection of Interviews with Refugees from China* (Hong Kong: Dragonfly Books, 1964), p. 63.

73. "A Greatly Hopeful New Generation," *People's Daily,* August 10, 1974.

74. Cheng Chu-yuan, *Communist China,* p. 160.

75. Chen Yung-kuei, "The Revolutionary Spirit of Tachai People," in *Irrigation and Electricity, 1964,* no. 4, reprinted in *People's Handbook 1964* (compiled by *Takung Pao* and published by Hsinhua Book Store), p. 86.

76. "A 'Tachai' in the Water Country," *China Reconstructs* 19, no.3 (March 1970): 41.

77. Ibid.

78. "Poker Game Criticism Session," *Hsin Ming Evening News* (Shanghai), October 17, 1965.

79. Cheng Chu-yuan, *Communist China,* pp. 159–160.

80. "Let Mao Tse-tung Thought Lead Labor Management," *Agricultural Technique Monthly,* November 1967.

81. Macciocchi, *Daily Life,* pp. 245–246.

82. Ibid., p. 255.

83. "Workers Study Philosophy," *China Reconstructs* 19, no. 12 (December 1970): 34.

84. Macciocchi, *Daily Life,* p. 136.

85. Ibid.

86. Ibid., p. 137.

87. Tuchman, *Notes from China,* p. 35.

88. "Develop the Functions of Workers' Philosophy Teams—Nanping Textile Factory Pushes Forward the Movement to Learn the Philosophy of Proletarian Dictatorship," *People's Daily,* July 14, 1975.

89. Macciocchi, *Daily Life,* p. 137.

90. Terrill, *800,000,000,* p. 96.

91. "Interview with a Commune Member," *China Monthly* 28 (June 1966): 32.

92. Francis Harper, *Out of China,* p. 65.

93. "Propelled by Proletarian Dictatorship Philosophy, Industries in Shanghai Accomplish First Half-Year Production Goals Ahead of Schedule," *People's Daily,* July 14, 1975.

94. "Continue Advancing—Or Rest with Our Title?" *China Reconstructs* 19, no. 12 (December 1970): 35–36.

95. Macciocchi, *Daily Life,* p. 126.

96. Ibid., pp. 241–242.

97. Ibid., p. 126.

98. "Liaoning Commune Big-Character Poster Criticizes Work Point System," Shengyang, Liaoning Provincial Broadcast, April 20, 1974, in FBIS-CHI-74-80, p. L3-4.

99. Ibid.

100. The results of a psychological experiment recently conducted by Abaineh Workie of Haile Selassie I University, Ethiopia, may be seen in the light of the relative effectiveness of the system of cooperation and competition in China. Using high school students in New York City as his subjects, Workie compared the productivity of six situations of cooperation and competition. Material incentives were employed in all situations. Highest productivity was achieved by intragroup cooperation without reference to another group (M=8.640), followed by intragroup cooperation with intergroup cooperation (M=8.337), intragroup competition with intergroup cooperation (M=7.188), intragroup cooperation with intergroup competition (M= 5.440), intragroup competition without reference to another group (M=4.307), and lastly, intragroup competition with intergroup competition (M=2.074). See Workie, "The Relative Productivity of Cooperation and Competition," *Journal of Social Psychology* 94 (1974): 225-230. Although generalizations from Workie's findings must be treated with great caution, his results do suggest the possibility that a system primarily based on intragroup competition and intergroup competition, which the Chinese leaders seem to prefer, does not normally promote productivity as long as material incentives are still revelant.

101. The extent to which the state dominates the economic life of the Chinese is revealed in an article by Vice Premier Chang Chun-chiao, "On Total Dictatorship against the Capitalist Class," in *Red Flag* 4 (1975): 3-12. According to Chang, more than 90 percent of agricultural productions are collectively managed by communes. In addition, a small, unspecified percentage is under the management of state farms. Commune members are allowed to keep small private plots and some family sideline productions. In industries, state-operated industries account for 97 percent of all assets, 63 percent of industrial workers, and 86 percent of all industrial productions. Industries operated at the commune level constitute 3 percent of assets, 36.2 percent of industrial workers, and 14 percent of industrial productions. Only 0.8 percent of workers engage in individually operated handicrafts. In commerce, 92.5 percent of all retail sales are managed by the state, 7.3 percent by the communes, and only 0.2 percent by individual peddlers.

102. The new constitution states that nonagricultural laborers may now engage in individual labor activities under the overall arrangements of urban street committees or commune production teams, provided that such individual labor activities are permissible by law and do not exploit others. How this provision will be implemented remains to be seen. See "Constitution of the People's Republic of China," Article no. 5, *People's Daily*, January 20, 1975.

103. "Constitution of the People's Republic of China," Article no. 7, *People's Daily*, January 20, 1975.

104. The "three-in-one" union sounds somewhat similar to the procedures for joint planning described by Delbeq. Ordinary citizens with little expertise, trained professional experts, and local officials were brought together to collaborate in reaching a decision. In this way, each of the three groups could contribute its best wisdom to the problem. See A. Delbeq, "A Group Process Model for Program Planning," *Journal of Applied Behavioral Science* 7 (1971): 466-492.

CHAPTER V

1. See Siao Yu, *Mao Tse-tung and I Were Beggars* (Syracuse: Syracuse University Press, 1959), pp. 9-23; also "Historical Commentary and Notes" by Robert C.

North, in Emi Siao, *Mao Tse-tung, His Childhood and Youth* (Bombay: People's Publishing House, 1955), pp. 217–218. Mao was born in 1893. It was in 1909 that he went to Tungshan School in Siangsiang.

2. For a description of Communist China's educational system before the Cultural Revolution, see Leo A. Orleans, "Communist China's Education: Policies, Problems, and Prospects," in *An Economic Profile of Mainland China* (Studies Prepared for the Joint Economic Committee, Congress of the United States, vol. 2, February 1967), pp. 499–518. For a bibliography on education in the first ten years, see Stewart E. Fraser, *Chinese Communist Education: Records of the First Decade* (Nashville: Vanderbilt University Press, 1965), pp. 422–496.

3. Mao Tse-tung, *On the Correct Handling of Contradictions among the People* (Peking: People's Press, 1957), p. 23.

4. In "East Is Red," no. 27–28, May 7, 1967 (published by Red Delegates of Peking's Universities and Colleges, Peking Mining College, reprinted in Chung Hua-ming, "Education Revolution in Universities and Colleges in Mainland China"), *China Monthly*, October 1969, pp. 466–467.

5. Mao Tse-tung, "Talks with Party Leaders Concerning Educational Work at Spring Festival" (February 13, 1964), in *Current Background* 891 (October 8, 1969): 42–44. (See Appendix B for text.)

6. Koide Yoshio, "New Direction of Reform for College Education in Communist China," Chung Huan-wen, trans. *China Monthly*, December 1970, p. 588.

7. New China News Agency release, October 23, 1968.

8. New China News Agency release, October 25, 1968.

9. "Ministry of Education Announces Rules on Admission to Universities and Colleges for This Year," *People's Daily*, June 4, 1964.

10. "The Road of Engineering and Technological Training as Seen from the Shanghai Machine-Tools Plant," *People's Daily*, July 22, 1968.

11. According to provincial radio broadcasts from Hupeh and Fukien, in 1971 and 1972 the Party allowed the admission of some children from the oppressor classes after students from peasant, worker, and soldier families had been given priority consideration. See Chen Feng, "College Admission and the Case of Chang Tieh-sheng," *China Monthly*, December 1973, pp. 37–38. An announcement on October 15, 1974 in the *People's Daily*, indicated that only students with peasant, worker, and soldier backgrounds were admitted for 1974. The total number of new students admitted into universities and colleges in 1974 exceeded 160,000. See "More Than 160,000 Peasants, Workers, and Soldiers Admitted as College Students," *People's Daily*, October 15, 1974.

12. Kuan Shan-meng, "The Higher Education of Communist China," *China Monthly*, October 1972, pp. 478–481.

13. The following was from "A Thought-Provoking Answer," *Liaoning Daily*, July 19, 1973.

14. "A Thought-Provoking Answer" (reprinted from *Liaoning Daily*), in *People's Daily*, August 10, 1973; "The Anti-Main Current Spirit," *People's Daily* editorial, August 16, 1973.

15. New China News Agency, "Chang Tieh-sheng Has Been in College almost a Year," *Takung Pao* (Hong Kong), July 25, 1974.

16. Fang Cheng, "Education in Communist China in 1964," *China Monthly*, May 1965, p. 209.

17. Mao Tse-tung, "Talks With Party Leaders," 1969.

18. "Establish a New Proletarian Examination and Evaluation System," *People's Daily*, August 16, 1969.

19. Tillman Durdin, "China's Universities Graduating First Students in New System," *New York Times*, December 26, 1973.

20. "Destroy the Sharp Pagoda System of the Revisionists," *People's Daily,* December 17, 1967.

21. "Contrast Two Schools to Demonstrate the Superiority of Peasant-Operated Schools," *People's Daily,* October 27, 1968.

22. "Understand how Poor and Lower-Middle Peasants Manage Schools from the Experiences of Three Agricultural Brigades," *People's Daily,* October 28, 1968.

23. Hu Yi-ming, "Revolutionary Education in Urban High Schools in Mainland China," *China Monthly,* October 1969, p. 479; Fang Cheng, "Education in Communist China in 1967," *China Monthly,* April 1968, p. 176.

24. Koide Yoshio, "New Direction."

25. Fang Cheng, "Education in Communist China," p. 208.

26. The Chinese term for "exchanging revolutionary experiences" is *chuan lien.* Literally it means "to string up and connect." The term came into prominence during the Red Guard movement of 1966 and 1967.

27. *Wen Hui Pao* (Shanghai), February 17, 1967.

28. "Brigade Schools Are Schools for Poor and Lower-Middle Peasants," *People's Daily,* November 17, 1968.

29. New China News Agency, "Shih Ching Shan High School of Peking," February 16, 1968.

30. "Lanchou May 7 High School—Factory Runs Schools, Both Hooked Up," *Red Flag,* 1969, no. 2, pp. 30–35.

31. Naito Yosaburo, "Education in Communist China After the Cultural Revolution," Kao Chieh, trans., *China Monthly,* August 1970, p. 376.

32. Lishu Revolutionary Committee, Kirin Province, "Education Programs for Elementary Schools and High Schools in Rural Villages," *People's Daily,* May 12, 1969.

33. Kuan Shan-meng, "Elementary and High School Education in Mainland China at Present," *China Monthly,* November 1972, p. 534.

34. "Textbook Prepared by Poor and Lower-Middle Peasants Is Wonderful," *People's Daily,* November 1, 1968.

35. Ibid.

36. "Teachers and Students Together Settle Blood Debts," *People's Daily,* January 30, 1969.

37. People's Radio of Shanghai, January 30, 1969, cited in Hai Feng, "Children's Education in Communist China at the Present Stage," *China Monthly,* September 1969, p. 435.

38. Editor's note to "The Road of Engineering and Technological Training as Seen from the Shanghai Machine-Tools Plant," *People's Daily,* July 22, 1968.

39. *Kuang Ming Daily,* (Peking), April 1, 1969.

40. "Use Revolutionary Criticism to Reform a University—Investigation Report by the May 7 Experimental Class of Futan University," *Red Flag* 6 (1971): 67–74.

41. "Curriculum Reform Is a Deep and Thorough Ideological Revolution—Report by Chiaotung University on Curriculum Reform," *Red Flag* 6 (1971): 105–110.

42. *Kuang Ming Daily* (Peking), September 6, 1971.

43. *Kuang Ming Daily* (Peking), August 28, 1972.

44. Ibid.

45. *Wen Hui Pao* (Shanghai), May 27, 1965; *Wen Hui Pao* (Shanghai), November 10, 1965; *Kuang Ming Daily* (Peking), April 14, 1965.

46. Pei Yu, "Solidly Accomplish the Task of Hook-up Between Factory and School," *Red Flag* 9 (1972): 777–779.

47. "Lanchou May 7 High School," *Red Flag* 2 (1969): 30–35.

48. Fang Cheng, "Education in Communist China," 1965.

49. New China News Agency release, October 27, 1968.

50. Chen Yung-kuei, "The Revolutionary Spirit of Tachai People," in *Irrigation and Electricity*, 1964, No. 4 (reprinted in *People's Handbook 1964*, compiled by *Takung Pao*, Peking, Hsinhua Book Store), p. 85.

51. "Agricultural Education Must Gradually Reform through Half Work and Half Study," *Kuang Ming Daily*, August 19, 1965.

52. "Half Work and Half Study System Is An Important Development in the Educational Revolution of Our Country," *People's Daily*, September 28, 1965.

53. "We Must Organize High School and Elementary School Graduates to Engage in Productive Labor," *People's Daily* editorial, August 11, 1955.

54. "Set Our Roots in Villages, Blossom, and Bear Fruits," *Chungkuo Ching Nien* (China's Youth) 2 (1964): 8–11.

55. "Obey Chairman Mao, Go Where Our Motherland Needs You Most," *Kuang Ming Daily* editorial, June 8, 1968; "Obey Chairman Mao, Go and Unite with Workers, Peasants and Soldiers," *People's Daily* editorial, August 18, 1968. This movement has sometimes been referred to as the "rustification" of urban-educated Youth. See Pi-chao Chen, "Overurbanization, Rustification of Urban-Educated Youth, and Politics of Rural Transformation: The Case of China," *Journal of Comparative Politics*, April 1972, pp. 361–386.

56. "Go to the Villages, to the Borders, to the Factories and Mines, to the Grassroots," *People's Daily*, July 22, 1968.

57. "Graduates of Peking High School No. 60 Actively Go up to the Mountains and down to the Villages," *People's Daily*, December 21, 1968.

58. "Cadres Should Take the Lead in Sending Children to the Villages," *People's Daily*, December 25, 1968; "Family Study Class Helps Her Overcome Self Concern—The Story of Tien Shu-hua of Peking High School No. 34," *People's Daily*, December 25, 1968.

59. "Resolutely Respond to Chairman Mao's Great Call for Educated Youth to Go to Villages," *People's Daily*, August 18, 1969.

60. "Hsi Hsiang County Revolutionary Committee Organizes to Send Students up to the Mountains and down to the Villages," *People's Daily*, December 22, 1968.

61. New China News Agency release, May 4, 1969.

62. *Revolutionary Youth*, Changsha, Hunan Province, Serial no. 1, 1st edition, November 10, 1967, cited in Hai Feng, "The Movement for Educated Young People to Settle down in the Countryside," *China Monthly*, November 1969, p.22.

63. Yang Chun-fa (student sent back home from Shanghai), "Study for the Proletarian Revolutionary Task," *People's Daily*, May 15, 1969.

64. "Is School Useless?" *Red Flag* 3/4 (1969): 31–34. This article was attributed to Wang Wei-ming and Li Yi-chun, two poor peasants in Chiatung County, Kiangsu Province.

65. Hsueh Chao, "Communist China's General Plan for High School and Elementary School Education in the Villages," *China Monthly*, July 1969, particularly pp. 9–10.

66. Yao Wen-yuan, "The Worker Class Must Lead Everything," *People's Daily*, August 26, 1968, also in *Red Flag* 2 (1968): 3–7.

67. Ibid.

68. "Workers Class Just Wants to Occupy the Educational Battlefield," *People's Daily*, September 10, 1968.

69. "Capital Workers Propaganda Team at Tsinghua University Organizes Mao Tse-tung Thought Classes," *People's Daily*, September 11, 1968.

70. "Old Workers at Futan University Propaganda Team Have Heart-to-Heart Talks with Red Guards," *People's Daily*, September 19, 1968.

71. "How to Run a Socialist University? Report No. 1," *People's Daily*, March

29, 1969; "How to Run a Socialist University? Report No. 2," *People's Daily,* March 31, 1969.

72. Naito Yosaburo, "Education in Communist China."

73. "Fully Develop the Political Functions of the Propaganda Team Under the Leadership of Party Secretary—Report from Chiaotung University," *People's Daily,* December 9, 1971.

74. "Firmly Grasp the Struggle between the Two Educational Policies and Never Deviate," *People's Daily,* November 7, 1968.

75. "Investigation Report on the Educational Revolution in Three Communes in Lao Shan County, Shantung Province," *People's Daily,* September 11, 1970.

76. "Teach Our Young Generation to be Revolutionaries Forever," *People's Daily* editorial, July 8, 1964.

77. For the six strategies, see "Proletarian Family History Must Be Passed on from Generation to Generation," *Chungkuo Ching Nien Pao* (China Youth Daily) editorial, June 27, 1963.

78. "A Meal of Bitter Memory—The First Lesson from the Poor and Lower-Middle Peasant Lecturer," *People's Daily,* January 11, 1969.

79. "Revolutionary Education in the Villages Must Depend on Poor and Lower-Middle Peasants," *Red Flag* 3 (1968): 27–31.

80. "Rental Collection Hall—A Model Socialist Art," *China Monthly,* October 1966, pp. 967–969.

81. *Chungkuo Ching Nien Pao* (China's Youth), June 27, 1963. One such stone monument is shown in Rewi Alley, *Travels in China—1969—1971* (Peking: New World Press, 1973), between p. 60 and p. 61. Engraved on the monument is a verse: "Never forget class bitterness, remember debts of blood and tears."

82. "Little Red Soldiers Follow the Glorious Traditions of Red Army Children Corps," *People's Daily,* August 2, 1974. For another example of these strategies, see "Use the Characteristics of School Children to Organize Criticism of Lin Piao and Confucius," *People's Daily,* September 5, 1974.

83. *Kuang Ming Daily* (Peking), March 3, 1969.

84. Chia Chun-soh, "Children of Tachai Growing up Strong by Feeding on Mao Tse-tung Thought," *Kuang Ming Daily,* May 31, 1968.

85. "Little Red Classes in a Mining District," *People's Daily,* June 2, 1969.

86. Ibid.

87. "Education of Children Consolidates the Proletariat Dictatorship," *People's Daily,* June 1, 1969.

88. Ibid.

89. Hai Feng, 1969, "Children's Education," p. 437.

90. "Study Mao Tse-tung Thought at Home, Help Mother Struggle against Self and Criticize Revisionism," *People's Daily,* February 6, 1969.

91. "Students Must Be Reeducated by Workers—Young Warriors from Shih Ching Shan Visit Capital Steel Works," *People's Daily,* September 15, 1968.

92. *Wen Hui Pao* (Shanghai) editorial, September 27, 1968.

93. "Struggle for the Solid Realization of Chairman Mao's Proletarian Policy," *Red Flag* 5 (1969): 66–72.

94. "Grasp Criticism of Lin Piao and Confucius: Promote Work of Trading," *People's Daily,* August 17, 1974.

95. "Criticize Reactionary Sayings, Speak Revolutionary Sayings," *People's Daily,* September 25, 1974.

96. "The Change in Meng Shiu-cheng," *People's Daily,* October 20, 1974.

97. "Criticize Reactionary Sayings," *People's Daily,* September 25, 1974.

98. Ibid.

99. Ibid.

100. Ibid. Chuko Liang (A.D. 181–234) was reputed to be China's most brilliant strategist during the Three Kingdoms period.

101. "We Must Not Let the Bad Books Poison Our Young People," *People's Daily*, July 21, 1969.

102. "Little Red Soldiers," *People's Daily*, August 2, 1974.

103. "The Progress of Communist China's Thought Reform," *Democratic Forum* (Hong Kong) 2, no. 17 (March 15, 1951).

104. Chang Tun-hsiao, "How North China University Reached a Climax for Its Study Programs," in *Hsueh Hsi* 1, no. 2 (October 1950).

105. Li Yu-yi, "A Most Abundant, Most Vivid Lession—Impressions from Participation in Land Reform Work outside Peking," *People's Daily*, February 27, 1951.

106. Adapted from Frederick T. C. Yu, "Campaigns, Communications, and Development in Communist China," in Daniel Lerner and Wilbur Schramm, eds., *Communication and Change in the Developing Countries* (Honolulu: East-West Center Press, 1967), pp. 199–201.

107. "Luan Chih-cheng Grows from an Apprentice to a College Lecturer," *Kuang Ming Daily*, January 13, 1962.

108. "Mathematics Department of Dr. Sun Yat-Sen University Organizes Old Professors to Train Young Teachers In Seminars," *Kuang Ming Daily*, January 22, 1962; "South China Agricultural College Cadres Sit in on Lectures," *Kuang Ming Daily*, December 15, 1961; "Experienced Teachers in Peking High Schools and Elementary Schools are Assigned Assistants," *Kuang Ming Daily*, January 27, 1962; "Associate Professors at Wuhan University Function as Links Between Superiors and Subordinates," *Kuang Ming Daily*, December 4, 1961.

109. Yao Wen-yuan, "The Worker Class."

110. Kuan Shan-meng, "Elementary and High School Education in Mainland China Today," *China Monthly*, November 1972, pp. 533–537.

111. "Establish a New Corps of Proletarian Class Teachers," *People's Daily*, February 10, 1969.

112. "Poor and Lower-Middle Peasants Demonstrate Superiority on Rostrum—Report by San Chang Commune, Tung Tai County, Kiangsu," *People's Daily*, November 16, 1968.

113. "How to Run a Socialist University? Report No. 1," *People's Daily*, March 29, 1969; "How to Run a Socialist University? Report No. 2," *People's Daily*, March 31, 1969.

114. "Workers and Army Propaganda Team at Peking University Help Reform Students and Teachers," *People's Daily*, March 18, 1969.

115. Chinese Communist Party Committee of Dr. Sun Yat-sen Medical College, "Let Intellectuals Contribute Their Knowledge Through Service and Reform," *People's Daily*, April 11, 1972.

116. "Red Guards and Students Distinguish Two Types of Contradictions, and Correctly Handle Teachers Who Have Committed Errors," *People's Daily*, June 22, 1969.

117. "Understand How Poor and Lower-Middle Peasants Manage Schools from the Experiences of Three Agricultural Brigades," *People's Daily*, October 28, 1968.

118. John Burns, "Chinese Girl, 12, Is Student Hero," *New York Times*, January 2, 1974.

119. Hsiang Hui, "Hunan Opera *A Song of Gardeners* Reviewed," *People's Daily*, August 2, 1974. Hsiang Hui, apparently a pseudonym, means "the bright light of Hunan."

120. Ibid.

121. See S. E. Asch, "The Effects of Group Pressure," in Alex Inkeles, ed.,

Readings on Modern Sociology (Englewood Cliffs: Prentice-Hall, 1966), pp. 206–215.

122. The strength of the "revisionists" in the universities and high schools is suggested by a renewed attack launched by the Party in early 1976. See for instance, "Tapienlun Promotes Revolution in School Education: Teachers and Students in Shanghai No. 2 High School Refute Rightist and Revisionist Fallacies," *People's Daily*, February 3, 1976; and "Teachers and Students at Wuhan University Praise Revolution in Education and Criticize Queer Talks and Absurd Ideas," *People's Daily*, February 4, 1976. It is evident from these and other articles that various "queer talks and absurd ideas" are circulating among educational workers and are being severely criticized and refuted.

CHAPTER VI

1. "Chairman Mao Visits Villages in Shantung," *People's Daily*, August 13, 1958.

2. Liu Shao-chi, "The Present Situation, the Party's General Line for Socialist Construction and Its Future Tasks," in *Second Session of the Eighth National Congress of the Communist Party of China* (Peking: Foreign Language Press, 1958), pp. 16–66.

3. Chang Kuang-yuan, Kao Ching-chi, and Li Chin-jui, "An Investigation of One People's Commune," *People's Daily*, September 3, 1958.

4. Mao Tse-tung, *On the Correct Handling of Contradictions Among the People* (Peking: People's Press, 1957), p. 17.

5. "Resolution of the Second Plenary Session of the Eighth Central Committee on National Agricultural Development from 1956 to 1967" (May 23, 1958); also Tan Cheng-lin, "Report on the National Agricultural Development Plan for 1956–1967" (May 17, 1958), reprinted in *Xin Hua Ban Yue Kan* 11 (1958): 14–17.

6. In Honan Province, for instance, there were 26,211 agricultural producers' cooperatives in 1956, with an average size of 358 families. See Wu Chih-pu, "From Agricultural Producers' Cooperative to People's Commune," *Red Flag* 8 (1958): 5–11.

7. Ibid. The following data were presented by Wu Chih-pu, governor of Honan and a member of the Central Committee in charge of agriculture.

8. Editor's note to "Tentative Regulations of the Chayashan Sputnik People's Commune," *People's Daily*, September 4, 1958.

9. Chang Chu-chuan, "At a People's Commune in Hsushui (Hopeh)," *Chungkuo Ching Nien Pao* (China's Youth), August 23, 1958; "People's Commune Is Good," *People's Daily*, August 18, 1958; "Changchou Village, Shangchih County (Heilungkiang) Has Established a Commune," *Heilungkiang Daily*, August 24, 1958; "Chaoying People's Commune Advances by Leaps and Bounds," *Honan Daily*, August 26, 1958; "Shansi Has Established a Huge Labor Army That Unites Workers, Peasants, and Soldiers," *People's Daily*, August 15, 1958; "The Advantages of Big Cooperatives as Seen From Sunrise Cooperative (Liaoning)," *People's Daily*, August 20, 1958.

10. For the name *Lao Tung Ta Chun*, see "An Important System in the Socialist Reconstruction," editorial in *Shansi Daily*, August 12, 1958.

11. The term *Big Cooperative* was used in Liaoning. See *People's Daily*, August 20, 1958.

12. "District Commissars in Hsinyang Called On-the-Spot Conference, and Discussed the Organization of the Commune, Distribution, and Party Leadership," *People's Daily*, August 21, 1958.

13. "The Regulations of the Sputnik Commune and Suggestions on How to Manage a Commune," *People's Daily* editorial, September 4, 1958.

14. Kang Chuo, "Chairman Mao Visits Hsushui," *People's Daily*, August 11, 1958.

15. Ibid.

16. "Chairman Mao Visits Villages in Honan," *People's Daily*, August 12, 1958.

17. "Chairman Mao Visits Village in Shantung," *People's Daily*, August 13, 1958.

18. Tan Chi-lung, "Rather Think the Commune Would be Better," *Red Flag* 9 (1958): 21–24.

19. "Receive the High Tide of the People's Commune," *Red Flag* (editorial) 7 (1958): 13–15.

20. "People's Commune Is Good," *People's Daily*, August 18, 1958.

21. "Chaoying People's Commune Advances by Leaps and Bounds," *Honan Daily*, August 26, 1958.

22. Ibid.

23. "How to Lead the People's Commune Movement," *People's Daily*, September 22, 1958.

24. "Chaoyang People's Commune," *Honan Daily*, August 26, 1958.

25. Ibid.

26. "How to Lead," *People's Daily*, September 22, 1958.

27. Ibid.

28. "Villages in Honan Have Been Communized," *Chin Jih Hsin Wen (Today's News)* September 2, 1958, reprinted in *Xin Hua Ban Yue Kan* (Peking) 18 (1958): 65–66.

29. "How Ankuo County Solved Economic Policy Problems in Its People's Commune Movement," *Hopeh Daily*, September 4, 1958.

30. Ibid.

31. "An Investigation of One People's Commune," *People's Daily*, September 3, 1958.

32. Kang Chuo, "In Praise of Hsushui Commune-II," *People's Daily*, August 26, 1958.

33. "Resolution of the Central Committee on the Establishment of the People's Communes in the Rural Areas (Peitaiho Resolution), August 29, 1958," *People's Daily*, September 10, 1958.

34. "The Central Political Bureau Called on the Party and the People to Struggle for the Production of 10,700,000 tons of Steel," *People's Daily*, September 1, 1958.

35. "Villages in the Entire Country Have Basically Adopted Communes," *People's Daily*, October 1, 1958.

36. "Chianghuai Commune Refutes 'Let's Eat Up Till We All Become Poor'," *People's Daily*, September 18, 1958.

37. "Honan Took Five Steps to Consolidate the People's Commune," *People's Daily*, September 19, 1958.

38. "How to Lead the People's Commune," *People's Daily*, September 22, 1958.

39. Li Hsien-nien, "What I Saw in the People's Communes," *Red Flag* 10 (1958): 4–8.

40. Ibid., p. 5.

41. Ibid., p. 7.

42. Ibid., p. 8.

43. Kang Chuo, "In Praise of Hsushui Commune-III," *People's Daily*, August 27, 1958; also *Ta Kung Pao* (Peking), October 25, 1958.

44. Cheng Chu-yuan, *Communist China—Its Situation and Prospect* (Hong Kong: Free Press, 1959), Appendix, pp. 17–18.

45. *Ta Kung Pao* (Peking), December 7, 1958.

46. *Ta Kung Pao* (Peking), December 8, 1958.

47. Hsu Li-chun, "On Whether We Have Attained Communism—Two Comments on Socialist and Communist Educational Movements in Rural Villages," *Red Flag* 12 (1958): 23.

48. "Manage the Commune Kitchens Well," *People's Daily* editorial, October 25, 1958.

49. "Experiences in Operating Commune Kitchens," *People's Daily*, October 29, 1958; "What Kinds of Commune Kitchens People Like Best," *People's Daily*, November 3, 1958; "Huahsien Commune Kitchens Provide Eight Services," *People's Daily*, November 11, 1958; "Introducing a Very Well Run Commune Kitchen," *Red Flag* 12 (1958): 38–41.

50. "We Must Pay Attention and Guarantee Rest for Peasants," *People's Daily* editorial, November 9, 1958.

51. "How to Adopt a System of Half Free and Half Wage Supply—The Experience of Hsuanchuang People's Commune," *Ta Kung Pao* (Peking), October 25, 1958.

52. "Rice Good, and Meat and Vegetables Good Too,—Additional Comments on Commune Kitchens," *People's Daily* editorial, November 10, 1958.

53. "Communiqué of the Sixth Plenary Session of the Eighth Central Committee," *People's Daily*, December 18, 1958.

54. "Decision Approving Comrade Mao Tse-tung's Proposal that He Will Not Stand as Candidate for Chairman of the People's Republic of China for the Next Term of Office," *People's Daily*, December 18, 1958.

55. New China News Agency release, December 19, 1958.

56. "Resolution on Some Questions Concerning the People's Commune (Wuhan Resolution)," *People's Daily*, December 19, 1958.

57. Ibid.

58. For a description of commune organization, see John C. Pelzel, "Economic Management of a Production Brigade in Post-Leap China," in W. E. Willmott, ed., *Economic Organization in Chinese Society* (Stanford: Stanford University Press, 1972), pp. 387–414.

59. "In Agriculture, Learn from Tachai," *People's Daily* editorial, September 23, 1970. The Tachai brigade abandoned private plots during the Cultural Revolution in 1966. See H. V. Henle, *Report on China's Agriculture* (Food and Agriculture Organization of the United Nations, 1974, Annex III, "A Model Agricultural Community: Tachai Production Brigade, Hsiyang Hsien, Shansi Province"), pp. 219–224.

60. George Chaplin, "Most Chinese Spend Life in a Commune," in *24 Days in China*, the Honolulu Advertiser, October 24–November 7, 1972.

61. "Constitution of the People's Republic of China," Article no. 7, adopted on January 17, 1975 by the Fourth National People's Congress, *People's Daily*, January 20, 1975. It may be noted that Chang Chun-chiao, who made the official report to the People's Congress on the amendment of the constitution, blamed Lin Piao for the "absurd idea" of wanting to abolish private plots while condemning Liu Shao-chi's policy of setting agricultural production quotas on individual families *(Pao Chan Tao Hu)*. See Chang Chun-chiao, "Report on the Amendment of the Constitution," *People's Daily*, January 20, 1975. According to the new constitution, only commune members are allowed to keep private plots and operate family sideline productions. These privileges are not extended to nonmembers, mostly individuals with family backgrounds as ex-landlords or ex-rich peasants.

CHAPTER VII

1. "How to Handle Contradictions Among the People," *People's Daily* editorial, April 13, 1957.

2. Ibid.

3. Mao Tse-tung, *On the Correct Handling of Contradictions Among the People* (Peking: People's Publishing House, 1957). This was the edited official version of a speech Mao gave at the eleventh session of the Supreme State Conference on February 27, 1957. The official version was released on June 18, 1957 after some passages of the alleged original version were published in the *New York Times* on June 13, 1957. The Chinese term, *mou tun,* though officially translated as "contradictions," seems to refer to different concepts in different contexts. When Mao was speaking of *mou tun* between the people and the class enemies, as well as among the people, he was referring to conflicts in the sense of rival claims to scarce resources and decision-making status. When Mao emphasized the fundamental *mou tun* between the relations of productions and the forces of production, he was referring to a different kind of conflict, in the sense that the old relations of production are incompatible and restrictive to the development of the forces of production. The conflicts analyzed in this paper refer to these rival claims.

4. Mao Tse-tung, *Correct Handling,* p. 2.

5. Mao Tse-tung, *Correct Handling,* p. 7. This principle of "unity—criticism—unity" has been reaffirmed. See Li Hsin, "Correctly Handle the Relation between Unity and Struggle," editorial in *Red Flag* 11 (1974): 14–17; reprinted in *People's Daily,* November 9, 1974.

6. Georg Simmel, *Conflict,* Kurt H. Wolff, trans. (Glencoe, Ill.: Free Press, 1955).

7. "How to Handle Contradictions," *People's Daily* editorial, April 13, 1957.

8. Cheng Chien, "Don't Fail to Appreciate Blessings When You Live in Blessings," *Worker's Daily,* November 15, 1957.

9. "Deep and Thorough Debate on Livelihood Problems at Shanghai's First Fountain Pen Factory," *People's Daily,* November 27, 1957.

10. "Food Problems and Ideological Problems," *People's Daily* editorial, August 5, 1957.

11. Ibid.

12. Ibid.

13. "Grain Sales in Shang Kao Village, Tai An County," *People's Daily,* August 5, 1957.

14. For a detailed description of the Hundred Flowers movement and the Antirightist campaign, see Theodore H. E. Chen, *Thought Reform of the Chinese Intellectuals* (Hong Kong: Hong Kong University Press, 1960); Roderick MacFarquhar, *The Hundred Flower Campaign and the Chinese Intellectuals* (New York: Praeger, 1960).

15. Chang Hui-ting, "How Come the Rightists Talk Like the Landlords?" *People's Daily,* July 2, 1957. This article singled out Chang Po-chun as supporting the rich peasants and opposing the agricultural collectivization movement.

16. Yen Hsin-ming, "Chang Po-chun Is Determined to Start a Rebellion," *People's Daily,* August 4, 1957. Yen was a member of the Central Executive Committee of the China Peasants and Workers Democratic Party.

17. "Expose the Treacherous Activities of Chang Po-chun's Small Group of Rightists," *People's Daily,* July 9, 1957.

18. Yen Hsin-ming, "Listen to the Mad Talk of Chang Po-chun: 'I Want to Contest with the Communist Party for Leadership'," *People's Daily,* July 3, 1957.

19. *People's Daily,* July 1, 1957.

20. Hu Yi-ho, "Chang Po-chun's Erroneous Thinking Has a Long History," *People's Daily,* June 16, 1957.

21. *People's Daily,* June 26, 1957.

22. Teng Chu-ming, "Let's See the True Face of Chang Po-chun; Also Refute the Absurd Utterances of Lo Lung-chi and Chen Jen-ping," *People's Daily*, June 19, 1957.

23. *People's Daily*, June 20, 1957. Lo's remarks were revealed by Shen Tzu-chiu, a fellow member of the Democratic League.

24. Chang Nai-chi, "A Few Problems About Aiding the Reform of Industrial and Business Personnel," *Takung Pao* (Peking), June 9, 1957.

25. The proposal for extending interest payments to 20 years was made by Li Kang-nien, a Shanghai industrialist. Chang Nai-chi encouraged Li's proposal. See Shen Pei-hua, "The Rightists Are Thinking of Dragging China Back to the Capitalist Road," *People's Daily*, July 8, 1957.

26. Chien Chia-chu, Sun Hsiao-chun, Wu Ta-kun, and Feng Ho-fa, "Why Is This a Conflict Between Two Roads?—A Criticism of the Anti-Socialism Thinking of Chang Nai-chi," *People's Daily*, June 20, 1957.

27. "What Is This All About?" *People's Daily* editorial, June 8, 1957.

28. Ibid.

29. "The Workers Are Speaking Up," *People's Daily* editorial, June 10, 1957.

30. "Expose the Treacherous Activities of Chang Po-chun's Small Group of Rightists," *People's Daily*, July 9, 1957; "Lo Lung-chi and Chao Wen-pi, Acting Like a Pair of Wolves, Are Attempting to Turn the Ministry of Timber Supply into an Independent Rightist Kingdom," *Worker's Daily*, July 20, 1957; "Ministry of Food Supply Holds Meetings to Criticize Chang Nai-chi," *People's Daily*, August 13, 14, 16, 19, 1957.

31. After Lo Lung-chi had proposed the redress committee, he received more than 130 letters providing details of mistrials. See "Democratic League Central Committee Meeting Exposes the Treacherous Activities of Lo Lung-chi," *People's Daily*, July 4, 1957.

32. S. E. Asch, "The Effects of Group Pressure," in Alex Inkeles, ed., *Readings on Modern Sociology* (Englewood Cliffs: Prentice-Hall, 1966), pp. 206–215.

33. Mao Tse-tung, *Correct Handling*, pp. 1–13.

34. Li Shu-chih, "From Rice Plants to People—A Few Problems About Political Leadership in the Villages," in *Chuntsung* (Masses) 7 (1958), reprinted in *Xin Hua Ban Yue Kan* 23 (1958): 11–13. Li's report cited only nine "too many and too few."

35. Ibid.

36. "Go Deep to the Masses of People," *People's Daily* editorial, September 23, 1957.

37. Kao Hsiao-ping, "Discover Conflict, Resolve Conflict, and Continuously Move Ahead," *Chuntsung* (Masses) 7 (1958), reprinted in *Xin Hua Ban Yue Kan* 23 (1958): 9–11.

38. Ibid., p. 9.

39. Ibid.

40. Li Shu-chih, "Rice Plants to People," p. 12.

41. Lu Chien-chung, "What Problems Have Been Resolved by Hsiung Ho Cooperative During the Production Tapienlun?" *People's Daily*, November 2, 1957.

42. Joseph LeLyveld, "Notes on China," *New York Times*, April 4, 1974.

43. Lo Keh-ming, "A New Development of the Tatzepao Movement," *People's Daily*, July 17, 1958.

44. Siao Yu, *Remembering My Boyhood* (Taipei, Taiwan: Yih Wen Chih Monthly Publications, 1969), pp. 77–80. Since Mao's village, Shao Shan, was close to Siao's home, Mao was probably aware of the custom of *hsi kuang yueh*. For the boyhood friendship between Mao and Siao, see Siao Yu, *Mao Tse-tung and I Were Beggars* (Syracuse: Syracuse University Press, 1959).

45. Yu Ming-sheng, "The Power of Tatzepao," *People's Daily,* March 28, 1958.

46. "Tatzepao, A Good Format for Promoting the Rectification Campaign," *Peking Daily* editorial, September 15, 1957.

47. Ibid.

48. Yu Ming-sheng, "Power of Tatzepao."

49. Ibid.

50. Ibid.

51. Chou Wen, "How the Industrial and Business Circles in Shanghai Organized Their Rectification," *Takun Pao,* December 30, 1957.

52. Ibid.

53. *Peking Daily* editorial, September 15, 1957.

54. Ibid.

55. Yu Ming-sheng, "Power of Tatzepao."

56. Lo Keh-ming, "New Development."

57. *Peking Daily* editorial, September 15, 1957, *op. cit.*

58. Yu Ming-sheng, "Power of Tatzepao."

59. Chou Wen, "Industrial and Business Circles."

60. Ibid. (The monk Fa Hai is an unsympathetic, unpopular character in Chinese folklore. He plagued Lady Pai Shu-cheng, a beautiful, tender-hearted white serpent demon who had fallen in love with Hsu Hsien, a young scholar. Using his magic power, Fa Hai destroyed their romance and placed Lady Pai under eternal torture. The story, known as "The Tale of the White Serpent," is the theme of a popular Chinese opera which has been banned since the Cultural Revolution.)

61. Yu Shu, "Fully Utilize the Mass Line Approach," *People's Daily,* July 11, 1958.

62. Ibid.

63. For an analysis of the use of tatzepao in the Cultural Revolution, see Godwin C. Chu, Philip H. Cheng, and Leonard L. Chu, *The Roles of Tatzepao in the Cultural Revolution: A Structural-Functional Analysis* (Carbondale, Ill.: Southern Illinois University, 1972).

64. For some of the reports, see Reuters, Peking despatch, June 13, 1974, "Posters in Peking Cite Shortcomings of City's Leaders," in *New York Times,* June 14, 1974; Agence France Presse, Peking, June 16, 1974, "Posters Attack Hua Kuo-feng," in Foreign Broadcast Information Service, FBIS–CHI-74-117, p. E10; Reuters, Peking, June 17, 1974, "Posters Criticizing Hua Torn Down," FBIS–CHI-74-117, p. E11; "Largest Wall Posters in Peking Attack Factory Chiefs," *New York Times,* June 23, 1974; Reuters, Peking despatch, June 23, 1974, "Posters in Peking Tell of Bloodshed In Rightist Uprising," in *New York Times,* June 24, 1974. For a discussion of the 1974 poster campaign in Peking, see Shih Chih, "Briefly Discuss the Latest Tatzepao Campaign," *China Monthly,* August 1974, pp. 31–32.

65. "The Change Induced by a Tatzepao," *People's Daily,* August 21, 1974.

66. "After a Tatzepao Is Posted," *People's Daily,* August 30, 1974.

67. Yu Ming-sheng, "Power of Tatzepao."

68. Discussed in chapter 3.

69. Emmett Dedmon, *China Journal* (New York: Rand McNally, 1973), p. 140.

70. The following is based on Godwin C. Chu and Leonard L. Chu, "Social Structure and Conflict Resolution in Mainland China—An Analysis of Letters in *People's Daily,*" presented at Annual Convention, Association for Education in Journalism, Fort Collins, Colorado, August 1973. Mimeographed. University of Hawaii, Honolulu, Asia Collection, Sinclair Library, or Hamilton Library.

71. Inkeles has suggested that letters published in the Soviet press serve the function of tension release. See Alex Inkeles, *Public Opinion in Soviet Russia* (Cambridge: Harvard University Press, 1962), pp. 197–203, 207–222.

72. A Poor Old Peasant, "Co-op Stores Should Provide the Masses with Convenience and Help with Production," *People's Daily*, May 12, 1968.

73. "The Mass of People Demand that the Use of Broadcast Trucks and Loudspeakers be Discontinued," *People's Daily*, June 16, 1967.

74. Tsui Cheng-yao and Heh Kuang-shan, "Fewer and Shorter Meetings during Busy Times," *People's Daily*, April 26, 1968.

75. Hsiang Chun and Hsin Hung, "Do Not Violate Auditing and Accounting System," *People's Daily*, March 14, 1968.

76. A Young Worker, "Thoroughly Repudiate the Old Educational System," *People's Daily*, December 12, 1967.

77. A Reader, "In Harvest Time, Do Not Forget Austerity," *People's Daily*, June 23, 1968.

78. A Reader, "Prohibit Waste in Pursuit of Formality,"*People's Daily*, July 17, 1967.

79. A Cadre, "Let Revolutionary Cadres Understand Revolution and Promote Production," *People's Daily*, October 27, 1967.

80. A Cadre, "Lower Level Cadres Should Boldly Lead in Production Work," *People's Daily*, March 13, 1968; A Cadre, "Wheat Crop Must be Tightly Grasped," *People's Daily*, June 6, 1968; Hsuan Tung, "Cadres Must Pay Attention to Coal Saving," *People's Daily*, February 9, 1968.

81. The numbers in these categories add up to more than 126 because some letters referred to more than one kind of conflict. Of the total of 182 letters published in 1967 and 1968, 46 did not express conflict or grievance, but sought or provided information. For details, see Chu and Chu, "Social Structure."

82. Inkeles noted the same function in his analysis of letters published in the Soviet Press. See Inkeles, *Public Opinion*.

83. Tu Chien, "Attention Must be Paid to Letters and Visits by the People," *Red Flag* 11 (October 1971): 69.

84. Ibid., p. 67.

85. See Chu and Chu, "Social Structure."

86. "Factories in Liaoning Are Reforming After Big Blooming and Blossoming," *People's Daily*, November 13, 1957.

87. Siao Yu, *Boyhood*, pp. 79–80.

88. Liu Chien, "How to Organize Tapienlun," *Worker's Daily*, December 26, 1957.

89. "We Must Rely on the Masses, Must Strengthen Leadership—The Big Debate Experience of Pai Chuan Village, Ho Hsun, Shansi Province," *People's Daily*, August 21, 1957.

90. Ibid.

91. Ibid.

92. "Village Broadcasting Network in Our Country Is Getting Better and Better," *People's Daily*, September 21, 1974.

93. "New Scenery at Chiang Chun—An Unfinished Broadcast Meeting," *People's Daily*, August 30, 1974.

94. "Constitution of the People's Republic of China," Article nos. 5,7, adopted on January 17, 1975 by the Fourth National People's Congress, *People's Daily*, January 20, 1975.

95. Ibid., Article no. 13. The industrial strikes in Chekiang Province in the summer of 1975 provided the first test of the implications of these constitutional provisions. At the moment, little is known about these strikes except that they were serious enough to require the dispatch of military troops numbering more than 10,000 to keep production going and prevent the strikes from spreading. (See United Press International report from Hong Kong dated August 8, 1975, "Strikes in Red

China," in *Honolulu Advertiser*, August 9, 1975.) Even though the cause of the strikes was not revealed, it most probably was related to wages, fringe benefits, and worker-cadre relations. If so, the strikes would be a manifestation of the basic conflicts between individual and collective interests, and between the leaders and the led, which we have discussed in this chapter. Although the initial press report made no mention of tatzepao, it is inconceivable that the big character posters were not extensively used by the workers who either initiated or responded to the calls for strikes. Nor was it known whether the leadership cadres in the factories made an attempt to resolve the conflicts through tapienlun. If they did, the debates were apparently ineffective, as troops had to be called in. We speculate that once the Party has been able to put down the strikes with the help of troops, it would most probably use tapienlun in an effort to resolve the differences with the majority of workers. It may be interesting to note that the term *tapienlun* gained renewed currency in early 1976 in articles on proletarian education published in the *People's Daily*.

CHAPTER VIII

1. See Daniel Lerner, *The Passing of Traditional Society: Modernizing the Middle East* (Glencoe, Ill.: Free Press, 1958). Also Lerner, "Technology, Communication and Change," in Daniel Lerner and Wilbur Schramm, eds., *Communication and Change: The Past Ten Years and the Next* (Honolulu: The University Press of Hawaii, 1976).

2. Yu has aptly called it the *Tao* of Mao. See Frederick T. C. Yu, "The *Tao* of Mao and China's Modernization," in Harold D. Lasswell, Daniel Lerner, and John Montgomery, eds., *Values and Development: An Asian Symposium* (Cambridge: The M.I.T. Press, 1976).

3. Wilbur Schramm, personal communication.

4. Letter to the editor by Chi Hui and Liu Hua, Sun Wa Commune, Ching Ho County, Hopeh Province, "Overall Planning Needed for Agricultural Construction," *People's Daily*, January 14, 1975.

5. Herbert Spencer, *The Principle of Sociology*, vol. 1 (London: Williams and Norgate, 1897), pp. 557–564.

6. "An Interview with a Commune Member of Pung Tao Commune, Nan An County, Fukien," *China Monthly* 28 (June 1966): 30–32.

7. The first such hero was Lei Feng, who was praised in the "Lei Feng" campaign in 1963. Lei, an army truck driver, was killed at age 22 while directing a driver to back a truck. This was followed by "Learn from Ouyang Hai" in 1964. Ouyang, a corporal in the Liberation Army, died at age 23 in an effort to prevent a collision of a passenger train and an artillery piece. In 1965 came "Learn from Wang Chieh." Also an army corporal, Wang was killed at age 23 when he threw himself over an exploding bomb in order to save his comrades. Two movements were launched in 1966: "Learn from Mai Hsien-teh," and "Learn from Liu Ying-chun." Mai, a mechanic in a gunboat, distinguished himself in a sea battle with the Nationalists. Despite a brain wound, he stayed on his post for three hours until the battle was over. Liu, an artillery soldier, was fatally injured at age 21 when he tried to restrain a horse drawing an artillery cart from running into six children.

8. A recent example is furnished in a report in the *People's Daily*, November 21, 1974, entitled: "Such High Work Spirit Never Seen Before." The report tells of a production contest at the Tientsin Bicycle Factory. In order to increase the 1974 total production by 110,000 bicycles over the 1973 record of 860,000, the workers engaged in a contest "where you chase me, and I chase you." Many workers did not go home, but lived and ate in the factory in order to work day and night.

9. Max Weber, *The Protestant Ethic and the Spirit of Capitalism* (New York: Scribner, 1958).

10. How economic behavior is motivated by institutionalized values is illustrated by Talcott Parsons, "The Motivation of Economic Activities," *Canadian Journal of Economics and Political Science* 6 (1940): 187–203.

11. Emile Durkheim, *Division of Labor in Society,* George Simpson, trans. (Glencoe, Ill.: Free Press, 1947), pp. 129–131.

12. Ibid.

13. Ibid., p. 131.

14. The Party's initial attitudes toward the children of ex-landlords and ex-rich peasants were exemplified in an article entitled: "Do not Discriminate Against Students from Landlord and Rich Peasant Families," published in *Chung Kuo Ching Nien (China's Youth)* 2 (1956):16. In that article, the question was asked as to whether high school graduates with family backgrounds as ex-landlords or ex-rich peasants could be allowed to join the agricultural cooperatives and teach in village public schools upon return to their own villages. The Party's answer was: yes, if they lived away from their parents; otherwise no. Living away from one's own parents in the village amounted to a renunciation of class background.

15. The 10 to 15 percent is a rough estimate. Official statistics prepared by the government of the People's Republic during the land reform put the number of landlords and rich peasants at less than 10 percent of China's rural population. See Liao Lu-yen, "The Dazzling Achievement on the Agricultural Battlefront in Ten Years," in *The Glorious Ten Years* (Hong Kong: San Lien Bookstore, 1959), p. 120. Reports on two villages made during the Cultural Revolution, however, suggest that the percentage of families subsequently identified as ex-landlords and ex-rich peasants could be higher than 10 percent. At Taiping Ling Brigade, Lung An County, Kirin Province, 41 of the village's 235 families were so classified. (See "Contrast Two Schools to Demonstrate the Superiority of Peasant-Operated Schools," *People's Daily,* October 27, 1968.) At Sungshu Kou Brigade, Ai Hui County, Heilungkiang Province, 12 of the 66 families in the village were classified as ex-landlords and ex-rich peasants. (See "Understand How Poor and Lower-Middle Peasants Manage Schools from the Experiences of Three Agricultural Brigades," *People's Daily,* October 28, 1968.) The inclusion of former capitalists, rightists, and loosely defined "bad elements" would probably bring the total close to 15 percent.

16. The provisions on private plots in the new constitution adopted in January 1975 seem to reflect this awareness. See "The Constitution of the People's Republic of China," Article 7, *People's Daily,* January 20, 1975.

17. The transferability of China's experience has been discussed by Wilbur Schramm, Godwin C. Chu, and Frederick T. C. Yu, "China's Experience with Development Communication: How Transferable Is It?" in Daniel Lerner and Wilbur Schramm, eds., *Communication and Change: The Past Ten Years and the Next* (Honolulu: The University Press of Hawaii, 1976).

18. Stephen Uhalley, Jr., "China as a Model of Revolutionary Development," *China Notes* 10, no. 3, (1972): 25.

19. According to provincial radio reports monitored in Hong Kong, the strikes apparently started in Chekiang Province sometime in July. Troops numbering more than 10,000 were sent into the factories in mid-July at the direction of central authorities in Peking to keep production going and prevent the strikes from spreading. In late July more troops were dispatched to the factories to reinforce those already there. See United Press International report from Hong Kong dated August 8, 1975, "Strikes in Red China," in *Honolulu Advertiser,* August 9, 1975.

20. For a discussion of authoritarian submission as part of the Chinese personality, see Francis L. K. Hsu, *Under the Ancestors' Shadow* (London: Routlege & Kegan Paul, 1949), and *American and Chinese, Two Ways of Life* (New York: Abelard-Schuman, 1953). It should be pointed out that as a personality trait, authoritarian

submission characterized those Chinese who were brought up in the old society. They were the ones who had to bear much of the burden of adjusting to the demands of the new regime in the 1950s. The modal personality of the younger generation is largely unknown. In view of their experience in the Cultural Revolution as well as in the many campaigns they have participated in, it is conceivable that those Chinese who have been raised under the new regime are not as submissive as their parents. This hypothesis needs to be tested by empirical evidence.

21. See Martin M. C. Yang, "Familism and Chinese National Character," in Yih-yuan Li and Kuo-shu Yang, eds., *Symposium on the Character of the Chinese, An Interdisciplinary Approach* (Institute of Ethnology, Academica Sinica, Monograph Series B., no. 4, Taipei, Taiwan, 1973), pp. 127–174.

22. The riots started on the morning of April 5, 1976, when a crowd, estimated at one time to be close to one hundred thousand, gathered at Tienanmen Square to pay homage to the deceased Premier Chou En-lai on the traditional day of *Ching Ming* (ancestors' day). An official release did not say how the crowd turned into a mob. (See "The Anti-Revolutionary Political Incident at Tienanmen Square," *People's Daily*, April 8, 1976). The rioting started around 8 A.M. when some of the demonstrators overturned a loudspeaker van of the Peking Municipal Security Bureau. After 9 A.M. more than ten thousand people gathered in front of the People's Auditorium, and soon fighting broke out between the mob and the security guards. Four trucks used by the security bureau were burned. Meanwhile, the situation got out of control. In the afternoon, a group of demonstrators stormed into a barracks of the People's Liberation Army on the southeast corner of the square, beat up the guards, destroyed some of the windows and doors, and burned the personal effects of the soldiers. Around 6:30 P.M. Mayor Wu Teh of Peking broadcast a plea for the demonstrators to leave the square, but had no success. The rioting did not subside until after the police and the Worker-Militia of Peking moved in at around 9:30 P.M. to disperse the demonstrators. The Party blamed Teng Hsiao-ping for instigating the riots and removed him from all his official posts, including the vice premiership. (See "Resolution of the Party's Central Political Bureau on Dismissing Teng Hsiao-ping from All His Positions," *People's Daily*, April 8, 1976.)

23. Simon Kuznets, *Toward a Theory of Economic Growth* (New York: W. W. Norton, 1968, p. 81).

APPENDIX C

1. Michel Oksenberg, "Sources and Methodological Problems in the Study of Contemporary China," in A. Doak Barnett, ed., *Chinese Communist Politics in Action* (Seattle: University of Washington Press, 1969), pp. 577–606.

2. For instance, stories published in the People's Republic have been analyzed to shed light on family relations in mainland China in comparison to those in Taiwan. See Ai-li S. Chin, "Family Relations in Modern Chinese Fiction," in Maurice Freedman, ed., *Family and Kinship in Chinese Society* (Stanford: Stanford University Press, 1970), pp. 87–120.

3. Ann Keatley and Albert Feuerwerker, "Scholarly Exchange with the People's Republic of China," *Social Science Research Council Items* 27, no. 3, (September 1973): 28.

4. Ibid.

5. Francis L. K. Hsu, "Introduction—How to Understand China," in Eileen Hsu-Balzer, Richard J. Balzer, and Francis L. K. Hsu, *China, Day by Day* (Yale University Press, 1974), p. xxviii.

6. For the concept of social structure, see A. R. Radcliffe-Brown, "On Social Structure," in *Structure and Function in Primitive Society* (New York: Free Press, 1965), pp. 188–204. Also, Claude Levi-Strauss, "Social Structure," in Sol Tax, ed.,

Anthropology Today (Chicago: University of Chicago Press, 1962), pp. 321–350.

7. The structural-functional approach is based on Talcott Parsons, *The Social System* (Glencoe, Ill.: Free Press, 1951); Marion J. Levy, Jr., *The Structure of Society* (Princeton: Princeton University Press, 1952); Robert K. Merton, *Social Theory and Social Structure* (Glencoe, Ill.: Free Press, 1961), particularly chap. 1, "Manifest and Latent Functions," pp. 19–84; and David F. Aberle, et. al., "The Functional Prerequisites of a Society," *Ethics* 60 (January 1950): 100–110.

8. For the concept of social structural change, see Parsons, "The Processes of Change of Social Systems," in Parsons, *Social System,* pp. 480–535; also see Neil J. Smelser, "Toward a General Theory of Social Change," in Smelser, *Essays in Sociological Explanation* (Englewood Cliffs: Prentice-Hall, 1968), pp. 192–280.

Index

About the Author

Born in Peking, GODWIN C. CHU did his undergraduate work in China and received his Ph.D. in communication research from Stanford University. He has taught in the fields of communication, sociology, and anthropology in Taiwan, Canada, and the United States. Before joining the East-West Center in 1973, first as a senior fellow and now as a research associate, Dr. Chu was professor and research director in the School of Journalism, Southern Illinois University. He has done extensive work in communication and social change, and has published articles in a number of scholarly journals, including *Rural Sociology, Sociology and Social Research, Sociometry, Journal of Experimental Social Psychology*, and *International Journal of Psychology*. He is the senior author of *The Role of Tatzepao in the Cultural Revolution: A Structural-Functional Analysis*, and coeditor of *Communication and Development in China*, and *Communication for Group Transformation and Development*.

☩ *Production Notes*

The text of this book was designed by Roger J. Eggers and typeset on the Unified Composing System by the design and production staff of The University Press of Hawaii.

The text and display typeface is Garamond No. 49.

Offset presswork and binding is the work of Vail-Ballou press. Text paper is Glatfelter P & S Offset, basis 55.